Peel and the Victorians

Peel mourning medal, 1850: *top* obverse, *bottom* reverse

Peel and the Victorians

Donald Read

Basil Blackwell

Copyright © Historical Association 1987

First published 1987

Basil Blackwell Ltd
108 Cowley Road, Oxford, OX4 1JF, UK

Basil Blackwell Inc.
423 Park Avenue South, Suite 1503
New York, NY 10016, USA

British Library Cataloguing in Publication Data
Read, Donald
Peel and the Victorians.
1. Peel, *Sir* Robert 2. Great Britain—
Politics and government—1837–1901
I. Title
941.081′092′4 DA536.P3
ISBN 0-631-15725-5

Library of Congress Cataloging in Publication Data
Read, Donald.
Peel and the Victorians.
Includes index.
Bibliography: p.
1. Peel, Robert, Sir, 1788–1850. 2. Public opinion—
Great Britain—History—19th century. 3. Prime
ministers—Great Britain—Biography. 4. Great Britain—
Politics and government—1837–1901. I. Title.
DA536.P3R42 1987 941.081′092′4 87-12147
ISBN 0-631-15725-5

Typeset in 10 on 12 pt Sabon
by Joshua Associates Limited, Oxford
Printed in Great Britain by Billing and Sons Ltd, Worcester

Let this merit never be forgotten in Sir Rt., that he could do without articulate backing, and depend upon the inarticulate; which indeed argues a strong man.

Carlyle on Peel

To L. B. C.

Contents

Illustrations

Preface

I

Sir Robert Peel was arguably the greatest peacetime Prime Minister in British history, even though his tenure of office (1834–5, 1841–6) totalled little more than five years. His greatness came to be widely recognized in his own lifetime, although such recognition was gradual and became complete only late in his career, at and after repeal of the Corn Laws in 1846. Twenty-five years ago, in my book *Press and People, Opinion in Three English Cities 1790–1850*, I drew attention to the mellowing of opinion towards Peel in the newspapers of Manchester, Leeds and Sheffield during the crisis of the 1840s. In that book, however, discussion of Peel's relationship with public opinion was kept within the context of newspaper history. This book has been conceived more boldly. It centres not upon newspapers, but upon Peel himself. The contemporary press, London as well as provincial, has been explored not for its own sake but as the medium through which Peel's developing offer of political leadership to the Victorian people, and their increasingly favourable response, were each actively publicised during two decades.

That historians would one day read these newspapers was indeed foreseen by one of them, the Whig *Morning Chronicle* of 3 January 1846. Writing at the time of the crisis of repeal of the Corn Laws, the *Chronicle* poked fun at newspaper reports of what was being said at protectionist meetings against Peel for becoming the advocate of repeal. It suggested that country gentlemen should think twice 'before allowing reporters to take down their after-dinner conversation':

> Even the *Morning Herald* goes into the library of the British Museum, and, once there, is always there. There is no saying at what distance of time the dust may not be wiped off, and the ponderous tome handed down . . . The fact that in the winter of 1845–6 the whole squirearchy of England was in a perfect fever and *furore* of panic at the thought of there being too much to eat, and dreamed, night and day, that England was

coming to an end with the Peel pivot, is now fairly booked for the future historian.

Source material for any study of Peel and the Victorian public is embarrassingly plentiful. No one will ever read every contemporary comment or report about Peel. Tens of thousands of files survive in the British Library newspaper collection at Colindale, and in local libraries. I have tried to take account of the leading London daily papers, headed by *The Times*, and also of many of the more interesting provincial papers, especially such leading titles as the *Manchester Guardian* and *Stamford Mercury*. Attention has also been paid to evidence from pamphlets, street ballads and sermons. Many letters to, from or about Peel are to be found in manuscript collections up and down the country. But the biggest collection consists of Peel's own voluminous private papers in the British Library (Additional Manuscripts 40181–40617). These papers, which include Peel's little-used 'general correspondence', have proved invaluable. Particular mention may also be made of the records in the library of University College, London, of 'The Working Men's Memorial of Gratitude to Sir Robert Peel', to which over 400,000 working men contributed after his death.

Anyone who writes about public opinion, even of the present day, would be foolish to claim that he can answer all questions with certainty, or some questions at all. This is even more the case for the student of Victorian public opinion. There was no Gallup opinion poll taken at the time of repeal of the Corn Laws. The only continuous statistics to hand are the newspaper stamp duty returns, whose apparent precision may be misleading about circulations, when newspaper circulation is itself only an uncertain measure of public opinion. Nevertheless, the attempt to explain Peel's relationship with his public has turned out to be well worth making, even if historical explanation cannot claim the character of proof. And just as the example of *Press and People* appears to have helped some historians of local opinion in other places than the three cities there studied, so perhaps the method employed here may be found helpful by those interested in other Prime Ministers than Peel. Certainly, the fluctuating reputation of Lord John Russell would lend itself to close analysis, as would the long popularity of Lord Salisbury.

II

Her Majesty The Queen has given gracious permission for use of material in the Royal Archives at Windsor Castle, for which I express my humble thanks. Elsewhere, I am indebted to archivists and librarians in more places than I can mention. But, in particular, I would like to thank the staffs of the Manchester Central Library (notably, Mr Harry Horton); of the manuscripts and newspaper departments of the British Library; of the Goldsmiths' Library, University of London; of the Library of University College, London; and of Nottingham University Library. For diversely valuable assistance I am grateful to the following: Miss Ann Hay of the Scottish Conservative and Unionist Association; Lord Blake; Lord Briggs; Professor Ian Christie; Professor Ian Cowan; Professor Maurice Crosland; Professor F. C. Mather; Professor Keith Robbins; the late Professor J. T. Ward; Mrs Irene Collins; Mr Rex Collins; Dr Maurice Milne; Dr Hugh Cunningham; Dr David Turley; and Dr Grayson Ditchfield. My son, Fergus, has been particularly helpful with regard to material in the *Illustrated London News*. Assistance with research expenses came from a British Academy small grant, which I am glad to acknowledge. The burden of typing was undertaken with characteristic dedication by Mrs Yvonne Latham and Mrs Sue Macdonald of the University of Kent. Without their help the book would have been much longer in the making.

The indebtedness of historians of the age of Peel to the work of Professor Norman Gash is well known, but deserves reiteration. I have given few specific references to his great two-volume life of Peel (1961, 1972) only because its continuous relevance has been taken for granted. What I have found new to say about Peel and his times has emerged, not because I have discovered shortcomings in Gash's interpretation, but because I have followed a novel line of approach. This has allowed me to add, without need to subtract.

Abbreviations

Add. MSS	Additional Manuscripts, British Library, London
Derby Papers	Papers of the fourteenth Earl of Derby; recently in the custody of Lord Blake, Queen's College, Oxford
Ellenborough Papers	Papers of the second Baron (first Earl of) Ellenborough, Public Record Office, London
Goulburn Papers	Papers of Henry Goulburn, Surrey Record Office, Kingston upon Thames
Graham Papers	Papers of Sir James Graham (Harvester Press microfilm, 1984)
Hardinge MSS	Papers of Sir Henry (first Viscount) Hardinge, Kent Archives Office, Maidstone
NeC	Papers of the fifth Duke of Newcastle, Nottingham University Library
NLS MS	Blackwood Papers, National Library of Scotland, Edinburgh
Peel, *Memoirs*	*Memoirs by the Right Honourable Sir Robert Peel* ... Part I (1856), II (1857); reprinted as one volume (New York, 1969)
Peel, *Speeches*	*The Speeches of the Late Right Honourable Sir Robert Peel, Bart. delivered in the House of Commons* (1853); reprinted (New York, 1972)
RA	Royal Archives, Windsor Castle
Stanhope MSS	Papers of the fifth Earl Stanhope, Kent Archives Office, Maidstone

1

Introduction:
Leadership and Response

I

I

On 2 July 1850 Sir Robert Peel died in agony as the result of a fall from his horse three days earlier. His passing immediately provoked a breadth and depth of grief such as had never been seen before at the death of any British political figure. The sense of loss ran so deep that the anonymous author, 'One Who Thinks for Himself', of a twelve-page pamphlet entitled *Peel A Mystery, The Man And His Motives Made Plain*, published in August 1850, complained that the month since Peel's death had been 'the most panegyrical one on record':

> Even at the expense of being thought guilty of an Irishism, we must own that we should have liked Peel to have lived a month after his death, in order that he might have enjoyed to the full his posthumous fame. How he would have revelled in every daily and weekly newspaper, how blandly he would have pondered over every review, how charmed he would have been with the bright light thrown on his darkest actions, and how surely would the close of the month have found him feeling in his pockets to subscribe to every one of his intended statues.

Among the press, the tone of the *Nonconformist*, the weekly organ of Radical dissent, which had long been suspicious of Peel in life, was particularly revealing at his death. On the last day of July it was so conditioned by the Peel 'panegyrical' mood that it admitted 'we scarcely like to write his name'. A whole leading article, headed 'THE GREAT STATESMAN AND "THE PROUD NOBILITY",' which praised Peel for refusing all honours, deliberately did so without once naming him. To call Peel simply 'the great statesman' seemed the best way both to control emotion and to heighten praise.

On 13 July the number of the *Manchester Guardian* which reported Peel's funeral also carried a farewell editorial which commented upon the many proposals for monuments to his memory. The *Guardian* drew particular attention to the wide social range of support for these projects. The rich were offering their pounds, the poor their pennies. 'We hope the historian will record, with a full sense of all that it conveys to a reflecting lover of his country, this most striking and extraordinary expression of popular feeling.' In the event, although these hopes were expressed so early, historians have not seriously discussed the response to Peel's death. It has been mentioned, but not explained. And yet, as the *Guardian* sensed, it may be taken as the starting point for an enquiry which can reveal much both about Peel himself and about the great Victorian public which he served. Fifty years ago Elie Halévy, the distinguished French historian of nineteenth-century England, apparently collected extensive notes about reactions to Peel's death, both at home and abroad.[1] Unfortunately, Halévy did not live to complete the book in which he would have analysed this material. The present study therefore attempts what Halévy probably intended, to relate the emotion expressed at Peel's death to the course and character of his public career in life.

This attempt cannot be briefly made, for the intensity of mourning sprang from the gradual coming together of many factors, both from Peel's side and from public opinion. Moreover, in any explanation of Peel's ultimate popularity numerous shifts and contradictions have to be accommodated. For example, Peel was a shy man who sometimes appeared cold in his dealings with individuals. Yet this does not seem to have mattered in the growth of his popular reputation. He opposed the great Reform Act of 1832, one of the most popular measures of the age. Yet this opposition was almost forgotten. He disliked and distrusted the two greatest political agitations of the 1830s and 1840s, not only the working-class Chartist movement but also the middle-class Anti-Corn Law League. In the end, this did his reputation no harm even with many Chartists or Leaguers. After 1832, he saw built up a new Conservative party to operate within the reformed political system, only to let it split over his 1846 scheme for repeal of the Corn Laws. Yet this sacrifice of party to policy positively did his reputation good. Only a minority complained that he had been brought into power at the 1841 general election in order to retain the Corn Laws. Peel was indeed repeating in 1846 what he had done in 1829, when he had promoted Catholic Emancipation despite his own earlier articulate opposition. The Roman Catholic *Rambler* for August 1850 took it for virtue that what it rightly called the 'six great acts' of Peel's career had all been passed 'either without or against that mighty power of party which is the ordinary instrument by which vast political changes are brought about'.

The six acts listed by the *Rambler* were: (a) currency reform; (b) reform of the criminal code; (c) formation of the Metropolitan Police; (d) Catholic Emancipation; (e) reform of the tariff; (f) repeal of the Corn Laws. That so many major reforms were needed in so short a time was a measure of the social, economic and political crisis of Peel's day. He was Prime Minister (1834–5,

[1] E. Halévy, *Victorian Years 1841–1895* (1951), p. 305.

1841–6) when the modern British political system had just begun its century-long course of piecemeal construction, and while the spread of towns and industry was first coming to dominate the lives of most Englishmen. These major reforms constituted Peel's energetic response to the contemporary crisis. They made his political career significant and successful. But it is the unprecedented popularity which he eventually won in the process of promoting these reforms, and the manner of its winning, which give his career its particular fascination alongside its obvious significance.

II

It is easy to say that Peel came to lead Victorian public opinion. It was said in his lifetime. 'The wonderful anomalies that are centred in his person,' claimed *The Times* on 23 December 1845, when Peel had resumed office with the intention of proposing Corn Law repeal, 'give him the key of many classes and influences, which no other man can command. Sir Robert Peel is Minister again, and the nation is re-assured.' But why? What did Peel's name come to mean to the Victorian public, and what did the Victorian public mean to Peel? What, indeed, constituted public opinion in Peel's day? How did it reveal itself? How did Peel seek to influence it? Why did the public follow him? How did the relationship develop? How did the public regard 'party' in politics? How did Peel himself regard it, at Westminster or in the constituencies? To what extent and how did his attitude change over the years? And why, at the end, long after he had ceased to be a party leader, was mourning for Peel so intense?

Any attempt to answer these questions must search not only inside the head and heart of Peel himself, but also inside the heads and hearts of many early Victorians of all classes. It is well to begin therefore with the Victorian class system itself, which so strongly influenced contemporary thought and action. Class was as much a feature of the industrial revolution as were the new machines and new techniques. Indeed, the cotton and woollen factories of Lancashire and Yorkshire were forcing grounds for class separation, where 'middle-class' masters employed 'working-class' men, women and children for cash wages without any other obligation. Significantly, the word 'hands' came into common usage to reflect this new narrow relationship. Peel's own father had been one of the largest and least oppressive of the early cotton masters who emerged during the last years of the eighteenth century. It was about this same time that the word 'class' in the social sense seems to have been first used, during the very years when young Robert Peel (born in 1788) was growing up. It was not a word or a concept which he was ever to accept easily. As late as 1849 he spoke of 'what is called the "middle class"', and of the risk that increased provision of education for the poor without increased attention to the education of middle-class children might be 'laying the foundation for an inversion of the orders of society'. Peel's preference for the word 'orders' here was old-fashioned and revealing. 'Class' carried overtones of social separation and perhaps of hostility. The older idea of society based upon 'order', 'rank', 'degree', assumed a long chain of social 'connection', even though not of social equality.[2]

Such a linked social system was what Peel preferred, but he was well aware that it was more readily sustainable within an agricultural community than within the new industrial society. Although his family's fortunes had been made in industry, Peel himself lived the life of a country gentleman on his large estate at Drayton Bassett, near Tamworth in Staffordshire. The Drayton atmosphere was one of traditional, rural connection rather than of class separation. This was noticed by Guizot, the French statesman, who stayed there in 1848. 'Out of doors, between the landlord and the surrounding population, a great distance, strongly marked in manners, but filled up by frequent relations, full of equity and benevolence on the part of the superior, without any appearance of envy or servility on the part of the inferiors.'[3] Drayton was a model of what can be categorized as an estate village. Not all villages were controlled by landlords in this way. Peasant villages, with their land shared out among many small proprietors, were freer in atmosphere but often also poorer. Drayton's fair rents, sufficient wages and adequate housing were favourably described in a long *Morning Chronicle* article on 8 June 1844, of which Peel himself kept a cutting. He was a good landlord for his time; but, characteristically, he was not so advanced that he stood ahead of his time.[4]

By the 1840s less than a quarter of the national workforce was engaged in agriculture, compared with one-half or more in the eighteenth century. Nevertheless, absolute numbers upon the land were still rising overall, and the 'landed interest' remained in its own eyes what it had always been – the most important social, economic and political grouping in the state. It was led by landlords, many but not all titled, whose family tenure of large estates was buttressed by strict laws of inheritance and primogeniture. Complementary spiritual support came from the parish clergy of the Church of England, which found its greatest strength in the countryside. Freehold and tenant farmers formed a middle rank within this rural society, while at the bottom came the landless labourers. In the 1840s these labourers totalled some three-quarters of all those associated with the land, a higher proportion than ever before or since. But their voice was little heard, whereas the landlords were closely linked with the centres of government both at Westminster and in the counties. After the

---

[2] *The Times*, 27 January 1849. See A. Briggs, 'The language of "class" in early nineteenth-century England', in M. W. Flinn and T. C. Smout (eds) *Essays in Social History* (1974), ch. 7; and 'The language of "mass" and "masses"', in D. E. Martin and D. Rubenstein (eds) *Ideology and the Labour Movement* (1979), ch. 4.

[3] F. P. G. Guizot, *Memoirs of Sir Robert Peel* (1857), p. 339.

[4] Add. MSS 40608, f. 356. See also J. Caird, *English Agriculture 1850–51* (1852), ch. 30.

passing of the 1832 Reform Act, the agricultural south of England remained over-represented in the Commons in proportion either to electoral numbers or to total population, compared with both London and the new industrial areas. Many small country towns returned agricultural Members, who joined the representatives of the landed interest who sat for the county seats. These seats had actually been increased in number under the Reform Act, from 188 to 253. Peel had welcomed this increase, 'as the means of maintaining the wrecks of aristocratical influence', even while he opposed the Act in general.[5] Land-owners were to remain much the largest group within the reformed Parliament, which helps to explain why almost all the English county Members felt able to vote for reform in 1831–2. They were not always reactionary in their views. But the evidence and symbol of their influence at Westminster were the contentious Corn Laws. Legislation passed in 1815, and modified but confirmed in 1828 and 1842, was designed to maintain corn prices at comfort-able levels by restricting the importation of foreign corn. 'Protection' was the aim; and the Conservative party, which Peel led, saw itself as especially the landed protectionist party.

Yet in 1846 Peel was dramatically to break with two-thirds of his parliamentary followers, and to propose repeal of the Corn Laws. He was well aware that the national economy had been transformed during his lifetime, and that the realities of an increasingly industrialized and urbanized society could not be ignored. 'If you had to constitute new Societies, you might on moral and social grounds prefer Corn fields to Cotton factories, an agricultural to a manufacturing population. But our lot is cast, and we cannot recede.' In these blunt terms Peel wrote in 1842 to his doubting friend, J. W. Croker, seeking to explain his tariff liberalization policy.[6]

The population of England doubled between 1801 and 1851, from 8,300,000 to 16,900,000. Most of the countryside's natural increase was being drawn into the towns, where the growth rate was further inflated by heavy Irish immigration. Between 1801 and 1851 the population of London grew from some 1,000,000 to about 2,400,000. And whereas in 1801 no provincial city had contained 100,000 inhabitants, by 1851 seven did so. From about 1845 more people in England were living within an urban environment than within a rural one. Rapid population growth meant that young people were much in evidence; 45 per cent of the population of England and Wales in 1841 were aged under twenty, only 7 per cent over sixty. 'The masses' was a significant new term of the 1830s – a word not only with demographic meaning but also one which carried overtones of social and political challenge. 'We wish to reach the Masses, the unknown multitude, "sine nomine Vulgus".' So wrote Peel's Home Secretary, Sir James Graham, during the tense year of 1842.[7]

[5] Peel, *Speeches*, II, pp. 370–2.
[6] Peel to Croker, 27 July 1842 (Add. MSS 40512, f. 147).
[7] Graham to Peel, 15 December 1842 (Add. MSS 40448, f. 71).

Not that 'the masses' below the middle classes existed as a unity. There were plural working classes, not one working class. An article in *Fraser's Magazine* for July 1850, on 'The English in the Nineteenth Century', made the point that while one social novelty of the century had been the emergence of an aristocracy of wealth, an equally important development had been the separation of poorer people into a multitude of jobs, each with its own wage range and status. Richard Burnet's *A Word to Members of Mechanics Institutes* (1826) pictured a 'Spiral of Success', which embraced a hierarchy of fifteen social categories. The ninth and highest working-class category consisted of 'mechanics and others earning more than forty shillings a week'; four productive working-class categories lay below this, and two more of paupers.[8]

At the top of the working classes, the numbers of labour aristocrats in safe and well-paid jobs were comparatively small. Below them were many more craftsmen and semi-skilled workers, whose wages and employment were at the mercy of the trade cycle. And below them again stood many domestic industrial workers, whose trades were often 'sweated' or were being squeezed out (as in the case of handloom weaving) by the introduction of machinery. Yet really large factories, employing thousands, remained comparatively few even in the textile districts; and elsewhere most people still worked in workshops or at home. Home work of another kind – domestic service – constituted much the largest single national occupation for women.

What many of the industrial working classes did have in common during the deep trade depression of the late 1830s and early 1840s was a heightened sense of insecurity. This brought many of them together, first in the agitation against enforcement of the New Poor Law in the industrial districts, and then in the Chartist movement. Peel was deeply concerned at this time lest economic depression should turn into permanent stagnation, so making social and political unrest equally permanent. In his 1842 letter to Croker already quoted he noticed how the declared value of exports of cotton goods had fallen by over £1,000,000 in 1841 compared with 1840.

> Look at the state of Society in ·this Country, the Congregation of manufacturing Masses, the Amount of our Debt, the Rapid increase of Poor Rates, within the last 4 years, which will soon, by means of Rates in Aid, extend from the ruined Manufacturing districts to the Rural ones, and then judge whether we can with safety retrograde in Manufactures.

The great need, in Peel's view, was not for any socialist redistribution of existing wealth, but for the creation of new wealth. Increased production would raise wages by stimulating demand for labour, at the same time as higher wages, by expanding demand for food, goods and services, would further encourage increased production. 'Inability to consume' was at the heart of the problem.[9]

---

[8] Maxine Berg, *The Machinery Question* (1980), pp. 156–8.
[9] Peel to Arbuthnot, 30 October 1842 (Add. MSS 40484, f. 160).

III

Peel was greatly worried in case the industrial revolution might be preparing the way for political revolution. The example of the French Revolution was always in the mind of Peel's generation. It was a hopeful example to advanced reformers, but an alarming one to conservatives (inside and outside the Conservative party), who believed that the maintenance of a balanced constitution of King, Lords and Commons, spiritually supported by an established Church of England, represented the only security for life, liberty and property. Peel noticed in 1836 how over seventy volumes of memoirs of the French Revolution had recently been published. He had read the memoirs of Bailly, and could hardly believe that he was not reading a history 'of more recent transactions in our own Country'.[10] Peel was highly suspicious of the Chartist movement, with its Radical demand for universal suffrage, annual parliaments, vote by ballot, and the other 'six points'. Even if the Chartists were not plotting violent revolution (which he long suspected), he was sure that the effect of their reforms, if adopted, would be revolutionary in the sense that they would destroy the institutions of stable government, undermine ownership of property and shatter business confidence. He spoke against the Chartist petition of 1842 'as neither more or less than an impeachment of the whole constitution of this country'. He believed universal suffrage to be incompatible with the maintenance of 'mixed monarchy'; and he refused to substitute 'mere democracy' for a form of government which had secured 150 years of 'more practical happiness and of true liberty than has been enjoyed in any other country that ever existed'.[11] From the Whig side in the same debate Macaulay made his celebrated speech which demonstrated how applied Chartism would mean seizure of property, destruction of institutions and collapse into an anarchy which could only then be overcome through the establishment of a military despotism. Seven years earlier *The Times* (10 January 1835) had taken credit for first describing the ultra-Radicals as 'the destructives'.

Peel had spoken more fully and strikingly against the Radical demand for vote by ballot in 1833. He had then argued that voting secrecy would be impossible to maintain; that bribery would not be prevented; and that therefore, since unenforceable law was bad law, a Ballot Act would be bad law. Beyond this, however, Peel opposed the ballot because of its implied challenge to security of property. 'It was merely absurd to say, that a man with ten thousand pounds a year should not have more influence over the legislature of the country, than a man of ten pounds a year.' Yet each was only entitled to a

[10] Peel to Goulburn, 22 August 1836 (Goulburn Papers).
[11] Peel, *Speeches*, IV, pp. 57–60.

single vote. 'How could this injustice, this glaring inequality, be practically redressed, except by the exercise of influence.'[12]

Peel's determination to reduce the economic pressures which won mass support for Chartist political demands underlay his great economic reforms of 1841–6, of which repeal of the Corn Laws was only the last part. Some recent historians of Chartism, writing almost with an air of discovery, have accepted that Peel's success in removing obstacles to production and consumption did undermine the Chartist picture of an uncaring state; and, therefore, did weaken the appeal of the movement.[13] From taking office as Prime Minister in 1841 until his retirement five years later, Peel repeatedly claimed to be acting above all sectional interests – whether of landlords, financiers or manufacturers. In 1846, the leading Chartist newspaper, the *Northern Star* (31 January), came out boldly in support of Corn Law repeal; and did so in language which showed how persuasively Peel had argued his case for acceptance as a Minister genuinely above sectionalism and truly interested in improving the lot of working people. The *Northern Star* noted with approval how Peel was proposing not only abolition of the Corn Laws but also tariff and other changes which would increase the demand for labour, at the same time as they lowered the price of food and other necessaries:

> Now, had free trade been proposed in Whig style – had it been granted as a boon to the increasing power of the League, and as a sop to the monied interests, unaccompanied by those wise, salutary, and statesmanlike adjustments proposed by Sir Robert Peel, not all the power at the disposal of government could have averted the horrors of revolution.

Social control through high economic policy was intended to complement existing attempts at social control through the diffusion of a broad everyday morality, defined by the middle classes. Religion and education made major contributions towards the formulation of this morality, while the new railway network assisted its circulation throughout the country. Church and chapel tried to set standards of behaviour, and tried to exercise influence by example even over those millions of the working classes who rarely attended religious worship. Since the end of the eighteenth century, the Sunday schools had spread simple religion, morality and instruction among working-class children. By the 1830s a strong effort was being made to prolong this contact into adult life, albeit with limited success. The president of the University of Glasgow Peel Club noticed with satisfaction in 1836 how religious enterprise was 'extending her churches to meet the demands of increasing population, planting her Bible schools in every village, and teaching her people that, notwithstanding the

[12] Ibid., II, pp. 681–3; III, pp. 486–93.
[13] See G. Stedman Jones, 'Rethinking Chartism', in *Languages of Class* (1983), ch. 3; and Dorothy Thompson, *The Chartists* (1984), ch. 14.

march of intellect, it is still proper that they should "be subject to the higher power" – that they should "fear God and honour the King".' Sadly, the very belief in the potential influence of national elementary education led the Church of England and the Nonconformists to squabble about ways and means for forty years, so delaying until after 1870 the completion of a network of schools. Peel deplored this delay, not least because he shared the view that education should be encouraged on account of its value for social control. He praised the Tamworth Library and Reading Room, when he opened it in 1841, as an institution for bringing together 'intelligent men of all classes and all conditions in life . . . harmonising the gradations of society and binding men together by a new bond'.[14]

In the years of Peel's 1841–6 administration United Kingdom railway mileage nearly doubled, from 1,700 miles to over 3,000; and the number of passengers carried annually grew from 24,000,000 to 44,000,000. Gladstone's Railway Act of 1844 introduced third-class 'parliamentary trains', which were required to run at low fares of no more than a penny a mile. The social effect of railways was visible, as people of all classes but the poorest began to travel as never before. *The Sunday Times* (8 September 1850), a paper with a mainly lower middle-class readership, noticed condescendingly how cheap excursion trains had introduced 'A New Era in Locomotion', and provided 'a check to idle debauchery amongst the working classes on Sundays'. During the mid-1840s railway expansion had indeed got out of hand, as speculators scrambled to support many foolish schemes during the 'railway mania'. But Peel continued to be an enthusiast for sensible development. With considerable publicity and ceremony, he cut the first sod for the Trent Valley Railway in 1845, near his own home, and spoke strongly in favour of such direct lines of communication between major centres. At the line's opening in 1847 he praised the 'wonder-working' effect of railways through rapid communication of people, goods and ideas, and (interestingly not least) of troops: 'it will promote the moral and social welfare of this country, and add to its political security.'[15]

Peel was here addressing audiences of middle-class and superior working-class Tamworthians – gentlemen, employers, shopkeepers and artisans. Their 'respectability' was confirmed by their presence at such celebratory occasions. This idea of respectability crossed social boundaries, reaching both up to the aristocracy and down to the artisans and aspiring working men. It has been argued that in some places respectability was not given to the workmen by the middle classes, but was derived from long-standing craft experience; it was therefore accepted without sacrifice of independence. Be this as it may, a

---

[14] *Proceedings of the Peel Club, University of Glasgow, Session 1836–37* (1837), pp. 17–18; *The Times*, 26 January 1841.
[15] *The Times*, 15 November 1845, 28 June 1847.

numerous respectable Victorian public existed; and both locally and nationally Peel sought to be heard by the respectable of all classes.[16]

'Respectability' properly understood was dynamic, not static; it carried with it a commitment to self-help. It did not depend upon possession of more than a modest minimum of material possessions. According to Edward Baines's *History of the Cotton Manufacture* (1835), cotton spinners, for example, could 'pass through life with much of humble respectability'. An article on 'The False Respectable' in *Eliza Cook's Journal* (1 December 1849), which served lower middle-class and artisan readers, attacked those who were interested only in owning fine clothes and houses, and 'keeping a gig'. On the other hand, social rising was accepted as a hoped-for reward for those who practised self-help. In his Tamworth Library address, Peel praised the hard-working example of George Stephenson, the great railway engineer who had risen from nothing. Six years earlier Peel had spoken with pride of his own rise; how the son of a cotton spinner had become Prime Minister. He was glad that honest hard work could lead to 'opportunities of elevation and distinction in this great community'. Two years later he assured the Conservative operatives of Glasgow that 'industry, sobriety, honesty, and intelligence will as assuredly elevate the low, as idleness, profligacy, and vice will depress, and justly depress, those who are in high stations.'[17]

Nevertheless, individual social rising did not diminish the need for the social and political cement of 'deference'. Walter Bagehot's discussion of deference is well known. It has been pointed out, however, that Bagehot risked confusing his readers by using the word in two senses.[18] Sometimes he meant non-intellectual deference, which was instinctive and which did not necessarily operate within any active public opinion. Yet, he was well aware of the role of opinion in Victorian politics. Deference in politics as part of public opinion he came to describe in his 1877 essay on 'Lord Althorp and the Reform Act of 1832' as 'intellectual deference'. John Stuart Mill in his *Political Economy* (1848) had likewise contrasted what he called 'ancient deference', still to be found in rural southern England, with the more considered deference towards those with superior intellect or knowledge which was to be found among some urban working men. 'Such deference is deeply grounded in human nature; but they will judge for themselves of the persons who are and are not entitled to it.'[19] Possession of a title certainly made it easier for individuals to attract either

---

[16] G. Best, *Mid-Victorian Britain* (1971), xvi, ch. 4. See also T. R. Tholfsen, *Working Class Radicalism in Mid-Victorian England* (1977); and G. Crossick, *An Artisan Elite in Victorian Society* (1978).

[17] *The Times*, 12 May 1835; Minute Book of the Glasgow Conservative Operatives' Association 1837.

[18] See D. Spring, 'Walter Bagehot and deference', *American Historical Review*, 81 (1976), pp. 524–31.

[19] J. S. Mill, *Principles of Political Economy* (Pelican ed., 1970), pp. 121–5.

'ancient deference' or 'intellectual deference'. Edward Miall, the Noncon-formist politician, complained in 1849 that as soon as a few peers 'or even a baronet, if he be but a distinguished man' came out in favour of some opinion, then it gained 'an amazing accession of force – old and oft-repeated trains of reasoning immediately produce, one sees not why, the most convincing results.'[20] How Sir Robert Peel, the most distinguished baronet of his generation, benefited from 'ancient deference' on his estate has already been indicated: how he may have benefited from 'intellectual deference' in politics remains to be considered in due place.

The Reform Act of 1832 did not put an end to deference in elections. It was not intended to do so. The electorate was still relatively small, and voting was by public declaration at the hustings. In 1854 the ratio of English electors to population was only 1 : 20.7 in the counties and 1 : 18.0 in the boroughs. There were still only just over 400,000 borough electors in England and Wales, and just over 500,000 county electors. And among the latter the Reform Act had diluted the old freeholder electorate with £50 tenants-at-will, who were said to be more vulnerable to landlord pressure. It may be that farmers were willing enough to agree with their landlords on matters which seemed remote from their concerns and to vote accordingly as a social gesture. But when many farmers felt strongly – as they did against the malt tax in the mid-1830s, or for the Corn Laws in the 1840s – their views were loudly heard even where landlords felt differently.[21]

Tenant farmers constituted the largest single occupational group of voters. In some constituencies substantial numbers of labouring men qualified to vote; but in most places the franchise did not reach below shopkeepers and craftsmen. In other words, despite the progress of the industrial revolution, the borough electorate remained predominantly pre-industrial even after 1832. The influence of local social leaders – landowners, employers, men of Church and chapel – often coloured the constituency response to national political issues. These, however, were not necessarily so important as local issues or personal rivalries. Out of the conflict of rival interests the final choice of representatives might fairly reflect local opinion. Property and numbers each played their parts. Such was the case even in constituencies where, after assessment of comparative strengths by the rival parties, no contests took place. One-third of United Kingdom seats remained uncontested even in 1832, nearly one-half in 1835, well over one-third in 1837, and well over one-half in 1841. The pendulum did not swing dramatically in early Victorian general elections, but there was still movement. Peel's breakthrough in 1841 was the culmination of shifts over three general elections, plus by-election gains.

[20] E. Miall, *The British Churches in Relation to the British People* (1849), pp. 205–6.

[21] See especially J. R. Vincent, *Pollbooks, How Victorians Voted* (1967); C. R. Dod, *Electoral Facts* (1853), edited by H. J. Hanham (1972), introduction; N. Gash, *Politics in the Age of Peel* (2nd ed., 1976); and R. Stewart, *The Foundation of the Conservative Party 1830–1867* (1978).

Influence might be supplemented by bribery and corruption, and in smaller boroughs where voters numbered only hundreds this might be the main impetus. Maidstone was one such venal borough. The Whig diarist, Charles Greville, claimed (1 January 1835) that the people there were 'generally alive to public affairs – look into the votes and speeches of members, give their opinions – but are universally corrupt'. So, political opinions might be held and yet have little to do with the way electors voted. The position in Maidstone was not quite so entirely corrupt as Greville suggested. But Dod's *Electoral Facts* (1853) did comment: 'Influence. – Little or none of a personal kind prevails . . . pecuniary resources constitute the best recommendation.'[22]

Peel himself sat from 1830 for his small home borough of Tamworth, which his father had earlier represented. The electorate numbered only 528 in 1832, and had fallen to 307 by 1852. Peel ostentatiously stood aside from nominating for the second seat, but candidates acceptable to his family were usually returned. Despite many offers of support, he never contested a large, popular constituency, relishing 'that independence which the representation of a small place enables a man to exercise'.[23]

IV

The implication here was that the bigger the local electorate, the more a Member of Parliament might be expected to respond to constituency opinion. Analysis of voting in the House of Commons has certainly suggested that what was reflected in the division lists was often not so much Members' social backgrounds or business interests as the kinds of constituencies which they represented. Constituency opinion could not be ignored in the aggregate. Peel's famous Tamworth Manifesto of 1834 was hardly needed to persuade opinion in Tamworth itself: rather, as will be seen, it was published as a novel attempt to sway opinion in constituencies elsewhere.[24]

The power of public opinion had become increasingly recognized in Britain and Europe during the eighteenth century, notably after Rousseau's persuasive exploration of the 'general will'. He was the first influential writer to employ the term 'public opinion' itself, which was being used in England by the 1760s. Jeremy Bentham followed with the first detailed discussion in English, arguing that the press made the most important contribution towards the formation of public opinion.[25] But there were always many opinions and many publics. In

---

[22] See J. A. Phillips, 'The many faces of reform: the electorate and the Great Reform Act', *Parliamentary History*, I (1982), pp. 115–35.

[23] Peel to Brougham, 19 April 1847 (Add. MSS 40482, f. 358).

[24] See W. O. Aydelotte, 'Constituency influence on the British House of Commons, 1841–1847', in W. O. Aydelotte (ed.), *The History of Parliamentary Behaviour* (1977).

[25] See P. A. Palmer, 'The concept of public opinion in political theory', in C. Wittke (ed.), *Essays in History and Political Theory* (1936).

Britain during the 1830s and 1840s the mixture was especially strident. At one extreme of opinion lay the noisy and sometimes threatening demands of the political and trade unions, of the anti-Poor Law campaigners, of the factory agitators for a ten-hour day, and of the Chartists. Almost as loud were the complaints of some self-made manufacturers, whose contempt for traditional aristocratic government came to be voiced through the Anti-Corn Law League. Opposite extreme opinions were to be found within the 'landed interest', which grew to fear the League. Sophisticated but radical ideas about government came from the Benthamites, who were few in number but influential behind the scenes. And within the religious public, intense and conflicting shades of opinion ranged from the 'Oxford movement' at one end of the Church of England to 'Exeter Hall' on the Evangelical wing.

Only occasionally did public feeling solidify for or against some measure or policy with sufficient volume and breadth of support to deserve the singular label, to make it valid to say that 'public opinion thinks . . .'. But that this could happen at certain times was recognized by young Robert Peel as early as 1820 in a perceptive letter to his friend, J. W. Croker. 'Do not you think that the tone of England – of that great compound of folly, weakness, prejudice, wrong feeling, right feeling, obstinacy, and newspaper paragraphs, which is called public opinion – is more liberal – to use an odious but intelligible phrase – than the policy of the Government?'[26] This was written while everyone was awaiting the verdict in the trial of Henry Hunt, the Radical, for his part at the Peterloo meeting. Peel sensed that 'respectable' majority opinion was shifting in favour of 'reform':

> Do not you think there is a feeling, becoming daily more general and more confirmed – that is, independent of the pressure of taxation, or any immediate cause – in favour of some undefined change in the mode of governing the country? It seems to me a curious crisis – when public opinion never had such influence on public measures, and yet never was so dissatisfied with the share which it possessed. It is growing too large for the channels that it has been accustomed to run through. God knows, it is very difficult to widen them exactly in proportion to the size and force of the unrest which they have to convey, but the engineers that made them never dreamt of various streams that are now struggling for a vent.

In the previous autumn Peel had been reported as asking similar questions of another friend. Clearly, his assessment of the state of public opinion was carefully considered.[27]

Peel now accepted 'the public' as an expanding force in terms of numbers as well as of influence. How far down the social scale should politicians look for

[26] L. J. Jennings (ed.), *Correspondence and Diaries of . . . John Wilson Croker* (1884) I, p. 170.
[27] E. Phipps (ed.), *Memoirs of . . . Robert Plumer Ward* (1850) II, p. 25.

'publics' and their opinions? This was a crucial question. Radicals such as J. S. Mill asserted plainly that 'the working classes are now part of the public.' He argued that concentration of their numbers in towns, plus newspaper and other reading, along with the influence of dissenting sermons and the effects of railway mobility, had all combined to make the working classes better informed and therefore entitled to be heard.[28] An article on 'English Journalism' in *Fraser's Magazine* for December 1846, the year of repeal of the Corn Laws, emphasized how two millions had been added to the population since the passing of the 1832 Reform Act, and how the character of that population had much changed. It was no longer largely brutish and un-educated, even if not yet properly educated. 'A criticism of political personages has come into play, which it would be easier to conciliate than to suppress.' The attitudes of political parties were now analysed 'by classes who were formerly supposed to be blind and indifferent to the progress of the political drama'. Every club and public house had 'its oracles and its declaimers. Almost everybody reads a newspaper, and those who do not read listen with attention to those who do.'

Conservatives (with and without the capital letter) were not to be convinced by such claims. They feared that the working classes were still inclined to act violently, that they were excitable and vulnerable to manipulation by demagogues. Peel, as will be seen, long held this view; but by 1846 he was addressing at least the 'respectable' working classes, notably in the famous peroration to his resignation speech where he asked for remembrance by 'those whose lot it is to labour'. Nevertheless, even during this final crisis of his career he was careful not to call upon the working classes for active support, for any organization and agitation in favour of Corn Law repeal.

If the working classes were indeed not to be regarded as part of the public, this left the way open for the middle classes, who might then even be called 'the people'. In his *Letters on a Regicide Peace* (1796) Edmund Burke had numbered at about 400,000 in England and Scotland 'those who, in any political view, are to be called the people . . . of adult age, not declining in life, of tolerable leisure for such discussions, and of some means of information, more or less, and who are above menial dependence'. At least one historian has concluded that Burke's guess fell only a little short of the actual numbers of the contemporary political nation.[29] The 1832 Reform Act, with its predominantly middle-class franchise, was formally 'An Act to amend the Representation of the People'; and during the debates, Lord Brougham, the Lord Chancellor, firmly equated the middle classes with the people. 'By the people, I mean the middle classes, the wealth and intelligence of the country, the glory of the

---

[28] Mill, *Principles of Political Economy*, pp. 123–5.

[29] See J. A. Phillips, 'Popular politics in unreformed England', *Journal of Modern History*, 52 (1980), pp. 599–625.

British name.' It has been estimated that the Reform Act did enlarge the franchise fairly accurately to embrace 'the people' so defined, by giving the vote to a mainly middle-class 20 per cent of the adult male population.[30]

Growing middle-class awareness was reflected in the increase of petitioning to the Sovereign or to Parliament, especially from the time of the first parliamentary reform movement in the 1780s, which was soon followed by the campaign against the slave trade. In the five years ending 1789, the number of petitions was 880; in the five years ending 1831, it reached 24,492, and in the five years ending 1841, 70,369. In 1845, 10,253 petitions with 1,288,742 signatures were presented against Peel's proposed increased grant to Maynooth College; and in 1846 there were 1,958 petitions with 145,855 signatures against repeal of the Corn Laws, but 467 petitions with 1,414,303 signatures in favour of repeal.[31]

The presentation of petitions, with right of discussion, was absorbing an excessive amount of parliamentary time by the 1830s, and Peel was prominent among those who pressed for restriction. From 1839, debate upon presentation to the Commons was finally given up. During the 1830s and 1840s the causes most strongly backed by petitions were the Chartist 'six points'; local government reform; Poor Law reform; factory reform; trade union reform; Corn Law repeal; and repeal of the newspaper taxes. Significantly, these were causes with strong extra-parliamentary support, but with at least initially limited support inside Parliament. Peel was suspicious of organized petitioning, even for policies which he favoured. Referring to petitions in favour of repeal of the Test and Corporation Acts in 1828, he remarked that if he were sure that these petitions had been 'quite spontaneous, and not set in motion by any external influence' he would 'pay much more attention to them'.[32]

Peel was to address himself during the 1830s and 1840s repeatedly to middle-class opinion. In 1840 he listed in the Commons 'those intelligent and powerful classes' which ought particularly to influence governments, 'the clergy, the magistracy, the commercial classes, the yeomanry'. Within such middle-class groups he sought to win the non-partisans, the silent majority, men who, though they might vote for party candidates at elections, did so not on partisan grounds but on the merits of rival arguments and personalities. 'Though extremes may not be reconciled, and many continue irreconcilable,' declared Peel in a speech on the Corn Laws in 1842, 'yet, after the old practice in this country, reason and moderation will gravitate towards that which is just.' A few weeks later, proposing an income tax, he admitted that he was appealing 'not so much to gentlemen opposite, as to the deliberate judgment of

---

[30] Briggs, 'Language of "class"', pp. 161–2.

[31] T. Erskine May, *Constitutional History of England* (5th ed., 1875), p. 67. See C. Leys, 'Petitioning in the nineteenth and twentieth centuries', *Political Studies*, 3 (1955), pp. 45–64.

[32] Peel, *Speeches*, I, p. 553.

the country, on which I rely for ultimate support – that deliberating class who
are enabled to form a just judgment of the financial difficulties in which we are
now placed'.[33]

This was not meant as flattery. Peel genuinely admired the middle-class
virtues, and wrote in private as he spoke in public. Just before the opening of
the first reformed Parliament in 1833, he told his lieutenant, Henry Goulburn,
that Conservative policy 'ought to be to conciliate the good will of the sober-
minded and well disposed portion of the Community, and thus lay the
foundation of future strength'.[34] And so it turned out. Peel's increasing success
in attracting support from the silent, 'respectable' majority (not exclusively
middle class) will be explored in later chapters. Suffice it to cite here the
Maidstone Gazette of 6 January 1846, which commented perceptively when
Peel was about to propose repeal of the Corn Laws:

> Sir Robert Peel knows well that the corn law question must and will be
> settled; not at the instance of the persons or classes who are most directly
> interested either in maintaining these laws or getting them abolished;
> but by the means of moderate men, who may be said to be the
> depositories of that strong common sense for which our nation is
> celebrated; who seldom take an active part in politics, but who invariably
> throw their weight into the scale in opposition to every proved and
> tangible public grievance. Such the present corn laws are now admitted
> to be.

V

If, as Peel said in the peroration to his 1842 budget speech, 'the empire of
opinion' now prevailed, that empire always felt the need for an emperor. The
early Victorians were great seekers after heroes, not least in politics. Thomas
Carlyle (himself the sage as hero) gave his lectures on 'Hero-Worship' in 1840.
'Hustings-speeches, Parliamentary motions, Reform Bills, French Revolutions,
all mean at heart this; or else nothing. Find in any country the Ablest Man that
exists there; raise him to the supreme place, and loyally reverence him.' Could
Peel be the man? Soon after the passing of the Reform Act, Lytton Bulwer
regretted that Peel had not placed himself 'in his natural position among the
ranks of the people'. If he had done so, 'he would have been undeniably what
he now just fails of being – a GREAT MAN.' But by the mid-1840s Carlyle
himself had decided that Peel had reached the level of a political hero who
deserved reverence because of his self-sacrifice. In gratitude for Corn Law

---

[33] Ibid., III, pp. 703, 848; IV, p. 18.
[34] Peel to Goulburn [postmark 3 January 1833] (Goulburn Papers).

repeal he sent Peel a copy of his study of Cromwell, 'our most conspicuous citizen'.[35]

The Victorian need for heroes was reflected in a readiness to make lists of candidates. Anthony Trollope, the novelist, wrote in 1850 to his mother and brother requesting them to compile such lists; Trollope added that he was asking friends to do the same. He reported later that only two living people had been named in the returns, Metternich and Wellington. Peel was not mentioned; and Trollope, as will be seen later, was not an admirer.[36]

'Pitt' (presumably the younger) figured in all Trollope's lists. Pitt's death in 1806 was followed by extensive mourning, although apparently not equal to the grief at Peel's death. Lord Aberdeen, who lived through both events, compared the two after attending Peel's funeral. 'I well recollect the death of Mr. Pitt. On that occasion there was a general impression that the country had become less secure; and that we had been deprived of our chief means of protection and defence; but the spirit of party was by no means extinguished.' In this spirit The Times, which had opposed Pitt's return to office in 1804, remarked how the 'melancholy event' merely confirmed 'in the public opinion, the necessity of a change in his Majesty's Councils'. It reported that 'a vast number' viewed Pitt's lying in state in the Painted Chamber, but that the crowd watching the funeral procession to and from Westminster Abbey was 'by no means great'.[37]

The death of Charles James Fox six months later was received by friends and supporters, especially in London and Westminster, with deep sadness. At Fox's funeral, as apparently not at Pitt's, the streets to the abbey were crowded with people.[38] Fox's outgoing personality, his readiness to address public meetings in Palace Yard, Covent Garden, even in London taverns, made him a much more visible figure than Pitt, who rarely spoke outside Parliament. The opening of G. O. Trevelyan's major Victorian biography described Fox as 'our first great statesman of the modern school'. The reputations both of Pitt and Fox, it is important to notice, seem to have expanded after their deaths. By 1812 an intensification of partisanship had encouraged fervent Pitt and Fox cults. Fox was remembered as a martyr for liberty, Pitt as 'the pilot who weathered the storm'. Pitt clubs were formed in some fifty towns. Pitt or Fox dinners were held on appropriate anniversaries. Busts, pictures and other memorial artefacts were widely sold for many years after 1806.[39]

---

[35] E. Lytton Bulwer, *England and the English* (1833), edited by S. Meacham (Chicago, 1970), pp. 386–7; Carlyle to Peel, 19 June 1846 (Add. MSS 40593, f. 453); J. A. Froude, *Thomas Carlyle* (1884) I, pp. 375–7.

[36] B. A. Booth (ed.), *Letters of Anthony Trollope* (1951), pp. 17–18.

[37] *The Times*, 27 January; 21, 24 February 1806; Lady Frances Balfour, *Life of . . . Aberdeen* (n.d.) II, p. 158; J. Holland Rose, *William Pitt and the Great War* (1911), pp. 559–60.

[38] *The Times*, 11 October 1806; L. Reid, *Charles James Fox* (1969), pp. 428–31.

[39] F. O'Gorman, *The Emergence of the British Two-Party System 1760–1832* (1982), pp. 68–9.

The younger Pitt's father, 'the great commoner', had by the time of his death in 1778 outlived by almost twenty years his peak of popularity during the Seven Years War. Nevertheless, it can be claimed for him that he was the first man, other than a king and excepting Cromwell, to be generally recognized as a national leader. Remarkably by later practice, this recognition was achieved without the elder Pitt ever addressing a large public meeting.[40]

George Canning, a protegé of the younger Pitt, himself died as Prime Minister in 1827. His brilliance was not matched by balancing qualities of judgement or consistency. Nevertheless, his death within months of taking office came as a national shock; and The Times (17 August) reported that 'thousands of the most respectable classes' lined the funeral route. The paper claimed that mourning was more intense than at any subject's funeral within living memory. Taken literally, this claim meant that mourning for Canning surpassed that for Pitt or Fox. But in 1850 the Examiner (6 July) remembered the occasion only to remark that, much as Canning had been mourned, regret for Peel was 'much more general and intense'.

In the 1820s comparisons were sometimes made between Canning and Peel as candidates for the highest office. Peel's reliability and tact were set against Canning's variability and levity. One commentator noticed after Peel's death how both Canning and Peel had tried to justify the Peterloo massacre of 1819 to the Commons; but how Canning's tone had been insolent and unfeeling, whereas Peel had remained calm and judicial. 'The language of Canning on that occasion was never forgotten or forgiven: after a few years no one remembered that Peel had ever had the misfortune to defend so bad a cause.' Bagehot, in his 1856 essay on 'The Character of Sir Robert Peel', remarked how 'old Liberals' still grew angry at the recollection of Canning's 'dexterous insincerity'.[41]

From his early days in politics Peel was recognized both inside and outside Parliament as a man of good character. The Times obituary on the death of Fox (15 September 1806) had emphasized how vital an acceptable reputation now was for success in politics. In a free country, wrote The Times, the people weighed the characters of public men, 'and while their personal similitudes are seen in every part of the kingdom, the portraits of their characters . . . are hung up in the minds of all its inhabitants.' In the still relaxed moral climate of 1806 The Times was able to gloss over Fox's unconventional private life, and to concentrate upon his statesmanlike talents. Peel's private life, by contrast, was impeccable, it being well known that he was a devoted husband and the solicitous father of five sons and two daughters. This was just as well, since during Peel's lifetime private as well as public behaviour came to matter in

---

[40] See Marie Peters, Pitt and Popularity (1980).
[41] W. R. Greg, Essays in Political and Social Science (1853) II, p. 324; E. B. Chancellor (ed.), Diary of Philip Von Neumann (1922) I, p. 90.

relation to public reputation. The compiler of Peel's collected speeches, published in 1853, remembered him as 'a good man, over whose destiny home affection had one holy sway, and public duty another'.[42]

By the 1840s, the brilliance alone of a Fox or a Canning would hardly have sufficed to sustain them in the eyes of the world, as the collapse of the reputation of Henry Brougham demonstrated. He reached a peak of popularity during the Reform Bill crisis as a brilliant man of the people; but within a few years his reputation had disintegrated when his restlessness became apparent to the public. Macaulay had, indeed, forecast that this would happen. *Punch* in 1843 carried a cartoon which depicted Brougham as 'The Image Seller', desperately offering for sale models of himself in such roles as Harlequin, Clown or Pantaloon. 'The chosen champion and Goliath of the people,' concluded one Kent newspaper, 'is transformed into the Grimaldi of the State.'[43]

In this same *Punch* cartoon Peel and Wellington looked on in sadness at Brougham. Peel matched Brougham in social concern, and Peel's drive (unlike Brougham's) was always well directed. Brougham strove always to be lively: Peel was willing to risk seeming to be dull. This latter quality was, indeed, almost a recommendation among statesmen by the early Victorian years. 'The British People being subject to fogs and possessing a powerful Middle Class require grave statesmen.' So Disraeli ruefully and facetiously observed.[44] The real background to this Victorian liking for seriousness was religious, the influence of the evangelical conscience. Peel's own conscience became increasingly visible, as he repeatedly emphasized how he was less concerned with party politics than with the public good. The conclusion to one of his speeches at the end of the 1842 session was revealing in this respect beneath its careful phrasing. Peel thanked his backbenchers for their support, but placed this support only third among his priorities: 'next to the approval of our own conscience, and to the hope of future fame, the highest reward we can receive is their cordial support and their personal esteem.'[45]

'Conscience' mattered, and it was expected to produce positive effects which were clearly beneficial. A statesman's policies were required to be both 'good' and to be readily seen as good. Emerson's 1847 lecture on 'The Uses of Great Men', in his series on 'Representative Men', complained about able individuals who spent their time answering difficult questions which most contemporaries lacked the skill even to put. Great men, he emphasized, 'must be related to us ... They satisfy expectation and fall into place.' How Peel came to satisfy much Victorian expectation is the theme of this book.

[42] Peel, *Speeches*, I, p. 2.
[43] *Punch*, IV (1843), pp. 116–17; *Dover Telegraph*, 2 March 1844; G. O. Trevelyan, *Life and Letters of Lord Macaulay* (World's Classics ed., 1932) I, p. 174.
[44] R. Blake, *Disraeli* (1969), p. 766.
[45] Peel, *Speeches*, IV, p. 138.

Great men were by definition strong men in their fields, and a great statesman was expected to provide strong government. This was partly a matter of actions, but also a matter of communication. A statesman's measures needed to be not only strong in detail, but also strongly felt and strongly presented. As late as 13 October 1845, only weeks before the final Corn Law crisis, *The Times* was still not accepting Peel's greatness as a political leader when judged by these standards:

> Where is the man among us capable of guiding the nation aright, of giving to public opinion that healthful tone which can alone render it harmonious with eternal truth, of deciding for the best the course and character of our rapid career? Lord Brougham and Mr. Carlyle have made the attempt, each in his own particular mode, and each has signally failed. It is in vain that we try to point to a single individual, to a clique, or to the leaders of a party, as likely to make any permanent valuable impression on the character of the people. But we have leaders who are availing themselves of the opportunities within their reach. In Ireland the passions of the people are sedulously cultivated by Mr. O'Connell, and in Great Britain the principle of expediency is embodied and exhibited in action in Sir Robert Peel.

In other words, although Peel's attachment to expediency might be producing useful reforms, such lack of heroic leadership did not provide a foundation for greatness of mind either in Peel himself or in the nation. The absence of a truly great man, concluded *The Times*, was leaving the country in danger:

> Under such leaders, with the examples set by them, with the encouragement they give by precept and practice, who will be bold enough to say that the social and moral condition of the nation, stimulated by the feverish excitement under which it labours, and suffering at the same time from a plethora of wealth in its upper extension, and the atrophy of poverty in its lower, may not, by one of those accidents to which the body politic is at all times liable, be suddenly brought into a state of the most imminent peril?

So exclaimed *The Times* in 1845. But an article in *Fraser's Magazine* for May 1842, on 'The Premier at Home and Abroad' had already suggested that Peel's greatness was becoming apparent after less than a year in office. It welcomed his bold policies and his assertion of authority from the centre. It asked specifically whether Lytton Bulwer would now deny Peel's claim to greatness. 'For the first time in his life Sir Robert Peel has been seen to act from the impulses of his own mind, and therefore for the first time ought the question of his being "a great man" to be considered.' Formerly, the article continued, Peel had been merely the servant of party: now he had brought forward '*his own* measures, and, in legal parlance, "put himself on the country".'

VI

The same article in *Fraser's* had dwelt upon the importance of public speaking in British life, from the parish level upwards. The entire nation, claimed the article, could be divided into 'those who speak, and those who have only learned to cry, "Hear, hear"'. The House of Commons was simply the highest of all forums for speaking and listening, where a Prime Minister was expected frequently to explain himself to Members and to the nation. He must be able, continued the article, 'not merely to plan his measures in the closet, but also to give a lucid and satisfactory oral explanation of the most complicated details at St. Stephens'. And Peel, the article concluded, possessed this double capacity for conception and communication to an eminent degree.

Peel himself readily accepted the necessary link between speaking and leading. In 1838 he was described as remembering in conversation how he had heard the younger Pitt address the Commons in 1805. 'The image of the man, his voice and manner, had constantly since been present to his mind, giving him altogether the idea of a man "born to be the Ruler of a People".'[46]

In an 1838 *Edinburgh Review* article on Sir William Temple, Macaulay claimed that 'parliamentary talent' was the most valuable qualification which a statesman could possess: 'a Minister who can make a successful speech need trouble himself little about an unsuccessful expedition.' But this required more than merely repeating a party line. It meant rallying and pleasing one's backbenchers, and gaining the attention and even the respect of the opposite side of the House. The rallying function of a Commons speech was especially important, as Sidney Herbert, a young Peelite, remarked to Lord Lincoln, another young Peelite, during the 1846 Corn Law debates: 'I hope Peel will speak tonight, for we have had two nights without a speech from our bench, and it is important to fix wavering opinions.'[47] To achieve a change of voting through the persuasiveness of a speech was rare, the more so as party attitudes solidified after the passing of the Reform Act. But when opinion was closely divided, as over the Reform Bill itself in 1831, even a few switched votes could count. 'I look to Peel's speech,' wrote Lord Ellenborough in March 1831. 'If he makes a successful speech we shall throw out the bill.' In the event the second reading was carried by a single vote.[48]

What was said in Parliament was reported through the newspapers to the country. Brougham asked in 1812, 'who is so romantic as to fancy that all the speaking in any one parliamentary debate ever influenced half a dozen votes?'

---

[46] A. Aspinall (ed.), 'Extracts from Lord Hatherton's diary', *Parliamentary Affairs*, 17 (1963–4), p. 262.

[47] Herbert to Lincoln, 16 February 1846 (NeC 11931).

[48] A. Aspinall (ed.), *Three Early Nineteenth Century Diaries* (1952), p. 62.

Speeches by parliamentarians mattered because their words 'decide their character in that body and in the country ... debates in parliament are a regular series of appeals to the people.'[49] The country, in other words, listened to Parliament. But increasingly, as 'pressure from without' became a part of the political process, Parliament found itself, however reluctantly, listening to the language of agitation in the country. *The Times* of 11 February 1845 noted how the force and effect of any excitement even in remote parts was now known almost immediately. 'Not only the words and voices of the speakers, but their tone, their gestures, their effect, the enthusiasm of their audiences, the zeal and the numbers of their followers, their unanimity, their combination, are all as well known within a few hours in St. Stephens or on 'Change as in the nearest market town.' G. H. Francis observed in *Orators of the Age* (1847) that all the great agitators depended upon repeated speech-making; and that organized pressure from reformers had provoked counter-organization from supporters of the status quo. He noted that the Anti-Corn Law League had been matched by agricultural protection societies; working-class Radical agitation by operative Conservative associations; Chartist meetings by 'ministerial speeches at anniversary dinners'.[50]

The style of speaking in Parliament had much changed by the early Victorian period compared with the days of Pitt and Fox; and it was a change which suited Peel. He remarked with satisfaction in 1845 that 'the speaking in simple unaffected language on subjects thoroughly understood by the Speaker, is becoming very popular.' Tom Moore noted in his 1825 biography of Sheridan how the old rhetorical style was already passing. When Canning, as late as 1826, ventured upon his famous antithesis of calling the New World to redress the balance of the Old, it was doubtful whether the Commons would break into sounds of approval (as it did) or burst out laughing.[51] Disraeli's bitterly brilliant personal attacks on Peel in the mid-1840s stood out not only because of their penetrating phrases but also because they aimed at character assassination. This went far beyond the limits of what was normally heard in Parliament by the Victorian period. Disraeli's sallies were the more dramatic for being delivered from Peel's own side of the House. Many years later Gladstone (a friend of Peel and no friend of Disraeli) admitted that the latter's invective had been quite as wonderful of its kind as reports suggested. 'Peel altogether helpless in reply. Dealt with them with a kind of "righteous dullness".' But though Disraeli's sparkle briefly excited the Commons, Peel's steadiness counted for more, especially in the country. The *Spectator* (9 May 1846) shrewdly acknowledged and dismissed Disraeli's speeches in a single

---

[49] [H. Brougham], 'Rights and duties of the people', *Edinburgh Review*, 20 (1812), pp. 423–4.
[50] G. H. Francis, *Orators of the Age* (1847), pp. 6–7.
[51] Peel to Thomas Baring, 13 January 1845 (Add. MSS 40557, f. 354); T. Moore, *Memoirs of ... Sheridan* (1825), pp. 463–5; J. McCarthy, *Sir Robert Peel* (1891), p. 11.

phrase as 'the ideal of pert presumption'. A visitor to the Commons described one of Peel's speeches as the finest he had ever heard, 'a predominant appearance of conviction and resolution . . . D'Israeli's was a mere baying at the moon in comparison with all his talent.'[52]

G. H. Francis noticed with approval that measures were now usually attacked rather than men. 'The House had become the property of the public; and deference is paid to the public, by public men merging their private quarrels in the more important contests of the class interests which they represent.'[53] Peel himself usually avoided personalities in his speeches, although he was capable of speaking *ad hominen* when he felt it to be deserved. Thus in August 1842 he castigated Palmerston, who had tried to draw unfavourable comparisons between Peel's new policies and those of the previous weak Whig administration. 'I am grateful to him for enabling the public to draw a contrast between the imperfect, bungling efforts at legislation of himself and his colleagues, and the extent and value of the comprehensive measures proposed by the present government.' Peel told his wife that he 'never saw a man look so foolish.'[54]

But Peel was under great pressure at this time, and such was not his usual style, which was constructive rather than destructive. He was fairly described as a great speaker rather than a great orator. His best speeches were clear in their language, sequential in argument and cumulatively persuasive. Mary Shelley noted that they had a beginning, a middle and an end: 'he rises with his subject & carries the hearer along with him.' Peel's grandson explained how Sir Robert liked to explore alternatives, 'until the last remaining appeared to be dictated to his audience by necessity rather than to have been chosen for them by the minister'. Francis Jeffrey made the same point less appreciatively in conversation in 1832: 'the liberality he always parades towards his opponents – the large concessions he makes, when he feels he has a strong case – the cards he throws away – always, however, keeping a good hand.' Peel himself admitted good humouredly to the Commons in 1847 that he had 'more than once excited a smile' when he had said 'that there were three courses which it was open to me to adopt'.[55]

Peel was usually clear if he wanted to be so. But he understood the uses of opacity. 'His language was cloudy only when it dwelt on matters which, however clear to himself, were not fitted or not ripe for Parliamentary inspection.' So explained an obituary article in *Tait's Edinburgh Magazine* for

---

[52] Blake, *Disraeli*, pp. 236–8; Betty Miller (ed.), *Elizabeth Barrett to Miss Mitford* (1954), p. 263.

[53] Francis, *Orators of the Age*, p. 18.

[54] Peel, *Speeches*, IV, pp. 127–38; N. Gash, *Sir Robert Peel* II (1972), pp. 337–8.

[55] *Sir Robert Peel and His Era* (1843), pp. 256–8; G. Peel, 'Peel, Sir Robert', *Dictionary of National Biography* (1895); Aspinall, *Early Nineteenth Century Diaries*, p. 190; Betty T. Bennett (ed.), *Letters of Mary Wollstonecraft Shelley* (1983) II, pp. 223–4.

August 1850. Even his supporters sometimes grinned 'at the balancing of reciprocally destroying negatives', and at the catholic generosity of the truisms to which he pledged himself. Thus he apparently once described Louis Philippe as the greatest ruler of France 'since Napoleon', a prime example of how to say something and yet nothing.

The danger with such use of language, and also with the method of proof by elimination, was that critical hearers might ask whether speakers of this kind possessed any real convictions. That Peel was nearly always 'plausible' was generally agreed; but for many contemporaries this long meant that he was hardly to be trusted. The speeches of his later years, however, when he was throwing off the restraints of party to advocate free trade, the increased Maynooth grant and repeal of the Corn Laws, left him no longer open to the charge of plausibility without conviction. His sincerity now stood out, as he proved himself ready to risk his own future in office for the sake of bold policies. G. H. Francis noticed the 'magical change' which came over Peel at this time.[56]

During the crisis of 1846 a parody of Peel's method of argument by elimination appeared in *The Struggle*, a Preston anti-Corn Law journal. A cartoon pictured Peel holding Cobden with one hand and gesticulating with the other towards 'Sir Harkaway', a landlord:

> Now, Mr. Cobden, you say that two and two make four. – You, Sir Harkaway, maintain that two and two make eight. – Now there are three courses open to me. I may coincide with Mr. Cobden. I may concede his point to Mr. [sic] Harkaway, and I may take a middle course; therefore, my dear friends, let us suppose that two and two make six – we must have compromise, and expediency must be listened to by any man who is minister.[57]

Peel irritated some listeners and readers by the seeming egotism of his speeches, in which the first person singular could occur with above-average frequency. In 1843 *Punch* wrote 'A Speech for Sir Robert', which was peppered with 'I's. *Punch* added punningly that the Queen had commanded Sir Robert to attach 'Argus' to his Christian names 'in commemoration of his *hundred I.'s*'. Peel was certainly conscious of his considerable capacities, but he also felt very seriously his heavy responsibilities; and it may have been the latter rather than the former which led him to speak so much in the first person. He wanted the public to know that he was fully concerned and fully in charge. 'I will not stand at the helm during such tempestuous sights as I have seen, if the vessel be not allowed fairly to pursue the course which I think she ought to take.'[58]

---

[56] Francis, *Orators of the Age*, pp. 38–9.
[57] *The Struggle*, no. 220.
[58] *Punch*, V (1843), pp. 202–3; Peel, *Speeches*, IV, p. 581.

"I will hold office unshackled by any other obligation than that of consulting the public interest, and providing for the public safety."—*Sir R. Peel.*

Compromise; or, Two and Two make Six.

Sir Robert.—Now, my dear Cobden, not so violent if you please. Now do, I pray, Sir Harkaway, listen to moderation. Now, Mr. Cobden, you say that two and two make four.—You, Sir Harkaway, maintain that two and two make eight.—Now there are three courses open to me. I may coincide with Mr. Cobden. I may concede his point to Mr. Harkaway, and I may take a middle course; therefore, my dear friends, let us suppose that two and two make six—we must have compromise, and expediency must be listened to by any man who is minister, and, therefore, umpire between conflicting interests.

'Compromise': *The Struggle*, no. 220 (1846)

VII

Yet if Peel was quite often blamed for egotism in the presentation of his policies, he was still more often praised for their 'practical' strength. 'Practical' was a word frequently used both by Peel and about him. The phrase 'practical politics' seems to have been coined by Disraeli in the fourteenth chapter of his novel, *Vivian Grey* (1826). Thereafter this expression, and the adjective alone, quickly slipped into everyday English usage in a spirit of decided approval. Most early Victorians liked to think of themselves as practical in thought and deed; and they were glad to find that Peel shared the same cast of mind. Prince Albert said publicly after Peel's death that his great influence sprang 'from the nation recognising in him qualities of the true type of the English character, which is essentially practical'. The *People's Journal*, which circulated widely among the lower middle classes and artisans, praised Peel in 1847 as 'the *beau ideal* of a practical man. That is the pivot on which all his weight in the country rests.'[59]

In 1842 Gladstone, from his close vantage point as Vice-President of the Board of Trade, was impressed as he watched Peel's practical method in action; initially with regard to the details of Corn Law modification, and then in manoeuvring the necessary legislation through Parliament.[60] Gladstone was struck by the tenacity with which Peel, first, retained as much as possible of the old arrangements so as to minimize alarm; and then, after announcing the plan to Parliament, steadily resisted any changes. In this way he 'narrowed the ground and reduced in number the points of attack and thus made his measure practicable in the face of a popular excitement and a strong opposition'. Speaking in support of this same measure, Peel himself summed up his purpose as 'to effect as much practical good as I can'. He then added a characteristic gloss: 'and not by pronouncing panegyrics upon general principles, which might win temporary popularity' but which would 'delay even a partial remedy'.[61]

Practical policies needed to be based upon full information. 'Facts are ten times more valuable than declamation'; so wrote young Peel in 1816.[62] He possessed a very good memory for details, and his command and presentation of statistics in his financial speeches were particularly impressive. The *Manchester Guardian*'s London correspondent (6 July 1850) remembered after Peel's death how

> round the details of a tariff he threw a charm from which none could escape; and, after listening to him for hours on cotton wool, copper ore, the duties on glass, exports and imports, bank issues, national income and expenditure, you wondered by what magic he contrived to fascinate you with topics so heavy in the hands of other men.

Peel's perorations were carefully prepared, although sometimes too obviously so. Certainly, he did not offer striking phrases or images, as did Disraeli. Yet Peel's inherent good sense and clear mind could lead him into crisply expressed truths; and Professor Gash has collected nearly six pages of these, drawn from his speeches and private letters.[63] Though not a humourist, Peel was capable of humour. He liked to poke gentle fun at the foibles of fellow parliamentarians, although some of this was not readily intelligible to outsiders.

---

[59] *People's Journal*, III (1847), pp. 201–3; *The Times*, 26 October 1850.
[60] Gladstone memorandum, 26 February 1842 (Add. MSS 44819, f. 79).
[61] Peel, *Speeches*, III, p. 841.
[62] Peel to W. Gregory, 9 April 1816 (Add. MSS 40290, f. 205).
[63] Gash, *Peel*, II, pp. 717–22.

Tait's obituary writer remembered how Peel's 'transient allusions to individuals, his smiles and gestures, and quotations, used to convulse the House with laughter, which seemed unaccountable when reported in the newspapers'.

Peel's voice was strong, and therefore easily heard across the floor of the Commons. His elocution was pronounced, and he added further emphasis by banging the dispatch box in front of him. His accent was slightly provincial, often remembered as 'Lancashire'; but William Huskisson described Peel's speech on the address in 1819 as 'very well . . . except that he *oped* too often, and talked of the *ouse*, as we Staffordshire men are apt to do'. Peel seems to have eventually schooled himself not to drop his 'H's at the start of words; but he continued to drop them in the middle. Carlyle praised Peel's voice as 'extremely good, low-toned, something of *cooing* in it, rustic, affectionate, honest, suitably persuasive'. A Lancashire accent is not usually recognizable as 'cooing'; so perhaps Peel's voice was not that of his county of birth but that of the county where he spent much of his life. The public schools had not yet imposed 'Oxford' English accents upon the upper classes. Both Lord Stanley and young Gladstone among Peel's Cabinet colleagues spoke with Lancashire accents.[64]

The *People's Journal* described Peel at work in the Commons: 'The way in which he "puts it" to the honourable member for so-and-so is perfection – it would melt a stone. You almost think you could be persuaded by his very tones and gestures only – that to hear the words he is uttering is only an unnecessary ceremony.' Peel's countenance, continued the *Journal*, added to the effect of his voice. 'It speaks a speech in itself. The bland smile, the exquisite irony of the arched and elevated eyebrows, the power of expressing scorn when to do so is part of the *role*, and yet the intellectuality, the refined shrewdness, and the commanding intelligence of the whole expression.'[65]

Peel usually began his important speeches with his left hand resting on his side, as he is pictured in the portraits by Lawrence and by Pickersgill. His tall, well-dressed figure, his handsome face with curved nose and intelligent blue eyes, his head topped by red hair abundant into middle age, combined to make him a striking figure. He was patently a man of authority. His legs were his one physical shortcoming. They were slightly out of proportion to his body, which caused him to walk awkwardly and to point his feet at unusual angles when standing. This is discreetly shown in Wintehalter's joint portrait of Peel and the Duke of Wellington.

For forty years Peel voiced his opinions at frequent intervals in the House of Commons. He reminded the house in 1841, with some satisfaction, that no politician had more explicitly revealed himself 'upon all the great

[64] Huskisson to Mrs Huskisson, 29 January 1819 (Add. MSS 39949, f. 30); Lord Campbell, *Lives of the Lord Chancellors* VIII (1869), p. 166; T. Carlyle, *Reminiscences* (1881) I, p. 433; G. Kitson Clark, *Life and Work of Sir Robert Peel* (1951), pp. 1–2.

[65] *People's Journal*, III (1847), pp. 201–3.

Peel in the Commons – a humorous view: *Punch*, 12 May 1849

constitutional questions'. *The Opinions of the Right Hon. Sir Robert Peel Expressed in Parliament and in Public*, a compilation by W. T. Haly, was first published in 1843; and went into a second edition after Peel's death in 1850. His collected speeches in Parliament, published in 1853, ran to four large volumes. One count of the number of times that Peel addressed the Commons has confirmed Peel's great activity there: he spoke 4,850 times. Some of these were only interjections, but the total is impressive when set beside Cobden's 482, or even Graham's 2,492. A count has only been taken for those early nineteenth-century politicians who were closely interested in economic questions, and so such leaders as Palmerston or Russell have not been assessed. But among those covered, only the chatterboxes Joseph Hume and Henry Brougham spoke more often than Peel. Peel heads the list for membership of parliamentary committees.[66]

[66] Peel, *Speeches*, III, p. 770; F. W. Fetter, *The Economist in Parliament, 1780–1868* (1980), appendix IV.

Peel was well aware of the need to suit his language and line to his Commons audience. He wrote in 1828 of 'House of Commons arguments ... of arguments for People who know very little of the matter, care not much about it, half of whom have dined or are going to dine, and are only forcibly struck by that which they instantly comprehend without trouble'.[67] The character of his Commons audience thus encouraged Peel into simplicity of argument. Brevity, however, did not necessarily accompany simplicity. When asked by Gladstone on one occasion whether he should be concise, Peel urged Gladstone instead to be long and diffuse, because of the need in the Commons 'to state your case in many ways, so as to produce an effect on men of many ways of thinking'.[68] Such an audience did not want to hear theoretical discussion. Peel himself was well read in contemporary social, economic and political theory, but he took care only to hint at this in his speeches. Indeed, he showed himself impatient at too much purely theoretical debate. Towards the end of the first session of the reformed Parliament he complained that there had been more motions for the consideration of abstract resolutions than at any former period. 'We should consider the difficulties surrounding practical questions before we entered into engagements on principles which we were not certain that we might be able to carry into execution.'[69]

Peel's control of the Commons was impressive. Disraeli, who himself briefly disturbed Peel's sway, admitted that he had played on Members of Parliament 'as on an old fiddle'.[70] Charles Greville noted in his diary (19 January 1834) that no matter how unruly or tired the House, as soon as Peel rose all was quiet and he was sure of being heard with attention. The compiler of Peel's collected speeches remarked that his speaking style was particularly geared to the House of Commons, and that his speeches outside Parliament were less impressive. 'He was not festive at festivals; he was only grateful, but never enthusiastic at ovations.' Nevertheless, Disraeli was exaggerating when he claimed that Peel could not address a public meeting or make an after-dinner speech 'without being ill at ease, or generally saying something stilted or even a little ridiculous'.[71] It will be seen in later chapters that Peel delivered several effective major speeches outside the House of Commons. But the parliamentary atmosphere suited him best. It is often forgotten that after the great fire of 1834, which destroyed the old Palace of Westminster, the Commons chamber in which Peel achieved all his later triumphs was a temporary construction which was still in use at the time of his death.

A sharp description has survived of Peel speaking at the opening of the Trent Valley Railway in 1847. It comes from the diary of a Manchester middle-class

---

[67] Peel to Lloyd, 19 February 1828 (Add. MSS 40343, f. 150).
[68] J. Morley, *Life of William Ewart Gladstone* (1905) I, p. 192.
[69] Peel, *Speeches*, II, p. 744.
[70] B. Disraeli, *Lord George Bentinck* (1852), p. 69.
[71] Ibid., p. 69; Peel, *Speeches*, I, p. 2.

THE GREAT CORN-LAW DEBATE IN THE HOUSE OF COMMONS. — A SKETCH FROM THE MINISTERIAL BENCHES.

Peel in the Commons – a serious view: *Illustrated London News*, 30 January 1846

reformer, Absalom Watkin, who had never before heard Peel, and who was 'much pleased', albeit with qualifications:

> He has a gentle, manly bearing, and carries his head well; his features are good, the mouth being well-formed and the eye not bright, yet not dull. He seems to smile habitually, but the lines of care, and as I thought of cunning, are very visible in his countenance. His voice is good, his utterance extremely distinct. and his sentences well formed.[72]

Watkin had been told that Peel had made a few notes, and 'the allusions he made to the ancient state of Tamworth and to Ethelfreda, the sister of Alfred, as well as his closing eulogy of the Queen, all seemed to have been pre-arranged.' Peel's action, thought Watkin, was not good: 'though he stood well, and, while his hands were loosely clasped before him, also looked well, he soon placed one hand behind him under his coat-tail, and when he threw out his right hand, it was not the opened hand, but two fingers extended, and the others were doubled in as if he were about to poke somebody.'

---

[72] A. E. Watkin (ed.), *Absalom Watkin, Extracts from his Journal* (1920), pp. 246–7.

VIII

Peel was very selective about attending public gatherings. He followed what he called a 'general rule' of only accepting invitations to events with which he had a particular connection, as with local election or other occasions at Tamworth. He refused to join meetings where he might be associated with extreme opinions expressed by other speakers. Thus in 1839 he even declined to attend a meeting at Willis's Rooms 'for the extension and improvement of popular Education in connection with the Church', presided over by the Archbishop of Canterbury. He told Gladstone that although 'we might answer for ourselves at a public meeting', it would be difficult 'to control others'. As the education question was shortly to be raised in Parliament, he preferred to express his opinions in his place there.[73]

Peel well knew that what he said at Westminster would carry weight not only within the Commons but nationally. In 1843 Gladstone carefully analysed what he believed to be Peel's view of the value of parliamentary speeches:

> Fremantle judges a speech according to its influence on those whom he has to *whip*: Peel's is a more complex view made up of the direct influence upon his voting supporters, the good aspect in argument towards the Opposition for debate, and the general relation to public opinion and the character of the Administration out of doors.[74]

This last aspect was very important to Peel. Although he refused merely to follow public opinion, or to allow it any veto over measures or policies which he judged to be in the public interest, he was always anxious for public approval in general, sensitive about the 'character' of himself and his colleagues. There ought to be, he declared in the Stockdale *v*. Hansard debates in 1840, 'a general sympathy' between constituents and their respective Members of Parliament. This made it vital for parliamentary speeches to be well and widely reported. There was no major question, he reminded the Commons, which 'had not been carried in the first instance by the free publication of the proceedings of parliament'. Moreover, ministerial explanations, or votes to spend taxpayers' money, needed to be understood in the country as well as in Parliament.[75]

The compiler of Peel's collected speeches claimed in his introduction that 'no man was ever more faithfully reported than Sir Robert Peel'. By the 1830s most

---

[73] Peel to Stanley, 18 May (?1835) (Derby Papers, 129/1); Gladstone to Peel, 18 May 1839 (Add. MSS 40426, f. 447); Peel to Gladstone, 22 May 1839 (Add. MSS 44275, f. 28).

[74] J. Brooke and Mary Sorensen (eds), *The Prime Ministers' Papers: W. E. Gladstone II: Autobiographical Memoranda 1832–1845* (1972), p. 194.

[75] Peel, *Speeches*, III, pp. 672–4.

speeches in *Hansard's Parliamentary Debates* were given in third-person extended reports; while major speeches, sometimes corrected by the speakers themselves, were increasingly given in the first person. Peel twice praised in the Commons the quality and impartiality of parliamentary reporting.[76]

The parliamentary reports which most people read appeared not in Hansard, but in the newspapers; either in the London daily or evening papers, headed by *The Times*, or in local weekly papers. *Hansard*'s reports were themselves supplied by reporters for the London papers. Into the 1820s the fullness and accuracy of Commons reporting had been variable. The position of the reporters' gallery long made it difficult for them to hear members whose voices were less than strong; and Canning, even though he could be heard, spoke so fast that reporters could not easily keep up with him. But improved positions and speedier forms of shorthand allowed more accurate and fuller reporting by the end of the 1820s. In 1833 the number of parliamentary reporters was between forty and fifty, and their 'respectability' was now accepted. Some of them, Peel reminded the Commons, were former army or naval officers, several were barristers and most had received 'an academical education'. One of their number in the 1830s was young Charles Dickens.[77]

These same London reporters were available, outside the parliamentary session, to attend major public meetings. Robert Lowery, the Chartist, remembered how well they covered the Chartist meeting in Palace Yard, Westminster, on 17 September 1838. The reporters for the various papers each took notes for about a quarter of an hour and were then relieved. The speech-making started at 1 p.m. and lasted until nearly 6 p.m. By 4.30 p.m. copies of the *Sun* were already circulating on the platform, with detailed reports of the speeches up to an hour earlier.[78]

Peel and his colleagues did sometimes complain about misreporting. Statistics in financial speeches were particularly difficult to get right at a single hurried hearing.[79] One way of ensuring circulation of a version satisfactory to the speaker was to publish in pamphlet form. Many of Peel's major speeches were printed in this way, although not all were authorized and corrected by him. The earliest Peel pamphlet speech in the British Library dates from 1817 (a speech against Catholic Emancipation); during the 1830s and 1840s one or more pamphlet versions of Peel's speeches in or out of Parliament appeared nearly every year. W. E. Painter of 342 Strand set out to issue in cheap form the speeches of Peel and other Conservative leaders 'the day after they are spoken'. For example, Painter published a version of Peel's Tamworth election

---

[76] Ibid., II, pp. 206, 742. See A. Aspinall, 'The reporting and publishing of the House of Commons' debates 1771–1834', in R. Pares and A. J. P. Taylor (eds), *Essays Presented to Sir Lewis Namier* (1956).

[77] Peel, *Speeches*, II, p. 742.

[78] B. Harrison and Patricia Hollis (eds), *Robert Lowery, Radical and Chartist* (1979), p. 108.

[79] Croker to Peel, 8 September 1842 (Add. MSS 40515, f. 104).

nomination speech of 28 June 1841: 'Price Three pence, or Twelve Shillings and Sixpence per Hundred, for Distribution'. An advertisement on the back announced that Painter undertook 'to print, publish, and advertise in London and Provincial Papers, Conservative Speeches, Addresses to Electors, &c., on condition of the Party taking Five Hundred copies at the selling price'. Joseph Planta wrote to Peel from Hastings, where he was a Conservative candidate, that he had made great use of Peel's Tamworth speech, and 'have had a Quantity down for Distribution'. Fremantle, the Conservative whip, recommended Painter to Peel as 'an intelligent man and much disposed to do good'. But a greater publisher than Painter, John Murray, had already reminded Peel of his readiness to issue pamphlet speeches, and did so down the years.[80]

Peel recognized the value of accurate and full speech reports, and on at least one occasion took considerable pains to assist. After he had spoken at a Tamworth dinner on 16 January 1835 to celebrate his re-election, the editor of the *Staffordshire Advertiser* sent him a draft report which Peel's estate steward, Thomas Hill, had said Peel would be willing to revise. Peel did so immediately. This corrected version first appeared in the *Advertiser*; but Peel urged publication also in pamphlet form: 'if you please you may print 600 copies of it separately & send them to Mr. Hill if you think it will not interfere with the circulation of your Paper. The copies will be only sent to the Voters at Tamworth who are desirous to have them.' Peel concluded that he had rejected other applications so as to favour the *Advertiser*, 'and I am very glad I did so after referring to your very accurate Report.'[81] A report of Peel's speech, 'abridged from the *Staffordshire Advertiser*', then appeared in *The Times* of 26 January 1835. Thus Peel's words now achieved national publicity. Lord Londonderry wrote enthusiastically two days later to tell Peel about a large Conservative public meeting held that day in Durham. 'Your glorious Speech arrived happily before we went into the Hall. It has had a most extraordinary effect here, so conciliatory to all, so bold in purpose, so fine in Logick.'[82]

This example illustrated how, although pamphlet versions might have their uses, it was the reports in the newspapers which most people read. John Henry Newman's anonymous attack in letters to *The Times* of February 1841, on the bad social philosophy which he claimed to find underlying Peel's speech at the opening of the Tamworth Library and Reading Room, was specifically directed at the text of the speech as circulated in *The Times*, 'since in that shape it will have the widest circulation'. Newman noticed that the pamphlet version

[80] *Tamworth Election. Third Edition. Sir R. Peel's Speech at the Nomination at Tamworth on Monday, June 28, 1841*; Planta to Peel, 19 July 1841 (Add. MSS 40485, f. 222); Fremantle to Peel, 4 November 1841 (Add. MSS 40476, f. 72); Murray to Peel, 19, 29 May 1841 (Add. MSS 40429, ff. 256, 290).

[81] C. C. Mort to Peel, 19 January 1835; Peel to Mort, 20 January 1835 (Add. MSS 40410, ff. 261, 267).

[82] Londonderry to Peel, 28 January 1835 (Add. MSS 40412, f. 134).

contained qualifications not in *The Times* text. He commented tartly that a public man 'must not claim to harangue the whole world in newspapers, and then to offer his second thoughts to such as choose to buy them at a bookseller's'.[83]

Because Peel's speeches in Parliament were well addressed to listeners who wanted simplicity and clarity, even with repetition, this meant that they were better suited to being read in newspaper reports than more rhetorical effusions. Certainly, it was sometimes complained that many parliamentary speeches were too long. The Whig *Morning Chronicle* (5 March 1844) urged Peel to set an example in this respect. *Punch* (15 March 1845) complained that whereas previous generations had fought for the right to read the debates, the present generation was abandoning that right because speeches were too drawn out. The London papers, however, tried to meet this difficulty by publishing condensed reports of debates on their editorial pages as well as more or less full reports elsewhere. These condensed versions, with their sharpening of language and argument, were probably what readers read first and best remembered. Peel's speeches readily lent themselves to being condensed, for they could be trimmed down to the clear argument which usually lay underneath any detail or reiteration. *The Times* on one occasion (14 May 1846) admitted that scrutiny of its full parliamentary reports required a mental effort; it spoke of readers who 'buckled on their harness for the study of the factory debate'. Lord Rosebery, the late Victorian Prime Minister, remembered that when he was a boy in the 1850s his family sat down after breakfast to read through the speeches. Rosebery's was, of course, an aristocratic family with leisure; but a Norwich newspaper proprietor assured the Select Committee on Newspaper Stamps in 1851 that the working classes too were interested in the parliamentary reports.[84]

How the condensing of debates seems to have benefited Peel's reputation in one important instance may be studied in connection with his Commons speech of 6 May 1844, which introduced his plan for major reforms in the banking and note-issue systems. His speech was necessarily long and elaborate, although masterly in argument. The *Annual Register* praised 'the skill by which controverted points were disposed of' and the 'happy elucidation' of details, which won the attention and admiration of the House. All this could be found in the extended reports in *The Times* and other daily papers, but what the public came to remember was simply Peel's mastery in general, and one passage in particular. The speech became known as Peel's 'what is a pound?' speech. The obituary article in *Tait's Edinburgh Magazine* (August 1850) remembered it as such, 'with its plain-spoken materialistic solution, used to

[83] *History of The Times* I (1935), pp. 405–7.
[84] *Report from the Select Committee on Newspaper Stamps* (1851), pp. 334–5; *British Historical and Political Orations* (Everyman ed., 1945), pp. 330–1.

sweep away the foggy masses of Birmingham financial metaphysics'. The full version of the relevant passage ran to three columns in *Hansard*'s 'corrected report', where the question was more wordily reported as, 'What is the meaning of the "Pound" according to the ancient monetary policy of this country?' *The Times* extended report, however, phrased the question as simply 'what is a pound?', and its condensed version then put this into reported speech:

> First, he would enquire what was a pound? and what was the engagement to pay a pound? Surely the word 'pound' meant something more than an abstraction; in his opinion it meant a certain weight of precious metal of a certain fineness; and the engagement of a maker of a promissory note to pay on demand a definite amount of that metal and fineness. A real measure of value in that just sense had existed till the year 1797.

Interestingly, this same condensed version was used, source unacknowledged, by the Chartist *Northern Star* of 11 May, published from Leeds.

Provincial weeklies, pressed for space, usually confined themselves to such condensed reports. But at the beginning of the 1842 parliamentary session the *Northern Star* of 12 February decided to report Peel's Corn Law speech at length in the first person, so that its readers might 'judge what *all* the stir has been about'. And during the long-running Corn Law crisis of the first half of 1846 many papers made special efforts to obtain and to print extended and even verbatim reports of Peel's main speeches. For example, the *Preston Guardian*, the highest circulating paper in north Lancashire, published Peel's speech on the address (22 January) 'at the greatest possible length' in its issue of 24 January; the report covered nearly two full columns, with long passages given in the first person. The *Preston Gazette* was a weekly; but four days later it issued a *Preston Gazette Extraordinary* to report Peel's speech of 27 January, which introduced his Corn Law repeal proposals:

> Aware of the intense anxiety felt by the public respecting the financial and commercial propositions of Sir Robert Peel, last night, in the House of Commons, we have, at very considerable expense, by the aid of extraordinary expresses from the three London papers (the *Sun*, *Daily News*, and *Standard*), for which we are considerably indebted to Mr. Wheeler of Manchester, in conjunction with our own special messengers, prepared an Extraordinary Edition of the *Guardian*, which contains a verbatim Report of the Premier's comprehensive and momentous announcement. By this effort, scarcely twelve hours will elapse between the delivery of this important speech in London last night, and its perusal in our own sheet by the public of Preston, the speech of the right hon. baronet having been *twice* committed to type during the interval!

The *Sun* and *Standard* were London evening papers; the *Daily News* was a brand-new morning paper. The efforts made to rush copies of the London prints throughout the country on this occasion were remarkable, with the new railway network playing an essential part. The *Daily News*, which was eager to make an impact, and *The Times*, as the premier newspaper, made the greatest efforts. The *Daily News* arranged to send copies containing the speech report 'by Special Engines to every town on every line in England'. So wrote Charles Dickens, who was at this time briefly the first editor of the paper. 'My speech will, no doubt, be in the possession of everyone tomorrow morning', remarked Peel to the Commons. And so it was. Peel began speaking at 5.20 p.m. and finished at 8.05 p.m. By 5 a.m. copies of the *Daily News* containing the speech were on sale in London, and by midday they had reached Scotland. John Dickens, the editor's father, took copies by rail to Exeter, and then by chaise to Plymouth. The *Daily News* of 3 February printed extracts in praise of its enterprise from some forty provincial papers. *The Times* adopted similar methods, and printed 54,000 copies between 3 and 8 a.m. on 28 January; but it was apparently not quite so fast in nationwide distribution as the *News*.[85]

John Dickens had written privately to Peel to ask for copies to be supplied at the close of his speech 'of the Documents, or references to them' as used by Peel. The aim was obviously to ensure both speed and accuracy in reporting. Peel obligingly supplied the one set he had, on the understanding that it would be available to all reporters without distinction.[86]

IX

One advertisement for the *Daily News* claimed in 1846 that newspapers had become 'the intellectual life of the Nineteenth Century'. They provided 'moral and political safeguards', and they placed everyone, regardless of variations in wealth, 'on a level as to information'. A leaflet from T. Mudie & Sons, stationers and newsagents of 15 Coventry St, London, preserved in Peel's papers, promised to supply London publications to any parts of the capital or country, with morning papers to be forwarded by the morning mails if required. Mudie listed the main London morning papers as *The Times*, *Morning Herald*, *Morning Chronicle*, *Morning Post* and *Morning Advertiser*; and the evening papers as the *Globe*, *Standard*, *Sun* and *Shipping Gazette*. Over sixty other weekly, bi- and tri-weekly publications were also named.[87]

---

[85] *The Times*, 28, 30 January, 4 February 1846; W. J. Carlton, 'John Dickens, journalist', *The Dickensian*, 53 (1957), pp. 5–11; Kathleen Tillotson (ed.), *Letters of Charles Dickens* (1977), vol. 4, p. 480.

[86] John Dickens to Peel, 26 January 1846; Peel to John Dickens, 28 January 1846 (Add. MSS 40583, f. 139).

[87] Add. MSS 40556, f. 341; *Dover Telegraph*, 23 May 1846.

The business of publishing and circulating newspapers and other publications had clearly become an important activity, much encouraged by the reduction of the newspaper stamp duty in 1836 which had cut newspaper prices from 7d to 4d or 3d. During the debates on the stamp duty reduction Peel had exclaimed approvingly that 'of all the phenomena of civilized society' he doubted if anything was more remarkable as an example of capitalist enterprise than the way people were supplied with intelligence.[88]

Editors of leading London newspapers, such as Thomas Barnes of *The Times*, were now gaining entry into London political society; for it was becoming accepted that circulation brought influence, and publication of the newspaper stamp returns began to demonstrate to the world how *The Times* not only enjoyed much the largest daily circulation, but was drawing further and further ahead. Its sales nearly quadrupled between 1837 and 1850 (from about 10,000 a day to about 40,000 a day), whereas those of the Whig *Morning Chronicle* and of the Conservative *Morning Herald* and *Morning Post* were falling, and those of the *Morning Advertiser*, the organ of the licensed victuallers, were only slightly rising. Whereas in 1837 sales of these four papers had totalled nearly twice those of *The Times*, by 1850 they amounted to less than 40 per cent. It was estimated in 1851 that one-quarter to one-third of London newspaper sales were made outside the capital. In 1837 W. H. Smith, the newsagent, sent 148 copies of *The Times* daily to Liverpool and 117 to Manchester, compared with 577 and 606 copies of other London papers; but by 1851 Liverpool was taking 506 copies of *The Times* and Manchester 848, against only 411 and 434 copies respectively of other London papers. Thanks to the railways, *The Times* reached both towns by 2 p.m. Sales of all papers tended to peak at times of political crisis, with part of each surge then retained. A total of 53,897,926 newspaper stamps was issued in Great Britain in 1837; 85,671,566 in 1850. The Select Committee on Newspaper Stamps noted that 1845, 'the great League year', saw 9,500,000 extra stamps issued, and 1846 another 5,000,000.[89]

The Times was simply the best London paper in all departments – news, comment, advertisements. It had the most correspondents at home and abroad; it was the paper most likely to obtain inside information during a crisis. Its editorial comment was not only well informed but also carefully calculated to appeal to a wide public. During Barnes's editorship (1817–41) it had given up supporting the Government of the day, and began instead to seek at one and the same time to discover, to reflect and to guide middle-class majority opinion. Its rivals often complained that this led it into unprincipled trimming. The *Morning Advertiser* (12 November 1845) asserted that *The*

[88] Peel, *Speeches*, III, p. 320.
[89] *Select Committee on Newspaper Stamps*, pp. 166–7, 341, 428, 434–5, appendix no. 4; A. P. Wadsworth, 'Newspaper circulations, 1800–1954', *Transactions of the Manchester Statistical Society* (1954–5), pp. 8–11.

Times was only too well named: 'Its principles and its practice are ever varying.' *The Sunday Times* (23 March 1845) described *The Times* as 'a sort of grave political harlequin, performing intellectual tricks for the amusement of the public'. The Whig *Morning Chronicle* (1 March 1844) noticed how cunningly mixed were *Times* comments on unsettled questions. 'What has it said on the Irish question? – what has it not said . . . the Irish policy of the *Times* is a greater enigma even than Sir Robert Peel.'[90]

The Times of 14 January 1843 answered such attacks by presenting its unpredictability as a measure of its independence. 'The influence of this journal has been at the disposal of no Minister and no faction.' And obviously a large majority of early Victorian daily newspaper readers preferred such independence to the partisanship of the other London dailies. Mitchell's *Newspaper Press Directory* for 1846 summed up *The Times* approach:

> Other papers may be preferred by particular classes, but *all* read the *Times*, who can; just because it is not possible to predicate its course on any question as regulated by the interests of any party or class . . . *The Times* has done this by endeavouring rather to express the opinions of the more sensible of all classes . . . The moderate common-sense side of the case is almost certain to be taken up in this paper.

The London evening papers rivalled the dailies in the 1830s; but their circulations were steadily falling during the forties. The Conservative *Standard*, which had been the best-selling evening paper in 1837 (almost 4,300 daily), was down to 1,600 by 1850. The range of the London evening papers reached far into the provinces, even before the spread of the railways. The *Standard*, for example, was printing letters in 1835 from 'a subscriber' in Manchester and 'A Tradesman of Exeter'.[91]

Awareness of London's evening and daily papers was greatly reinforced by the regular practice of copying news and comment from their columns into the provincial press. In this way the views of *The Times*, in particular, gained much wider notice than its (by twentieth-century standards) modest sale might suggest. The *Stamford Mercury*, for example, with the largest provincial circulation of 10,000 copies weekly in 1846 extending throughout the eastern counties, carried a regular feature entitled 'Spirit of the Public Journals'. The *Mercury* reported Peel's speech of 27 January 1846 under a small headline, 'The Great Disclosure', with the text condensed to a column and a quarter in the third person. Alongside stood three-quarters of a column of favourable editorial comment from *The Times*. The common practice was to borrow

---

[90] A. Aspinall, *Politics and the Press c.1780–1850* (1949), pp. 380–1. See especially *History of The Times*, I; and D. Hudson, *Thomas Barnes of The Times* (1943).

[91] *Standard*, 28 January, 28 February 1835.

editorial opinions from London papers of similar views. But the superiority of *The Times* in all departments made it tempting even for papers of other political persuasions sometimes to copy from it. The protectionist *Maidstone Journal* of 9 July 1850 offered only four column-inches of guarded editorial comment of its own on Peel's death; but it printed two and a half columns of much friendlier material from *The Times* – an editorial, an account of Peel's accident, details of funeral plans, and a review of Peel's character, political services and last speech.

Copying was not all one way. London papers were ready to repeat news and opinions from provincial papers, where the news was interesting or the opinions adjudged to be significant. For example, the *Standard* of 25 November 1834, at the time of Lord Melbourne's sudden dismissal, published a column headed 'STATE OF PUBLIC FEELING' which gave extracts (all, of course, favourable to the Conservatives) from one Scottish, one Irish and seven English newspapers. There were some 225 English provincial newspapers in 1842; but nearly half had circulations below 1,000 per week, and the failure rate was high. The *Manchester Guardian* went bi-weekly after the reduction of stamp duty in 1836, when its price fell from 7d to 4d; but price still ruled out any daily publication outside London. The *Guardian* averaged an overall sale of 5,000 copies in 1837, well over 9,000 by 1850.

Mitchell's *Newspaper Press Directory* for 1846 emphasized how provincial newspapers were important to their localities. 'The family resident in the country looks with the same eagerness to the delivery of the local newspaper, as we in London do for *The Times*, and other morning journals.' Mitchell also suggested that copies of the London papers which were sold outside the capital circulated mostly in exchange rooms and places of business. It certainly seems that a single copy of any paper, London or provincial, was likely to be handled by large numbers of readers. Newspapers were expensive items to be made the most of; and since they were printed on rag paper, they were more durable than twentieth-century prints. Copies were exchanged between friends and neighbours, so that one copy might be seen by several families, perhaps ten or more people. Customers at public houses, barbers' shops or coffee houses could read copies there, and Richard Cobden remarked that the main attraction of mechanics' institutes lay in their newsrooms. Nearly every town had at least one subscription newsroom, where a range of London and local papers would be taken. In 1842 the Manchester Exchange newsroom served about 1,800 subscribers, most of them presumably in the cotton trade. Each day 24 copies were taken of the *Morning Chronicle*, 22 of *The Times*, 12 each of the *Morning Herald* and *Morning Post*, 10 each of the *Standard* and the *Globe*, 9 of the *Sun*, and 6 of the *Courier*. Of the *Manchester Guardian*, *Manchester Chronicle* and *Manchester Courier* 12 copies were taken, 4 each of the *Manchester and Salford Advertiser* and *Manchester Times*; 9 Liverpool papers were taken, 26 other provincial papers, 6 Irish papers, 12 foreign papers, 14 Sunday papers, and 18 magazines and reviews.[92]

Through such various channels the *Leeds Mercury* of 7 December 1839 estimated that each of its copies was being read by an average of fifteen to twenty people. This would have multiplied its sale of 9,700 copies per week into a reading public of perhaps 150,000, spread over the West Riding woollen district. In agricultural east Kent, the *Dover Chronicle* of 7 August 1841 suggested an average of twelve readers for every copy of the local papers, thereby lifting modest circulations of only a few hundreds into worthwhile notice. At the other end of the range, *The Times* by the same multiplication would have been addressing a daily readership of 500,000 by 1850.[93]

Richard Cobden suggested to a Manchester audience in 1850 that most businessmen lacked the time to read anything but newspapers, perhaps 400 or 500 each year.[94] How far down the social scale did newspaper reading reach? Not down to most agricultural labourers. The *Dover Chronicle* article already cited complained that not one in a dozen of the local rural labourers could read a newspaper. An evening class of such labourers was found to be unable to understand a *Times* editorial even when it was read out to them. But among industrial workers, and in the towns, newspaper reading was more extensive. Evidence that many working men and women could read was provided by the large quantity of cheap literature – fictional, sensational, improving – which was being produced by the 1840s. It has been estimated that between two-thirds and three quarters of the early Victorian population could read, although far less could write.[95] This is not to say that such a high proportion regularly perused newspapers. It was working-class men who read newspapers, when they read anything, whereas their womenfolk preferred light journalism with a high fiction content, notably such penny weeklies as the *Family Herald* and *London Journal*. Both were selling over 100,000 copies weekly by the end of the 1840s, and were to go much higher in the 1850s. Although avowedly non-party, they each contained some political matter which mixed deference with explicit support for reform. Thus in 1846 the *London Journal* ran a series of 'Political Sketches', and the first of these (16 May) was devoted to Peel. How the *Journal* came out strongly in his support, even while still insisting that it was non-party, will be considered in due place.[96]

[92] B. Love, *Hand-Book of Manchester* (1842), pp. 230–2.
[93] See A. Aspinall, 'The circulation of newspapers in the early nineteenth century', *Review of English Studies*, 22 (1946), pp. 29–43.
[94] J. Morley, *Life of Richard Cobden* (1903), pp. 892–3.
[95] *Select Committee on Newspaper Stamps*, pp. 468–9. See especially R. K. Webb, 'Working class readers in early Victorian England', *English Historical Review*, 65 (1950), pp. 333–51; and 'The Victorian reading public', in B. Ford (ed.), *From Dickens to Hardy* (1972).
[96] See Anne Humpherys, 'G. W. M. Reynolds: popular literature and popular politics', *Victorian Periodicals Review*, 16 (1983), pp. 79–89; and B. E. Maidment, 'Magazines of popular progress and the artisans', *Victorian Periodicals Review*, 17 (1984), pp. 83–94.

A printed statement of the objects of the new Leeds Operative Conservative Association, sent to Peel in 1835, announced that it had been formed to resist the drift to anarchy; 'and to furnish our minds by means of newspapers and other publications with correct views on political subjects, and to furnish an antidote to those publications of a dangerous tendency which are everywhere obtruded upon us'.[97] The assumption was clearly that Leeds working men were well able to read newspapers and to base their politics upon such reading. Nevertheless, the limited success of these Conservative efforts in Leeds was to be strikingly demonstrated when the *Northern Star*, the national newspaper of the Chartist movement, began to be published there only two years later. The rapid success of the *Star*, which achieved sales of over 42,000 copies per week during the spring of 1839, was the more remarkable in view of its selling price of 4d per copy. Not all readers of the *Star* were necessarily Chartists. It was a good paper for political news, and C. D. Collet told the Select Committee on Newspaper Stamps in 1851 that some working men took it because it was the only paper which reported popular movements, not because they shared the views of its proprietor Feargus O'Connor, the Chartist leader.[98] The circulation of the *Northern Star* slowly declined during the 1840s. Readers transferred to popular Sunday papers such as the *Weekly Dispatch*, *Lloyd's Weekly*, the *News of the World* and the *Weekly Times*, which were each selling 40,000–50,000 copies per week by the end of the decade. These papers cost only 3d, and this low price was important to working-class readers, who were short of both money and time and for whom a Sunday paper was often the only paper seen. Prominence was given to detailed reporting of crime and to other more or less sensational news, but there was also a page of parliamentary reporting. Articles about the Sunday press in the *London Journal* (19 and 26 July 1845) spoke of a new reading public found by the Sunday papers, 'that vast section of society which craved political information, and had hitherto been unable to obtain it in consequence of the price of the newspaper press'. The popular Sundays were all in favour of 'reform', but their colour varied from Liberal to Radical.[99]

Reading a newspaper might be a communal matter, with those who were able to read passing on the contents to those who could not. Some public house landlords employed people to read out the news. At times of political excitement reading aloud became a feature of political meetings, Chartist and otherwise. During the Corn Law crisis of 1846 arrangements were apparently made in Liverpool to have public readings at the Commercial Hall of all important debates, 'at a small charge', for the benefit of the working classes.

[97] C. Richardson to Peel, 26 March 1835 (Add. MSS 40418, f. 172).

[98] *Select Committee on Newspaper Stamps*, p. 152. See J. Epstein, *The Lion of Freedom* (1982), ch. 2.

[99] See Virginia Berridge, 'Popular Sunday papers and mid-Victorian society', in G. Boyce et al. (eds), *Newspaper History* (1978), ch. 13.

When *The Times* report of the Queen's speech reached Liverpool on the evening of 22 January it was read out in the hall. Some 3,000 were said to be present, 'many of them gentlemen of wealth and influence'. Loud cheers followed those parts of the speech which referred to the free-trade intentions of the Peel ministry. *The Times* leading article in support of repeal was also heard, and likewise received with loud applause.[100]

Political news and comment could be not only read out but also sung out. Street ballads were composed, published and hawked within hours of any event occurring of public interest. Ballad language was necessarily simple, and the rhyming was often crude; but such ditties could catch and encourage the popular mood. Henry Brougham sent to Peel a single-sheet ballad called 'John Bull and the Corn Bill', 'which I bought last night to prevail on the minstrel that was crowing it to leave the street':

> Oh! what advantage we shall reap,
> Penny loaves and butter cheap,
> Puddings in country, pies in town,
> And apple dumplings six for a brown,
> And the Queen declares if time should come
> That she should have another son,
> Stamped in gold should be upon his b–
> Sir Robert Peel and the Corn Bill.

Alas, there is no record of Peel's response to this ditty.[101]

At the other end of the range of occasional publications were the many more or less weighty political pamphlets, which were published not only in London but in provincial towns. Pamphlet publication seems to have been easy and swift. One Leeds author in 1829 read a Peel speech in support of Catholic Emancipation on a Monday, sent the first pages of his reply to the press on the following Wednesday, and expected publication on the Thursday of the next week.[102] Pamphlets might run to a hundred pages or more, and were intended to be studied carefully by readers able to pay 1s or 2s for each title. Peel himself was a frequent reader of pamphlets, many being given to him by authors who hoped to influence him. One such pamphlet was sent by Christopher Wordsworth to Peel in April 1845 in the middle of the Maynooth crisis. Wordsworth, whom Peel had promoted to a canonry of Westminster in the previous year, was strongly anti-Catholic; and this was apparent in his two anonymous Maynooth pamphlets, *Maynooth, The Crown, And The Country*

---

[100] *Liverpool Albion*, 26 January 1846; *Blackburn Standard*, 28 January 1846.

[101] Brougham to Peel, 10 July 1846 (Add. MSS 40482, f. 321). See also J. Ashton, *Modern Street Ballads* (1888).

[102] W. R. Ward (ed.), *Early Correspondence of Jabez Bunting 1820–1829* (Camden fourth series, 1972), vol. 11, pp. 204–5.

and *A Review of the Maynooth Endowment Bill, Shewing Its Fatal Tendencies*. Wordsworth sent the first of these to Peel, in the hope that he would peruse it without finding its spirit and language unacceptable, whatever he might think of its arguments. Peel, however, wrote back very strongly. He said that he would not have replied, but that silence might have seemed to imply agreement that there was nothing wrong with the tone of the pamphlet. On the contrary, Peel told Wordsworth that it was likely to encourage agitation and endanger good relations between Protestants and Catholics in Ireland. Those without public responsibility might find it easy to write pamphlets; but those who had to allay agitation 'had better beware before they take your advice'.[103]

Pamphlets supplemented the extended discussion of issues to be found in the weekly, monthly and quarterly journals and reviews. Lytton Bulwer believed that whereas daily papers rarely did more than represent political opinion, these publications aspired to create it. Newspapers, he argued, needed good sales, and they could not risk offering new opinions whose very novelty meant that they were not yet popular. So new ideas were left to the journals and reviews.[104] The leading weeklies in the 1830s and 1840s were the *Spectator* and the *Examiner*, ably edited by R. S. Rintoul and Albany Fonblanque respectively. The circulation of the *Examiner* in 1845 was about 6,000 copies weekly, and that of the *Spectator* 3,500. But, as the *London Journal* pointed out (30 August and 6 September 1845), articles from both were often copied into *The Times* and other London and provincial papers; and so they exerted an influence far beyond their direct sales or readership. A Nottingham stockinger wrote to Peel during the Corn Law crisis to remark that he had seen from the *Spectator* how Peel was intending to retire after enactment of repeal. He wrote to express the hope that Peel would stay in office to protect the working classes. Perhaps the stockinger had read the *Spectator* at a newsroom, or he may have seen it quoted in a London or local paper.[105]

Mitchell's *Newspaper Press Directory* for 1846 described the *Spectator* as cold but sagaciously anti-Whig; the *Examiner* as more human and strongly Whig. Peel seems to have read both every Sunday. The *Spectator* gave him strong support from 1841, and the *Nonconformist* (16 November 1842) complained because it had called his Government 'God-given'. The *Nonconformist* itself had been successfully launched in 1841 by Edward Miall as the weekly mouthpiece of politico-religious dissent.

The leading political monthlies were *Blackwood's Edinburgh Magazine*, *Fraser's Magazine* and *Tait's Edinburgh Magazine*. *Tait's* was Whig,

---

103 Wordsworth to Peel, 3 April 1845; Peel to Wordsworth, 7 April 1845 (Add. MSS 40564, ff. 48, 49).
104 Lytton Bulwer, *England and the English*, p. 237. See Joanne Shattock and M. Wolff (eds), *The Victorian Periodical Press: Samplings and Soundings* (1982).
105 S. Broomhead to Peel, 24 March 1846 (Add. MSS 40588, f. 91).

Blackwood's and *Fraser's* Conservative. *Fraser's* was edited in the 1830s by the brilliant but wayward William Maginn, who before his death in 1842 had received charity from Peel.[106] He chose to forget that Maginn, an Irish Orangeman, had fiercely attacked him for his switch over Catholic Emancipation. *Blackwood's* had likewise strongly opposed Catholic Emancipation, but eventually forgave Peel. It finally broke with him over repeal of the Corn Laws. It was selling perhaps 8,000 copies monthly during the early 1830s, although under 6,000 by the time of repeal. These were significant and profitable figures for the period.[107]

The Whig *Edinburgh Review* and the Conservative *Quarterly Review* were the great quarterlies. Peel was in touch with the *Quarterly* through his friend, J. W. Croker, who was its chief political writer. Its circulation reached a peak of over 9,000 in 1841, the year of Peel's election victory; but it had fallen to about 8,000 by the end of the decade. Croker described the *Quarterly* to Peel in 1842 as 'a kind of *direction post* to a large body of people, particularly in the Country'.[108] An article, anonymous as usual, in the *Quarterly Review* for January 1830 seems to have first popularized the name 'Conservative party': 'what is called the Tory, and which might with more propriety be called the Conservative, party; a party which we believe to comprise by far the largest, wealthiest, and most intelligent and respectable portion of the population'. Most of these people, the article concluded, were 'as anxious to promote any prudent and practicable amelioration of the state, as any of their fellow-subjects'. These were Conservative sentiments which Peel himself would have been glad to acknowledge.

X

Newspaper content may be categorized under three headings: news; editorial and other discussion of opinion; and items of amusement. Peel, as already noticed, praised the intelligence gathering and reporting achievement of the press. *The Times* (9 March 1846) claimed that because everything was now exposed to publicity, there would be nothing left to discover 'a century hence hid in old trunks'. All political activity was now quickly revealed through *Hansard* and the newspapers. 'The Minister can do nothing in secret.' This was, of course, an exaggeration. Yet Peel himself remarked in 1846 how 'the Newspapers generally spoil the interest of Blue books, by the previous publication of anything worth Reading.'[109]

---

[106] Maginn to Peel, 10 February 1841 (Add. MSS 40429, f. 65); *Notes and Queries*, first series, V (1852), pp. 433–4.

[107] See J. M. Milne, 'The politics of *Blackwood's*, 1817–1846'. Unpublished Ph.D thesis, University of Newcastle upon Tyne, 1984.

[108] Croker to Peel, 20 February 1842 (Add. MSS 40502, f. 326).

[109] Peel to Lincoln, March 1846 (NeC 11980).

Here was a compliment in the form of a complaint. But Peel felt less easy about possible press influence over opinion, at least in its boldest pretensions. Thus during the Reform Bill debates he voiced the fear that the press was assuming direct control over the Whig Government. This he could never accept as constitutional. The press should never be allowed to make or unmake measures or ministries. It needed to be read with caution, both by politicians and the public, in the knowledge that it was a force without the restraint of responsibility; also that its most successful appeals were 'to the passions, and not to the reason of mankind'.[110]

This last charge was made during the excitements of 1831-2; but the general level of political discussion in the press of the 1830s and 1840s was usually reasonable, even if often partisan. Leading articles were now well-established features in many provincial newspapers as well as in the London dailies and evenings. It was often asked whether such articles shaped reader opinion, or whether readers favoured newspapers which contained editorials that reflected their existing views. 'Politically speaking, what is this "public opinion?" Are the newspapers the sources of it, or the mere channels and conductors? – are they the real thunder, or merely the echo?' So asked an article on 'The Influence of Newspapers' in *Fraser's Magazine* for September 1831. *The Times* seems to have achieved its unique success as a journal of opinion by saying what its readers expected (but saying it well), and by sometimes (but not too often) offering a seemingly bold lead when it judged that its readers were either already changing or were willing to change their minds. *The Times* description of the Anti-Corn Law League as 'a great fact' (18 November 1843) was a notable instance of such a bold (but yet carefully phrased) lead, as will be seen in due place. Earlier in the same year *The Times* (19 January 1843) had itself explained how if a newspaper enjoyed the 'general confidence' of its readers, it might lead opinion upon particular topics 'in a degree not easy to be ascertained'.

Successful provincial newspapers of the period, such as the *Leeds Mercury* or *Manchester Guardian*, seem to have used the same method locally. Just as *The Times* gave the most national and international news, so the leading local papers became known for the fullness of their regional news coverage. This was the essential basis. Readers were then ready to ponder any editorial opinions on offer; these must mainly reflect, but could sometimes prompt, their thoughts. Influence of this kind was reinforced where local editors were personally well known and respected, as were both Edward Baines of the *Leeds Mercury* and J. E. Taylor of the *Manchester Guardian*. When two or more provincial papers were published in competition this often intensified the local debate. In Manchester the Liberal *Manchester Guardian* (1821) was challenged, but not equalled, from 1825 by the Conservative *Manchester Courier*, and from 1846

---

[110] Peel, *Speeches*, II, p. 401.

by the middle-class Radical *Manchester Examiner*. Political rivalry was often sharply expressed. But the Peelite *Nottingham Journal* of 4 January 1850 benevolently referred to its 'respectable neighbours', the Radical *Nottingham Review* and Liberal *Nottingham Mercury*. 'We could not be the organ of all opinions, and they arose to meet the wants of different portions of our townsmen.' The protectionist *Nottinghamshire Guardian* was not included in this embrace.

Letters from readers, often under pseudonyms, were prominent mirrors of opinion in many papers, London and local. Thomas Barnes greatly increased the number of letters in *The Times*. Charles Greville noted in his journal for 16 January 1843 how the Corn Law and condition of England questions were running in people's minds. 'The newspapers are full of letters and complaints on these subjects.' Not all letters to editors were upon political topics. One Christmas address from the editor of the *Preston Guardian* (26 December 1846) gave thanks for the wide-ranging vigilance of his correspondents. 'They pick holes in the character of statesmen, and find dangerous holes in street pavement, with equal facility.' Selection of letters for publication exposed editors to the temptation of bias; and no doubt letters were sometimes composed to editorial order, or even by the journalists themselves.

As well as disseminating news and views, early Victorian newspapers were expected to carry advertisements, and also items included for amusement. Numerous advertisements made an important direct contribution to news-paper revenue, and were also essential to win circulation. Here again *The Times* led the way. Trivial but colourful items of news might be included in the knowledge that these helped to sell newspapers. One experienced journalist admitted in 1851 that a report of a balloon ascent might sell more copies of a paper than any piece of political writing.[111] 'A Constant Reader' reminded the over-earnest editor of the *Manchester Times* (5 February 1831) that even the heartiest reformers had wives, sisters and daughters to whom 'a little more LIGHT READING . . . would be *most acceptable*'.

Publications such as the *Satirist*, largely devoted to scurrilous personal attacks on public figures, were fading out during the 1840s. But the early Victorians remained eager to read gossip. Peel himself naturally became a prime subject for treatment in personal terms. The newspapers thought it legitimate and interesting, for example, to discuss the state of his health during the Corn Law crisis. 'Health of the Premier – Sir Robert Peel's health is improved, he having derived great benefit from cupping. – *Daily News* of Thursday. – Sir Robert Peel was again cupped on Friday, previous to his going to the house of commons. – *Daily News* of Monday.' So ran a paragraph in the *Manchester Guardian* of 18 February 1846. Peel disliked such items, although he was resigned to them. He did not realize how such harmless gossip was helping to humanize his public image, and thereby to strengthen his appeal. An instance of how a titbit of trivial information could be brought into happy support of his political policies occurred a month later, again circulating through the columns of the *Daily News* and *Manchester Guardian* (14 March 1846):

> Appropriate. – Sir R. Peel returned from Brighton by the mail train on Sunday. The Duke of Richmond was a passenger by the same train, but these two distinguished personages did not travel in the same carriage. As if to illustrate the positions they respectively occupy in the country, Sir Robert placed himself in the leading *coupe*, and the duke got into the *coupe* which was at the tail of the train. – Daily News.

This paragraph drew the explanatory *Guardian* comment that the places assumed were entirely appropriate: Peel, the free trader, leading and looking forward: Richmond, the protectionist, in the rear and looking behind.

Peel tried in 1843 to keep back the news of the Queen's intended visit to Belvoir Castle, the seat of the Duke of Rutland. 'Of course in these times,' he told the duke, 'when every action of every man's life is speculated on by the Press, conjectures will soon be formed.' Two years later, when the Corn Law crisis was beginning, he was instructing the Queen herself about press methods. She had sent him a newspaper cutting, which said that a nobleman in high office was about to retire. The Queen asked, 'What can this Paragraph mean?' Peel replied that it was mere speculation. 'As no particular name is mentioned the failure of the prophecy is not regarded, and suppose the event predicted should happen to occur the Newspaper claims credit for its superior information.' In a postscript Peel added that he had now heard that rumour in the clubs was saying that Wellington and Stanley had resigned, which was presumably the inspiration for the paragraph.[112]

Just before taking office in 1841 Peel had even read to a Tamworth audience a paragraph of this type from the Whig *Globe*. This claimed that he had boasted how he would make the Queen a Conservative in six weeks:

> Now you observe, gentlemen, it is not confidently said, it is a report only, *on dit*, that the Queen has heard of the boast; but that I made the boast there is not the slightest doubt expressed . . . and having attributed to me the expression, that I would make the Queen a Tory, in order to seem perfectly just, he puts in parenthesis, "or Conservative, as he said," and all for the purpose of begetting the impression, that a writer who was so very particular, must be one of scrupulous veracity.

The press, concluded Peel, possessed great influence. 'I know its influence in public affairs; I know its influence on public men.' But the circulation of false

---

[112] Peel to Rutland, 11 November 1843 (Add. MSS 40535, f. 29); Queen Victoria to Peel, 2 December 1845; Peel to Queen Victoria, 3 December 1845 (Add. MSS 40440, ff. 358, 360).

stories would diminish public confidence in the press, and reduce its influence.[113]

If Peel expressed mixed feelings about the press, the Duke of Wellington was suspicious of it. While he was Prime Minister from 1828 to 1830, and then during the subsequent Reform Bill crisis, nearly all the London papers were hostile to his party. Yet Wellington long remained reluctant to admit any need to conciliate press opinion. 'The Duke has nothing to say to the newspapers,' he wrote as late as 1833 to a journalist who had offered his services to the Conservatives, 'and he is desirous of avoiding to have any communication of any description with any of them.'[114] But others were more aware of the need to promote Conservative opinions. After Wellington's resignation in November 1830, a Conservative press committee seems to have begun paying one George McEntagart to act as party press agent; but he turned out to be as ungentlemanly as Wellington might have supposed, eventually threatening legal action against the party, and in 1834 being awarded damages by an arbitrator.[115] An article in *Fraser's Magazine* for September 1833, on 'The Press and the Tories', gave the case for awareness a striking twist by arguing that, although it was now agreed that power was in the hands of the people, 'the Tories neglect – absolutely neglect – the only efficient means of guiding and directing that power to the attainment of good, and act as if they really thought the rabble capable of judging for themselves.'

The same article emphasized the importance of provincial newspapers in shaping local opinion. From the mid-1830s Conservative papers were set up in various parts of England under the guidance of Alaric Watts; their leading articles and main political news were supplied centrally. Many of these papers, however, proved to be short-lived, and few achieved large circulations. Conservative prints remained in a decided minority both for numbers and circulation. But Watts told Peel in 1843 that over twenty years he had 'established or renovated' twenty-one Conservative papers, headed by the *Manchester Courier*. This had gained the largest sale of any provincial Conservative paper. Watts claimed to have spent over £8,000 on newspapers (it is not clear whether he meant money of his own); but now his health was failing, and he asked for some official employment for his son. Peel granted this request, thereby recognizing the value of Watts's services, although his reply was brief and in the third person.[116]

Peel had disliked the activities of the Conservative press committee, and he opposed all proposals to invest party funds in newspapers. In 1840 he firmly

---

[113] *The Times*, 30 July 1841.

[114] Duke of Wellington, *Political Correspondence I: 1833–November 1834* (1975), p. 5.

[115] Aspinall, *Politics and the Press*, pp. 198–9, 329–41, 460–2, 480; Aspinall, *Early Nineteenth Century Diaries*, pp. viii–xiv.

[116] Watts to Peel, 1 February 1843; Peel to Watts, 7 February 1843 (Add. MSS 40524, ff. 118, 122).

rejected a scheme to buy the support of the *Courier*, a London evening paper, even though the proposal was strongly backed by F. R. Bonham, the party organizer. Peel expressed his 'horror of money transactions with Newspaper Proprietors'. If an editor were left with complete freedom (as was desirable on general grounds), what happened if he took a line which Peel, as party leader, did not like? 'What remedy should I have but communication with the Editor, remonstrance against the Course taken, menaces probably of withdrawing my subscription. All this places me in the man's power.'[117] Two years later, when the *Courier* was finally about to collapse, W. E. Painter wrote to Peel saying that it had been offered to him, and asking if 'any encouragement' would be forthcoming. Peel tersely answered that this was 'not in his power'. In 1843 Sir James Graham summed up the stance of the Peel Government as 'not to buy the Press but to leave it to its own free agency, thinking on the whole that Government free from the trammels of a newspaper alliance fares better than one which renders itself subservient to this, the most degrading of all tyrannies'.[118]

Peel was sometimes accused of having said that he never read newspapers at all. In reality, he read more than most people, even though he refused to be directed by any of them. He told the Commons in 1837 that he bought many papers, and that others of interest were sent to him by friends. He accepted newspaper reading as a public man's duty: 'after long experience he had got so callous that he could read them without the slightest disturbance.' Upon one Sunday in 1840 he was being urged by Bonham to study leading articles in *The Observer* and the *Examiner*, plus the *Spectator*, and *The Sunday Times*, 'and other radical papers'.[119]

Like most readers, Peel was pleased when he found his own views reflected in what he read. In 1844 he praised to Graham an attack upon Daniel O'Connell in the *Examiner*. 'I wish the Article in the Examiner could be extensively circulated in Ireland. It hits in just the right place.' The article in question (21 December 1844) gave O'Connell's definition of truth as 'Something that we wish to be thought or believed'. The *Examiner* was not at this date a journal which favoured Peel, and this example confirms that he did not confine himself to reading Conservative publications.[120]

Peel believed that the press and politicians should be free to react to each other in complete independence. This ruled out bought support, but it left room for what he once called 'impartial and discriminating support'. These

---

[117] Fremantle to Peel, 17 October, 23 November, 3 December 1840 (Add. MSS 40428, ff. 304, 331, 405); R. Stewart, 'The Conservative Party and the "Courier" newspaper, 1840', *English Historical Review*, 91 (1976), pp. 346–50.

[118] Painter to Peel, 22 June 1842; Peel to Painter, 23 June 1842 (Add. MSS 40511, f. 12); C. S. Parker, *Life and Letters of Sir James Graham* (1907) I, p. 360.

[119] Bonham to Peel, 'Sunday Morning' [1840] (Add. MSS 40428, f. 496).

[120] Peel to Graham, 24 December 1844 (Add. MSS 40450, f. 438).

were Peel's words in a letter of thanks to Thomas Barnes of *The Times* for his backing during the course of the 1834–5 Conservative administration. Peel was always conscious of the particular importance of *The Times*. In this knowledge, he drew the attention of the Queen to an article in the issue of 7 February 1843 which attacked the policy of Lord Ellenborough, Governor-General of India. 'Such an article in the Times is not a bad index of the prevailing opinion.'[121] Peel was aware of the care taken by *The Times* to align itself with middle-class non-party majority opinion, and of its success in doing so. Therefore, what *The Times* said *about* Peel and his policies was important *to* Peel: not because he was willing to be controlled by *The Times*, but because it both reflected and influenced a large part of that middle majority opinion to which Peel himself also wished to appeal. *Times* buyers and their families must have been largely drawn from the top half of such middle opinion; while its bottom half – the lower middle classes and some artisans – must have included many who saw *The Times* in newsrooms, or who often read extracts from it in local newspapers.

The interplay between Peel's policies and *Times* comments becomes therefore of central interest to the present study. Would Peel have achieved his great final reputation if *The Times* had been steadily hostile towards him from 1834? In the event its tone towards Peel varied from time to time and issue to issue. 'Independent of all parties, we have never refused our support to any which seemed anxious to forward the true interests of the country. Happy to have aided the Conservative cause, when it required our aid, we have never abandoned those principles which we hold distinct from the majority of the Conservative party.' So *The Times* of 14 January 1843 explained its attitude in the middle of Peel's second premiership. By its end he too was adhering to principles which he held 'distinct from the majority of the Conservative party'. How much, and with what reservations, *The Times* supported him at this critical stage will be discussed in due place, as will its flow of comment over the preceding dozen years.

The relationship between Peel and *The Times* first became close during the short Peel Ministry of 1834–5. By the summer of 1834 *The Times* had grown tired of Whig rule. The paper was quarrelling with Brougham and Palmerston, and was particularly disgusted by the New Poor Law, against which its proprietor, John Walter, was to campaign for years. In November William IV suddenly dismissed Lord Melbourne as Prime Minister. Thomas Barnes, *The Times* editor, was privately sounded out on behalf of the Conservatives, who now found themselves offered office. Barnes promised his independent support, provided that the Reform Act and measures already sanctioned by the Commons for tithe reform and reform of municipal corporations were countenanced by the Conservatives. There was a delay while Peel came back

---

[121] Peel to Queen Victoria, 7 February 1843 (Add. MSS 40436, f. 14).

from Italy. He immediately accepted the premiership on his return; but he knew that Conservative candidates must now set out to win floating votes in the constituencies at the forthcoming general election. In such circumstances he recognized the particular importance of gaining the support of *The Times* and its readers; and he indirectly but speedily welcomed Barnes's offer. A suggestion from John Walter in a letter of 10 December to Sir James Scarlett that Peel should issue 'some frank explanation, some popular declaration, *previous* to a Dissolution of Parliament' was passed on by Scarlett to Peel. After much ministerial discussion of best ways and means, Peel's famous Tamworth Manifesto (to be discussed in the next chapter) was published in *The Times*, *Morning Herald* and *Morning Post* of 18 December.[122]

John Walter stood as a 'Liberal–Conservative' candidate for Berkshire in the general election, and Peel asked the King's secretary to use his influence with the Windsor clergy on Walter's behalf. 'I need say nothing as to the importance of keeping the *Times* & Mr. *Walter* in good humour.'[123] Peel was concerned lest *The Times* should withdraw or qualify its support, especially when a leading article on 7 January 1835 aired the idea of a grand alliance with Melbourne against the Radicals. In the event, *The Times* remained firm, despite irritatingly poor communications between Downing Street and Printing House Square. Finally, after complaints from the latter, at the end of February Peel appointed Sir George Clerk to deal with the paper. But the Ministry survived only six more weeks. On the day of his resignation (18 April) Peel felt free at last to express his gratitude directly to Barnes: 'Having this day delivered into the hands of the King the Seals of office, I can without any imputation of an interested motive, or any impediment from scrupulous feelings of delicacy, express my due sense of the powerful support which that Government over which I had the Honour to preside received from the Times newspaper.' Peel went on to remark how the fact that Barnes still remained personally unknown to him made plain the disinterestedness of his support. Peel concluded by expressing admiration for 'the daily exhibitions of that extraordinary ability to which I was indebted for a support the more valuable because it was an impartial and discriminating support'. Barnes in reply thanked Peel for his 'cordial & liberal' letter. 'Such an acknowledgement is the only one which an Independent Journalist should expect from any Minister.'[124]

Historians of *The Times* have implied that this exchange was unique. But on the same day Peel wrote a similar letter of thanks to S. L. Giffard, editor of the *Standard*, the London evening paper. Giffard prized his independence; but whereas *The Times* was simply 'independent', the *Standard* was committed in

---

[122] Walter to Scarlett, 10 December 1834 (Add. MSS 40405, f. 24); *History of The Times*, I, chs. 17–19; Hudson, *Thomas Barnes*, chs. 8–9; Aspinall, *Politics and the Press*, pp. 253–63.

[123] Peel to Sir H. Taylor, 1 January 1835 (Add. MSS 40302, f. 131).

[124] Peel to Barnes, 18 April 1835 (Add. MSS 40310, f. 41); Barnes to Peel, 19 April 1835 (Add. MSS 40420, f. 29).

its politics. In other words it was 'independent Conservative'; always somewhere on the Conservative side, protectionist, and a strong adherent of the Church of England Establishment. Its views down the years will be compared in subsequent chapters with those of *The Times*.

The *Standard* finally broke with Peel over repeal of the Corn Laws in 1846; but in 1834 the relationship was very different. On 8 December Giffard offered the backing of his paper in a letter to Peel, his only condition being that the Government should communicate exclusively with the *Standard* among the London evening papers. Peel answered encouragingly that he contemplated no communication with any other evening paper. As to the *Standard*, 'such has been my admiration of the Ability with which that Newspaper has been conducted that I have uniformly read it, being better pleased to bear with its occasional severities upon myself than to forego the satisfaction of reading its able and powerful & eloquent Comments upon public Affairs.' Peel's letter to Giffard on resignation four months later was even more friendly. Peel thanked him for 'powerful assistance':

> No one has better means of judging than he who was behind the scenes of the political Drama, of the tact and discretion and ability with which your daily exertions in the great cause were made, and no one can *so well* appreciate the pure and truly honourable motives from which those exertions spring, and from which their energy and vigour were mainly derived, as he who was in the possession of Patronage and Power from which you scorned to derive any advantage.[125]

Mitchell's *Newspaper Press Directory* for 1846 remembered how valuable the *Standard* had proved to be during Peel's subsequent years in opposition from 1835 to 1841 'in keeping alive the spirit of his party'; and how it had aided him in office, until the break in 1846, by 'combating with equal energy his old opponents and his disaffected allies'. Giffard wrote again to Peel when he was about to take office in 1841, repeating his offer of 1834. 'You will I hope have seen by my conduct during the last six years that it is not your accession to the high office, to which you are entitled, that commands my respect and service.' Peel replied that he was 'equally sensible of the disinterestedness and the value' of Giffard's offer.[126]

In the case of *The Times* there was no repetition in 1841 of the contact and correspondence of 1834–5. Thomas Barnes had died in May 1841, hoping for Melbourne's fall and Peel's return to office. But John Walter's dislike of the New Poor Law was to bring him into continuing conflict with Peel, and still

---

[125] Giffard to Peel, 8 December 1834; Peel to Giffard, 10 December 1834 (Add. MSS. 40404, ff. 304, 308); Peel to Giffard, 18 April 1835 (Add. MSS 40420, f. 23).

[126] Giffard to Peel, 31 August 1841; Peel to Giffard, 3 September 1841 (Add. MSS 40486, ff. 305, 306).

more with Sir James Graham, the Home Secretary, whose administration of poor relief was widely believed to be unfeeling. *The Times* opposed virtually every measure which Graham proposed. Walter's dissatisfaction was, however, not allowed automatically to colour the paper's attitude towards Peel's Government on other issues. In particular, Lord Aberdeen, the Foreign Secretary, kept in friendly touch with J. T. Delane, the new editor, over questions of foreign policy. When in 1844 Peel told Aberdeen that *The Times* was 'scandalous towards Graham' and suggested discontinuation of communications from the Foreign Office, Aberdeen sensibly did not take this irritated advice. He had read, no doubt, the sharp attack on Peel and Graham in that morning's *Times* (6 July) for 'shuffling and contradiction' over Poor Law reform. In March 1846 Peel admitted at last that there were fair grounds for complaint about the provision of medical relief under the Poor Law. *The Times* of 10 March took the chance to remember the clamour against itself for repeating this over nearly ten years. *The Times* accepted that Peel himself had not joined in the clamour; but neither had he spoken against it. 'We gladly receive his tardy assent to our general proposition.'[127]

The Times obviously required steady humouring. Peel, despite outbursts of annoyance, accepted that this must be attempted. One way was to supply the paper with exclusive information. Although the *Standard* and its sister paper, the *Morning Herald*, seem to have been sometimes preferred as committed Conservative organs, Peel was well aware how at critical moments a story publicised through *The Times* was likely to achieve maximum notice. Thus, while still in opposition in 1840, he sent for publication a long letter in favour of Church of England parish organization which he had originally written privately to the Bishop of Durham in 1835. *The Times* had published leaders in a similar spirit. Peel's letter appeared in full in the paper of 21 September 1840, with his name given at the end and with the laconic introduction: 'The following important letter has come into our possession; we have no doubt of its authenticity and therefore publish it.'[128] A similar initiative was tried in May 1844, at a time when Peel's Government was known to be at odds with the East India Company directors. Aberdeen told Peel that Delane had offered to help in calming public opinion. Peel supplied an announcement through Aberdeen, which revealed that Sir Henry Hardinge was to become Governor-General of India; 'and that this appointment will take place with the cordial approbation of the Crown and the Court of Directors, and in consequence of friendly concert between the authorities immediately responsible for the selection of a Governor-General.' Peel's soothing paragraph was printed

[127] *The Times*, 16 April, 12 May, 15, 22 June 1842; 6 July, 27 August, 7, 8 October 1844; 3 March, 6 May 1845; Peel to Aberdeen, 6 July 1844 (Add. MSS 43063, f. 275); *History of The Times*, II (1939), ch. 1, pp. 95, 550–1.
[128] E. Sterling to Peel, 21 September 1840 (Add. MSS 40428, f. 306).

without change in *The Times* of 4 May, on the leader page and with wide spacing.[129]

One way to help friendly London or provincial newspapers was to supply them with official advertisements, to the exclusion of their rivals. Peel expressed concern soon after taking office in 1841 that his own local paper, the *Staffordshire Advertiser*, seemed to have been omitted from the advertisement list – 'without being a party paper [it] has very conservative leanings'.[130] Peel had himself spotted the absence of official advertisements in the *Advertiser*. He was likewise vigilant about the state of press opinion. When in January 1845 Croker, who was growing increasingly uneasy about Peel's policies, claimed that only the *Quarterly Review* 'in the vast circle of periodical literature' supported the Government, Peel answered that this was 'very incorrect'. He mentioned *Blackwood's* and the *New Quarterly* as friendly; 'Fraser also I believe.'[131] Because of Peel's friendship with Croker, the *Quarterly Review* was long and fairly regarded as Peel's journalistic mouthpiece. Its opinions upon ministerial policy, wrote *The Times* tartly on 5 July 1845, 'are always interesting to those who wish to know what that policy really is'.

The Times seems to have known how, behind the scenes, Peel was ready to advise Croker and sometimes to afford him detailed assistance in the preparation of articles. A notable example of this occurred with the number for September 1842, to which Croker contributed a piece on the 'Policy of Sir Robert Peel'. For this he was given much help by the Prime Minister. Croker had written to him on 25 July to report continuing dissatisfaction within a section of the Conservative party at Peel's new commercial policy. 'You are accused of double dealing because you say that you will benefit consumers without injuring producers.' Peel passed this letter on to his secretary, Edward Drummond, with the instruction that it was 'very important' to assist Croker with his article. Peel replied on 27 July that he would supply materials to form the basis of 'a valuable Article'. He then ran into a defence of his policy, part of which has already been quoted (pp. 5–6). Peel wrote again on 3 August, sending paragraphs from 'the Papers of this day' which reported signs of reduction in the widespread economic distress. 'Without improvement we were on the brink of Convulsion.' Peel was particularly anxious to explain to Croker for the benefit of his country readers how the new Corn Law would help agriculturalists; how the saving of expenditure as wheat prices fell would not be money lost to farmers, but would enable more wheat and other agricultural

---

[129] Aberdeen to Peel, 3 May 1844 (Add. MSS 40454, f. 176); Peel to Aberdeen, (3 May 1844) (Add. MSS 43063, f. 262).

[130] Drummond to editor of *Staffordshire Advertiser*, 20 October 1841 (Add. MSS 40492, f. 357); Peel to Fremantle, 21 October 1841; Fremantle to Peel, 22 October 1841 (Add. MSS 40476, ff. 45, 47); *History of The Times*, I, p. 491.

[131] Croker to Peel, 18 January 1845; Peel to Croker, 20 January 1845 (Add. MSS 40558, ff. 39, 41).

produce to be bought. 'Lower the price of Wheat, not only Poor rates, but the cost of every thing else is lowered.' Moreover, explained Peel, economic logic was deliberately not being pushed to its limit; the new Corn Law was designed to maintain a moderate price.

Croker thanked Peel on 5 August for the papers, '& what will be more useful to me, your own points'. He sent 'a blank form of queries, which I should be glad if you would have filled up & returned to me, also one of the parliamentary returns to which I wish to have an addition made'. Croker also asked for 'your *new corn scale* as it passed . . . and tell me also (or tell me where to find) the explanation of *your sugar* & *timber* duties as compared with those of the whigs last year which were rejected. In which of your speeches shall I find the fullest exposition of your general principles on all these points?' Such was Croker's thoroughness. Two days later he sent to Peel 'a paper with my queries on one side to which you can easily procure answers & return me the paper'. Five days later Croker complained that all his questions had not yet been answered, although he thanked Peel for supplying a copy of his budget speech which was useful even though very ill reported. On 13 August Peel asked a shade restlessly, 'Surely you have got answers to every query you have sent me?' Finally, some time later, 'Tuesday', probably 30 August, Croker sent Peel a draft of the article for revision. As late as 27 August, with Peel 'absent', Croker had turned to Gladstone as Vice-President of the Board of Trade, for yet further information. 'I am particularly anxious that we should be correct in our facts.'

Not surprisingly, Peel's statistics and arguments dominated Croker's text. Peel's striking words to Croker – 'If you had to constitute new Societies, you might on moral and social grounds prefer Corn fields to Cotton factories, an agricultural to a manufacturing population. But our lot is cast, and we cannot recede' – were expressed much less effectively in the article as – 'We might on moral and social grounds prefer, and feel it our duty to encourage, an agricultural rather than a manufacturing population – but our present lot is cast.' Despite this pedestrian style, Graham praised the article to Peel as 'unfolding the real motives on which your Policy is based'. The *Quarterly* number was published on 17 September, and the next day Croker modestly expressed the hope to Peel that 'it may do some good in country houses'.[132]

That Peel should have thought it worth while to give so much attention to journalism at a time when his mind was much occupied with the danger of revolution showed how he recognized the power of the press, and how important it was to present his policies accurately and favourably through it. He knew that the *Quarterly* article would be read by the protectionist right-

---

[132] Add. MSS 40512, ff. 143, 147; Add. MSS 40513, ff. 60, 109, 185, 318, 355; Add. MSS 40514, f. 311; Add. MSS 40515, ff. 104, 216; Croker to Gladstone, 27 August, 1 September 1842 (Add. MSS 44359, ff. 173, 175, 181); Graham to Peel, 1 September 1842 (Add. MSS 40447, f. 112); Jennings, *Croker*, II, pp. 382–9.

wingers of his own party, who subscribed to the journal and who needed to be calmed; beyond this Peel was aware that the contents of *Quarterly* political articles were quickly circulated through the newspapers to many other categories of readers. In this instance, *The Times* of 20 September devoted its first leader to friendly discussion of what it called this 'Conservative manifesto on the subject of Sir R. Peel's financial measures'. *The Times* noticed particularly the successful operation of the new Corn Law. Given the restraints of party, Peel had 'done all that could be done at the moment', although the poor hoped for further reductions in the future since farmers had now been shown that they had not been damaged by less protection. On 22 September the *Manchester Guardian* quoted from *The Times* article in a leader of its own, which emphasized the need for further cuts in the corn tax. In its issue of 28 September the *Guardian* also reprinted a partisan three-quarter column attack upon the *Quarterly* article from the Whig *Examiner*. In such ways did one anonymous article enter into public discussion, an article carefully but anonymously inspired by Peel as Prime Minister.

XI

An unkind observer in the Whig *Morning Chronicle* of 14 November 1845 noticed how Peel's views had 'enlarged with his person'. At the time of the death of Fox, *The Times* of 15 September 1806 had remarked that the 'personal similitudes' of public men were to be seen all over the kingdom. By the later eighteenth century mezzotints taken from portraits of such celebrities as the elder Pitt, General Wolfe or Laurence Sterne could be bought for about 5s, and smaller engravings for 1s. Portrait busts were available for a few pounds. Josiah Wedgwood, the pioneer potter, had been an eager producer of commemorative plates to celebrate both great events and great men, of which perhaps the most famous was the jasper medallion of the kneeling slave asking, 'Am I not a man and a brother?'[133]

By Peel's day likenesses in the form of engravings more or less flattering, or cartoons more or less unflattering, were circulating in large numbers. But popular awareness of what Peel and other politicians looked like received great reinforcement with the weekly appearance from the early 1840s of two successful illustrated papers, *Punch* and the *Illustrated London News*. Both quickly became Victorian institutions by raising the art of engraving to a remarkable level of refinement, giving 'wings and spirit to ponderous and senseless wood'. So exclaimed the first number of the *Illustrated London News* on 14 May 1842. By 1850 it was selling some 67,000 copies per week, price 6d.

---

[133] N. McKendrick, 'Josiah Wedgwood and the commercialisation of the Potteries', in N. McKendrick et al. (eds), *The Birth of a Consumer Society* (1982), pp. 122–3.

Its readers came mainly from the upper and middle classes, as an article admitted on the last day of 1842; but 'hundreds' of letters from working people were claimed as proof that its championship of the poor had won their approbation. The *London Journal* (19 July 1845) asserted, however, that the *News* circulated chiefly among families 'where there are young persons' and possessed little political influence. At the least, it gave its readers some idea of the appearance of even minor politicians. During its first weeks, for example, it carried a series of 'Popular Portraits' of such varied parliamentarians as W. B. Ferrand, Colonel Sibthorpe, T. S. Duncombe, J. A. Roebuck, Sir Robert Inglis and Richard Cobden. The shrewd remark was made thus early (2 July 1842) that if Cobden had failed to convince Peel of the wisdom of Anti-Corn Law League policy, 'it is not because the right hon. baronet has failed to listen to him'.

Peel was aware of the *Illustrated London News*, and also of its short-lived rival the *Pictorial Times*, which was started in March 1843. He told Prince Albert in November that he had heard how there was nearly a street affray between employees and partisans of the rival papers on Lord Mayor's day.[134] The likenesses of Peel himself in the *Illustrated London News* were not nearly so good as those in *Punch*; but the *News* also tried to picture newsworthy situations. For example, the number of 31 January 1846 showed Peel arriving at Westminster four days earlier to deliver his Corn Law repeal speech. He was pictured having just stepped out of his carriage, his dispatch box in his left hand, raising his top hat to the surrounding crowd with his right hand, and being saluted by an attendant peeler. Such a regular sense of fleeting incident was new in Victorian journalism. The same issue included a sketch of Peel inside the Commons chamber on the great day and also printed, in a special supplement, an almost verbatim report of his speech.

It was suggested in 1850 that one reason why *Punch* cartoons of Peel were especially lifelike was that as he grew older his face took on 'a peculiar expression of refined and somewhat playful acuteness' which well suited cartoon representation.[135] The first number of *Punch* had appeared on 17 July 1841, while Peel was in the process of winning the general election. He therefore figured prominently in both its cartoons and its articles from the very start. In the number for 24 July a full-page article entitled 'Punch and Peel' appeared, which wondered how the bedchamber question, which had kept Peel out of office in 1839, would be overcome this time:

Reader. – They say the Queen doesn't like Sir Robert.
Punch. – I'm also told that her Majesty has a great antipathy
to physic – yet when the Constitution requires medicine, why –

---

[134] Prince Albert to Peel, 11 November 1843; Peel to Prince Albert, 13 November 1843 (Add. MSS 40437, ff. 320, 336).
[135] *Tait's Edinburgh Magazine*, XVII (1850), p. 463.

Reader. – Sir Robert must be swallowed.

Punch. – Exactly so.

Facing this article stood a full-page cartoon, which showed Peel snatching Lord John Russell from the Treasury Bench.

The likeness of Peel was a good one – 'that tall, fair-haired, somewhat parrot-faced gentleman' as the article described him. *Punch* artists such as Richard Doyle and John Leech were long remembered for drawing the most lifelike representations of Peel. It was even claimed in 1895 that when one Peel statue was undertaken, the sculptor had been given a Leech cartoon as the best guide to feature and expression.[136] At first, however, *Punch* was decidedly Radical in its politics, and strongly critical of Peel. As late as 29 November 1845 an article entitled 'Peel's Games' pretended that the Premier was about to bring out a book of card games:

> embracing all the new games and tricks which by a skilful knowledge of how to play his cards, Sir Robert Peel has become master. He intends devoting an entire chapter to shuffling . . . Tricks will occupy a very large space . . . Cribbage, as played at the expense of the Whigs, will be elaborately explained; and a chapter on revokes will explain how it is that there is nothing irrevocable in the games of the Premier. The work will be emblazoned with a splendid portrait of Sir Robert Peel as the Knave of Spades.

This supposed portrait was reproduced full-page. Peel was shown carrying a double-edged sword 'To Cut Both Ways', with one leg chained by 'Monopoly' but the other spurred by 'Free Trade' (see p. 159).

Harriet Martineau noticed how *Punch* reached every part of the kingdom.[137] It was soon selling 30,000 copies weekly, at 3d, to a mainly middle-class readership. During the later 1840s its Radicalism was mellowing; and a measure of this, as will be seen in due place, was the rapid softening of its line towards Peel during the Corn Law crisis of 1845–6. *Punch* began increasingly to reflect that same moderate and independent middle-class opinion as *The Times* also served, and whose support Peel always recognized to be important to himself.

Before *Punch* was started, the best political cartoons had been those drawn by 'H. B.', John Doyle. Between 1829 and 1851 he published 917 lithograph *Political Sketches*, which were issued separately and were at their peak of popularity during the 1830s. Their appeal was especially to those in touch with the London high political world, who could readily follow Doyle's gentle satire

---

[136] M. H. Spielman, *History of Punch* (1895), pp. 202–3. See also J. B. Jones and Priscilla Shaw, 'Artists and "suggestions": the *Punch* cartoons 1843–1848', *Victorian Periodicals Newsletter*, 11 (1978), pp. 3–14.

[137] Harriet Martineau, *History of the Thirty Years' Peace* (1878) IV, pp. 439–40.

upon topics of the moment. H. B.'s Peel was, in the words of the *Westminster Review*, 'the man as he is daily seen'. Doyle's drawings were, therefore, hardly caricatures at all, and contrasted with the destructive characterization which had been commonplace in the preceding age of Gilray. Significantly, *The Times* in giving the *Sketches* regular notice upon publication, welcomed 'their tendency to give a goodhumoured turn to the dissensions of party feeling'.[138]

The identity of 'H. B.' long remained a secret, which added to the interest. It seems not to have been noticed that John Doyle first revealed himself in a letter to Peel in 1841. 'Although conceived in sport, I soon became convinced from the extent of their sale & the importance attached to them in political circles, that I possessed in my hands an agent of some little influence.' Peel answered that he was 'very sensible of the great merit of your performances'; and in 1843 he praised them to Brougham as 'amusing and instructive'. At the time of his creation of the Metropolitan Police in 1829 Peel told his wife how he had laughed over a print by W. Heath displayed in a print-shop window. It was called 'Peeling a Charley', 'in which I am represented stripping one of the old watchmen of his great-coat, etc.'[139]

The *Westminster Review* article already quoted pointed to the paradox that whereas a portrait painter could be tempted for reasons of flattery to depart from fidelity, a cartoonist such as 'H. B.' could dare to be true to life. Yet Doyle's purpose in revealing himself to Peel had been to ask the Premier for help with a non-humorous likeness. He wanted this for a painting of the scene earlier that year when Peel had introduced his successful Commons motion of want of confidence in the Whig Government. Doyle wrote that an engraving from such a picture would be 'very acceptable to a large portion of the Public'. He expected to draw mainly from memory, but begged the favour of an interview. Peel, however, replied that he had no time to spare.

Peel seems to have been an increasingly reluctant sitter. He sat at the Queen's request for Wintehalter's double portrait of Wellington and himself in 1844. He also sat for Linnell's curiously fuzzy portrait in 1838. But he declined to sit for Pickersgill in 1841. Yet a Pickersgill portrait survives which, although presumably not done from life, was described by one of Peel's sons as the truest likeness.[140] Always the best-known Peel portrait was that of 1825 by Lawrence, which glowingly depicted a still young-looking and handsome figure, with that

---

[138] *Westminster Review*, XXVIII (VI, n.s.) (1838), p. 292. See also G. M. Trevelyan (ed.), *The Seven Years of William IV, A Reign Cartooned by John Doyle* (1952); and M. D. George, *English Political Caricature 1793–1832* (1959), vol. 2, ch. XIV, nos. 290, 831.

[139] Doyle to Peel, 11, 17 December 1841, 7 January 1842; Peel to Doyle, 12 December 1841 (Add. MSS 40497, ff. 116, 118, 119; Add. MSS 40500, f. 312); Peel to Brougham, 2 November 1843 (Add. MSS 40535, f. 81); G. Peel (ed.), *Private Letters of Sir Robert Peel* (1920), p. 117; George, *Political Caricature*, p. 227, plate 85.

[140] Pickersgill to Peel, 27 November 1841; Peel to Pickersgill, 28 November 1841 (Add. MSS 40496, ff. 35, 37); R. Ormond, *Early Victorian Portraits* (1973) I, pp. 368–73; II, nos. 721–31.

pleasantly amused expression which cartoonists later found so helpful. Several copies were made of this Lawrence portrait, and it was frequently engraved right down to the time of Peel's death a quarter of a century later. In that same year the *Gentleman's Magazine* for August 1850 named what it regarded as the ten most remarkable mezzotints and lithographs of Peel. The British Museum catalogue of engraved British portraits (1912) lists four engravings of Lady Peel and twenty-six of Peel himself; still not a complete total. The market for engravings was clearly large and lasting. The *Standard* of 27 October 1841 remarked how Walton's full-length portrait had obviously been done with subsequent engraving in mind, since it showed great breadth of light and shade. 'The Conservative world', the paper added, would look forward to obtaining the 'really authenticated likeness'. Yet it seems unlikely that Peel ever sat for Walton. A portrait bust of Peel was produced by Chantrey in 1833; another by Bienaimé in 1841, 'with only *one* view of your person'. This was offered by the sculptor to Peel himself, but declined. Busts by Graham were exhibited at the Royal Academy in 1846 and 1847.[141]

Peel featured prominently on the Opposition front bench in Heyter's group portrait of the House of Commons in 1833. He also appeared in Partridge's 1846 group of the Fine Arts Commissioners. In that same year *John Bull*, a protectionist weekly, carried on 6 June a malicious report that Peel, Graham, Ripon and Wellington were to appear in the group portrait of the Council of the Anti-Corn Law League, which had been commissioned to celebrate repeal of the Corn Laws. The problem, claimed *John Bull*, was how to include the four Ministers in the picture, since they were not Council members. 'It has been surmounted, however, by grouping them together in one corner, where they appear as if receiving their orders from Mr. Cobden, who is represented as addressing them.' Repeal, in other words, had been dictated to the Peel Government by the Anti-Corn Law League. The engraving, claimed *John Bull*, was to be sold for 10, 7 and 3 guineas.

Peel's new home, Drayton Manor, was illustrated in 'numberless engravings', as the *Morning Chronicle* of 10 July 1850 remarked the day after the departure from there of his funeral procession. One Drayton engraving appeared in the *London Journal* of 16 May 1846 at the head of an article on 'Sir Robert Peel and his Free-Trade Measures'. Such illustrations might be cut out and hung on their walls by humble admirers. Henry Mayhew noted how some artisan homes were decorated with engravings of Chartist or Radical leaders.[142] The *Northern Star* published down the years a succession of such engravings, large and small. On 1 January 1848 it announced a reprint at 4d each of ten small portraits and of eight large portraits at 1s each. The

---

[141] Bienaimé to Peel, 30 October 1841; Drummond to Bienaimé, 1 November 1841 (Add. MSS 40493, ff. 286, 288).

[142] P. E. Razzell and R. W. Wainwright (eds), *The Victorian Working Class* (1973), p. xxxiv.

significance of the fact that after his death in 1850 Peel's portrait was added to this number will be considered in due place.

More enduring than engravings were commemorative medals. The early Victorians were fond of these; but Peel gave no encouragement to A. J. Stothard, self-styled 'Medallic Historian of the Times', who twice asked for assistance over intended Peel medals. The Premier remained unresponsive, despite Stothard's assurance that he was a staunch Conservative.[143] With or without Peel's assistance, a medal available in gold, silver or bronze was produced in 1837 to commemorate his installation as Lord Rector of Glasgow University. Also in the British Museum collection are four medals made to celebrate repeal of the Corn Laws in 1846. The three most striking of these seem to have been commissioned by the Anti-Corn Law League. Each shows variations upon the same basic design. One contains a portrait of Peel on the obverse, surrounded by an elaborate background with two sheaves of wheat, a cornucopia, barrels, timber, sacks, manuscript, an artist's pallette, a key, a steelyard, palm leaves and laurel leaves. On the reverse appear cameo portraits of Cobden, Bright, Villiers and Wilson.

Staffordshire-ware representations of contemporary celebrities were being mass-produced by the early Victorian years, for sale at a few pence at markets and fairs as well as in shops. Their popularity seems to have reached a peak about 1850. At this time perhaps a score of representations of the Duke of Wellington were circulating, mostly showing him in civilian clothes as an elder statesman. At least eight figures of Peel were issued, some at the time of Corn Law repeal, others at and after his death. One seems to have been inspired by the engraving of Peel on horseback which appeared in the *Illustrated London News* four days after he died. Most Staffordshire likenesses were poor; but they were significant not for their artistry but for their popularity, because they were bought in tens of thousands by working people.[144]

This was the first age of photography. Was Peel ever photographed? A daguerrotype of the Duke of Wellington has survived, from which an oil painting and an engraving were copied. Shortly after Corn Law repeal Peel was asked to sit for a companion daguerrotype, to be engraved on steel. The request was couched in words obviously coloured by the peroration to Peel's recent resignation speech, in which he had hoped to be remembered by 'those whose lot it is to labour'. The daguerrotypist described himself as 'one whose income is earned by his own industry after long hours labour'. But Peel still refused the request.[145]

Peel therefore seems to have died as the last Prime Minister never to have

---

[143] Stothard to Peel, 25 March 1842; answered 28 March 1842 (Add. MSS, 40505, f. 142).

[144] T. Balston, *Staffordshire Portrait Figures of the Victorian Age* (1958), pp. 52–3, supplement 7.

[145] J. Lunsden to Peel, 14 July 1846 (Add. MSS 40596, f. 82); *The Times*, 26 October 1984.

been photographed. The growth of his reputation was to owe nothing to the medium of the camera. But Peel's great debt to the medium of the printing press will have begun to be apparent throughout this chapter; and it will become still more apparent in the chapters which follow, wherein the response from the press and the public during his later career is surveyed. This response was revealingly various, not only at any one time but over time. As G. H. Francis wrote with significant exaggeration after Peel's death, 'there was not a public man, or a public writer, whom he did not compel to think and say of him at one time the absolute reverse of what he had said at another'.[146]

---

[146] G. H. Francis, *The Late Sir Robert Peel, Bart.* (1852), p. 9.

2

Peel Mainly in Opposition: 1834–41

I

At the time of Peel's death Charles Greville, the Whig diarist (6 July 1850), described the four months of the first Peel Ministry, from December 1834 to April 1835, as 'the most brilliant period of his life'. During these months Peel laid claim to a reputation for disinterested statesmanship, which was to gain increasing acceptance throughout the subsequent fifteen years of his career. This reputation can indeed be traced back in embryo for several years before 1834. Gladstone, writing in 1851, argued that during and after the Catholic Emancipation crisis of 1829 Peel's political character had been 'forced into expansion and ripeness'. Gladstone was implying that until this time Peel had only been what the Canningite *Times* of 6 June 1827 described as a 'useful subaltern officer', who could ably execute what others suggested to him. 'To talk of such a person as a statesman! or a chief! is merely an idle abuse of words.' The *People's Journal* of 1847 made the same point as Gladstone, that when carrying Catholic Emancipation through Parliament against the 'envenomed opposition of his former followers', Peel had 'laid a deep foundation of national respect' by the moderation with which he bore attacks. This may have impressed public opinion even though a majority in the country probably remained opposed to his new policy. A sense of this public respect seems to have made it easier for *Blackwood's Edinburgh Magazine*, which had vigorously attacked Peel during 1829, suddenly to cease its fire. It noticed in its October number how Wellington and Lyndhurst had taken out prosecutions in reply to press attacks, whereas Peel, who had been most severely criticized of all, had not done so. 'From this manly conduct he will profit greatly . . . pressing indeed must the necessity be, which shall ever induce us again to say a syllable against him.'[1]

---

[1] *People's Journal*, III (1847), p. 203; J. Brooke and Mary Sorensen (eds), *The Prime Minister's Papers: W. E. Gladstone III: Autobiographical Memoranda 1845–1866* (1979), p. 77; Milne, 'The Politics of *Blackwood's*', p. 248.

Gladstone believed that the process of Peel's elevation to a higher level of political character was continued by his firm but temperate opposition to the Reform Bills of 1831–2. Peel told the Commons (17 December 1831) that he would maintain his resistance to the last, 'convinced that though my opposition will be unavailing, it will not be fruitless, because the opposition now made will oppose a bar to further concessions hereafter . . . not opposed to a well-considered reform of our institutions which need reform, but opposed to this reform'. Peel feared that the Reform Act would root up those feelings of social respect and attachment, 'which are the only sure foundations of government'.[2] The tone here was again 'manly'; and this helps to explain how within a few years Peel's opposition to the Reform Act had been widely forgiven, even if not forgotten. Even the Radical *Extraordinary Black Book* of 1832, while still describing Peel as a 'tiny statesman and better qualified for a peerage than premiership', conceded that his resistance to parliamentary reform 'was not distinguished by the factious spirit, which animated the subalterns of his party'. Gladstone's regular personal contact with Peel began when the reformed Parliament first met in 1833. By this date, Gladstone remembered Peel as 'already the profound statesman'.

Peel's career of disinterested statesmanship after the Reform Act can be divided into three phases. Up to 1841 he was the rising Conservative party leader, who none the less remained always careful never to let party leadership become partisan leadership. From 1841 to 1845 he served as an active and creative Prime Minister; but he became a Minister whose policies increasingly set him apart from many of his own party, in and out of Parliament, and who yet refused to be deterred by this fact. Finally, from 1846 to 1850, during the Corn Law crisis and after, Peel deliberately placed himself not merely apart from the protectionist Conservative party but apart from any party inside or outside Parliament, moving with much applause into a novel position above party. The first of these phases will be surveyed in this chapter; the second and third phases will be treated in the chapters which follow.

II

The year 1833 marked a new beginning for the British Parliament, and it marked a new beginning for Peel. Within a couple of years he was to become the leader of a new Conservative party at Westminster and in the country. This fresh label, 'Conservative', was intended to suggest a more positive attitude than that conveyed by the old name of 'Tory', which had lost its vigour by becoming linked with reactionary views factiously defended. Peel himself had by implication repudiated the Tory label in a speech of 1827. 'I may be a Tory –

[2] Peel, *Speeches*, II, p. 433.

I may be an illiberal – but the fact is undeniable, that when I first entered upon the duties of the Home Department, there were laws in existence which imposed upon the subjects of this realm unusual and extraordinary restrictions: the fact is undeniable, that those laws have been effaced.'[3]

Peel was here referring to the series of law reforms which he had promoted while Home Secretary (1822–7) in the Government of Lord Liverpool. Liverpool's administration from 1812 to 1827 had gradually developed a policy of conservative reform, which owed something to the example of the younger Pitt, but more to the good sense of Liverpool himself, aided by such able younger lieutenants as Huskisson and Peel. The successful commercial, financial and law reforms of the later Liverpool years prepared the way for much of what was to follow during Peel's reforming Ministry of 1841–6. Yet throughout Liverpool's long tenure of office he was never able to depend upon an assured majority in the House of Commons. His Government had always to top up its majorities by attracting votes from more or less independent Members who had been persuaded upon the merits of each case.[4]

Before, during and after the Reform Act crisis this spirit of independence remained very strong at Westminster, no less strong in the first reformed Parliament which met in January 1833 than in its unreformed predecessors. Even the rump of some 150 members who sat with Peel in opposition were far from united; and at least until he took office in December 1834, Peel knew that he was far from being certainly accepted as their leader. Yet from the first Peel spoke out decisively in the reformed House of Commons, with his eye as much on opinion outside Parliament as inside. In his 8 February speech on the Address he declared his firm opposition to further parliamentary reform; but he wisely perceived that the most likely way to prevent further 'democratic' change would be to make the system work as now reformed – to demonstrate how, without further alteration, it could produce good government. And he readily accepted that such good government must include prudent but significant amendment of institutions, always excepting further reform of Parliament or reform tending towards the disendowment or disestablishment of the Churches of England and Ireland. He told the Commons that he was against 'simultaneous change in every thing that was established'; but not against 'gradual and temperate reform', such as would leave undisturbed that public tranquillity which was essential for the encouragement of capital investment and the creation of jobs for the working classes. This able speech immediately established Peel's position in the reformed House as a statesman with a future as well as a past. He was plainly the man round whom the right-wing might rally, although not in a spirit of reaction.[5]

[3] Ibid, I, p. 509.
[4] See N. Gash, *Lord Liverpool* (1984).
[5] Peel, *Speeches*, II, pp. 604–13.

Peel's line of constructive prudence had been carefully considered; and he was to adhere to it through the period of the Tamworth Manifesto, right up to taking office in 1841. Thereafter, he began to put prudence into practice. In a letter to Croker in 1842 he looked back to his 1833 speech as the deliberate beginning of a sequence of public declarations of intent, which he had now set out to honour.[6]

A month before making the 1833 speech Peel had written privately to Goulburn anticipating its content, but making more explicit his rejection of ultra-Toryism. At the same time he refused to contemplate factious voting with the Radicals merely to embarrass the Whig Government. On the contrary, he defined to Goulburn the 'chief object of that party which is called Conservative' as 'to resist Radicalism'. Peel then made the important statement (already quoted) of his belief in the need to win the support of non-partisan middle opinion: 'our policy ought to be to conciliate the good will of the sober-minded and well-disposed portion of the Community, and thus lay the foundations of future strength.'[7]

During the 1833–4 sessions the Whig Government was hardly in control of the House of Commons. The influence of the Radicals, Dissenters and Daniel O'Connell's Irish seemed likely to force further radical reform in Church and state. In May 1834 Sir James Graham and Lord Stanley resigned from the Cabinet in opposition to the appropriation of surplus Irish Church revenues to non-church purposes. In June they and some twenty-four other moderate reformers joined with Peel and the Conservatives in opposing the second reading of a bill to admit Dissenters to the old universities. Then in July Lord Grey, who was widely respected, resigned as Prime Minister to be succeeded by Lord Melbourne, who was not so well regarded.

Peel viewed these Whig embarrassments with some satisfaction. But he was not eager to take office himself until the Whigs had become further discredited, and until the ultra-Tories had shown themselves willing to see the sense of his middle way. A revolt by the ultras in the Lords in August, which carried Wellington along with it, demonstrated that extreme gestures still appealed to the far right. Then suddenly the various elements in the party were brought together by an unexpected offer of office. In mid-November William IV dismissed the Melbourne Government. Ministers had been quarrelsome and at odds; the King also feared for the safety of the Irish Church at their hands. When Lord Althorp, the well-liked Whig leader in the Commons, was perforce elevated to the Lords by the death of his father, William IV seized the excuse to withdraw his confidence from the Ministry. This was to be the last time that the personal disfavour of the Sovereign has ended an administration. The King sent for Wellington, who declined the premiership in favour of Peel. But Peel was

---

[6] Jennings, *Croker*, II, pp. 386–7.
[7] Peel to Goulburn [postmark 3 January 1833] (Goulburn Papers).

touring in Italy, and so in the meantime the Duke held the offices of First Lord of the Treasury and Home Secretary. Peel did not return to London until 9 December, when he immediately accepted the King's commission. Friendly but firm refusals from Stanley and Graham of invitations to join the new Cabinet soon presented Peel with a major setback. He had hoped to form a broad-based administration of the centre as well as of the right. Instead, he was forced to narrow his range. This weakened his subsequent calls for non-partisan support both in the country and in Parliament.

Should Peel have tried to collect a working majority within the existing House of Commons, which had sat for less than two years? This became a matter of considerable discussion. Peel was very much in a minority. With only about 150 immediate followers, he would have needed to win at least an equal number of votes on every important division in order to make up his majorities. Lord Liverpool's majorities in the previous decade had never depended upon independent support to this extent. Yet it was a measure of the still limited commitment to party of many Members of Parliament that *The Times* now argued strongly for Peel not to seek an immediate dissolution, but to face the Commons. John Walter, the owner of *The Times*, may deserve credit for contributing (as will be shortly seen) towards the discussion which led to the publication of the Tamworth Manifesto in preparation for a general election. But as late as the day before the manifesto's publication, a *Times* editorial of 17 December was claiming that at least two-thirds of the existing Members of Parliament were 'rational and constitutional Reformers' who might support Peel. Even the next day, an editorial obviously written before receipt of Peel's manifesto in the small hours and printed incongruously alongside it, reiterated this argument against a dissolution. As late as 8 January 1835 another editorial looked back to these earlier remarks about 'the worse than doubtful policy of dissolving Parliament'. Perhaps this was Barnes's line as editor, in contrast to that of John Walter.

Peel's refusal to test the willingness of the existing Commons to support a programme of prudent reform ran him into the risk, in the eyes of *The Times*, of seeming to be insincere in his professed attachment to reform. The Liberal *Manchester Guardian* of 3 January 1835 developed this argument. 'Had Sir Robert Peel really meant his cabinet to be a reforming one, we should not now, in the depth of winter, and within two short years of the last general election, have been plunged into the excitement of a new one.' In his *Memoirs* Peel explained how he had found preparations for a general election well advanced on his return from Italy. Moreover, there was the risk that majorities in his support in the Lords would have placed the upper house in conflict with contrary majorities in the Commons. This would have been dangerous. 'The progress of the contest would have given to the administration the decided character of a Government supported by the Crown and Lords against the House of Commons.' Also, argued Peel in retrospect, his basis of only some 150 supporters was simply too small to hope for majorities by topping up.[8]

Peel did not air these arguments in public at the time. He contented himself when the newly elected Parliament met with taking full responsibility for advising a dissolution, on the ground that precedents from 1784, 1806, 1807 and 1831 suggested that when an extensive change of Government had occurred, it was proper to dissolve a hostile Parliament and to appeal to the judgement of 'a higher, and a fairer tribunal – the public sense of the people'.[9] So the appeal was made in January 1835. But how was a Conservative Prime Minister to try to win over tens of thousands of electors who only some two and three years earlier had voted for the Reform Bill, which he had then so steadily resisted? Peel saw clearly that he must demonstrate his trustworthiness and moderation. He must separate himself from all ultra-Tory attitudes, even though he had taken some ultras into his administration; and he must not seem to stand too close to the Duke of Wellington, even though he was Foreign Secretary. Wellington's brusque rejection of parliamentary reform had precipitated the crisis of 1830–2: and before and during the 1835 election he was being accused of an inclination towards dictatorship, as allegedly demonstrated by his readiness to hold more than one office in Peel's absence.

Goulburn had reported upon the state of public opinion in a letter which awaited Peel on his return from Italy: 'the property of the Country desires a conservative & not an *ultra Tory* Government, meaning by that a Government deaf to all improvement which comprises change, however much on other grounds to be desired.' On the same day Lieutenant-Colonel James Lindsay wrote from Fifeshire (where he was to be an unsuccessful Conservative candidate) to remind Peel of the unpopularity of Wellington's name, 'connecting it with the cry of no reform, but they readily accept of you'. Four days later Sir Thomas Lethbridge from Taunton reported Somerset opinion as strong for 'an Entire Reform of abuses, in Church & State', and ready to believe that Peel would introduce the '*right and proper degree of Reform*'. Lethbridge urged Peel to make an immediate declaration of his principles. He advised this, however, not as preparation for a general election but in order to influence the existing House of Commons, which (though pledged to reform) had passed the Irish Coercion Bill, 'a pretty good proof that when duty & *property called* upon, they had not only the power but the will, to *preserve* our Institutions'. If Peel did dissolve, Lethbridge expected no great alteration in the membership of the Commons: but 'a vast alteration of *Sentiment* among those returned', provided that before the dissolution the country had been told Peel's principles of government. 'All depends upon this, as far as I can learn public opinion.'[10]

---

[8] Peel, *Memoirs*, II, pp. 43–8.

[9] Peel, *Speeches*, III, p. 11.

[10] Goulburn to Peel, 8 December 1834 (Add. MSS 40333, f. 177); Lindsay to Peel, 8 December 1834 (Add. MSS 40404, f. 312); Lethbridge to Peel, 12 December 1834 (Add. MSS 40405, f. 89).

On 10 December John Walter, who was not only the proprietor of *The Times* but also a Liberal Member of Parliament and soon to be 'Liberal–Conservative' candidate for Berkshire, had written to Sir James Scarlett about the need to rally opinion in that county, which was inclined to be hostile to those making a shift towards Peel. Walter thought that such a rallying might be best achieved through 'some frank explanation, some popular declaration previous to a Dissolution of Parliament'. Peel was not so distrusted as Wellington, and 'the least violent among the party of which I speak may be inclined to give the King's Ministers a fair trial'. This letter was passed by Scarlett to Peel. It is interesting to notice how Walter, far from repeating *The Times* line against a dissolution, seemed to be expecting one.[11]

Peel needed little persuading that some sort of statement was desirable; but he was not yet sure about its best form. At a Cabinet dinner on 13 December there was discussion whether he should shape his forthcoming speech at the Mansion House banquet on 23 December into a statement of principles. The next day, however, one Cabinet Minister, Lord Ellenborough, urged Peel to think instead of addressing a public letter to those Members of Parliament who had supported him. A speech, Ellenborough warned, was liable to be misreported, a public letter much less so. In what seems to have been a variant of this proposal, John Walter, apparently with aid in drafting from Thomas Barnes, composed an address which was to be sent to Peel from friendly Members, to which Peel could reply with a statement of principles. A version of this proposed address was forwarded by Scarlett to Peel on 16 December. But Peel replied on the same day that the best way of achieving the desired publicity would be through a public letter to his own constituents, 'which I can issue on any day, on the ground that my seat is now vacant'. A draft was submitted to the Cabinet at dinner on 17 December, and after prolonged discussion it was sent to the three morning papers just in time for inclusion in the issues for 18 December. *The Times* remarked that there was no time to do more than 'give this document as conspicuous a position as its importance demands'.[12]

III

The Tamworth Manifesto was not innovative in form. Election candidates had often written addresses, even under the unreformed system. But Peel's letter was made into a great innovation by the way it was publicised – and was intended to be publicised – not just locally in his constituency, but nationally through the London press. Here was a Prime Minister speaking to the whole

[11] Walter to Scarlett, 10 December 1834 (Add. MSS 40405, f. 24).

[12] Ellenborough to Peel, 14 December 1834; Scarlett to Peel, 'Tuesday', [16 December 1834]; Peel to Scarlett, 16 December 1834 (Add. MSS 40405, ff. 202, 325, 327); Ellenborough journal, 13, 14, 16–19 December 1834 (Ellenborough Papers 30/12/28/5).

electorate for the first time. This was noteworthy. Yet the significance of the Tamworth Manifesto as a step on the road to democracy in Britain can easily be exaggerated. The content of the manifesto showed it to be in its day, and in the intention of its author, a rallying cry not *for* but decidedly *against* the progress of democracy. By asserting his commitment to moderate reform Peel did by implication distance himself from ultra-Toryism; but in the paragraph in which he promised to act in the spirit of the Reform Bill he distanced himself also, and more explicitly, from democratic Radicalism:

> if, by adopting the spirit of the Reform Bill, it be meant that we are to live in a perpetual vortex of agitation; that public men can only support themselves in public estimation by adopting every popular impression of the day, – by promising the instant redress of anything which anybody may call an abuse, – by abandoning altogether that great aid of government – more powerful than either law or reason – the respect for ancient rights, and the deference to prescriptive authority; if this be the spirit of the Reform Bill, I will not undertake to adopt it.

Only with this said, – with democracy denied, with 'deference to prescriptive authority' praised – did Peel become positive:

> But if the spirit of the Reform Bill implies merely a careful review of institutions, civil and ecclesiastical, undertaken in a friendly temper, combining, with the firm maintenance of established rights, the correction of proved abuses and the redress of real grievances, – in that case, I can for myself and colleagues undertake to act in such a spirit and with such intentions.

Significantly, the manifesto had begun by emphasizing how Peel was seeking to address non-partisan middle opinion: 'that great and intelligent class of society . . . which is much less interested in the contentions of party, than in the maintenance of order and the cause of good government'. Maintenance of the civil peace was thus placed first, a reflection of Peel's fear of a revolutionary outbreak which would threaten social harmony, the security of property and business confidence. He refused to admit that the passing of the Reform Act disqualified him from holding office because he had opposed it. Instead, he emphasized that he now accepted the act as 'a final and irrevocable settlement'. He reminded his readers how in the 1820s he had himself reformed the currency, the criminal law and the system of trial by jury. He offered, if confirmed in power, 'a careful review of institutions'. In particular, Peel went as far as he could to conciliate the Dissenters, reiterating his support for their relief from payment of Church rates and observance of Anglican marriage rites. He tried to soften his continuing refusal to back their admission to Oxford and Cambridge by offering, on grounds of civil equality, to promote their entry into the medical and legal professions on the same terms as Anglicans. He refused to contemplate the alienation of Established Church property in either England or Ireland; but he was ready for reform of tithe, for the reorganization of Church revenues, and for a full enquiry into the working of the Church Establishment, not with a view to its abolition but to improve its effectiveness. In the same spirit of positive enquiry, Peel proposed to let the Royal Commission on Municipal Corporations continue its work. Finally, he promised to maintain peace, to support the public credit, and to govern with strict economy and with 'just and impartial consideration of what is due to all interests – agricultural, manufacturing, and commercial'. Peel's very last words were to ask for 'a fair trial', the expression used in John Walter's letter of 10 December.

Neither the tone of the Tamworth Manifesto nor its specific commitments were new; quite the contrary. Peel's speech on the Address in 1833, and subsequent speeches to the reformed House of Commons, had already made it clear how strongly he was bidding for the support of non-partisan middle opinion. He was offering reassurance to the propertied that he could deliver stability; and he was promising the propertied and unpropertied alike, electors and non-electors, that he could bring them the benefits of good government.

The manifesto came under immediate discussion throughout the country, and it was to form the basis for innumerable Conservative election speeches. Charles Greville (20 December) noted how it had made 'a prodigious sensation' in London political circles. The Whigs tried to dismiss it as 'artful but shallow'. It was, commented Greville, 'rather too Liberal for the bigoted Tories, but all the moderate people are well satisfied'. The Whig evening *Globe* of 19 December argued that Peel's opposition to the Reform Act could not now simply be forgotten; it had been as extreme as support for the Holy Alliance or for Owenism. Moreover, claimed the *Globe*, neither the currency nor the law reforms, about which Peel was now boasting, had shown any originality. In contrast to this Whig carping, the *Globe's* Conservative evening rival, the *Standard*, was enthusiastic. It had written on 10 December of the desire among Conservatives for 'a reforming government'. On 16 December it had described Peel's Ministry as a last chance. Peel's overthrow would be 'almost instantly followed by the subversion of the Throne – the dissolution of the national Church, and a complete change in the property of the empire'. The Whig *Morning Chronicle* laughed at such fears; but the *Standard* replied by emphasizing the rapidity of 'the movement'. Look how much damage had been done in only two years – 'Ten bishoprics amputated from the Church!'; the East India Company 'prostrated'; 'the whole state of society in the West Indies revolutionized!'; the Reform Act passed. It was against this background of hopes and fears that the *Standard* reprinted the text of the Tamworth Manifesto on the evening of 18 December: 'this is a first instance of a minister throwing himself upon the judgment of the public; the first formal acknowledgement that the people, in their collective body, have a right to know beforehand, minutely and circumstantially, the principles upon which the government is to be carried on'. Here was 'the first homage offered to the popular principle of the Reform Bill', a step (added the *Standard* with relish) which Grey, Melbourne and Brougham had never dared to take.

The *Standard* of 19 December noticed how a majority of the London morning and evening papers had written favourably about the manifesto. *The Times* of that morning had praised Peel's 'uncompromising frankness'; he need not fear 'to meet a freely chosen English House of Commons'. The implication here was that Peel could reasonably hope to attract enough independent votes to carry his policies in the Commons. *The Times* returned to the point on 9 January 1835; 'the right sense and spirit of the nation will not endure from its representatives the unprincipled expedient of a sweeping vote against the Government'. Yet *The Times* was also fearing a factious alliance of the Whigs with the Radicals, 'the destructives', in which the latter would set the pace towards revolution. 'If there be no difference between Whigs and Revolutionists, then think twice before you vote for either' (12 January). An article by Croker on 'Sir Robert Peel's Address' in the February number of the *Quarterly Review* remarked that, before the passing of the Reform Act, to solicit support 'not from parliament but from the people ... would have been thought derogatory and impugned as unconstitutional'. Now, since the choice of Ministers was 'absolutely dependent on the choice of the several constituencies', such an appeal had become inevitable. Not, Croker emphasized, – and Peel, who was sent a proof for comment, must have emphatically agreed – that this required a Prime Minister who won an election to obey every whim of public opinion. 'Sir Robert Peel has undertaken a navigation which can be successfully accomplished as little by invariably yielding to public opinion, as by habitually disregarding it. He must know that it is – as the wind to the ship – his *primum mobile*, and that his course must be obedient to its *impulses*, though not always to its *direction*.'

The Tamworth Manifesto does not seem to have impressed many Dissenters. Peel was probably asking too much to expect them suddenly to trust him, especially as he had reaffirmed his belief in the Anglican Church Establishment even while making his careful gestures towards them. On 20 December the *Manchester Guardian* – which was Unitarian-owned, and which in 1839 was to be described to Peel by Lord Francis Egerton (who represented South Lancashire) as 'read by every whig & dissenter in Lancashire' – printed the text of the manifesto; but an editorial dismissed its 'forced concessions' as not to be compared with the 'spontaneous efforts' of the Whigs. A week later it described an election speech of Egerton's in Manchester as almost identical to Peel's 'vague professions', and called upon electors 'not to trust this ministry for an instant'.[13]

Five days after publication of the Tamworth Manifesto, Peel spoke at the

---

[13] Egerton to Peel, 16 May 1839 (Add. MSS 40426, f. 439).

Lord Mayor's Mansion House dinner. This was to be the first of four well-publicised speeches which he was to deliver, in and out of office, during the next few years – three in the City of London (December 1834, May 1835, May 1838) and one in Glasgow (January 1837). These were, of course, additional to speeches which he gave at intervals in his Tamworth constituency. The 1834 Mansion House speech repeated the pledges of the Tamworth Manifesto; but it was even more clearly a call for trust in himself and his colleagues. Men, emphasized Peel, mattered as well as measures: 'the heads which conceived, and the hands which are to execute those measures'. The speech also contained a rousing passage in which Peel proclaimed that the public wanted quiet and stability after the noise and upset of recent years. People wanted to say:

> We are tired of agitation (great cheering) – we are tired of that state of continual excitement, the effect of which in private life is to withdraw men from their proper business, and in public life to consume the energies of public men in other than their proper duties. We hate the pressure from without – (loud and protracted cheering, which drowned the conclusion of the sentence).[14]

The *Standard*'s report of this speech was the fullest version, and it may have been supplied or corrected by Peel himself. Certainly, a month later he gave the *Standard* of 23 January 1835 a great boost by allowing it to publish, in advance of presentation to Parliament, a two-column partial outline of his plans for Church reform in response to changed conditions, especially in the manufacturing districts. The *Morning Post* of 27 January suggested that this was a deliberate 'feeler' to test public reaction. Perhaps it was. The *Standard* of 28 January was pleased to notice the interested and mainly favourable response, adding that it had received far more letters than it could possibly publish.[15]

Peel did not win a majority at the general election. The gap in the Commons was too great to close. Nevertheless, it has been noticed how the 1835 election produced a greater change in relative party strengths than any other election until 1880.[16] Admittedly, since Conservative numbers had fallen so low at the last election it was likely that they would now recover noticeably. They had already gained seven seats at by-elections during 1834. But an extra impetus to recovery had been given by the Tamworth Manifesto. It had given Conservatism a newly attractive appearance in the eyes of many non-partisan voters, who paradoxically seem to have been persuaded by it to vote even for some

---

[14] *The Times*, 24, 25 December 1834; *Standard*, 24 December 1834.

[15] Giffard to Peel, 21 March 1845 (Add. MSS 40563, f. 135).

[16] See D. Close, 'The formation of a two-party alignment in the House of Commons between 1832 and 1841', *English Historical Review*, 84 (1969), pp. 257–77 and 'The rise of the Conservatives in the Age of Reform', *Bulletin of the Institute of Historical Research*, 45 (1972), pp. 89–103; both based upon his 1967 Oxford University D.Phil thesis, 'The general elections of 1835 and 1837 in England and Wales'; Stewart, *Foundation of the Conservative Party*, chs. 5, 6.

ultra-Tory candidates. Peel was told that this explained, for example, the success of Colonel Sibthorp at Lincoln.[17]

At the 1835 election Conservatives almost doubled their numbers in the Commons, from about 150 to just under 300. They gained especially well in the English boroughs, but made up some ground almost everywhere (tables 2.1 and 2.2). In 1835 the cry of 'the Church in danger' had rallied many Anglicans, albeit with the effect of keeping Dissenters suspicious of Peel. Agricultural depression encouraged a clamour from the grain-growing districts

TABLE **2.1**   Party strength after the general elections of 1832, 1835, 1837 and 1841

	Conservatives	Liberals	Waverers	Total
1832	146	456	52	654[a]
1835	291	342	25	658
1837	313	338	7	658
1841	375	281	–	656[b]

[a] Four seats remained vacant because of punitive suspensions of writ.
[b] Sudbury was disenfranchised.
Source: Close, 'Rise of the Conservatives', p. 90.

TABLE **2.2**   Conservative gains between 1832 and 1841

	England and Wales		Scotland	Ireland	Total
	Boroughs	Counties			
By-elections, 1832–3					10
General election, 1835	53	27	3	9	92
Changes of party, 1835[a]	25	10	2	6	43
By-elections, 1835–7					8
General election, 1837	−1	22	−1	−7	13
Changes of party, 1837					1
By-elections, 1838–41					10[b]
General election, 1841	19	23	3	5	50
Changes of party, 1841		2			2

[a] It is necessary to assume that MPs changed party at the start of each Parliament.
[b] Two by-elections resulting from petitions are included in the 1837 general election results.
Source: Close, 'Rise of the Conservatives', p. 90.

[17] R. Williams to Peel, 21 January 1835 (Add. MSS 40411, f. 1).

against the Whigs and the malt tax, although in the event Peel refused to repeal the tax on the ground that the revenue was essential and a malt tax could only be replaced by a property tax.[18]

In the middle of the elections Peel assured the King's Private Secretary that 'the people of England will at no remote period be satisfied that I have the power to do as much in the way of real salutary Reform, as the sincere friends to such Reform could wish'.[19] On 16 January he delivered the speech at the Tamworth dinner to celebrate his re-election which has already been noticed for attracting wide publicity. Peel emphasized that Ministers must now seize all such occasions for nationwide communication. 'It is by the result of public discussion that, as a Minister, I hope to succeed.' He refused to admit that the election result meant that he was sure to be outvoted in the new House of Commons: 'the representatives of the country will not refuse to give the King's Ministers a FAIR TRIAL.' Peel was here making the old assumption that Members of Parliament recognized as the first call upon them the duty to support the King's Ministers, whoever they were, if they were offering a prospect of good government; and that loyalty to party came second to this. 'I am not alarmed at the lists that are published, dividing the members of Parliament into "Conservatives" and "Reformers". I cannot but think that many of those who are classed as Reformers entertain opinions not far different from my own.'[20]

An estimated forty-three members who had sat in the previous Parliament as reformers were now returned as Conservatives; twenty-five 'Conservative–Whigs' had also been elected. Peel anticipated an addition of support from independents and waverers once he had explained himself to the Commons; he believed that in key divisions enough of them would vote with his Government's 300 supporters to produce working majorities. The Ministry would thus be able not merely to survive but to promote its programme of reforms, just as the Liverpool Government had done in the 1820s. The *Manchester Guardian* of 31 January certainly seems to have thought that something like this might happen, but with the Commons leading Peel rather than with Peel leading the Commons. The *Guardian* offered to support any well-considered measures which 'knowledge of the actual constitution of the house of commons' might extract from an otherwise supposedly reluctant Peel.

This was not to be. Although the Conservatives were the largest single party in the Commons, Whigs, Radicals and Irish began to come together in an alliance – sealed in the Lichfield House compact – which by the old standards could be regarded as factious or even disloyal; but which could be justified as an exasperated response to the outdated royal intervention which had installed

[18] Peel, *Speeches*, III, pp. 29–41.
[19] Peel to Taylor, 12 January 1835 (Add. MSS 40302, f. 184).
[20] *The Times*, 26 January 1835.

Peel in office. The Conservative candidate for Speaker was immediately defeated. This was far from conclusive, and Peel pressed on, encouraged by *The Times*. Defeats recurred. Could the King's business be done? Peel was not interested in simply holding office for its own sake, although he recollected ten years later how he had thought it right to uphold the constitutional position of the Crown by not yielding too easily to 'popular clamour or factious Combinations'.[21] Peel waited to be defeated on a major issue, where the voting was plainly a matter of confidence. Defeat by 322 votes to 289 came over the principle of appropriating surplus Irish Church revenues. On 8 April Peel resigned. He was sure that it would be wrong to seek another general election, because he saw little prospect of winning a Conservative majority; and since a general election was called by royal favour, for Ministers to fail would be damaging to the Crown: 'every failure is a mighty stride towards the complete destruction of all balance in the Government. There is in truth very little left.'[22]

IV

Peel had fallen after four months, but he had gained greatly in reputation during this first brief premiership. *The Times* of 8 April 1835 praised the remarkable development of his qualities, which made his ejection 'a grievous national calamity'. The *Annual Register* wrote that in personal terms Peel's tenure had been 'altogether triumphant', even though he had been 'placed in the difficult situation of a minister dependent on the public voice, and yet determined not to bow the knee to those idols on which democratical superstition bestows the name of popular rights'. The country, continued the *Register*, had been impressed by the energy and oratorical skill with which he had fought a losing battle in the House of Commons, where he clearly stood without a rival. A collection of Peel's *Speeches . . . During His Administration 1834–1835*, published along with the text of the Tamworth Manifesto, reached a second edition by August 1835 in response to 'extensive demand', even though it cost 10s. Joseph Parkes, in whose middle-class Radical circle Peel was known as 'Sir Joseph Surface', admitted by implication that Peel had made a great impact. Parkes contemplated writing Peel's political biography, 'as an antidote to the laudanum doses of Peel's hypocritical addresses and speeches'.[23]

Harriet Martineau claimed in her history of the period, written a decade later, that it was during these difficult months in office that old prejudices about Peel began to dissolve, as people began to appreciate his unusual but

---

[21] Peel to Brougham, 30 January 1845 (Add. MSS 40482, f. 147).

[22] Peel to Goulburn (May 1835) (Goulburn Papers).

[23] Jessie K. Buckley, *Joseph Parkes of Birmingham* (1926), pp. 145–6.

impressive character. 'Every one knew that he had had no option about undertaking office; and every one felt and said that he had failed only because parties had been as yet too strong for him.'[24] In other words, non-partisan opinion was beginning to turn towards him, opinion which might be coming to respect Peel even while continuing to dislike the Conservative party. Charles Greville (4 April) believed that public recognition of Peel's liberal yet safe views would soon bring him back to office. A letter from young Disraeli under the pseudonym of 'Loelius' in The Times of 25 May offered a shrewd characterization of Peel, undistorted by that personal hostility which was to underlie Disraeli's later assessments: 'a temperament essentially national, and a habit of life pleasing to the manners and prejudices of his countrymen, with many of the virtues of the English character, and some of its peculiarities; confident rather than sanguine; guided by principles, yet not despising expedients; fearful to commit himself, yet never shrinking from responsibility; proud, yet free from vanity'.

Addresses of regret on Peel's departure from office, sent to the King and to Peel himself, filled columns of The Times every day from 6 to 15 April, and of the Standard until 21 April. The Standard joyfully complained that it lacked the space to print all the texts, and had perforce to substitute long lists of placenames. The general complaint of the addresses was against the 'excess of party zeal' which had defeated Peel: 'a combination of parties who have hardly one sentiment in common'. Although many committed Conservatives must have signed these addresses, men of no party also added their names. Over 1,100 London solicitors addressed Peel to emphasize how his defeat was 'contrary to the wishes of the majority of your countrymen'. Peel wrote light-heartedly but with obvious satisfaction about this 'wonderful address' from a fraternity which he had not realized to be 'so nearly unanimous' in his support.[25]

Francis Place, in a letter to a fellow leading Radical, Joseph Hume, claimed that not one public meeting had sympathized with the Whigs upon their fall, and not one had congratulated them on their return to office. This was an exaggeration; but morale was certainly higher on the Conservative side. The Whigs and their allies were to be increasingly on the defensive. Francis Place went on to liken the unsettled political situation to that of France before the revolution. 'The frequent choppings and changings of ministers are producing a rapid conviction among the people inimical to the very form of the government in all its parts.' Peel would have agreed about this danger, and about the need for more stability, although he would have disagreed about the remedy which Place suggested – universal suffrage and vote by ballot. Peel emphasized to Goulburn how the Whigs must now be allowed to stay in office,

[24] Martineau, Thirty Years' Peace, III, pp. 198–9.
[25] Peel to Croker, 13 April 1835 (Add. MSS 40302, f. 260).

opposed over differences of principle but not harassed by opportunist manoeuvring.[26]

On 11 May Peel made another major speech out of Parliament, this time to the merchants, bankers and traders of London in the Merchant Taylors Hall. This speech dwelt upon two themes to which Peel often returned down the years – the interdependence of the industrial, commercial and agricultural interests; and the continuity of British politics and institutions. Both emphases were calculated to soothe contention and at the same time to raise the level of political discussion. Peel promised his audience 'plain opinions in plain language'. He vigorously threw down any barriers between the Conservative party and the new mainly middle-class electorate: 'we disclaim any separation from the middling classes of this country'. He was himself proud to be the son of a cotton spinner. It was good that such a man could become Prime Minister; not in any spirit of levelling 'democracy', but under the existing balanced constitution of King, Lords and Commons. As a public man he was willingly 'a man of the people'; but he sought no 'paltry and fleeting popularity'. He hoped instead to win the 'sound good opinions' of sensible people.[27]

This speech was widely noticed, and praised for its vigour and clear appeal to the middle classes. *The Times* of 13 May called it 'spirit stirring', and urged the immediate circulation of 100,000 copies in cheap pamphlet form. By 24 May Charles Greville was noting how this had been done throughout the country.

Not only the message but also the man now received close scrutiny whenever Peel spoke outside Parliament. In its number for October 1835 *Blackwood's Edinburgh Magazine* – which had once castigated Peel over Catholic Emancipation, had then suddenly ceased its attacks, and which by 1835 had returned to his support – published a short article which was obviously intended to encourage a cult of personality. It described Peel's behaviour at a Tamworth political dinner on 4 September, his first public appearance in his constituency since his resignation. 'A seat was assigned us so near the guest of the evening that much of his general conversation reached us. We watched him – we are not ashamed to avow it – narrowly and closely. We wished to gain an insight into the workings of that commanding mind.' At first Peel was gay and casual; but when the cloth was drawn he became serious and concentrated, in preparation for his speech. *Blackwood's* did not report this, since it had already been well publicised; but it did report the few words with which Peel had lovingly responded to the toast to his wife, 'which exhibited him to no small advantage as a private citizen and as a man'. In his main speech Peel recapitulated the constructive legislation which his Government had intended. He claimed – erroneously, but what became true after the 1837 general

---

[26] Place to Hume, 2 May 1835 (Add. MSS 35150, f. 36); Peel to Goulburn, [May 1835] (Goulburn Papers).

[27] *The Times*, 12 May 1835.

election – that the Conservatives had won a majority among the representatives of 'the English people'. In such circumstances he refused to accept that his attempt to stay in office had been 'so rash as some people have considered, nor that my hopes to settle those questions were so remote as many people thought'. He concluded by emphasizing the importance of the non-popular elements in the constitutional balance – the House of Lords and the King. Radicals sought to undermine both, and so to destroy that balance. 'I ask you whether the popular voice, represented through popular channels alone, is sufficient for you?' Peel professed himself 'almost sure' that it was not – that the people wanted to transmit a balanced constitution to future generations.

In January 1837 Peel became Lord Rector of Glasgow University, and this led to the most striking of all his extra-parliamentary initiatives during these years. His visit to Glasgow became a major public relations exercise, remembered by Gladstone over fifty years later as one of the most remarkable examples of the use of 'the platform'.[28] Peel had now thrown off his old-fashioned inhibitions about the propriety of addressing audiences outside Parliament and outside his constituency. Event succeeded event in Scotland, all well publicised. Peel began on 11 January with his non-political rectorial address to the Glasgow students. Then, over the next two days, he dined with the Principal and professors; presided over a meeting of the University Senate; visited the Glasgow Royal Exchange, where he made an impromptu speech standing on a chair; accepted innumerable addresses; was given the freedom of Lanark; and received also the freedom of Glasgow, which had been withheld by the Whig Council but which was purchased for him by the contributions of 2,003 operative Conservatives. Finally, on 13 January, Peel spoke at a great civic banquet, for which the demand for tickets was so great even at 25s each that – with no building in Glasgow big enough – a temporary hall of timber and tarpaulin had to be erected. Illuminated by two large gasoliers, it was able to seat over 3,400 guests, 'the most numerous and powerful festive gathering ever assembled in this country to do honour to a political leader and testify adhesion to his Party'.[29]

Here was visible evidence of how mercantile middle-class moderate opinion was now ready to listen to Peel, even though he was the Conservative leader. Graham assured him that in the west of Scotland 'the distinction between the old Tory Party and the Conservative Reformers' was much less marked than in Edinburgh: 'many most respectable Persons, who were friendly to the Reform Bill, will be found in Glasgow ready to meet you, and to bury all past differences in an earnest desire of making common cause against the tendency to a Republic.' Lord Aberdeen thought Peel's election by the students was a good sign for the future. The Radical *Westminster Review* conceded that there

[28] *Nineteenth Century*, XXXIII (1892), p. 688.
[29] *Spectator*, 21 January 1837.

was a drift of members of old Whig families at public schools and universities towards Conservatism. John Hope, a leading Scottish advocate, admitted to Peel that Scotland's £10 householders were still 'conceited Democrats'. He doubted (rightly as the 1837 general election in the city was to demonstrate) if the Conservatives would yet win a single seat in Glasgow, or gain overall in Scotland. None the less, he detected a movement towards Peel among the propertied, who were now ready to rally 'under the name & Banner of Him whom Ultra Tories, Conservatives and Reclaimed Whigs all equally look to'.[30]

Peel had not needed much persuading, first, that he ought to stand for the Rectorship; and secondly, that once elected he ought to allow an elaborate programme to be arranged, 'considering the State of public feeling in Scotland'.[31] He seems, indeed, to have worked himself into a rare state of visible elation during the visit. His rectorial address was received as a model exhortation, much admired not only in the hearing but in print. Lord Aberdeen told him that he had been reduced to tears upon reading it; Maria Edgworth, the novelist, praised it to Peel for its elegance of language, high tone and freshness of mind. A German translation was immediately issued, and a copy sent to Peel.[32] What he said was certainly sensible, but it was hardly original. Presumably, it was so much admired because it expressed what contemporaries wanted to hear being said to the youth of Britain. The mood was decidedly early Victorian, even though Victoria was not yet on the throne. Peel praised classical education, and noticed how many statesmen had been good classicists – North, Pitt, Grenville, Windham, Burke, Canning. He modestly did not add his own name to this number, but no doubt the students took the point. He praised religion and the Christian virtues of self-help and self-control. He praised industrial progress, and remarked how the steam-engine was accelerating communication, mental as well as physical, 'creating new demands for knowledge'.

Peel's main political speech at the banquet on 13 January was especially an appeal for support from those who had backed the Reform Bill, but who had no wish to use it as 'a platform from which a new battering is to be directed against the institutions of the country'. Peel took pains to emphasize that there need be no separation between middle-clas commercial opinion and that of the landed aristocracy. Neither wanted democracy. He pointed to the bad examples of the United States and France; and he quoted from the famous passage in de Tocqueville's *Democracy in America* (1835) about the tyranny of majority

---

[30] Graham to Peel, 21 November, 11 December 1836 (Add. MSS 40318, ff. 47, 49); Aberdeen to Peel, 29 November 1836 (Add. MSS 40312, f. 273); Hope to Peel, 16 November 1836 (Add. MSS 40422, f. 167).

[31] Peel to Stanley, 22 November 1836 (Derby Papers 129/1).

[32] Aberdeen to Peel, 15 January 1837 (Add. MSS 40312, f. 283); Maria Edgworth to Peel, 4 February 1837, Peel to Maria Edgworth, 9 February 1837 (Add. MSS 40423, ff. 30, 44); German translation (Add. MSS 40423, f. 168).

opinion and the threat to free institutions from the unchecked operation of majority rule. Both middle classes and aristocracy, claimed Peel, wanted a Government 'animating industry, encouraging production, rewarding toil, correcting what is irregular, purifying what is stagnant and corrupt'.

This speech was nationally and fully reported. *The Times* of 16 January devoted almost two pages to its account of the banquet, plus five columns to other events. Even the Liberal *Manchester Guardian* of 18 January devoted what it called 'a very considerable space' (four columns) to Peel's two main speeches; and it added an editorial which attacked him for lack of positive policies. But the fullest reports of all Peel's Scottish speeches and of the activities surrounding them, with an elaborate folding engraving of the scene at the banquet, were given in James Cleland's *Description of the Banquet in Honor of the Right Honble. Sir Robert Peel*, which ran to 144 pages. This lavish publication constituted a celebratory artefact in its own right; to be set alongside the Peel medal already noticed, and a striking engraving by J. Bouvier which showed Peel silhouetted against a background of the Glasgow Royal Exchange.

Peel was very well pleased with his reception in Glasgow. He knew that he was leaving behind him not only a favourable impression, but also two new Conservative organizations. The University of Glasgow Peel Club seems to have been the first – and to have remained the only – political club to bear Peel's name. It had been formed on 21 December 1836, both to commemorate Peel's election and to promote Conservative principles. On religious questions these were given a decidedly Orange Presbyterian emphasis. All graduates and students of the University were eligible for membership, which quickly reached 350. *Proceedings* for 1836–7 and 1839–40 were published, and a fourth annual dinner was reported in *The Times* of 28 December 1839. On the wall behind the chairman's table at the dinner was hung an allegorical painting, commissioned for exhibition at club meetings. 'Old time is represented in the act of removing a curtain and displaying a well-executed likeness of the patron of the club, Sir Robert Peel.' Elsewhere in the picture Britannia was seen relating to Fame 'the deeds of the right hon. baronet', whose coat of arms also occupied a prominent position.

The *Proceedings* for 1839–40 claimed that the influence of the club had now extended from the University into the city. Certainly, its influence seems to have aroused jealousy in the ranks of the local reformers to such a degree that Robert Wallace, Radical Member for Greenock, moved in the Commons on 17 March 1840 for a return about the club, with a view to the suppression of all political associations within universities. Wallace, supported by Joseph Hume, argued that because Glasgow University and its professors were partly supported out of public funds, involvement in politics was improper and 'tended to produce insubordination'. Peel spoke against the proposal in the name of free discussion; he added that political activity was likely in universities, such as Glasgow, where a rector was elected annually. Wallace withdrew his motion; but he left behind the surprising impression that the Radicals were more suspicious of political organization than the Conservatives. *The Times* of 17 March took the chance to publish a teasing editorial, which compared the visible strength of the Peel Club with the equally visible weakness of the University Liberal Club. This parliamentary publicity can only have reinforced the impression made three years earlier of Peel as the political hero of the younger generation.

Glasgow operatives as well as Glasgow students had organized themselves in support of the new Conservatism. The Glasgow Conservative Operatives' Association was founded on 23 December 1836, two days after the University Peel Club.[33] It too was strongly Presbyterian. Peel replied in friendly but careful terms to an address from the Conservative operatives, which praised his political career as 'worthy of the proudest days in our history'. There was no class, he answered, 'more deeply interested in the maintenance of peace and order, in the protection of property, in the respect for constitutional privileges, than the working and industrious classes'. It is unlikely, however, that Peel wished to encourage the formation of such bodies as more or less independent working-class organizations. He regarded the working-class Radical movement as dangerous not only for its extreme views, but also because of its substantial separation from the guidance of the upper and middle classes. He wanted society to remain linked through numerous gradations, not sharply divided into classes. 'How faint and imperceptible are the gradations between the different ranks!', he exclaimed to the Glasgow operatives. It was probably significant that his reply quickly turned from a one-sentence compliment to the Operatives' Association as such into much more extended praise of operatives in general as part of the linked social order.

Peel always found it easier to work *for* the working classes than to work *with* them, even when they proclaimed themselves Conservatives. When in 1834 he visited his estate near Blackburn, his hopes of passing unnoticed were disappointed. His comments about this were revealing:

> the only inconvenience I suffered was not from a radical but a conservative assemblage (mob I must not call them) headed by Pensioners who insisted for a long time in dragging me for about a mile into the Town, preceded by an enormous flag and a band of music. I escaped this infliction, but was pursued to the Inn by my friends, who of course congregated half the Town in front of the Inn.[34]

---

[33] Minute Book of the Glasgow Conservative Operatives' Association 1837. See also J. T. Ward, 'Some aspects of working-class Conservatism in the nineteenth century', in J. Butt and J. T. Ward (eds), *Scottish Themes* (1976).

[34] Peel to Goulburn, 3 September 1834 (Goulburn Papers).

The first Operative Conservative Association was formed at Leeds in March 1835, and the movement then spread rapidly through the manufacturing districts. A printed statement of the objects of the Leeds society was sent to Peel. It promised 'deference and respect to all who are in higher stations'; but deference was sugared by the assertion that 'the different degrees and orders of society are so closely united and interwoven with each other, that while we exalt them we raise ourselves'.[35] How Peel responded to this Leeds initiative is not known; but such sentiments must have reassured him that here was no dangerous spirit of social or political independence. Yet nine years later, when the Bury Operative Conservative Association sent him a large simnel cake in recognition of his political services, he still replied in terms which gave no direct commendation to the association as such. He loftily answered only in the third person. 'A token of regard & esteem from any portion of the Working Classes of the Town of Bury cannot fail to be gratifying to the feelings of Sir Robert Peel.'[36]

Others had been more enthusiastic than Peel. An anonymous article (by Archibald Alison) in *Blackwood's* for July 1835 advised the creation of a network of Conservative associations on a three-tier basis, from parish and ward committees through county-town and borough committees to national committees in each capital. In 1837 R. S. Sowler, son of the proprietor of the *Manchester Courier* – the leading provincial Conservative paper – published *Thoughts on the State and Prospects of Conservatism, with especial reference to the Associations of the Gentry, Tradesmen, and Operatives*. Sowler noticed how these bodies had first been formed among the county gentry, with that for South Lancashire leading the way in November 1834; but that they had soon begun to be copied among the operatives. The successful example of the Radical Birmingham Political Union, argued Sowler, could not be ignored. Such organizations were not to be condemned in general, only when they 'sought to exercise an authority in the affairs of the nation which ought only to belong to its legitimate rulers'. In resistance to this latter spirit Peel had written privately but strongly in 1828 against the ultra-Protestant Brunswick Clubs, which were then being formed to oppose Catholic Emancipation. 'I think Clubs or combinations of any kind to resist the decisions or influence the deliberations of the Legislature are dangerous Instruments.'[37]

Old-fashioned politicians found it difficult to distinguish between such bodies formed to exert 'pressure from without' and constituency associations linked with parties in Parliament. C. W. Wynn wrote to Peel from Denbighshire

---

[35] C. Richardson to Peel, 26 March 1835 (Add. MSS 40418, f. 172); Stewart, *Foundation of the Conservative Party*, ch. 7.

[36] G. Norris to Peel, 14 March 1844 (Add. MSS 40541, f. 208).

[37] Lord Talbot to Peel, 25 November 1828; Peel to Lord Talbot, 27 November 1828 (Add. MSS 40308, ff. 86, 88).

in April 1835 to ask his opinion about the new Conservative constituency associations. Wynn believed them 'always liable to be perverted from their original object and tending to produce irritation and reaction, and usually to check the exercise of individual judgement and opinion'. At the same time he saw 'our friends promoting them all over the country'. Unfortunately, Peel's answer to Wynn has not survived. But Peel kept his distance from constituency organization even in his own county of Staffordshire.[38] Nevertheless, constituency associations of gentry or middle-class tradesmen came to be established in most counties and many boroughs in time for the 1837 general election. They reflected spreading pro-Conservative feeling at the grassroots, since all were started upon local initiative without any direction from the party leadership. Of course, Bonham heard about them, and kept Peel informed as part of his continuous assessment of the state of public opinion. He reminded Peel in 1837, for example, that the Brighton Conservative Association had been set up in 1834 'with the hearty good wishes of the Court'; but was '*now* on the wane and requires every artificial support'. Royal influence had changed sides with Victoria's accession, and a rival association had been formed with her Whiggish uncle, the Duke of Sussex, as patron.[39]

The Times gave steady publicity to the work of the Conservative Associations. It did not fear them as potentially democratic, but, on the contrary, praised them (1 November 1836) as 'barriers against revolution'. At a meeting of the East Norfolk Conservative Association, reported in *The Times* of 31 October 1836, the chairman (the Earl of Orford) welcomed 'the celebrated Tamworth address', although he admitted that some might think it 'too liberal'. This remark showed how the Conservative Associations were far from bold in their opinions, even if novel by their very existence.

Whereas Peel tended to distance himself from working-class and even middle-class Conservative Associations, he gave a clear lead over electoral registration. He recognized the vital need for potential Conservative voters to be placed and kept on the lists, which were now revised annually. Registration work was both complicated and expensive for the parties. To press forward friendly names, to draw up objections to unfriendly names, and to counter opponents' objections became a never-ending activity, which stimulated the creation of local party machinery. In August 1837 at a dinner to celebrate his re-election for Tamworth Peel made an immediately celebrated call in deliberate imitation of a cry of Daniel O'Connell's. The *Morning Chronicle* of 9 August gave the passage in the first person, whereas *The Times* was for once

---

[38] Wynn to Peel, 25 April 1834 (Add. MSS 40420, f. 74). See G. B. Kent, 'The beginnings of party political organization in Staffordshire 1832–41', *North Staffordshire Journal of Field Studies*, 1 (1961), pp. 86–100.

[39] Bonham to Peel, 23 September 1837 (Add. MSS 40424, f. 140).

outdone, and could only use the third person: 'The advice which has been given to some persons was, "Agitate, agitate, agitate"; the advice which I give you in this, "Register, register, register".' This advice was not new. For example, an article (by Archibald Alison) in *Blackwood's* for May 1835 had urged Conservatives to build up their support in the press and to give attention to the registers. 'IT IS IN THE REGISTRATION COURTS THAT THE BATTLE OF THE CONSTITUTION IS TO BE FOUGHT AND WON.' Fifteen years later Alison was to claim in a *Blackwood's* obituary article (September 1850), that Peel – who 'regularly read' the magazine – had borrowed these words unacknowledged for a speech. Certainly, at Tamworth on his re-election in 1841 Peel was to remark: 'I said before, and I believe it has been proved to be true, that the battle of the constitution must be fought in the registration courts.' Peel may have been referring back here to his 'Register, register, register' call of 1837. Whether he knew that he was taking words directly from *Blackwood's* must remain doubtful; for if, as Alison suggested in 1850, this formulation had quickly passed into common usage, Peel can be accused of no more than lack of originality in repeating it.[40]

Peel's experience with the new 1835 Parliament had demonstrated that majorities could not now be collected through heavy cross-voting in the Commons. It had become essential to get as many declared Conservatives elected as possible at the next general election. In this process Peel's friend F. R. Bonham played a key part as linkman between the parliamentary party leadership and Conservatives in the constituencies. Peel, who did not praise lightly, told Bonham on the day of publication of the Tamworth Manifesto: 'I never could have accepted office without seeking your aid.' Another active party organizer was Lord Granville Somerset. Bonham and Somerset made their base at the Carlton Club, which had been opened in 1832 as the Conservatives' London social centre. *Ad hoc* central election committees met at the club in 1832 and 1835. After Peel's resignation in 1835 Bonham recommended the formation of a small but permanent committee. This was intended to complement the local efforts of the constituency associations. This committee, with Bonham as its chief executive, prepared the ground for the general election of 1837, which followed the death of William IV; and it was to continue through to the Conservatives' general election victory of 1841. During these years the committee dispensed money for elections; it supplied candidates; it monitored the day-to-day progress of general elections; it assessed by-election prospects; and it organized and helped to finance election petitions. At busy times Bonham was writing to Peel almost daily. Peel gladly left the details of political management to Bonham; but he was ready to receive, and sometimes to request, advice about political tactics based upon Bonham's

[40] *The Times*, 30 July 1841.

detailed knowledge both of opinion in the constituencies and of gossip at the Carlton and in the lobbies at Westminster.[41]

It would be going much too far, however, to claim that Bonham and the committee directed the Conservative party in the constituencies. Scotland and Ireland always remained special electoral cases; and in English seats local influences could always outweigh whatever Bonham, or even Peel himself, might suggest or prefer. In 1842 Peel's prestige as Prime Minister still failed to install J. C. Herries, a former Cabinet Minister, as the Conservative candidate at a Liverpool by-election. Herries found himself driven out by the local influence of John Gladstone, father of the rising young member of Peel's Government. The elder Gladstone's request for a baronetcy had been very recently rejected by Peel. 'My father always told me,' he wrote to Herries in frustration, 'that the *slyest* of all created beings was old Gladstone.'[42]

V

It was a measure of greater preparedness at both national and local levels that about 450 Conservative candidates stood in the general election of 1837 compared with only some 390 in 1835. Conservative zeal in the constituencies was widely noticed, even though not always favourably. The Liberal *Manchester Guardian* (26 August) wrote of the 'desperation' of the Conservatives and of their use of bribery and corruption. 'Not that we mean to claim for our own party absolute purity in these respects.' Party labels were now very prominent. The word 'Conservative' had been carefully not used by Peel in his Tamworth Manifesto; but in his equivalent although much shorter 1837 election address (published with a supporting editorial in *The Times* of 28 June) he spoke plainly of 'that powerful Conservative party, with which I am proud to boast my connexion'. He went on, however, to differentiate 'the defence of great principles' from 'the mere temporary interests of party'.

The Conservatives gained some twenty seats overall, chiefly in the English counties. This gave them a total of 313. But the Whig Government's 328 supporters were almost as numerous as before the election, thanks especially to gains in Ireland. Independents were almost squeezed out. In correspondence with Peel, and in the *Quarterly Review* for October 1837, Croker deplored 'the great constitutional change' involved in the disappearance of the independent members, who had traditionally numbered as many as a hundred. They had represented public opinion 'in contradistinction to party, or local interests . . .

[41] Peel to Bonham, 18 December 1834 (Add. MSS 40406, f. 104); Peel to Bonham, 4 May 1835 (Add. MSS 40420, f. 126). See N. Gash, 'F. R. Bonham: Conservative "political secretary", 1832–47', *English Historical Review*, 63 (1948), pp. 502–22.

[42] John Gladstone to Peel, 7, 15 January 1842; Peel to John Gladstone, 14 January 1842 (Add. MSS 40499, ff. 103–8); Herries to Peel, 28 January 1842; Peel to Herries, 29 January 1842 (Add. MSS 40501, ff. 95, 97).

On them every Government depended for its stability.' Now, grumbled Croker, the House of Commons had become merely an assembly of delegates.[43]

Yet Peel could hardly complain because his Opposition minority was now so very large. There was great hope for the future on the Conservative side, in the knowledge that the Government majority was only just sufficient and depended upon a coalition which might break up. But Peel's own ranks were far from homogeneous. The *Annual Register* reprinted a contemporary count which found only some eighty 'Conservatives' among Peel's followers, compared with 139 'Tories' and about a hundred 'Ultra-Tories'. These totals were not exact; but it was probably accurate enough to say that only a quarter to one-third of the parliamentary party were Peelites, much the same proportion as were to remain faithful to Peel in the split of 1846.

Differences within the parliamentary Conservative party over Peel's leadership showed themselves at intervals. The ultras inclined to partisan opposition, which their leader consistently refused to countenance. Speaking at Tamworth after his re-election in 1837, he had straightway promised to support the Whig Government, in the national interest, against Radical pressure for household suffrage, triennial Parliaments or vote by ballot.[44] Before Parliament met, Graham was warning Peel that it would be difficult 'to keep 320 Gentlemen together, at heart bitterly opposed to a Government, yet required to uphold the Minister, whom they despise, in constant struggles with his own Radical Friends'. Yet Graham was full of praise for the new Conservative party, into which he and Stanley were themselves being absorbed. It united, claimed Graham, 'more Talent, more Wealth, more public Virtue and more intelligence than ever yet was embodied in any Party'. Peel could be proud to lead such a combination. 'The proud eminence of this Position, as well as its Novelty, would seem to defy the ordinary Rules of Opposition Tactics.'[45]

Graham went on to emphasize how the Conservatives possessed 'the immense advantage of representing, not virtually by Nomination but really and directly by popular choice, the best Portion of the entire Community'. 'Popular' in this definition meant no more (but no less) than that the Conservatives represented 'a great preponderance of property, of learning, of decent manners and of pure religion'. Peel himself took up the claim to Conservative popularity in this sense when he delivered another major extra-parliamentary speech in the Merchant Taylors Hall on 12 May 1838 at a dinner given in his honour by 313 Conservative Members of Parliament, of whom 300 were present. *The Times* next day declared that nothing of this nature had been seen before – the representatives of four-fifths of the 'property, intelligence, and public virtue' of the nation coming together to demonstrate in favour of ancient institutions and

[43] Croker to Peel, 15 August 1837 (Add. MSS 40321, f. 229).
[44] *The Times*, 9 August 1837.
[45] Graham to Peel, 15 November 1837 (Add. MSS 40318, f. 103).

against 'a band of mercenary traitors who have assaulted them'. Peel's speech of 'vivid representation and luminous narrative' made plain, claimed *The Times*, why a short further period of patience and vigilance would see the Conservatives in power. A report and commentary in the same spirit appeared in the June number of *Blackwood's*, rejoicing in 'the tribute paid to one whom we love and honour'.

Peel reminded his followers in the Merchant Taylors Hall that his object had been to lay the foundations of a great party, 'existing in the House of Commons, and deriving its strength from the popular will', which would reduce the risk and the shock of collisions between the Lords and the Commons. Peel then dealt tactfully with those in his own party who wanted to oppose the Whig Government regardless. 'Our more impatient friends in the country must recollect, that our very name almost implies a contradiction; we are a Conservative opposition; we adopt the principles which used to be said to prevail in an Administration; we not only adopt the principles of a Government, but we perform many of its functions.' Peel then listed recent examples of how the Opposition had sustained the Whig Ministry under pressure from its own extremists – against a motion for excluding bishops from the House of Lords; against repeal of the Corn Laws; and against the demand for vote by ballot. In each instance Conservative Members had made up the greater part of Government majorities.

Support for the Corn Laws and for the protection of agriculture were thus noticed in Peel's speech by way of illustration of sound Conservative voting; but agricultural protection was not mentioned in Peel's peroration where he spelt out the basic principles of Conservatism. These he enumerated as (a) maintenance of the prerogatives of the Crown, and of the proper balance between King, Lords and Commons; (b) support for the Anglican Church Establishment, qualified only by equality of civil rights without reference to sect; and, (c) in general 'the preservation and defence of that combination of laws, of institutions, of usages, of habits and of manners which has contributed to mould and form the character of Englishmen'. Many in Peel's audience no doubt chose to regard agricultural protection as coming under this last umbrella of 'usages'. But for Peel protection was a policy not a principle, and policies (unlike principles) were changeable.[46]

Peel had referred only to 'impatient friends in the country', but he knew that there was also impatience among the Members of Parliament whom he was addressing. Occasional general meetings of the parliamentary party, sometimes at Peel's house in Whitehall Gardens, were called to restrain this restlessness, although Peel always preferred smaller meetings with prominent backbenchers. In March the possibility had arisen of a motion of censure against the Colonial Secretary being passed with Conservative support; this would have

[46] *The Times*, 13 May 1838.

led to the resignation of the Whig Government at a time when Peel did not want to take office only to repeat his experience of 1834–5. Conservative Members were therefore summoned to Peel's house, where they agreed to manoeuvres which provoked a direct confidence vote; and this, as anticipated, the Government won. Not a single Conservative acted out of line. Here was evidence of the new strength of party commitment, even against partisan inclination, carefully directed by Sir Thomas Fremantle, the party's Chief Whip.[47]

Peel relished this party discipline; but his men were open to control only because they were eager for their party to take power. Yet Peel's concept of Conservative Opposition resulted in the Whigs staying in office for six years from 1835. Could Peel be trusted? Such questioning became muted, but it never quite disappeared. In retrospect, Peel remembered the care necessary not to revive 'the half-extinguished animosities' associated with Catholic Emancipation. He did not find such humouring congenial. During the Reform Bill period, when he was following his own line without any wish to lead a party, he was reported as likening parties to serpents, 'in which the heads are moved by the tails', adding that he refused to be moved by the tail. This underlying inclination to think and act apart from party was to become submerged as Peel built up the Conservative position during the 1830s; but it was to reappear once he had taken office in 1841.[48]

For some time before this date, Peel's return to office had begun to seem likely, as Melbourne's Government floundered and as the morale of its supporters in the Commons sank still lower. There was a feeling that too much attention was being given to Irish issues – the Irish Church, the Irish Poor Law and the reform of Irish municipal corporations. The Government had also run into recurring budget deficits, deep trade depression and intense social and political unrest. From 1838 both the working-class Chartist movement and the middle-class Anti-Corn Law League were campaigning throughout the industrial districts.

The Whigs could do little right, at a time when strong government was much needed. But there was to be one false start before Peel took charge. This came with the 'bedchamber affair' of 1839. On 7 May in that year Melbourne resigned over the Jamaica question. *The Times* of 10 May compared the position with that of 1834, when William IV had dismissed the Whigs and called in Peel. But that, remembered *The Times*, had been 'conscription'. The King had been two or three months ahead of public opinion, and the attempt to introduce a Conservative administration had failed. Now, however, the Whigs had resigned voluntarily. Public opinion, claimed *The Times*, wanted Peel. The

---

[47] See Stewart, *Foundation of the Conservative Party*, ch. 6; and N. Gash, 'The organization of the Conservative Party 1832–1846, Part I: The parliamentary organization', *Parliamentary History*, 1 (1982), pp. 137–59.

[48] Add. MSS 40423, f. 300; Aspinall, 'Lord Hatherton's Diary', p. 135.

paper refused to admit that any problem over the Queen's ladies-in-waiting could possibly prevent him taking office. 'As some absurd rumours are about respecting the feelings of the Queen, we think it right to state that Her Majesty's manner to the Duke of Wellington and to Sir Robert Peel was most frankly gracious.' In reality, the young Queen remained a Whig partisan, whose manner towards Peel when inviting him to become Prime Minister had been scarcely gracious. By 11 May *The Times* was reporting that rumours had begun to circulate, which were then put into the London evening papers, of 'an extraordinary and unlooked for obstacle'. Rumour had it that Peel had demanded a clean sweep of all the Queen's ladies because they came from Whig families. *The Times*, with truth, denied that Peel had asked for a complete change, only for the removal of such a number as would show that the Ministry enjoyed royal confidence. *The Times* reprinted a *Standard* article which claimed that the Queen, under the influence of Lady Normanby, the wife of a Whig Cabinet Minister, had retracted a promise that Peel should enjoy a free hand. It was not, in fact, true that Victoria had ever given Peel such freedom. But it does seem to have been the case, as the *Standard* also claimed, that the Whig *Globe* of 9 May had published the news of the Queen's insistence upon keeping *all* her ladies even before she had told Peel himself of this unacceptable new condition.

The Times of 13 May returned bitterly to the attack against Lady Normanby. 'Will the people of England be stupid enough to uphold the saucy clamour of a household coterie?' A full-column 'Letter to the Queen', signed 'Loelius', Disraeli's pseudonym, criticized the royal conduct. By this date Peel had given up; but *The Times* declared that he should let the truth be known. 'The correspondence on this question must every line of it come forth.' In the event, Peel took care in explaining his actions to the Commons to protect the Queen by saying little about her. The newspapers divided on party lines, however, and some Conservative papers were not so quiet about the Queen as their leader. For example, the *Kentish Gazette* of 14 May deplored 'the pertinacious determination of her Majesty' in allowing herself, in her innocence, to be trapped by a Whig scheme to hold on to office. Recourse to the eighteenth-century idea of 'the King in toils' allowed the Whigs to be attacked without seeming to make a personal attack upon the Sovereign. Both *Blackwood's* and the *Quarterly Review* (in a Croker article) adopted this line in their issues for June 1839. *The Times* of 17 May was less restrained. It printed a two-verse poem entitled 'The Petticoat Government', of which the second verse ran:

> In so ticklish a cause I'll not be so bold
> As to venture to judge betwixt House and Household;
> But, whatever the decision, I think we may say,
> That henpecked John Bull yields to petticoat sway.

On the other side, the Liberal *Manchester Guardian* (15 May) denounced what it called the 'sheer Billingsgate and blackguardism' of *The Times* and *Morning Post*, an oblique reference to the Lady Flora Hastings scandal, which had overlapped with the bedchamber affair and had damaged the good name of Victoria for sense and humanity. The *Guardian's* own line was that, while it understood why Peel wanted 'to re-constitute the female part of the household', precedent did not require this; and that the young Queen was entitled to a free choice of friends such as 'the meanest subject possesses'. Next day Lord Francis Egerton, Conservative Member for South Lancashire, optimistically drew Peel's attention to 'the very moderate tone' of the *Guardian*.[49] The Chartist *Northern Star* of 18 May declared itself unimpressed by the manoeuvrings of either the Whigs or the Conservatives. How, it asked, was the country to be governed, 'both of them having confessed themselves incapable of governing it'? Certainly, since the full facts were not revealed, it seems likely that the bedchamber episode, by generating unjustified sympathy for Victoria, did temporarily damage Peel's reputation. None the less, in reply to an address from Shrewsbury which expressed approval of his conduct, Peel claimed that in a very short time his actions would be seen to have been constitutional and proper 'by a very large majority of that portion of the community whose deliberate sentiments ultimately prevail over misrepresentation and calumny, and constitute public opinion in this country'. *The Times* of 6 June published the Shrewsbury address, with an editorial in praise of Peel's 'grave and valuable' reply.

The Whigs had returned to office in curious circumstances. But it has been argued on their behalf that the course which they were following during these years, of depending upon occasional but sometimes crucial Conservative support against their own extremists, was not a symptom of weakness but a deliberate non-partisan middle policy, not dissimilar to that recommended by Peel. In the spring of 1839, however, when Peel came out in support of the Radicals over Jamaica, he had seemed to be abandoning that policy.[50] In reality, Peel had acted on the merits of the matter as he saw them. He never expected the Whigs to be defeated, and they did indeed win the critical division by five votes. Melbourne had resigned when he could have carried on, as after the bedchamber episode he was to do for another two years.

Peel was now more than ever determined not to take office without a clear House of Commons vote against the Government. In June 1840 a Conservative no-confidence motion was defeated by the unexpectedly large margin of 308 to 287 votes. Peel was dismayed. But by-elections were running the

---

[49] Egerton to Peel, 16 May 1839 (Add. MSS 40426, f. 439).

[50] See I. D. C. Newbould, 'Whiggery and the dilemma of reform: Liberals, Radicals and the Melbourne Administration 1835–9', *Bulletin of the Institute of Historical Research*, 53 (1980), pp. 229–41.

Conservatives' way, as he pointed out in another want-of-confidence division a year later. This time the Whigs lost by one vote on 4 June 1841. They had already been defeated 317 to 281 in a sugar duties division on 18 May. Peel claimed during the no-confidence debate that the Whig Government had suffered a net loss of at least 12 seats at by-elections since the last general election. Clearly, its majority was no longer viable. Rather than resign forthwith, Melbourne was persuaded to appeal to the country.[51]

VI

The general election of 1841 produced a comfortable overall Conservative majority in the Commons, estimated contemporaneously by Fremantle at about 78, 362 to 289.[52] This election victory was well grounded, being no sudden surge of opinion but one built upon the movement already visible in 1835 and 1837. The Conservatives had taken great pains to ensure the translation of this favourable tendency of opinion into votes. When the Whig *Morning Chronicle* perversely complained about the contrast in effort between the two parties over the placing of names on the electoral registers, the *Standard* (14 July 1841) answered that the Conservatives had simply 'brought out a reserve, because they had a magnificent reserve to bring out'. The obvious strength of the Conservatives in some constituencies meant that 113 seats went to them without a contest, compared with only 55 in 1837.

The Whigs had come out in favour of a fixed duty on corn in place of the existing sliding scale, which most Conservatives continued to prefer. One analysis of published election addresses has found that for both parties this was the main issue, noticed by about 60 per cent of candidates. Some 30 per cent of Whig candidates mentioned the related questions of adjustment of the sugar and timber duties; but for Conservatives the second issue (mentioned by about 40 per cent of candidates) was defence of the Church and resistance to the pretensions both of O'Connor's Irish Catholics and of English Dissenters. Criticism of the New Poor Law was voiced in over 20 per cent of Conservative addresses, criticism vigorously supported by *The Times* but not by Peel. Neither Whigs nor Conservatives were advocating free trade in corn, but the Whigs were seen by many agriculturalists as heading in that direction.

Conservative gains were made mainly in the counties, and especially in the corn-growing English counties. Fremantle calculated that Conservatives now held 137 English county seats out of 159, a gain of twenty-three; they also took

---

[51] C. Ross to Peel, 26 May 1841 (Add. MSS 40429, f. 287); Peel, *Speeches*, III, p. 766.

[52] See Betty Kemp, 'The general election of 1841', *History*, 37 (1952), pp. 146–57; Stewart, *Foundation of the Conservative Party*, ch. 8, p. 386; E. Jaggard, 'The 1841 British Election: A Reconsideration', *Australian Journal of Politics and History*, 30 (1984), pp. 99–114.

two more Scottish and four more Irish county seats. These gains went far towards giving Peel a safe majority. In addition, Fremantle noted a net gain of eight English borough seats plus one Scottish and four Irish boroughs. The forty-four Conservative Members who sat for larger boroughs with over a thousand electors represented older commercial centres rather than new manufacturing towns. Indeed, Conservatives held only one-third of the larger English borough seats, even though their great strength in the counties and smaller rural boroughs made them especially a party of England.

In the June number of the *Quarterly Review* Croker published an article on 'The Budget and the Dissolution' which he later claimed to have been adopted as virtually a Conservative manifesto.[53] It assumed that the Conservative party was above all the party of the land. 'The *landed interest* need not be reminded that they are the chief objects of ministerial hostility.' During the election campaign Whig proposals for corn, sugar and timber were criticized as having been formulated too late to carry conviction. The *Annual Register* suggested, however, that the election debate rose above the merits of all specific proposals, and became a discussion of the fitness of the Whigs to govern.

If this were so, Peel's high reputation as a man of political business must have helped the Conservative cause. Just how much then did Peel contribute to victory in 1841? He issued no new Tamworth Manifesto, for he was still acting in the spirit of 1834. His nomination speech at Tamworth was, however, widely circulated, being reported in the first person over four and a half columns in *The Times* of 29 June. Peel described how the Conservatives had gradually acquired strength; and how this had never been used factiously, or to encourage religious animosity. In this spirit he still refused to contemplate the abandonment of Catholic Emancipation. He spoke firmly against a fixed corn duty, but in favour of a sliding scale. He then added a careful criticism of free trade in corn. 'The proposition of buying corn in the cheapest market is certainly tempting in theory; but before you determine that that is just, you must ascertain the amount of the burdens to which land in other countries is subjected, and compare this with the burdens imposed on land in this country.' Poor rate, highway rate, church rate and tithe were recognized by Peel as being paid especially by landed occupiers.

Both the *Standard* (29 June) and *The Times* (30 June) praised this speech effusively as a model of its kind. If, claimed *The Times*, Peel were to reveal the same capacity in office as he had done in opposition, he would acquire a civilian reputation scarcely less great than Wellington's military reputation. But a month later (24 July) *The Times* took care not to claim that Peel had directly won the election for his side. The paper explained that Peel had not himself created the Conservative movement in the country. 'All that he could do was to train its outward energies in the way to conquest, and by Fabian tactics in

53 M. F. Brightfield, *John Wilson Croker* (Berkeley, 1940), p. 419.

Parliament to gain time for its consolidation, and development. That he has done.' On 27 July *The Times* rejoiced in the 'triumphant reaction of sound public opinion against the progress of a partially successful democratical movement.' As for Peel: 'No statesman ever before, in this or any other country, stood in the position of Sir Robert Peel.'

Peel, in short, was the beneficiary of victory. But *The Times* did not pretend that his version of Conservatism had carried the day in those agricultural constituencies which his party had captured. Peel had virtually admitted in his Tamworth nomination speech that his Conservatism differed from that of other less liberal Conservative candidates. He complained that Whig newspapers had publicised the statements of 'some Conservative candidate, and that was a manifesto of Sir R. Peel . . . But I am not allowed to speak my own opinions.' *The Times*, for its part, bridged the gap between Peel and less progressive Conservatives by blandly arguing that the party had been installed in power 'not for any pledges or promises which they had given, not for the sake of any measure or series of measures', but because of confidence in the capacity and disinterestedness of its leaders. Perhaps this was only what Croker meant when he told Peel that 'all turns on the name of Sir R. Peel', and that every Conservative elected 'professed himself in plain words to be Sir Robert Peel's man, and on that ground was elected'. Every candidate and every elector knew that Peel would become Prime Minister if the Conservatives won.[54]

Because Peel owed his majority largely to gains in agricultural constituencies, and because the number of Peelite Conservatives (found to total just over a hundred in this Parliament at the split of 1846) was not markedly increased in 1841, one historian has argued that this election victory concealed Peel's failure over the preceding years to convince many of his party and much of the electorate of the wisdom of his version of Conservatism.[55] Certainly, Peel personally was to become obviously more popular in 1846 than he was in 1841. He was to achieve this by acting increasingly apart from his party, and eventually by standing above party. Up to 1841, in contrast, he had vigorously advocated his Conservatism from within the Conservative party. In 1841 Peel was consciously asking many electors to vote for Conservative candidates of whom many were patently much less liberal than he was himself. That electors could like Peel and dislike his party was indicated by the *Annual Register* in its account of the general election. Here was a pointer for the future. As early as 1841 respect for Peel was winning him support on personal grounds even in spite of his party:

> Many, who still stood aloof from the Conservative party, and professed
> jealous suspicions of its future policy, were not averse to give it a trial in

[54] C. S. Parker, *Sir Robert Peel* (1891–9) I I, p. 475.
[55] See I. Newbould, 'Sir Robert Peel and the Conservative party, 1832–1841: a study in failure?', *English Historical Review*, 98 (1983), pp. 529–57.

the possession of power ... They saw clearly that the large and comprehensive mind of the distinguished leader of that party, Sir Robert Peel, had no sympathy with a narrow or ultra system; that he had, in all matters of trade and commerce, been the advocate of measures which tended to give free scope to the energies of the country, and had given his zealous co-operation, while at the head of the most powerful Opposition ever known in parliament, in furthering the cause of practical reform.

Thus although many electors of this persuasion had still not voted Conservative, they had come to trust Peel, and were ready to welcome 'practical reform' at his hands no matter how impractical or unreforming many of his followers might be. Greville summed up in his diary for 10 August 1841: 'All Peel's conduct for some time past, his speeches in and out of the House of Commons, upon all occasions, indicate his resolution to act upon liberal and popular principles, and upon them to govern, or not at all.'

The Whigs did not resign at once, but waited to be defeated in the House of Commons. Peel told his constituents at a celebration dinner in Tamworth on 28 July how, to use a medical metaphor, he would wait to be 'called in' before committing himself on action or legislation. But he confirmed that the principles upon which he intended to rule would be those of the Tamworth Manifesto. He took care to emphasize the breadth of his support in the country; how the Conservatives had gained seats not only in agricultural constituencies but in some important urban centres – he mentioned specifically the City of London, Westminster, Liverpool, Hull, Leeds, Belfast, Dublin – as well as in the manufacturing counties of South Lancashire and the West Riding. Most of the new industrial towns had, in fact, still rejected Conservative candidates; but Peel was obviously eager to make the most of the still limited progress of Conservatism beyond the agricultural districts. 'There must be some cause which has led to this expression of public opinion other than the influence of landlords over their tenants.' Peel rightly claimed that the Whig cries of cheap bread and cheap sugar had failed. Ministers had lost the confidence of the country. Victory had not been won by 'the dexterous manoeuvres of the leaders of the party', least of all by 'factious combination'. Victory had been won in the constituencies. Peel praised strongly the efforts of tens of thousands of Conservative constituency workers, 'men not known to public rumour'. They had laboured harder even than candidates themselves had hitherto been expected to labour, and had helped to translate anti-Whig feeling into Conservative votes. Here was a tribute from a party leader to his party workers of a kind which was eventually to become commonplace after Victorian elections, but which was novel in 1841.[56]

When the new Parliament met, the Whigs were defeated in the Commons by a Conservative majority of 91 on the address, 360 votes to 269; and on 30

---

[56] *The Times*, 30 July 1841.

August Peel kissed hands as Prime Minister. This time he was backed by a visible majority. This time, too, there were to be no difficulties with the Queen, who within a short period, prompted by Prince Albert, was to develop a deep admiration for her new Minister. When a collection of Peel's House of Commons speeches was published in 1853, it omitted. Hansard's 'corrected report' of Peel's long speech of explanation about his difficulties with Victoria in 1839. Peel, the Queen and the Victorian public had soon become keen to forget the whole bedchamber episode. By the 1850s most Victorians wanted to hear only of sympathy of mind between their great Victorian Minister and his grateful Sovereign.

3

Peel in Power: 1841–5

I

Peel quickly made it clear to Parliament and to the country that the days of weak Whig rule were over. He started upon a determined and constructive attempt to overcome the urgent problems of the day. The constitutional and religious issues of the 1830s had now been either solved or shelved; but they had been succeeded by a threatening social and economic crisis. This crisis had led to the emergence of two of the greatest political agitations of the nineteenth century, the working-class Chartist movement and the middle-class Anti-Corn Law League. Both were to continue to be active throughout Peel's five years in office.

The numbers of the early Victorian poor were visibly too many. Yet the problem was not simply one of maldistribution of wealth, which might have been solved by the speedy enactment of the Chartist demand for universal suffrage, followed by some form of socialist redistribution. In reality, even if the whole national income had been equally distributed in 1841, the average standard of living would still have been some 25 per cent below what later Victorian social scientists were to set as a subsistence minimum. The priority of the 1840s, in other words, was for wealth creation, regardless of whether the national wealth also required redistribution. Peel refused to promote any redistribution; but he was determined to encourage wealth creation by stimulating production, which would in turn increase the demand for labour.

Even before he had taken office, at the conclusion of his speech of 24 August 1841 during the debate which ended with the defeat of the Whigs, Peel had revealed his firm intentions about the use of power:

> If I exercise power, it shall be upon my conception – perhaps imperfect – perhaps mistaken – but – my sincere conception of public duty. That power I will not hold, unless I can hold it consistently with the maintenance of my own opinions; and that power I will relinquish the

moment I am satisfied that I am not supported in the maintenance of them by the confidence of this House, and of the people of this country!'[1]

Within weeks of winning the election Peel was thus emphasizing how he placed his sense of duty as Prime Minister well above his sense of commitment as leader of the Conservative party. The *Standard* of 21 July 1841 gave him some encouragement in this detached attitude by claiming that he had been chosen for office not 'by arrangement with this nobleman, and that gentleman, but upon the suffrages of the nation, ratified by the approbation of his Sovereign. He will therefore be more free than ever a minister was before to select his colleagues.'

From his early days in politics Peel had believed that the executive must give a strong lead to the House of Commons, rather than be subservient to it.[2] He regarded the Cabinet as the inheritor of the ancient executive role of the Crown. Cabinet members were Queen's Ministers in more than name. Although the Commons retained a reserve power of veto over Ministers, Peel's Cabinet expected to hold the initiative in the conduct of affairs; entirely so with regard to executive action, and largely so with regard to proposals for legislation. If Peel had not been leading the Conservative party in 1841, he would not have become Prime Minister. Yet he refused to accept that this placed him under any obligation to trim his policies to suit the opinions of his backbenchers. On the contrary, he treated his elevation to the highest office as placing the responsibility upon backbenchers to support the Queen's Ministers in policies which the Government chose to recommend in the national interest. The party behind him existed in this view to make majorities, not to make difficulties. 'The discipline exacted by Sir Robert Peel from his supporters may have been severe,' explained Lord Aberdeen to Guizot on one occasion in 1844, 'but it was indispensable.'[3]

Such discipline was, of course, asking a great deal of Conservative backbenchers. The eighteenth-century tradition of 'independence' was still strong in the House of Commons. Moreover, the amount of patronage available to humour Members and their constituents was now very limited. Peel often complained that too much of his time was being absorbed by patronage business, the more tiresome because it meant causing dissatisfaction. 'Such is patronage. It is the unhappy fate of a Minister to possess it nominally, and to be supposed ungrateful and insensible to real merit and equitable claims, when it is the want of power and not of inclination which precludes the recognition of them.' So wrote Peel despairingly in 1843. His difficulties with his followers in the Commons were also increased by his manner towards

---

[1] Peel, *Speeches*, III, p. 802.
[2] Stewart, *Foundation of the Conservative Party*, p. 20, and ch. 9.
[3] Aberdeen to Guizot, 2 July 1844 (Add. MSS 43134, f. 75).

them, which was distant and cold, a weakness caused partly by shyness and partly by preoccupation with business.[4]

But if Peel gave too little attention to his backbenchers, he supervised his colleagues almost too much. He dominated his Cabinet. This required continuous awareness of all the major concerns of every department. He told Croker in 1842 that he wished someone would give *him* a Ten Hours Bill. He found it necessary to write for over six hours even on Christmas Day 1842. After four demanding years in the highest office, Peel complained in 1845 that the burdens were incompatible with his strength. He then listed a Prime Minister's duties as (a) extensive reading; (b) constant communication with the Queen and Prince Albert; (c) 'to see all whom he ought to see'; (d) supervision of the grant of honours and the disposal of civil and military patronage; (e) 'to write with his own Hand to every person of note who chooses to write to him'; (f) 'to be prepared for every debate'; and (g) 'to sit in the House of Commons eight hours a day for 110 days'.[5]

Although Peel was in charge of one of the most purposeful administrations in British history, the secretarial provision for Ministers in the 1840s remained rudimentary. They were serviced by only a handful of civil servants, and there were no telephones, typewriters or computers to speed up the conduct of business. The machinery of state necessarily moved slowly. Peel was sometimes impatient with grumbling backbenchers who lacked his inside knowledge or his perception. In 1844, after a major backbench revolt over the sugar duties, he wrote a letter marked 'Most Private' to the wife of the Irish Viceroy, which revealed his thoughts with a frankness impossible in public:

> There is not time to confer with individuals to soften down objections by personal conferences, to flatter the vanity by showing confidence and appearing to consult . . . We must therefore presume upon *confidence*, not that sort of confidence which after a series of defeats will resume a Government by a general vote of confidence, and leave it to flounder on through unpopular details of Legislation, but that confidence which will enable it creditably to do the daily work which it has to do in the House of Commons in the face of the public.[6]

Peel emphasized how he felt no sympathy for backbenchers who had committed themselves in advance 'to vote for that which is popular before the argument against it is heard'. Ministers were urged to compromise. But one concession would lead to more concessions, 'transferring Government and the

---

[4] Peel to Devon, 26 March 1843 (Add. MSS 40526, f. 39). See also E. Hughes, 'Civil service reform 1853–55', *History*, 27 (1942), pp. 54–8.

[5] Peel to Croker, 21 February 1842 (Add MSS 40502, f. 326); Peel to Fremantle, 25 December 1842 (Add. MSS 40476, f. 211); Peel to Arbuthnot, 14 August 1845 (Add. MSS 40484, f. 197).

[6] Peel to Lady de Grey, 21 June 1844 (Add. MSS 40547, f. 136).

duties of Government, to parties wholly irresponsible and much less informed than Ministers'.

Peel insisted upon ruling in this spirit throughout his five years in office. Four days before the above letter was written, *The Times* of 17 June 1844 had complained sharply about his lack of contact with backbenchers. Peel probably read the complaint himself. 'He has succeeded in creating the opinion that he is a good man of business, an indefatigable Minister, a reputable dispenser of patronage, a dexterous Parliamentary leader ... but he has not identified himself – he has never attempted to identify himself – with the feelings or sympathies of his supporters.' He had avoided committing himself, *The Times* continued, on almost all points of policy, his intentions surrounded 'in an impenetrable mystery' until the moment of revelation in the Commons, when he was ready to tell his followers 'that they must swallow it'. In the end Peel was to ask too much, and his party was to split over repeal of the Corn Laws in 1846. Before then, however, although many of his supporters were sometimes uncomfortable and occasionally rebellious, the country was to benefit greatly from five years of purposeful government.

II

Everywhere during the last months of 1841 the question was being asked 'what will Peel do?' He had announced on 17 September, when he first met Parliament after taking office, that he would not prepare and propose new measures without careful deliberation. This meant that he would not be ready until the opening of the 1842 session. For several weeks *Punch*, the new Radical weekly, had taunted Peel for his insistence in his Tamworth speech of 28 July upon waiting to be 'called in' before committing himself. It portrayed Peel as 'Sir Rhubarb Pill', a quack doctor; and it continued in the same vein when Peel refused to prescribe hurriedly even after being 'called in'. 'For ourselves,' concluded *Punch*, 'we hope nothing from Sir Robert Peel.'[7] *The Times* of 4 August had been unimpressed by such Radical and Whig clamour for Peel to reveal his '*programme*', a word still sufficiently un-English for it to be printed in italics. The Whigs, 'politicians of easy virtue', would only claim (wrote *The Times*) that they were preparing just such measures themselves, and that it would therefore be factious of Peel to turn them out. When after taking office Peel insisted upon careful consideration, *The Times* (18 September) likened him to a good builder, in contrast to the Whig jerry-builders. 'All his materials will be well seasoned.'

Despite *Punch*'s taunts, Peel's deliberate self-association with the image of a doctor may have done his reputation good. It has been noticed how in novels of

[7] *Punch*, I (1841), pp. 53, 67, 126.

the period doctors were growing in esteem. They were now treated as no less disinterested than clergymen, and with a more obviously immediate function in the new social conditions.[8] If a doctor of medicine was acceptable as a disinterested person, so a doctor-figure in politics might also claim acceptance, especially if he promised to rise above the prejudices of party. Peel had emphatically promised this, both in his Commons speech of 24 August before the defeat of the Whigs, and in his first speech as Prime Minister on 17 September. Richard Cobden, the chief of the Anti-Corn Law League, who had just been elected to the new House of Commons, was complaining in November how 'the profoundest apathy' prevailed with regard to party differences; the Whigs were rather more unpopular than the Tories. 'As for leaders, the masses have just as much love for Peel as for Russell.'[9]

Tait's Edinburgh Magazine for August argued that Peel would only survive if he became 'the Minister of the Middle Classes'; but this gave a class gloss to the idea of non-partisan politics which Peel was always to reject. During 1841 the *Spectator* had swung strikingly from strong opposition to steady support for Peel, as R. S. Rintoul, its editor, became impressed by Peel's readiness to separate himself from narrow party views.[10] Liberal newspapers remained unimpressed. The *Dover Chronicle* (21 August 1841) announced that Peel in office would follow his usual 'expediency policy', sometimes liberal but always sure first to serve party interests 'to the same factious lengths as any Sibthorp'. The *Manchester Guardian* anticipated on the first day of 1842 that 'force of circumstances' might drive Peel to propose some good measures which he had previously opposed. The *Guardian* promised to support any such reforms, but without 'much regard or gratitude' towards Peel personally. The *Nonconformist* (1 September 1841) anticipated that 'the wily premier will make a show of concern for the people, as he always does, and will attempt to cozen them out of every sound principle'. By contrast, Conservative county papers such as the *Derby Mercury* (4 August 1841) expressed confidence that their leader, 'heedless of popularity', would show 'firm adherence to political integrity in all he undertakes'.

Peel's concern for the condition of the people was not mere show, as the *Nonconformist* claimed. The long period of deliberation which he demanded at this time reflected not insincerity or lukewarmness but careful determination to find a course of Government action most likely to ease the prevailing economic and social distress. Long unemployment and consequent near-starvation reached a peak during 1841–2, unequalled during the nineteenth century. It persisted with particular intensity at Paisley, a handloom weaving town near Glasgow, where the depression was aggravated by a fashion change

---

[8] F. R. Leavis and Q. D. Leavis, *Dickens, The Novelist* (1980), pp. 242–7.

[9] S. Smiles, *Autobiography* (1905), p. 117.

[10] W. B. Thomas, *The Story of the Spectator 1828–1928* (1928), pp. 134–7.

which had reduced demand for Paisley's famous shawls. By autumn 1842 some 15,000 people, a quarter of the town's population, were living upon charity. Peel was to refer many times, both in public and in private, to the example of Paisley. 'I never shall forget,' he told the Commons in 1844, 'as long as I live the situation of Paisley in 1841 and 1842.'[11]

Soon after entering office, Peel arranged for private enquiries to be made about the town of Paisley. He was encouraged to find that the undoubtedly great distress was being borne 'with exemplary patience'. He refused to promote a public subscription because this would leave Ministers open to applications from other deserving places; but he gave his colleagues a lead by subscribing privately. In May 1842 he drew the attention of the Queen and Prince Albert to the state of Paisley and some parts of Lancashire where charitable resources were almost exhausted. He recommended the publication of a Queen's Letter to the archbishops and bishops inviting nationwide charitable contributions: 'the moral effect of a demonstration of formal Sympathy with the distressed and of approval of their peaceable conduct and submission to the Law might be very advantageous.' Peel also reactivated the Manufacturers' Relief Committee, which he had originally promoted with the archbishops when he was Home Secretary in 1826.[12]

Paisley's Radical town corporation had drawn up a petition in April 1842 in support of Peel's new commercial reforms. Peel welcomed the petition with the hope that his measures would bring relief to sufferings 'borne with so much fortitude and patience'. In October 1842 he repeated to Croker how his reforms were intended to help places such as Paisley by stimulating demand. 'For the *last year* there have been supported in that one Town of Paisley (and necessarily supported unless you choose to incur the Risk of wholesale death from famine, or a frightful outbreak and desperate assault upon Property) 9000 persons on a weekly average throughout the year by Charity.'[13]

Peel was here making clear how aware he was that intense and widespread distress might lead to violent outbreaks, that the patience of the poor in Paisley and elsewhere might run out. The very frequency of his commendations revealed his underlying uneasiness that distress might be exploited by demagogues interested in following the example of the French Revolution. Such he felt to be a real danger when he took office in 1841. Both the Chartist and Anti-Corn Law League agitations, which had first reached peaks in 1839 and then subsided, were now rising again. Peel distrusted all 'pressure from

[11] Peel, *Speeches*, IV, p. 344; I. Levitt and T. C. Smout, *The State of the Scottish Working Class in 1843* (1979), pp. 156–9.

[12] Peel to Hon. C. Murray, 31 October 1841 (Add. MSS 40493, f. 314); Peel to Prince Albert, 7 May 1842; Queen Victoria to Peel, 7, 20 May 1842; Peel to Queen Victoria, 20 May 1842 (Add. MSS 40434, ff. 65, 68, 81, 84).

[13] R. Farquharson to Peel, 21 April 1842; Peel to Provost J. Henderson, 26 April 1842 (Add. MSS 40507, ff. 18, 53, 56); Peel to Croker, 30 October 1842 (Add. MSS 40517, f. 342).

without', from the middle-class Leaguers as much as from the working-class Chartists. In October 1841 Lord Francis Egerton reported, in a letter passed on to Peel, about the state of opinion in Manchester, which was both a strong Chartist centre and the base of the Anti-Corn Law League. 'I always feel as if I were toasting muffins at a volcano,' wrote Egerton. He admitted that there were not 'any immediate signs of eruption'. Feargus O'Connor, the Chartist leader, had held a meeting without causing much alarm among Egerton's Conservative supporters in the town. 'Perhaps it ought to have done so.' Egerton remained fearful for the winter, even more because of the Leaguers than the Chartists. He believed that it was 'the policy of C. Villiers & his gang to excite positive disturbances if possible'; and because of the limited strength of the local police force, he feared that 'much mischief' would be done before it was checked.[14]

Local authorities in many places were hard pressed to maintain the peace during the political crises of the 1830s and 1840s. At first only London, where Peel had famously established the Metropolitan Police in 1829, possessed a civil police force of sufficient size and effectiveness to hope to maintain law and order under pressure of mass political agitation. London's 'peelers' had gained control of London's streets during the 1830s, to their credit with the propertied classes and to the great benefit of Peel's reputation.[15] Persons of small property, such as shopkeepers and artisans, seem to have welcomed the new protection against crime and disorder as readily as did the well-to-do. Working people were more suspicious of interference, and in some industrial areas open hostility to 'Bourbon police' was to outlast Peel's lifetime. In July 1839 a body of Metropolitan policemen was sent by the Whig Government from London to Birmingham, where the Chartist National Convention was sitting. Peel was doubtful about the wisdom of using policemen to deal with crowds in places unfamiliar to them. The introduction of outsiders might add to the tension. It would be better, argued Peel, to let order be maintained by the military, or better still by a sufficient local force known to the inhabitants. Peel lent strong support to the passing in that same year of the Birmingham Police Act, which created a force on the London model. Similar acts followed for Manchester and Bolton.[16] Birmingham was near enough to Drayton to give Peel a personal as well as a general interest in the state of the town. He was told in May 1839 of rumoured Chartist plans to march on Drayton Manor. Lord John Russell wrote as Home Secretary to assure him that steps were being taken to prevent any attack.[17]

[14] Egerton to Arbuthnot, 4 October 1841, with Arbuthnot to Peel, 7 October 1841 (Add. MSS 40484, ff. 66, 68); Peel, *Speeches*, IV, p. 110.

[15] See D. Jones, 'The new police, crime and people in England and Wales, 1829–1888', *Transactions of the Royal Historical Society*, fifth series, 33 (1983), pp. 151–68.

[16] L. Radzinowicz, *History of English Criminal Law*, vol. 4 (1968), pp. 253–9.

[17] S. Palmer to Peel, 13 May 1839; Russell to Peel, 14 May 1839 (Add. MSS 40426, ff. 417, 419).

Peel's high reputation as the founder of the Metropolitan Police in 1829 was linked with his reputation as a reformer of the English criminal law during the same decade. This last reputation, although deserved, now seems also to have been somewhat exaggerated. Peel did promote the repeal of many outdated statutes, and he simplified the law by consolidating some 300 Acts, relating to some 80 per cent of all offences, into four broad measures. For this he received in 1829 the freedom of the City of London, when he was hailed as 'the Justinian of the British empire'.[18] But it was pressure from backbench Members of Parliament, plus initiatives taken by Lord John Russell as Home Secretary from 1835 to 1839, which first markedly reduced the number of capital sentences. Russell himself complained in a memorandum of 1839 how little Peel had done to reduce the number of everyday capital crimes, rightly suggesting that comparative statistics of executions for the 1820s and 1830s would reveal how much more the Whigs had contributed in 'practical administration'. According to G. R. Porter's *Progress of the Nation* (1851), 1,385 persons were sentenced to death in England and Wales in 1829 and 74 executed, 13 for murder; by 1839, only 56 persons were being sentenced to death and only 11 executed, 10 for murder.[19]

Yet Peel was long credited with being the author of a bold policy of sentence mitigation, along with his successful codification. A favourable account of Peel's achievements up to 1843, entitled *Sir Robert Peel and His Era*, praised him for transforming 'a criminal code remarkable for its atrocious and debasing severity'. Peel's reputation as a law reformer was so great that even those who liked him for nothing else often praised him not only for simplifying but also for softening the law. 'In the amelioration of the Criminal law Sir Robert Peel certainly deserves commendation from any well-wisher to the good feelings of society, and also of humanity. In any other respect, I only regard Sir Robert Peel as a very *niggling* politician.' So declared *A Political Pamphlet By a Radical of the Olden Day*, published in 1842. In a mood which anticipated the famous peroration to his 1846 resignation speech, Peel had ended a Commons speech in 1826 on the consolidation of the criminal code by admitting that it was his ambition to win distinction for his name 'by connecting it with permanent improvements in the judicial institutions of the country'. His wish was certainly granted, even beyond his deserts.[20]

By 1841 it was not further law reform which was expected from Peel but answers to the widespread and diverse problems of economic distress, with their related social and political effects. How much could, or should, the state

---

[18] *The Times*, 9 April 1829. See Radzinowicz, *English Criminal Law*, vol. 1 (1948), ch. 18.

[19] D. Beales, 'Peel, Russell and reform', *Historical Journal*, 17 (1974), pp. 879–80; A. P. Donajgrodzki, 'Sir James Graham at the Home Office', *Historical Journal*, 20 (1977), p. 102, n. 21.

[20] Peel, *Speeches*, I, p. 410.

intervene? Peel accepted that Ministers had a major role to play in encouraging the economic and social well-being of the nation. He rejected dogmatic *laissez-faire* economics, which regarded mass poverty as a consequence of surplus population and offered large-scale emigration as the only solution. He had read the great political economists, and he became an advocate of free trade; but he refused to be dominated by theory. In this spirit he told Goulburn in August 1846 that, although he regretted the need for further government intervention in response to the great famine in Ireland, it was necessary on grounds both of humanity and of public order. 'Even the philosophers who agree to your arguments, will condemn you if you let people perish.' Three months later he reiterated how the most famine-stricken districts 'would require some better consolation than the doctrine of Adam Smith on the true Principles of demand and supply and the danger of Government interference'.[21]

On banking and currency policy Peel showed himself ready at two critical periods to intervene decisively and in detail, in order to promote a sound basis for economic enterprise. His chairmanship of the Currency Committee of 1819, which reported in favour of a return to cash payments, first made him widely known to the public. His recommendations were speedily enacted in a measure which became known simply as 'Peel's Act'. He now won an enduring reputation as an authority on currency and banking matters, which he was to reinforce with his Bank Charter Act of 1844. Opposition to Peel's deflationary policy did come in the 1820s and 1830s from farmers, encouraged by William Cobbett, and from Birmingham merchants and artisans, led by Thomas Attwood, who attributed their various economic ills to the rise in the value of money. At intervals down the years Peel defended his deflationary policy in the Commons. He claimed that the ending of abnormal wartime conditions would in any case have lowered agricultural prices. He did not deny that the return to a gold standard had brought temporary distress; but he argued that this must be borne in order to avoid the much greater evil of a depreciating currency: 'when you depreciate the standard, the prices of the necessaries of life rise much faster than the wages of labour ... one of the main causes of the gradually declining condition of the industrious classes arose from depreciated paper currency.'[22]

Peel was severe, perhaps too severe, in his dismissals of the views of Attwood and the Birmingham currency school. Attwood wrote privately to Peel in December 1841 advocating an immediate issue of notes, as during the financial crisis of 1825: 'if the policy then acted upon had been rendered permanent there would have been no *Distresses*, no *fluctuations* & no *discontents* in England.' Peel did not agree, but acknowledged Attwood's 'disinterested motives'. The Birmingham Chamber of Commerce sent four letters to Peel

21 Peel to Goulburn, 12 August, 21 November 1846 (Goulburn Papers).
22 Peel, *Speeches*, II, pp. 664–81; III, pp. 129–34.

between August and December 1842, which were published with Peel's approval in pamphlet form in January 1843 along with his replies. *The Times* of 20 January reprinted the whole pamphlet, and so gave the exchanges nationwide publicity. An accompanying editorial remarked that 'the quack medicine which unfailingly drives out the ague to-day may much more infallibly kill us of a fever tomorrow'.[23]

The considerable pains which Peel took with his replies is revealed by the endorsement on his office copy of one letter in December 1842: 'not sent but one shorter and to the same general effect'. To the end of his life Peel deplored the extent of what he regarded as gross misunderstanding about currency theory among otherwise intelligent writers. He believed that Joseph Harris's *Essay on Money and Coins* (1757–8) had long since settled the argument. Harris was a rigid monometallist. 'I verily believe that nine out of ten of the persons who write about monetary subjects have never mastered the first principles of the science; and do not comprehend the true relation in which a definite weight of gold stands to other commodities as a standard of value.' So wrote Peel vigorously in one of his last private letters. Five weeks later, in May 1850, the Whig Chancellor of the Exchequer, Sir Charles Wood, began a letter to him by admitting that he did 'not like taking steps in banking & currency matters without your knowledge & concurrence'. Such was Peel's high reputation in his lifetime, and long after. But in the twentieth century ideas of currency management and price stabilization have found a degree of favour which would have surprised him.[24]

If the currency question required state intervention to fix guidelines and to create machinery, so did the problem of pauperism. The New Poor Law of 1834 represented an elaborate piece of state social provision, locally implemented but centrally guided through a new bureaucracy. Peel would have won the warm approval of many of his own paternalist backbenchers if he had opposed this Whig measure, as they did; and if he had also supported the campaign for a ten-hour day in the factories. But he refused to be led by his followers. He always declined to seek party unity or advantage at the cost of his own convictions. He reminded the Commons in 1840 that 'the leaders of the Conservative party' had helped the Whigs to pass the Poor Law in 1834. He does not seem himself to have spoken on the question then, but he pointed out six years later that the Conservatives had not followed the factious example of earlier Oppositions: 'if we had availed ourselves of the unpopularity of the law, and of the facilities it afforded for exciting public discontent, the law could not have passed.' He promised continuing support for the New Poor Law 'out of

---

[23] Attwood to Peel, 3, 10 December 1841; Peel to Attwood, 7, 10 December 1841 (Add. MSS 40496, ff. 193, 197; 40497, ff. 75, 79; 40513, f. 69; 40518, f. 111; 40519, f. 250; 40520, f. 187).

[24] Peel to J. Pennington, 18 April 1850 (Add. MSS 40610, f. 64); Wood to Peel, 25 May 1850 (Add. MSS 40603, f. 257).

friendship for the poor', because it would check the demoralization which the old system had encouraged through lack of control. It would thereby 'raise the character' of the poor.[25]

The anti-Poor Law agitation, which was backed by many Tory Radicals in and out of Parliament, denounced the numerous shortcomings of the new system. Peel was ready to consider changes in detail, but no more. He attacked Richard Oastler by name in the Commons in 1840. 'I have never sanctioned his agitation – I deem it most pernicious.' In 1842 Peel's Government secured renewal of the Poor Law for a further five years with only minor alterations.[26]

Fifty-three Conservative backbenchers have been identified as both opponents of the New Poor Law and supporters of ten-hours factory legislation.[27] These Members of Parliament mainly represented North of England constituencies. The New Poor Law was unsuitable for strict enforcement in Lancashire and Yorkshire during periods of high unemployment among the textile workers. At busy times, on the other hand, twelve and more hours were worked each day in the cotton and woollen mills. The House of Commons leader of the ten-hours campaign was Lord Ashley. He was motivated by genuine Christian paternalism; but some of his associates were moved more by dislike of the new manufacturers. To the charge that wages would fall under a ten-hour day – the argument from political economy which Peel himself had adopted – the usual answer was that the workers would accept this in return for less work. Few attempts were made to argue the question within the context of general commercial policy. Yet for Peel this context was all important. 'It is said that we are not to take foreign competition into account. I am told that this is not to be viewed as a commercial question. I am told that it is a question between mammon and mercy. I am to disregard the effect which legislation will have upon the commerce of this country.' So complained Peel when speaking in opposition to Ashley's ten-hours amendment to the Government's Factory Bill of 1844. Even long hours, countered Peel, were preferable to no work, and to suffering such as that at Paisley in 1841–2. 'Did I not see that with a depressed commerce there is an addition to the material sufferings of the people of this country, infinitely greater than could be produced by twelve, thirteen or fourteen hours of the severest labour?' Peel argued that reduced hours would either reduce wages or would raise costs of production. This last would mean increased prices, which in the face of foreign competition might lead to falling sales and to operatives being thrown out of work and into distress. Peel took this argument from the political economists; yet he did so not on doctrinaire grounds, but because of his genuine concern for the prospects of the workers

---

[25] Peel, *Speeches*, III, p. 698.

[26] Ibid., p. 695.

[27] See D. R. Fisher, 'The opposition to Sir Robert Peel in the Conservative Party 1841–1846'. Unpublished Ph.D thesis, Cambridge University, 1969.

themselves. He repeated the same line to the Queen in private as he had developed in public. Wages would be reduced 'at a very early period'; textile exports, which contributed £35,000,000 by value to total national exports worth £44,000,000, would probably fall, so causing 'serious injury' to commerce. In the event, the eventual adoption of the ten-hour day did not produce these damaging effects. But if Peel was wrong in his analysis, he was right in his intentions.[28]

Peel could, of course, claim a special relationship with the cotton trade. When Edward Baines, jun., sent him a copy of his new standard *History of the Cotton Industry* in 1835, Peel thanked him with an expression of 'double interest' in the subject, as a private individual with family connections with the industry, 'and as a Public Man, from its importance to the Power and Welfare of this Country'.[29] In 1847 a memorial was sent to Peel by ten-hours delegates representing many North of England towns, which pointedly reminded him that his family fortunes had been made by the 'excessive Toil' of many workers in the mills of Peel's father; who had, however, introduced a Ten Hours Bill himself. Peel's reply, which was published in the *Northern Star* of 20 February 1847, admitted his 'special obligations'; but he argued that awareness of these obligations had only made him the more interested in the 'permanent welfare' of the operatives.[30]

Peel remained steady in his opposition right up to the passing of the Ten Hours Act in 1847. Yet during his first weeks in office in 1841 his genuine concern for the working classes had encouraged a West Riding short-time deputation into thinking that he might change his mind. The interview took place at Downing Street on 28 October 1841. The five-man deputation included Joshua Hobson, printer of the Chartist *Northern Star*, and the interview was to receive much more publicity than Peel anticipated. The deputation described the intensity of working-class suffering. To alleviate this, Peel was asked for a Ten Hours Bill to cover all operatives aged between thirteen and twenty years; for the gradual withdrawal of all female labour from factories; for the abolition, or at least major reform, of the New Poor Law; and for an enquiry into the causes of distress, with particular reference to the effects of machinery. A full pamphlet report of this discussion, carefully edited but still in the first person, gave the public a good sense of the exchanges between the ten-hours advocates and the Prime Minister. The deputation made plain its hopes that Peel might respond without regard to party. 'We are sick of party nicknames, and party contests, for party purposes.' They were 'prepared to

---

[28] Peel to Queen Victoria, 19 March 1844 (Add MSS. 40438, f. 156); Peel, *Speeches*, IV, pp. 344, 717–22.

[29] Baines to Peel, 31 January 1835; Peel to Baines, 22 February 1835 (Add. MSS 40412, ff. 246, 248).

[30] Add. MSS 40598, f. 90.

award our confidence, support, and gratitude, to any Government, or set of
men (no matter what their party name may be) who will show by their actions
that they sympathize with our wrongs.' Peel was praised for taking his time in
order to find right solutions. 'We have had too much legislation which can only
be fitly characterised as being from "hand to mouth".' He was described as
having listened 'with head bent down, in a manner expressive of very deep
thought and attention'. One of the deputation was reported in the last
paragraph as having remarked afterwards that 'at all events, it is clear that
Sir R. Peel has a heart.' These words assumed great importance, for they were
picked up and emphasized by sympathetic newspapers throughout the country.

Peel certainly did have a heart; but this did not mean that he had accepted
the proposals made to him. On the contrary, he had repeated to the deputation
his fear that shorter hours would raise costs and reduce competitiveness. He
accepted that if any measures could be devised to lessen distress, it was the
Government's duty to adopt them for the sake of the operatives. 'But we have
not only their case to consider, but also the effect which such measures would
have upon the employment of capital.' In Peel's view this ruled out most of
what the deputation proposed. His last remarks ought to have been more
noticed than they were: 'should I come to a different conclusion to that you
hold, I shall do so with a confident reliance on the intelligence, moderation,
and good feeling you have now displayed.'[31]

The Times of 30 December 1841 published what it called next day 'a full
and even dramatic account' of the Peel interview. It emphasized the importance
of the meeting 'as showing the opinions and feelings of the better and more
intelligent of the operative class'; their dismissive attitude towards party
politics was commended as 'the general view'. The *Northern Star* of 8 January
1842 also printed a full version of the interview, along with an editorial hailing
it as 'one of the most important documents ever presented to the British public'.
The Peel report was followed by an account of a meeting on the same day with
Sir James Graham, the Home Secretary. This interview was described by the
Star as 'less favourable', because Graham had shown himself to be under the
influence of Malthusian over-population theory. But the contrasting optimism
with regard to Peel was not destined to last long. As soon as Parliament met on
2 February, it became clear that the Premier had made up his mind for action
along lines of his own. The *Northern Star* of 12 February carried an unusually
full parliamentary report over eight columns. Its editorial was headed 'The Peel
Accouchement'. It exclaimed that the New Poor Law was to continue, and that
the Ten Hours Bill was to be opposed by Government. 'The 17,000 starving
poor of Paisley and the hundreds of thousands in a like condition through the

[31] *The Ten Hours' Factory Question* (1842), reprinted in *The Battle for the Ten Hours Day
Continues, Four Pamphlets 1837–1843* (New York, 1972). See also G. Kitson Clark, 'Hunger and
politics in 1842', *Journal of Modern History*, 25 (1952), pp. 355–74.

whole country, are to have no relief. New taxes are to be imposed!!! How long will Sir Robert Peel be Minister?'

So Peel was back under attack from the working-class Radicals. Meanwhile, the Whig Opposition in Parliament had pointedly drawn attention to the episode. When the Commons met, Lord John Russell immediately referred to Peel's 'somewhat theatrical interview' with the ten-hours delegates. The fact that the encounter had been enthusiastically reported in the Owenite *New Moral World*, and that Joshua Hobson of the *Northern Star* had been one of the deputation, led Russell to assume that all its members were 'Socialist editors'. Peel, claimed Russell, had promised that the Government would look into the factory question; but now it appeared from a public letter just published (3 February) in *The Times*, from Lord Ashley to the short-time committees of the North, that Peel had belatedly made plain his total opposition to ten hours.

Peel was obviously embarrassed by the widespread and misleading publicity which the interview had attracted. 'I conversed with them; but I am no party to the publication of what took place.' 'I am innocent of any intention to derive an advantage from the dramatic effects of which the noble lord spoke.' The *Manchester Guardian* (5 February) did not believe him. It claimed that the excitement in Radical and Conservative papers about Peel's 'heart' had been deliberately stimulated. 'The device served a temporary purpose, in detaching a few of the labouring classes from the anti-corn-law movement.' This had never been Peel's intention; but his brief contact with the working-class movement had certainly raised hopes, albeit mistakenly; and this made its subsequent hostility towards the Government during the tense year of 1842 all the deeper.

Although Peel was prepared to listen to working-class complaints, he did not believe that the workers were well qualified to suggest remedies for their own problems. He made this explicitly clear while opposing Ashley's ten-hours proposals in 1844: 'that will be a bad system if they take the popular feeling and the popular will as the guides to legislation.' Only Ministers and Parliament could take a properly comprehensive view of the national interest. But Peel did care deeply about the present and future of the working classes; and he was ready to countenance intervention to control working conditions when convinced that the moral case was irresistible. In this spirit, although he opposed Ashley over ten-hours legislation because he believed the moral case to be weaker than the contrary economic case, in the summer of 1842 he supported Ashley's Mines Bill, which excluded all females from work underground. Peel told Ashley that he admired 'equally the good feeling and the ability, the qualities of Head and Heart with which you have forced this matter upon public notice'.[32] Here was a revealing assumption by Peel, that tests of

[32] Ashley to Peel, 15 June, 2 August 1842; Peel to Ashley, 16 June, 4 August 1842 (Add. MSS 40483, ff. 68, 70, 78, 80); Peel, *Speeches*, IV, pp. 373–4. See also W. C. Lubenow, *The Politics of Government Growth, Early Victorian Attitudes Towards State Intervention 1833–1848* (1971).

'head' and 'heart' were both applicable to such legislation. 'Heart' alone was not enough, but neither was 'head' alone.

Public health questions were another proper field for state intervention in Peel's view. He emphasized the social psychological as well as the physical benefits. 'Whatever are our financial difficulties, the outlay will be true economy that promotes the health and improves the habits of your manufacturing population, and brings home to them the practical proof that they and their present comfort and enjoyment are the objects of your deep solicitude.' So Peel told the Commons in 1841. By 1845 the Peel Government was ready to introduce public health legislation. Gladstone noticed how Peel was emphasizing in Cabinet that 'what is now called the condition of the people question' was coming to the fore: 'however it may be a law of civilisation that the extremes of wealth and poverty should increase together – some effort should be made.' Publication of the final report of the Royal Commission on the Health of Towns left the way open for Lord Lincoln to introduce a comprehensive Health of Towns Bill. This was due for debate and enactment in 1846, but was submerged by the Corn Law crisis of that year.[33]

Peel had remarked in 1841 that public money should be used only as a stimulus to local and private effort. Such effort was increasingly vigorous in some of the big towns. Peel was glad in 1845 to lend pictures for an exhibition to raise money for public walks and baths in Leeds, and likewise to be named as a patron of a Manchester fancy dress ball in support of public baths and washhouses. He subscribed £1,000 towards the provision of public parks in Manchester and Salford; and Peel Park, opened in August 1846 within weeks of repeal of the Corn Laws, was named after him. The Mayor of Manchester rightly noticed, at the park's opening, the importance which Peel attached to the psychological implications of public health provision, 'the improvement and cultivation of the affections' of the masses being as important as the raising of their level of well-being.[34]

III

But back in 1841–2 Peel knew that the first need was to provide work and wages. The *Annual Register* for 1842 chronicled how the prevailing distress had 'engendered a restless and uneasy feeling in the public mind'; there was 'an undefined impression that some powerful and extensive remedies were required to restore the functions of society to a healthy and thriving state'. Here

[33] *Parliamentary Debates*, third series, LVII (1841), pp. 124–76; Brooke and Sorensen, *W. E. Gladstone II*, pp. 272–3.

[34] Add. MSS 40562, f. 268; 40564, f. 211; 40550, f. 347; *Manchester Guardian*, 8, 26 August 1846.

was the test and the opportunity for Peel. When he had seemed to be about to take office in 1839, one Soho tavern-keeper had written to express confidence that 'your fertile mind will easily imagine some Method to keep them employ'd and then good bye to all Chartists . . . give them employment and they will sleep away politics.' This was certainly Peel's aim in office three years later.[35]

By February 1842 his 'fertile mind' had put together proposals for tariff reform and for an income tax, with the purpose of stimulating the economy and so increasing the demand for labour. In general, Peel was moving towards free trade, but not in any doctrinaire spirit. When introducing his tariff proposals in May 1842 he approvingly quoted William Huskisson, the pioneering freer trade Minister of the 1820s: 'in the vast and complex interests of this country, all general theories, however incontrovertible in the abstract, require to be weighed with a calm circumspection.' In February, while introducing his Corn Law relaxations, which stopped short of repeal, Peel specifically refused to claim overall theoretical consistency for his various economic measures: 'the wisest and safest course for me to adopt is to effect as much practical good as I can, and not by pronouncing panegyrics upon general principles.' The key word, 'practical', was repeated in Peel's next sentence: 'I must try to effect a practical adjustment of this question as much to the satisfaction of the general classes of the community as I can.'[36]

Peel began with the Corn Laws. On 9 February he proposed reduced protection to the Commons, but not repeal. He rejected the Anti-Corn Law League argument that industrial distress was being increased because of dear bread caused by the Corn Laws. Those out of work had no money to buy bread at any price. They needed employment and wages. But Peel did tell the agriculturalists that they could afford to accept reduced cover under the Corn Laws. He proposed a new sliding scale, with protection decreasing from 20s. to 1s. per quarter as the corn price rose. Significantly, he emphasized that the landed interest could no longer expect protection on principle. Agriculture had its special burdens to bear, and so deserved protection. But it was one interest among many, all of which he sought to treat fairly. 'The only protection which can be vindicated, is that protection which is consistent with the general welfare of all classes in the country.'[37]

This sober middle way could not hope to satisfy either the repealers at one extreme or the ultra-protectionists at the other. Moreover, suspicion was widespread that it was only Peel's sense of what was practical politics which had prevented him from proposing repeal, perhaps gradual. The Radical *Birmingham Journal* (26 March 1842) observed how Peel was 'forced to work down his really clever capacity of understanding to the absolute dullness of

[35] W. M. Davis to Peel, 8 May 1839 (Add MSS 40426, f. 218).

[36] Peel, *Speeches*, III, pp. 841–2; IV, p. 76.

[37] Ibid., III, pp. 822–38.

their muddled perceptions'. For this reason Charles Greville, the Whig diarist (11 February), thought that Peel's introductory Corn Law speech had been 'the speech of an advocate rather than of a statesman'.

Peel confessed privately to Gladstone that he would indeed have preferred 'a lower protection', but that he could not have got this through the Lords. As it was, he was able to carry most protectionist opinion with him, in and out of Parliament. The ultra-protectionist Duke of Buckingham resigned from the Cabinet; but others were able to persuade themselves that, while reducing agricultural protection to the minimum, Peel had also confirmed his commitment to the principle. The *Birmingham Advertiser* (26 February 1842) thought that Peel had probably gone a shade too far in reduction; but it felt able to reassure its agricultural readers that a Conservative Government 'holds it as an axiom, that to efficient protection they are justly and clearly entitled'. *Blackwood's Edinburgh Magazine* took the same line in its August review of the parliamentary session. Lord De La Warr wrote to tell Peel that his proposals had been upon the whole favourably received by agriculturalists in Kent, satisfied that the Government accepted the case for some protection. Peel, while carefully saying nothing about the principle, answered that feeling was also favourable elsewhere. 'It is demonstrable that 20s. as a maximum is as effectual as 50s.'[38]

A core of about sixty Conservative Members of Parliament constituted a more or less permanent opposition to Peel on major agricultural questions between 1841 and 1845.[39] They were not organized as a group, but they did constitute a tendency. Forty-seven were English county Members; some two-thirds represented constituencies in the corn-growing southern and eastern regions. Another eighty Conservative Members voted against the Peel Government at least once on an agricultural issue. A substantial minority within Peel's ranks was thus uncomfortable about his agricultural policies. But the second reading of the new Corn Law was carried by 286 votes to 178, with 279 Conservatives supporting Peel and only two in the minority. In 1842 loyalty to the leader was still strong. Peel's tariff changes likewise received overwhelming Conservative support, despite a panic among cattle farmers about lower duties on imported foreign cattle. Peel received a deputation of Members of Parliament, but was dismissive about the alarm. He reminded the Commons that population was increasing more rapidly than the supply of food; there was no need for high protection.[40]

The reduction in cattle duty was one of the many tariff relaxations proposed in the great budget of 1842, introduced on 11 March by Peel himself rather

[38] De La Warr to Peel, 14 February 1842; Peel to De La Warr, 15 February 1842 (Add. MSS 40502, ff. 180, 186).

[39] Fisher, 'Opposition to Sir Robert Peel', ch. 2.

[40] Peel, *Speeches*, IV, p. 85.

than by Goulburn, the Chancellor of the Exchequer. Peel proposed to levy an income tax for the first time in peace, at a rate of 7d. in the pound. It was to last for three years, as an emergency measure. The policy of tariff reductions, which had been started by the Liverpool Ministry in the 1820s, was to be vigorously resumed. The income tax was expected to contribute £3,700,000 towards new revenue of £4,000,000. This sum would be sufficient to cover the anticipated deficit, and to meet the fall in receipts from the reduction of the corn duties. Some £500,000 was expected to remain in hand, and Peel proposed that this should be used to finance the new tariff policy. No duty on raw materials was henceforth to exceed 5 per cent; on partly manufactured articles to exceed 12 per cent, and on manufactured articles 20 per cent. The contentious sugar duty was left untouched for the time being.

Peel's new policy meant that out of some 1,200 items in the tariff, the duties were reduced on about 750. This, as Peel explained, was commercial reform with a social purpose. 'The real way in which we can benefit the working and manufacturing classes is, unquestionably, by removing the burden that presses on the springs of manufactures and commerce.' The peroration to Peel's budget speech reminded the Commons of the financial sacrifices made by their fathers during the long wars with France. He called for equal sacrifice now in peacetime, in recognition that this was 'no casual and occasional difficulty'. Alongside increasing national wealth had come increasing mass poverty. This dangerous spread of distress had to be rolled back: 'you will not impair the character for fortitude, for good faith, which, in proportion as the empire of opinion supersedes and predominates over the empire of physical force, constitutes for every people, but above all for the people of England – I speak of reputation and character – the main instrument by which a powerful people can repel hostile aggressions and maintain extended empire.'[41]

Greville (13 March) described Peel's speech of three hours forty minutes as 'a masterpiece'. The Premier had dominated the whole House, noted Greville, his own backbenchers and the Opposition alike. 'This just measure, so lofty in conception, right in direction, and able in execution, places him at once on a pinnacle of power.' *Blackwood's Magazine* in its August review of the session, remembered 'the moral sublimity' of the occasion, as Peel called for sacrifices from the better-off in the national interest. 'Let us be proud, as we ought to be, of such a leader.'

One Conservative Member of Parliament wrote to assure Peel that Radicals and Conservatives on Liverpool Exchange had shared in the 'universal satisfaction'. Peel answered that he was 'much pleased'.[42] His concern was even more with opinion outside Parliament than within, for he was both calling

---

[41] Ibid., III, pp. 865–87.

[42] T. Hawkes to Peel, 12 March 1842; Peel to Hawkes, 13 March 1842 (Add. MSS 40504, ff. 102, 104).

for sacrifices from the propertied and offering hope to the unemployed. In answer to a petition of support from the Bristol Chamber of Commerce, he referred to 'my reliance on the public spirit of which their petition is an example'.[43] The *Morning Post* (23, 25 April) gave prominence to this address and to Peel's answer. The *Post* of 15 April had already voiced Conservative support in lofty language similar to that of *Blackwood's*. 'The great Conservative party of Great Britain – the real aristocracy and gentry, led by a bold Minister who confided in their *genuine* liberality – propose to restore the finances of the country by taxing their own class.' The *Post* (14 April) was sure that public opinion backed Peel: 'the country is impatient to try the practical working of these measures.' The anonymous author of *Sir Robert Peel and His Era* (1843) remembered the deep impression made by Peel's proposals despite cries from the Whigs that he was stealing their measures. The country 'looked on with indifference as to the claims of paternity. The "New Tariff" was the general theme; and great was the rejoicing amongst the commercial community.'

The Opposition at Westminster, and also the Anti-Corn Law League in the country, tried to work up feeling against the imposition of an income tax. It was attacked as inquisitorial and unnecessary. *The Struggle*, a Preston anti-Corn Law paper, contended that the tax was required only because of the deficiency in revenue caused by the Corn Laws. The new tax was not designed to help the poor, rather 'to rivet upon them the galling fetters of monopoly'. In reality, Peel had the poor greatly in mind. He had advocated an income tax ever since his period in office in the 1820s, on grounds as much of social justice as of economic policy. Lord Ellenborough noted in 1830 how Peel wanted 'to reconcile the lower with the higher classes, and to diminish the burthen of taxation on the poor man'.[44]

What Peel had wanted for 1831 he got for 1842. He was busy discussing the idea in the summer of 1841 even before he took office. Goulburn doubted whether a reformed Parliament would prove sufficiently unselfish to accept an income tax except in wartime. Peel answered that the arguments in favour preponderated.[45] Peel was determined to press the tax through the Commons, in the confidence (as he told the House on 23 March) that the middle classes in the country would understand the need, even though they would be the new taxpayers: 'it is for the interest of property that property should bear the burden.' By July Peel was able to draw attention to the willingness with which the tax had been accepted. He took this as a reflection of confidence in his Government: 'grievous as an Income-tax is, unusual as is the proposal of such a

---

[43]   Peel to J. Vining, 23 April 1842 (Add. MSS 40507, f. 32).
[44]   Lord Ellenborough, *A Political Diary, 1828–1830* (1881), II, pp. 213, 215; A. Aspinall (ed.), *Correspondence of Charles Arbuthnot*, Camden third series, 65 (1941),p. 124.
[45]   Goulburn to Peel, 22 July 1841; Peel to Goulburn, 28 July 1841 (Goulburn Papers).

measure in time of peace, objectionable as is the inquisition which it establishes, yet so convinced are the people of this country that some vigorous and decisive steps are necessary, that they willingly submitted to the impost.'[46]

The Radical *Birmingham Journal* (2 April) had attacked the income tax as 'pure tyranny', whereas the Conservative *Birmingham Advertiser* (17 March) had recommended it as 'the most just tax that can be laid'. A private letter to Peel assured him that, although 'respectable' Birmingham opinion did not like the inquisitorial nature of the income tax, it was accepted as necessary. 'Besides, we believe that as relates to persons of small income, whose expenditure is mainly in the necessities of life, what they pay to the income Tax will be fully returned to them by their decreased expenditure arising out of the other able and excellent measures by which the Income tax is to be accompanied.'[47] A song called 'The Income Tax' in the August issue of *Blackwood's* made the same points, among others:

> A pleasant medicine's sure to kill,
> Your only cure's a bitter pill:
> The drugs of base deluding quacks
> Made Peel prescribe his Income tax.
>
> Yet now I hope the new tariff
> Will something save in beer and beef.
> If that be so, you'll all go snacks,
> And half escape your Income tax.

H. W. Tancred, the Liberal Member for Banbury, was admitting by 14 April that 'If there is any steam in the country we neither for love nor money can get it up, & must allow our triumphant enemies to ride over us.' Conversely, a Hitchin Quaker was blaming the politicians: 'not even Peel's income tax can raise any spirit of resistance to conservatism.' The Whigs, he complained, appeared to be 'spiritless', while Radicals such as Roebuck and Raikes Currie 'laud Peel to the skies and contrast his vigour and liberality with the feebleness and irresolution of the late Ministry'.[48] Raikes Currie's praise was described by Harriet Martineau as especially influential, the more so because he rarely addressed the House. Currie, a London banker, welcomed Peel's measures on 18 April for their comprehensiveness. He supported the appeal to the propertied to make sacrifices, and urged Peel 'to continue to act above party'; if he did so, concluded Currie, he would become known not merely as an able Minister but as 'among those master spirits who have achieved supreme power, and used it like gods, to do justice to mankind'. *The Times* next day gave the

---

[46] Peel, *Speeches*, IV, pp. 17–27, 106.

[47] W. Chance to Peel, 13 April 1842 (Add MSS. 40506, f. 179).

[48] B. S. Trinder (ed.), *A Victorian M.P. and his Constituents* (1969), p. 7; G. E. Bryant and G. P. Baker (eds), *A Quaker Journal* (1934), p. 275.

speech a full column report. Harriet Martineau remembered how Currie's words 'served as an exposition of a widely spread view, and as a guide to some who were still perplexed what to think and do'.[49]

The Conservative *Kentish Gazette* of 19 April noticed how the country generally, including the agricultural districts, had accepted Peel's 'general scheme', despite reservations on particular points. Fox Maule, a Liberal Member for Perth, admitted that there and 'in all other towns' in Scotland 'there was a class of persons whom the right hon. Baronet had captivated by his measures'. Joseph Brotherton, the middle-class Radical Member for Salford, conceded that in the Manchester area opposition to the income tax was much less than the League had expected. 'Loud cries of "Hear, hear," from Sir Robert Peel and the Treasury Bench.' Some 24,000 people had signed a Manchester petition in support of the tax, admitted Brotherton, including both Anglican clergy and Dissenters, who had been moved by the overwhelming need to feed and clothe the poor. Revealingly, the *Manchester Guardian* of 20 April remarked that no real alternative to an income tax had been suggested, 'with its adjuncts of the corn bill and the tariff'. The *Guardian* therefore supported Peel's plan as 'the best existing means of proceeding for the actual and expected financial deficiency'. Its line was reported to Peel by Lord Francis Egerton as being maintained 'against all remonstrances from its Whig subscribers'. Egerton also forwarded a Bury petition, which claimed that Peel's measures had won 'universal approval in this County'. Peel replied that he was 'very much pleased by the intelligence from Lancashire'.[50]

The Times of 12 March gave Peel its influential support in enthusiastic terms:

> We do not hesitate to say, that the proposals made by Sir Robert Peel last night, and the speech in which he developed them, would be sufficient, if they stood alone, to place him in the first rank of financial statesmen. They are a complete justification of the confidence which the country has reposed in him; and the nation will respond to the appeal made to it, not only with satisfaction, but with enthusiasm.

The Times agreed that an income tax, although inquisitorial, was unavoidable. There remained the consolation that it was not intended to be permanent. By 26 March, however, while pressing for improvements in detail, *The Times* was already wondering about that 'speedy withdrawal which the people and the Premier hope for'. As for the Corn Bill, *The Times* of 9 April warmly praised Peel's agricultural backbenchers for accepting a bolder measure than they could have anticipated. Few of them were competent to judge precisely the best

[49] Martineau, *Thirty Years' Peace*, IV, pp. 184–5.
[50] Egerton to Peel, 8 April 1842, enclosing J. Hutchinson to Egerton, 7 April 1842; Peel to Egerton, 9 April 1842 (Add. MSS 40506, ff. 63, 65, 66).

level of protection, and they were right to take Peel's advice. At the other extreme of opinion, *The Times* of 18 May dismissed the agitation of the Anti-Corn Law League as 'senseless and seditious'.

The *Dover Telegraph* of 21 May perceptively noticed how press support for Peel was divided between those who welcomed his measures 'for their boldness and comprehensiveness', and those who accepted them merely as 'the best compromise'. Those inclining towards free trade took the former view, those who preferred protection took the latter. For the moment Peel had managed to combine the support of these two very different categories of opinion, both within Parliament and in the country. But the contrast was apparent. So was Peel's masterfulness in the face of both supporters and opponents. On 6 April he described, rather complacently, the course of his recent 'political and parliamentary campaign' to Lord Ellenborough in India. Peel emphasized how he had refused to temporize. He felt confident that real achievement depended upon 'unflinching perseverance in that cause, which, having ample means of judging, you are convinced is the right cause'.[51]

IV

It was impressive that many of the propertied classes were ready to support Peel's policies even though they were being asked to make financial sacrifices. On the other hand, many of the working classes remained unconvinced, even though they were promised material benefits from Peel's policies. Approval did come, however, from operative Conservatives in Derby and Glasgow.[52] And one Leicester stockinger assured Peel that the prevailing feeling at two local meetings of working men had been that 'Sir Robert Peel is the best minister we have ever had.' Because the Leicester operatives were 'not the slaves of party', they were willing to support any fair Government, whatever its label. The stockinger hoped for future reductions in the corn and sugar duties. 'The working classes have, for many years, looked upon the government with hatred as their oppressors; by perseverance in the course which you have adopted, you will remove that feeling.'[53]

So even the stockinger was not claiming that Peel had yet overcome all working-class suspicion. Confusion in the minds of working men was reported to Peel from Manchester. At first he had been burned there in effigy, for not repealing the Corn Laws; yet when the details of his income tax and tariff were known 'the very same parties say that they are very sorry for what they did and

---

[51] Peel to Ellenborough, 6 April 1842 (Add. MSS 40471, f. 177).

[52] Add. MSS 40505, f. 14; J. T Ward, 'Some aspects of working-class Conservatism in the nineteenth century', in J. Butt and J. T. Ward (eds), *Scottish Themes* (1976), p. 150.

[53] W. Jackson to Peel, 3 April 1842 (Add. MSS 40505, f. 364).

said and that you are a much better man than Lord John Russell.'[54] A broadside, published in July 1842, entitled 'Peel's Income Tax, or A Miss at Popularity', was gently hostile:

> Poor Bob! what a scrape you have got into at last,
> You are paying at present for sins that are past,
> And well you deserve it – such ratting acts, sink-em,
> The Corn Tax on one hand, on the other the Income.

But another broadside, published in Norwich, called 'A Rare Row About the Income Tax', praised the measure for taxing publicans and other tradesmen who exploited the poor:

> We reckon your income at two hundred a year,
> Because three parts are water what you sell for beer.

Manchester was only one of many towns where Peel was burned in effigy by the Leaguers. When this happened at Caernarvon in March, it stimulated the signing of a pro-Peel address from the 'respectable' inhabitants. Peel commented, with a light-heartedness rare at this period, that he did not mind being burned 'when the flames excited so gratifying a demonstration in my favour'. An effigy of Peel was whipped through the streets of Birmingham on 27 February, the figure bearing the words 'Sir Robert, the Artful Dodger, "He that witholdeth corn, the people shall curse him." – Proverbs.'[55]

Where might such strong language lead? Peel was deeply worried by what he believed to be the violent inclinations of the League and Chartist leaders. In particular, he blamed them for the 'plug strikes' of August 1842, which were regarded by Ministers as a potential national revolutionary outbreak. In reality, the strikes did no more than bring together local restlessness throughout the manufacturing districts. But Peel, his nerves strained by months of over-work, feared the worst.

On 31 May an attempt was made upon the life of the Queen. A second attempt followed on 3 July. Both were found to be the deeds of unbalanced men acting alone. But the fact that they were not revolutionaries would have given little consolation if the Sovereign had been killed. When Peel brought the news of the first attempt to the Commons, 'excitement well nigh overpowered his utterance'.[56] His home at Drayton Manor was put into a state of defence during the plug strikes. Because he was necessarily kept in London during the crisis, he wrote often and anxiously to his wife. She reassured him that 'no men actually attacking doors and windows would have left this place alive'.[57]

[54] M. Ramscar to Peel, 5 April 1842 (Add. MSS 40506, f. 10).

[55] T. Assheton Smith to Peel, 11 March 1842; Peel to Smith, 19 March 1842 (Add. MSS 40504, ff. 86, 88); J. A. Langford, *Modern Birmingham and its Institutions* (1872), I, pp. 22–3.

[56] Peel, *Speeches*, IV, p. 89.

[57] T. Hill to Peel, 21 August 1842 (Add. MSS 40514,f. 132); Peel, *Private Letters*, pp. 202–4.

Was there some direct connection between the Anti-Corn Law League and the strike outbreak? Many magistrates in the industrial districts, especially in Lancashire, were League supporters; and Sir James Graham, the Home Secretary, suspected that for this reason they were slow to put down violence. Troops therefore had to be employed on a large scale. The official organ of the Anti-Corn Law League, the *Anti-Bread Tax Circular*, was placed by Peel and Graham in the same category as advanced Radical and Chartist papers, which they watched with a view to prosecution. 'I think public opinion would support us just now,' Peel told Graham on 15 October, 'after the experience of recent events, in worrying by prosecution the Editors and publishers of some of the worst papers. I would select political articles and provocations to tumult.'[58]

In his speech of 11 July against Villiers's annual motion for total repeal of the Corn Laws, Peel mentioned a placard headed 'Murder' which was apparently being sold by the Anti-Corn Law League in Manchester.[59] Threatening language towards Peel seems to have become commonplace in the industrial districts. League speakers made indirect threats; and at a League meeting in London in July the Rev. R. S. Bayley, a Sheffield Dissenting minister, exclaimed that he knew of one gentleman who had voiced his willingness to kill Peel if a hundred men were balloted and he chanced to be the chosen assassin. Bayley emphasized his opposition to assassination; but added that when Peel went to his grave there would be 'few to shed one tear over it'.

Bayley's story achieved immediate national notoriety, and must have come speedily to Peel's notice. It was repeated in the article on 'Anti-Corn-Law Agitation' by Croker in the December *Quarterly Review*. As with the article on Peel's policy in the September number, the content and argument of this piece owed much to help given personally by Peel and Graham. The tone of the September article had been one of exposition and defence: the tone of the December article was one of exposure and attack. Croker quoted at length from League publications to demonstrate that, despite protestations to the contrary, the Anti-Corn Law League regarded violence or threats of violence as legitimate. He concluded that the plug strikes were 'prepared, commenced, and, to a certain point, guided, by emissaries of the League'. He claimed that the League encouraged the strikes so long as there was hope of using them as violent pressure against the Corn Laws; 'but when they discovered that the people were holding steadily to the contrary course, and insisting on their former rate of wages, the Leaguer magistrates were ready to suppress the insurrection, which they found themselves unable to direct.' This reversal of role did not remove, in the view of Croker (or Peel), the moral responsibility of

---

[58] Peel to Graham, 15 October 1842 (Graham Papers, 54A); A. Briggs (ed.), *Chartist Studies* (1959), pp. 385–94.

[59] Peel, *Speeches*, IV, p. 119.

the Anti-Corn Law League for creating an atmosphere within which violence was likely to erupt.

The evidence which Croker used had been collected for Graham as Home Secretary, with encouragement from Peel, by a young barrister named Montague Smith. Four copies of the whole dossier were privately printed. Croker worked from a copy for his article, with help from Graham and final revision by Peel, who found the end-product 'excellent'. A shortened version was issued in pamphlet form, to be read (Graham explained to Peel) by 'the Masses, the unknown multitude'. On 16 December Croker reported to Peel that the article had been well received: 'more people were intimidated by Cobden & Co. than I had at first supposed.' Croker thought that they would be encouraged to firmer resistance in the future. Peel and Graham had little doubt that this would prove necessary, for they expected the League to try incitement and intimidation again.[60]

Manchester, the home town of the Anti-Corn Law League, became the centre of Peel's especial attention during the plug strikes of August 1842: 'we felt that the example of Manchester, whether for good or evil, would exercise a most powerful influence on the other parts of the country.' Troops were poured into the district, and within a few days the outbreak had begun to collapse there and elsewhere.[61]

Peel had warned Graham in August to put the Queen even more upon her guard. 'The spreading of Reports of assassination at such a time as this suggests the policy of Caution.'[62] In the event, it was to be Peel himself who was nearly murdered a few months later. On the afternoon of 20 January 1843 his private secretary, Edward Drummond, was shot in the back while walking in Whitehall. He died four days later. The murderer was Daniel McNaghten, a mechanic from Glasgow. Two questions immediately arose – was Peel himself the intended victim; and if so, was McNaghten acting alone or as the instrument of some revolutionary group? Peel was certainly the target. McNaghten felt that he had been persecuted by the Conservatives at Glasgow, who had challenged his right to a vote. Peel was reluctant, however, to admit that this explanation removed the likelihood of McNaghten being linked with a conspiracy. 'The Evidence of his mental delusion is strong,' Peel told the Queen, 'but it must be borne in mind that he was exactly the Instrument which others wd. Employ.' Peel and the Queen were both keen for McNaghten to be hanged, and were shocked when he was acquitted as insane on the basis of what became the long-used 'McNaghten rules'. The Queen's reactions at this

---

[60] Graham to Peel, 18, 22 November 1842 (Add. MSS 40447, ff. 344, 359); Graham to Peel, 15 December 1842 (Add. MSS 40448, f. 71); Croker to Peel, 9, 16 December 1842 (Add. MSS 40520, ff. 180, 213); Jennings, *Croker*, II, pp. 389–93.

[61] Peel to G. W. Wood, 22 August 1842 (Add. MSS 40514, f. 143).

[62] Peel to Graham, 16 August 1842 (Add. MSS 40447, f. 74).

time were probably intensified by the fact that she was pregnant; Peel's by the response of his wife, who for a time was completely prostrated by thoughts of what might have happened.[63]

The newspaper-reading public was much excited by the crime, and became absorbed by the subsequent trial. Delane of *The Times* asked Peel for, and was supplied with, early information. The paper's first report on 21 January was described as 'from information on which perfect reliance may be placed'.[64] An editorial two days later emphasized how Peel himself had been the intended victim. McNaghten's trial early in March was covered at length, with the disapproving editorial comment (6 March) that the verdict would encourage murder because an easy defence of 'monomania' would now be available. The Chartist *Northern Star* (18 February) tried to fix responsibility for Drummond's death upon the Anti-Corn Law League. The Conservative *Manchester Courier* (28 January), in a comment which was given national circulation when copied by *The Times* three days later, made a show of not blaming the League as an organization by blaming some of its speakers instead. Bayley's story was again cited; and the question was asked whether McNaghten, sane or insane, might not have been encouraged by 'such hints'? In *The Times* of 25 February a letter from Bayley denied that his anecdote had been told in order to encourage assassination.

This climate of tension provoked a direct personal clash between Peel and Richard Cobden, the League leader, in the House of Commons on 17 February 1843. Cobden accused Peel of being 'individually responsible for the present condition of the country', especially by refusing to repeal the Corn Laws. Peel was instantly stung by this personalized emphasis, which Cobden had employed at League meetings but never before in the Commons. Could it be interpreted as meaning that Peel deserved to be assassinated? Peel sprang up to answer that he would not be 'influenced by menaces either in this House or out of this House'. Amidst uproar, Cobden tried to claim that he had meant no more than that Peel was responsible as head of the Government, for which he often spoke in the first person. 'He sums up the whole cabinet in his person.' Peel reluctantly accepted this apology; but his supporters remained angry, while Cobden's followers claimed that he had been deliberately misunderstood by Peel who wished to discredit the League leader. Radical *Punch* published a cartoon which showed Peel astride a keg of gunpowder, smoking a cigar while saying 'I am not responsible'; Cobden sat perched on a sack marked 'Anti-Corn Law League', while he offered Peel some ears of corn.[65] The Whig evening *Globe*, in an article copied by the *Manchester Guardian* (25 February), gave its

---

[63] Peel to Queen Victoria, 24, 25 January 1843 (Add. MSS 40435, ff. 301, 309); Peel to Queen Victoria, 5, 6, 7, 27 March (Add. MSS 40436, ff. 69, 75, 77, 107); Queen Victoria to Peel, 5 March 1843 (Add. MSS, f. 71). See also R. Moran, *Knowing Right From Wrong* (New York, 1981).

[64] Delane to Peel, 20, 24 January 1843 (Add. MSS 40523, ff. 217, 233).

[65] *Punch*, IV (1843), p. 107.

own twist to the claim that Peel bore personal responsibility. This must be the case, wrote the *Globe*, because he insisted upon following a policy which was 'neither that of the landed nor the trading interest'.

V

Certainly, Peel entered 1843 determined to continue with his own chosen line, as observers were well aware. 'H. B.' published in March a cartoon entitled 'Race between the Hare and the Tortoise'. Russell was the hare, Peel the tortoise. The suggestion was that Peel in his steady way seemed to be moving towards free trade and repeal of the Corn Laws; whereas Russell, having made the gesture of proposing a low fixed duty, had since lost the initiative. In 1843 the Peel Government's measure to admit Canadian corn at a nominal duty aroused considerable opposition in the corn-growing counties, especially from tenant farmers. This dissatisfaction was transmitted to Peel's backbenchers. Peel called a party meeting at his home, and resistance in Parliament eventually petered out. But the formation in the constituencies of local agricultural protection societies was ominous for the future.

These bodies were as much suspicious of Peel as hostile to Cobden. A speaker at a Kent county meeting in June 1843 asked whether, with the example of Catholic Emancipation in mind, agriculturalists could trust Peel. The question carried the more weight because the speaker had lived in Ireland, and had supported emancipation: 'but for the man who had always opposed it to suddenly come forward and introduce and carry the measure, was a course which would for ever destroy all confidence in him.'[66] Lord Talbot, Lord Lieutenant of Staffordshire, wrote to his friend Peel in January 1844 to report that he was under pressure to join the Staffordshire protection society. He asked 'whether as a real supporter of Yourself & your Government' he should do so, especially as he was well known to be a free trader. Peel gave him the same answer as he had given to his son-in-law, Lord Villiers. 'Consult entirely your own feelings.' Talbot reluctantly became president of the society, resigning to support Peel during the repeal crisis of 1846.[67] In January 1844 Croker described to Peel the state of opinion on his own estate near Cheltenham. 'Some of them seemed to think that you were actually an anti corn law leaguer, & above all they seemed in dread of Canada.'[68] Yet on

---

[66] *Kentish Gazette*, 13 June 1843. See Fisher, 'Opposition to Sir Robert Peel', pp. 114–46, ch. 3.

[67] Talbot to Peel, 20, 29 January 1844; Peel to Talbot, 29 January 1844 (Add. MSS 40539, ff. 99, 101, 102); Peel to Queen Victoria, 31 January 1846 (Add. MSS 40441, f. 46); *The Times*, 6 February 1846.

[68] Croker to Peel, 2 January 1844; Peel to Croker, 8 January 1844 (Add. MSS 40538, ff. 16, 145).

Croker's estate, and elsewhere, suspicion was being restrained by present prosperity, for agriculture and industry were now moving out of the depression of the early 1840s. But when in October 1844 Peel was told of 'Agricultural Good humour' in Shropshire, his answer was revealing. The news, he wrote, was especially satisfactory 'when such good humour coexists with prices of Agricultural produce sufficiently low to place an abundant supply within the reach of the Great body of the community'. The implication was that 'abundant supply' came first, above agricultural good humour.[69] A year earlier Peel had spoken at the Tamworth Farmers' Club. He had explained how important the Birmingham market was to Tamworth; how manufacturing and agricultural prosperity were thus linked. Harriet Martineau remembered that it was noticed nationally how Peel was here repeating 'League doctrine'.[70]

Although Peel had defended the revised Corn Law in the Commons in 1843, and promised to make no change during the session, he had refused to bind himself for longer, or in principle. His sole test was the practical working of protection. A Hitchin Quaker thought that Peel had spoken 'very doubtfully' about the Corn Laws at the start of the session; still opposed to a fixed duty, 'but seeming to imply a preference for perfect free trade gradually attained to'.[71] Peel was privately admitting to Gladstone by the end of the session that, if not hampered by party considerations, he would have liked to include in the Government programme for 1844 a new Corn Law which united the fixed duty with the sliding scale at a much lower rate. By December Gladstone was noting that Peel had expressed in passing 'a strong opinion that the next change in the Corn Laws would be to total repeal'.[72] Yet at the start of the 1843 session the Nonconformist of 15 February had argued that Peel could never hope to carry total repeal, even if he were to announce his conversion. Not more than a hundred of his own party would follow him. 'The whigs would not adopt him . . . those who are now his masters would take affairs into their own hands. The Premier himself could not get what the League wants out of the present House of Commons.' Here was a perceptive anticipation of what was to happen in 1846, except that the Whigs did then decide to back Peel, which made the vital difference.

How carefully Peel had to tread while publicly under pressure from both extremes, and while his own private opinions were shifting, was well illustrated by the 'velveteen plot' of January 1843. A Manchester free-trade cotton manufacturer, W. Barlow, sent Peel two pieces of velveteen of a new and beautiful fashion, patterned with a stalk and ear of wheat under which lay a

[69] Lord Clive to Peel, 11 October 1844; Peel to Clive, 12 October 1844 (Add. MSS 40552, ff. 212, 214).

[70] The Times, 25 October 1843; Martineau, Thirty Years' Peace, IV, pp. 296–7.

[71] Bryant and Baker, A Quaker Journal, p. 303.

[72] Brooke and Sorensen, W. E. Gladstone II, pp. 191, 195; M. R. D. Foot and H. C. G. Matthew (eds), The Gladstone Diaries, III (1974), p. 195.

small scroll inscribed with the word 'FREE'. Peel accepted the gift, but without noticing this contentious wording. The *Manchester Guardian* of 4 January reported the episode, mentioned the wording, and gave the text of Peel's letter of thanks. 'Lady Peel admires it so much, that she will convert one of the pieces into a cloak for her own wearing: the other I will apply to my own use.' All this was next day copied into *The Times*, and into other papers. Intense press speculation followed, Peel's opponents professing to find great significance in his readiness to accept the cloth. *Punch* poked fun at Peel's mistake. 'Great, indeed, would have been the triumph of the League, if the Minister had donned the insidious trousers, and, taking his seat in the House of Commons, had, without knowing it, based his Ministry upon – "free" corn!' Peel hurriedly returned the velveteen, complaining that he had not noticed how it 'bore any allusion to matters that are the subject of public controversy'. Barlow answered that he had not acted under any political motivation. This further correspondence appeared in the *Manchester Guardian* of 11 January, and in *The Times* of the next day. This trivial but revealing episode was long remembered. Three years later, when Peel had finally declared for repeal, *Punch* (21 February 1846) composed a letter, supposedly from the Prime Minister, asking for the velveteen to be given again.[73]

Another and much greater difficulty for Peel in 1843 was the deeply hostile reception given to Graham's Factory Bill, and especially to its education clauses. Peel and Graham were agreed about the importance of improving educational provision for the working classes. Graham had emphasized this in a wide context when writing to Peel in September 1842. 'Insurrectionary movement' must be suppressed, but 'the moral feeling' of the people must be raised:

> We must augment the means of Education; we must keep down the price of Articles of first necessity; we must endeavour to redress the wrongs of the Labourer; we must mark our honest sympathy with his wants; and while we uphold the authority of the Law with firmness, we must temper it with mercy. All this is in the exact Spirit of your Government.[74]

Graham's proposals for state assistance in the education of factory children were thought by Nonconformists, Wesleyans and Roman Catholics unfairly to favour the Church of England. Over 13,000 petitions with more than two million signatures protested against the plan in its original form, and almost the same number then petitioned against an amended version. Members of Parliament hesitated to ignore such intense constituency feeling. Clearly, the Church of England could not now be given any special role in education even

---

[73] Peel to W. Barlow, 7 January 1843; Barlow to Peel, 9 January 1843 (Add. MSS 40522, ff. 229, 230); *Punch*, IV (1843), p. 36; Martineau, *Thirty Years' Peace*, IV, p. 300.

[74] Graham to Peel, 8 September 1842 (Add. MSS 40447, f. 130).

though it remained the state Church. In the end, the whole bill had to be abandoned for the current session. Peel deeply regretted this, in the knowledge that adequate provision for working-class education was being delayed, and also because such a major legislative setback seemed to damage the business reputation of his administration.[75] Peel did not give up entirely, however. By 1846 the education estimates had reached £100,000. The Minutes of 1846, which set up a pupil–teacher system, although published after Peel had left office, were being formulated as early as 1844. Ideas from Peel for 'some plan of public Examination' for elementary schoolboys seem to have been reluctantly abandoned because the cost promised to be much more than he had anticipated.[76]

In the *Quarterly Review* for September 1843 Croker defended Peel's policies. The article chastised the agricultural interest, 'whether in the country or in the press', for suspecting that the Cabinet might be meditating 'any anti-agricultural projects'. 'Its political existence is interwoven with the principle of agricultural protection.' Nevertheless, two months later, *The Times* of 18 November published its widely noticed leader which accepted that the Anti-Corn Law League had now become 'a great fact'. The Leaguers quickly turned this article into a major boost for themselves by seizing upon the most striking phrase. That *The Times* was still not recommending repeal, and that it had expressed continuing dislike for 'gregarious collections of cant and cotton men', was blandly ignored.[77] The main thrust of *The Times* article lay in its criticism of Peel for allegedly mishandling the corn question. The League had flourished because Peel preferred a sliding scale to a moderate fixed duty. *The Times* made clear its liking for a fixed duty in further major editorials on 21 and 28 November. Peel was urged to propose a duty before it was too late, to detach moderate opinion from the League side. Frustration among moderates – not the rhetoric of Cobden and Bright – was giving the League its strength. Peel possessed the power 'to propose such a measure as the landowner will not reject nor the merchant contemn'. With Ireland disturbed by O'Connell's agitation for repeal of the union, it had become the more necessary to unite opinion in England. 'The integrity of the British empire is at stake. Let us not add to this the discussion and dissensions of the English people.'

Other newspapers could not fail to notice this series of articles. The *Manchester Guardian*, for example, copied the whole leader of 18 November,

---

[75] Gladstone, *Diaries*, III, pp. 289–90, 294; G. I. T. Machin, *Politics and the Churches in Great Britain, 1832 to 1868* (1977), pp. 151–60.

[76] Peel to Wharncliffe, 5 October 1844 (Add. MSS 40551, f. 329); Wharncliffe to Peel, 29 November 1844; Peel to Wharncliffe, 30 November 1844 (Add. MSS 40554, ff. 449, 451); F. Smith, *Life and Work of Sir James Kay-Shuttleworth* (1923), pp. 162–71; R. Aldrich, 'Peel, politics and education, 1839–46', *Journal of Educational Administration and History*, 13 (1981), pp. 11–21.

[77] A. Prentice, *History of the Anti-Corn-Law League* (1853), II, pp. 136–41.

and quoted the others extensively. On 2 December it described the third article as 'another solemn warning to the premier'. *The Times* was, of course, read by Peel and his colleagues; and Graham wrote to Peel on 29 November arguing for 'an authoritative contradiction', to emphasize that Ministers were not contemplating doing what the paper wanted. Recourse to a fixed duty would, in Graham's view, be 'inconsistent with our political Honor':

> I can understand the change in circumstances which may utterly supersede the necessity of Protection, and which may render the supply of Food for increasing Multitudes to be drawn from any Quarter of the Globe the first care of the British Government: but while Protection lasts we cannot advocate a fixed duty, which is more than nominal.

Peel, in reply, expressed surprise that people should be 'duped by Newspaper paragraphs into a belief that we could propose a fixed duty'. He thought that an official denial would only encourage unwelcome discussion. He recommended instead an inspired paragraph in the *Standard*, 'not appearing from authority, but *confidently predicting* that there will be no proposal of a fixed duty'. Such a paragraph does not seem to have been published. But an editorial in the *Standard* of 4 December reassured landlords and farmers that their protection had been reduced only to make a surer defence of the remainder. 'We tell the agriculturists that they may place the most implicit reliance upon the present minister.'[78]

This *Times* pressure closed a difficult year for the Government. Greville had noted (1 August) how Peel had 'fallen immensely in public opinion' because he was thought to have failed in his general administration of affairs, especially in Ireland. Greville suggested (6 June) that religious feuds associated with the Puseyites in England, and with the Seceders in Scotland, had added to middle-class unease. Croker's September *Quarterly Review* article complained about exaggerated expectations of what Ministers could do. Peel had refused 'to purchase dishonest popularity, either in parliament or the country, by professing to cure diseases which he knows to be beyond the reach of ministerial remedies'. Greville (15 September) noticed how sharply *The Times* of 11 September had attacked this article. The paper argued that the people rightly expected to see 'something done' by an administration with a large majority and all the resources of the state at its disposal. Peel confessed to his wife in August that he found the labour of government 'too severe for me in the present state of the country'. The 'eternal agitation' meant that the recess of Parliament no longer brought its former relief.[79]

---

[78] Graham to Peel, 29 November 1843; Peel to Graham, 30 November 1843 (Add. MSS 40449, f. 241).

[79] Peel, *Private Letters*, p. 244.

Peel found it the more difficult to act early and firmly against O'Connell's agitation in Ireland because of its similarities with that of the Anti-Corn Law League in England. The Cabinet decided that, since it could not move against Cobden, it had better hold off from O'Connell, at least until he was clearly committed to seditious courses. The Anti-Corn Law League also influenced Conservative by-election policy. When in January 1844 the sitting Member for Dudley, Thomas Hawkes, contemplated retirement, Peel urged him to delay. 'Whenever there is a vacancy Dudley will, I fear, be a tempting field for them.' The seat was eventually held by the Conservatives in August.[80] But a year earlier the League, in the person of John Bright, had won a by-election at Durham City. A split in the local Conservative ranks, which Peel tried but failed to close, had let Bright in.[81] The biggest Conservative by-election failure came, however, with the City of London contest in October 1843. Victory in such a significant seat, Peel had agreed with Bonham, 'would be a very decisive indication of public opinion, and defeat, considering the vacancy, would be as discreditable'. Defeat, admitted Graham to Peel after the event, would 'go far to seal the fate of the Corn Laws'; it would 'give great additional impetus to the power of agitation, while it weakens the power of resistance on the part of the Government.' The deputy chairman of the local Conservative Association attributed the setback especially to assiduous doorstep canvassing by the League.[82] Even a by-election victory might not bring Peel certain support, least of all from Birmingham. Peel was told how Richard Spooner, who was elected there in July 1844, opposed the Government on banking, Poor Law and factory questions, three of the major issues of the day.[83]

A particularly colourful expression of dissent within Peel's party had erupted in 1843 in the shape of the 'Young England' group. This comprised four romantic Tories, informally led by Disraeli. They first came into notice by opposing the Government's Irish Arms Bill, on the exaggerated and personalized ground that Peel was behaving as badly towards the Irish as had Cromwell. Croker told the group in the September *Quarterly* that they had attracted 'more of wonder than respect'. Certainly, they posed no numerical threat to Peel. On the other hand, they were a striking symptom of the increased questioning of his leadership among Conservative backbenchers.[84]

---

[80] T. Hawkes to Peel, 3 January, 9 February 1844; Peel to Hawkes, 15 January 1844 (Add. MSS 40538, ff. 38, 40, 41).

[81] Peel to Lord Londonderry, 18, 28, 30 July 1843; Londonderry to Peel, 25, 29, 31 July 1843 (Add. MSS 40531, ff. 156, 291, 297, 298, 300, 301). See also D. Large, 'The election of John Bright as Member for Durham City in 1843', *Durham University Journal*, 47 (1954), pp. 17–23.

[82] Peel to Bonham, 28 September 1843 (Add. MSS 40533, f. 308); Peel to Graham, 21, 22 October 1843; Graham to Peel, 21 October 1843 (Add. MSS 40449, ff. 115, 117, 123); J. W. Powles to Peel, 3 January 1844; Peel to Powles, 6 January 1844 (Add. MSS 40538, ff. 42, 47).

[83] G. Whiteley to Peel, 14 July 1844 (Add. MSS 40548, ff. 104, 107).

[84] Blake, *Disraeli*, ch. 8.

VI

Dissent within the Conservative ranks in the Commons was to express itself during 1844 in two major revolts; first, over the Government's Factory Bill, and secondly over its proposed revision of the tariff on imported sugar.[85] In February, Graham's Factory Bill proposed to limit children in textile mills to no more than six hours work per day; but it did not seek to reduce the permitted twelve-hour day for young persons and women. Ashley moved a ten-hours amendment, which was carried with ninety-five Conservatives voting for it. Peel refused to accept ten hours, or even to settle for an eleven-hours compromise. The bill was withdrawn; but later in the session a twelve-hours measure was passed.

The Government's proposals for reduced sugar duties were regarded as a challenge to the whole structure of colonial preferential tariffs. The problem was also complicated by the desire to tax foreign slave-grown sugar more heavily than foreign free-labour sugar. On 14 June Philip Miles, who represented Bristol and the West India interest, proposed a wrecking amendment which was carried by twenty votes, with support from sixty-two Conservatives. Three nights later, amid much tension, Peel risked the whole existence of his administration by insisting upon a reversal of this vote.

Peel was able to save his measures by taking a high line; but only at the price of adding bitterness about his leadership to the questioning which had first produced these adverse votes. Few Conservative backbenchers had wanted to turn him out; on the other hand, none of them relished being dragooned by the whips. Hardly any were persuaded to reverse their votes. Some abstained on the second sugar vote, and forty-three absentees from the first division came back to vote for Peel. This gave him a majority of twenty-two. *The Times* complaint about Peel's remoteness from his party, published on the morning of the reversal of the sugar vote (17 June 1844), has already been quoted.

If Peel was hardly popular in Parliament, he was not necessarily unpopular in the country. John Rudge of Salford published in Manchester, under the pseudonym of 'Civis', a pamphlet with a long self-explanatory title: *On Patriotism, A Letter To Richard Cobden, Esquire, M.P. and John Bright, Esquire, M.P., Or A Friendly Remonstrance With Them, On What May Be Truly Called Their Incessant Persecution Of The Prime Minister*. This claimed that the 1842 Corn Law was working well. 'Did Messrs. Cobden and Bright ever enquire of their housekeepers whether they ever remembered provisions so reasonable?' Peel's successful commercial policy, which served the interests of all, was being matched by his equally successful foreign and colonial policies.

---

[85] R. Stewart, 'The ten hours and sugar crises of 1844', *Historical Journal*, 12 (1969), pp. 35–57; Stewart, *Foundation of the Conservative Party*, pp. 187–90.

Thankfulness should be felt for 'that great and godlike mind which, under God, guides and directs the destinies of England.' *The Times* of 9 August did not describe Peel so exaltedly. It complained that he lacked the traditional Tory concern for the poor, being interested in no persons less than £10 householders with the vote. On the first day of 1845 it admitted that the English industrial districts were prosperous; but it emphasized, in contrast, how Irish peasants and English agricultural labourers were still suffering. The *Standard* of the same day, however, came close to matching the enthusiasm of the Salford pamphlet: 'the whole of our political horizon scarcely presents a cloud.' While commercial prosperity was unequalled, disturbing influences such as the Anti-Corn Law League, O'Connell's Repeal Association and the Tractarian heresy were all described as fading.

A Conservative protectionist county Member, A. S. O'Brien of Northampton, who was chairman of the publications committee of the Agricultural Protection Society, sent Peel a set of its tracts in August 1844. Somewhat ominously, O'Brien remarked in a covering letter that the society's great object was 'to keep the farmers in good humour'. The tracts included a printed review of the progress of the cause during the first half of 1844. The abolition of the wool duty in the budget was welcomed by the review as likely to benefit agriculture; and success was claimed in obtaining modifications to the Bank Charter Act with regard to country banks.[86]

The Bank Charter Act had been the major measure of the 1844 session. Peel regarded it as one of the chief legislative achievements of his career, 'the complement and defence of the act of 1819'. But some contemporary economists, and some twentieth-century historians, were to point out that in framing his measure as a defence of bullionism Peel was fighting old battles. The gold standard was not under serious attack by the 1840s. Yet Peel thought that it was being questioned by contemporary 'banking school' advocates of monetary management, whose real views he failed to understand, perhaps because he confused them with those of the Attwoodites. This made the Bank Charter Act into a less commanding measure than Peel imagined it to be. Paradoxically, it has been suggested that a major reason why it seemed to work quite well up to 1914 was because Peel had failed to take account of the high volume of bank deposits. As a result, the Bank of England quickly learned to manage such deposits so as to influence the money supply. The Act, in short, left great room for manipulation, such as Peel and the 'currency school' professed to find horrifying.[87]

The Bank Charter Act strictly separated the 'issue' and 'banking' depart-

---

[86] O'Brien to Peel, 1 August 1844 (Add. MSS 40549, ff. 174, 176).

[87] Peel to Brougham, 9 May 1844 (Add. MSS 40482, f. 42); Peel, *Speeches*, IV, pp. 365–6; B. Hilton, 'Peel: a reappraisal', *Historical Journal*, 22 (1979), pp. 592–6; D. K. Adie, 'English bank deposits before 1844', *Economic History Review*, second series, 23 (1970), pp. 285–97.

ments of the Bank of England; and it laid down that the specie reserves of the former, which covered the note issue, were not to be used to sustain the latter. Any note issue above £14,000,000 was to be backed by bullion. The issuing of notes was to be gradually concentrated in the hands of the Bank of England. Thereafter, country and joint-stock bank notes slowly began to fall out of circulation, as planned. Unexpectedly, however, at each commercial crisis of the Victorian period, the Bank of England almost exhausted its banking department reserves, even while its issue department was left with ample bullion. As early as the crisis of 1847, the Treasury perforce granted permission for this to be drawn upon, although in the event no drawing was needed. In the 1857 crisis, however, such a transfer in contravention of Peel's rules became unavoidable. Yet Peel's Act was very successful in psychological terms. In the mind of the public at large, and of the City of London in particular, it was accepted as a final measure which closed all debate. Such acceptance reflected Victorian confidence in Peel as a statesman, a general confidence which overlooked the imperfect working of his measure in detail.

In 1844 praise for the Bank Act was expressed throughout the whole country, except in Birmingham. The *Manchester Guardian* (11 May) dismissed the complaints of the Attwoodites, and emphasized how opinion in Manchester had always favoured a single bank of issue. 'We have not met with a single dissentient.' *The Times* likewise warmly welcomed Peel's proposals, although it complained that his explanatory speech of 6 May was 'scarcely so good as his propositions'. Peel, the paper felt, had failed to argue the best case for checking the issue of notes by country banks. In another speech on 20 May Peel referred to this complaint, without mentioning *The Times* by name. The paper then answered that Peel had still omitted to explain how country banks had failed to regulate their issues by reference to the state of the foreign exchanges. 'The assertion of this or some equivalent duty is *par excellence* the principle on which the measure is supported.'[88] Although *The Times* might find fault with Peel's advocacy, the public did not, perhaps (as *The Times* itself noticed on 11 May) because non-specialists could hardly begin to understand the complexities of banking. Peel was trusted, regardless of whether his speeches stated the full case. The widely noticed 'what is a pound?' passage in his introductory speech at least showed him bravely trying to speak in simple terms.

What were the everyday benefits which people expected from the Bank Charter Act? The *Banker's Magazine* for April 1844 concluded that the mercantile community anticipated 'greater steadiness in the money market, and greater uniformity in prices'; while the wider public expected that banks would become safer. 'This general approbation of measures deeply affecting every transaction of which money forms a part, reflects infinite credit upon the

---

[88] *The Times*, 7, 8, 11, 22 May 1844; Peel, *Speeches*, IV, p. 379.

talents and sound judgment of the eminent Statesman by whom they were introduced.' By January 1845 Peel was already claiming 'a decided check' upon the issue of paper by country and joint-stock banks, 'which but for the operation of the new Law, would have been stimulated by the hot fit for Railway Speculations'.[89]

VII

Peel was sustained throughout these difficult years by his genuine Christian faith. After his death in 1850 a copy of a prayer was found among his personal belongings in a box on his dressing-room table. Six years later it was published in the *Staffordshire Advertiser*, and from there into *The Times* and *Manchester Guardian* of 1 December 1856. Two days later *The Times* explained how the prayer had been sent by a Midlands Nonconformist minister when Peel was under severe attack during the Corn Law crisis of 1846. Although not Peel's own composition, *The Times* felt – and the Victorian public immediately agreed – that the care with which he had kept these words meant that he had found them especially inspiring:

> Great and Merciful God, Ruler of all nations, help me daily to repair to Thee, for wisdom and grace suitable to the high offices whereto thy Providence has called me. Strengthen, O Lord, my natural powers and faculties, that the weighty and solemn interests with which Thy servant is charged may not greatly suffer through weariness of body and confusion of mind. Deign, I beseech Thee, to obviate or correct the ill effects of such omissions or mistakes in my proceedings as may result from partial knowledge, infirmity of judgment, or unfaithfulness in any with whom I may have to do.
>
> Let Thy blessing rest upon my Sovereign and my country. Dispose the hearts of all in high stations to adopt such measures as will preserve public order, foster industry, and alleviate distress.
>
> May true religion flourish, and peace be universal.
>
> Grant that, so far as may consist with human weakness, whatsoever is proposed by myself or others for the general good may be viewed with candour, and that all wise and useful measures may be conducted to a prosperous issue.
>
> As for me, Thy servant, grant, O merciful God, that I may not be so far engrossed with public anxieties as that Thy Word should become unfruitful in me, or be so moved by difficulty or opposition as not to pursue that narrow way which leadeth me to life. And, O most gracious Father, if notwithstanding my present desires and purposes, I should

[89] Peel to R. Rush, 1 January 1845 (Add. MSS 40554, f. 476).

forget Thee, do not Thou forget me, seeing that I entreat Thy constant remembrance and favour, only for the sake of our most blessed Advocate and Redeemer, Jesus Christ, to whom with Thee and the Holy Spirit be glory for ever. Amen.[90]

Peel was a firm supporter of the established Church of England, and saw it as the duty of the Government to sustain it: 'not for any miserable purpose of maintaining its emoluments for individual interests', but for the sake of providing a church open to all.[91] Nevertheless, he was well aware of the strength of Nonconformity. About half the churchgoing population of England, and perhaps 20 per cent of the reformed electorate, consisted of Nonconformists. Most of them voted for Peel's opponents, although a significant minority of Wesleyans do seem to have favoured Peel at the 1841 election. In 1843, however, the Wesleyans shared in the fierce opposition to Graham's factory education plan.[92]

This episode confirmed Peel in the belief that the power of non-Anglican opinion was now so great that the Church of England could never again be singled out for support by the Government, even in a good cause. In this knowledge, when the bishops asked for more public funds to build churches in the manufacturing districts, Peel admitted the need but finally decided that new churches could not be paid for out of taxpayers' money, much of it from non-Anglicans. If this were attempted, so much protest would result that the cause of religion in general and of the Anglican Church in particular would be damaged: 'peace and charity would be sacrificed'.[93] As an alternative, the Populous Parishes Act of 1843 permitted separate districts to be formed out of present parishes even where no district churches existed; and it empowered the Ecclesiastical Commission to borrow up to £600,000 from Queen Anne's Bounty to pay the stipends of clergy in these new districts.

Peel gave £4,000 from his own pocket for churchbuilding in London and the manufacturing counties. News of his generosity was leaked by *The Times* (11 October 1843), with the remark that Peel's 'noble example' required no elaboration 'to give it full weight and influence with the public'. The next day, however, *The Times* quoted a paragraph from The *Standard*, which noticed how the Premier had now given back his whole annual salary of £5,000 – £4,000 for churchbuilding, £1,000 to the education fund. 'We admire and

---

[90] *Notes and Queries*, second series, 8 (1859), p. 147; Ethel Peel (ed.), *Recollections of Lady Georgiana Peel* (1920), pp. 206–7.

[91] Peel, *Speeches*, III, p. 421.

[92] Graham to Peel, 13 April 1843 (Add. MSS 40448, f. 269); Vincent, *Pollbooks*, pp. 67–70; R. Anstey, 'Parliamentary reform, Methodism and anti-slavery politics, 1829–1833', *Slavery and Abolition*, 2 (1981), pp. 211–26.

[93] Peel to Graham, 22 December 1842 (Add. MSS 40448, f. 116). See also P. J. Welch, 'Blomfield and Peel: a study in co-operation between church and state, 1841–1846', *Journal of Ecclesiastical History*, 12 (1961), pp. 71–84.

respect Sir Robert Peel in all his relations,' concluded the *Standard*; 'but in this instance we have real pride in presenting the Prime Minister of England to the nations of Europe.'[94]

When Peel took office in 1841 he was most respected by religious moderates, both within and outside the Church of England, and most suspected by those at the extremes. Thus the *Nonconformist* of 1 September 1841, the organ of the disestablishment movement as well as a voice for Corn Law repeal, described his accession to office as 'the setting in of political winter'. An article in *Fraser's Magazine* for October on 'Sir Robert Peel's Claim to the Confidence of the Clergy' argued that he would be given support by all but partisan Whigs; or by those who had not forgiven him for Catholic Emancipation; or by the Tractarians. But *Fraser's* estimated that these totalled only some 2,000 out of 18,000 clergy. The article praised Peel for the major Church reforms which had been inspired by the Ecclesiastical Commission. Peel had himself sponsored its creation while in office in 1835. He had emphasized that the Church of England must extend its usefulness, and so 'confirm its just claims upon the Respect and affection of the People'. The Commission saved the Church as an establishment by showing that it could reorganize itself from inside, notably by beginning to redistribute its great resources to meet the needs of the new industrial society. The success of the Ecclesiastical Commission proved to be one of Peel's greatest achievements.[95]

Peel's personal beliefs placed him in the undogmatic and broad middle of the Anglican spectrum. He was not demonstrative in his religion, much preferring quiet faith to unquiet argument. He found Gladstone's early brand of high Anglicanism difficult to understand and harder to justify. It is often forgotten how the celebrated first sentence of Macaulay's damaging notice of Gladstone's *The State in Its Relations with the Church*, published in the *Edinburgh Review* for April 1839, included the suggestion that Gladstone's views on politics and religion were contrary to Peel's. Macaulay described Gladstone as 'the rising hope of those stern and unbending Tories who follow reluctantly and mutinously a leader whose experience and eloquence are indispensable to them, but whose cautious temper and moderate opinions they abhor'. Peel certainly regretted that Gladstone had seen fit to publish his book; and told him so.[96]

In a letter to Croker in 1842 Peel defined what 'the sense of the Government' should be in religious affairs: 'in favour of that which is reasonable and just, in favour of the Church of England. Protestant Principles as they have been

---

[94] Peel to Blomfield, 3 September 1843 (Add. MSS. 40533, f. 12).

[95] Peel to Rev. J. C. Franks, 9 March 1835 (Add. MSS 40416, f. 141); Peel, *Memoirs*, II, pp. 69–85; O. Chadwick, *The Victorian Church* (1966) I, pp. 101–6.

[96] T. Wemyss Reid, *Life, Letters, and Friendships of Richard Monckton Milnes* (1890) I, p. 316; R. Shannon, *Gladstone* (1982), pp. 81–2.

understood for the last hundred years, the via media between Popery and Dissent.'[97] This meant that Peel was entirely out of sympathy with the Tractarian movement within the Church, and the Tractarians with him. He privately charged them with 'levity, or vanity, or the love of singularity', although he never made public the strength of his dislike. The Tractarians from their side were not so reticent. The *British Critic*, their mouthpiece, declared in July 1841 that Peel's name was 'a nullity in any question in the least concerned with religion'. He was dismissed as a mere politician, concerned only with expedients. Newman's hostile anonymous letters to *The Times* earlier in the year, denouncing Peel's alleged secularism, have already been mentioned. Peel took great care to promote no Tractarians to bishoprics or to other influential positions. He deplored the continuing disharmony within the Church, and was relieved when Newman finally seceded to Rome.[98]

Most shades of Anglican opinion were represented within the House of Commons. Some 230 Conservative backbenchers have been found who went into the lobbies against Peel's Government on at least one religious vote. But the hard core of his critics on religious questions numbered just under fifty, still a sufficient number to be troublesome.[99] During his first two years in office a disruptive crisis within the Church of Scotland required much anxious attention from Peel. The scale of the eventual secession seems to have surprised him. He had characteristically hoped that moderates would 'pluck up courage enough to avow their own conscientious opinions, & to disregard the menaces of Newspapers and of factious Leaders'.[100]

A religious dispute in England led to the passing of the Dissenters' Chapels Act of 1844. This allowed Unitarians to retain chapels from which they were in fear of being ejected under the Law of Charitable Trusts, in cases where the property had originally been endowed with the implicit assumption that Trinitarian worship would be practised. Unitarians naturally welcomed the measure, which Peel defended in the Commons on grounds of 'individual justice'. Law, he contended, should not be exploited in a spirit of religious prejudice to take property from any sect. He emphasized that the Act did not interfere where Trinitarian belief had been explicitly required in the original endowments. Nevertheless, feelings ran high in the country; and about 2,600 hostile petitions were sent to the Commons, chiefly from Nonconformists. This encouraged 106 Conservatives to vote against the second reading. The evangelical Anglican, Lord Ashley, complained excitedly to Bonham that

---

[97] Peel to Croker, 27 February 1842 (Add. MSS 40502, f. 328).

[98] Peel to Rev. T. Henderson, 13 Novemebr 1844 (Add. MSS 40553, f. 307); Peel to Henderson, 18 November 1845 (Add. MSS 40578, f. 345); Brooke and Sorensen, *W. E. Gladstone II*, p. 93.

[99] Fisher, 'Opposition to Sir Robert Peel', ch. 5.

[100] Peel to Rev. R. Buchanan, 20 June 1842 (Add. MSS 40509, f. 235); Peel to Sir G. Sinclair, 20 June 1842 (Add. MSS 40510, f. 188); Machin, *Politics and the Churches*, ch. 4.

Ministers had passed a law 'against the will of the Country to give to Socinians the funds assigned to the spiritual teaching of the Believers in the Holy Trinity. *They will pay the penalty of this Sin*.'[101]

VIII

The middle and later years of Peel's Ministry were to be increasingly troubled by problems associated with Ireland – successively, O'Connell's agitation for repeal of the union; the Maynooth grant crisis of 1845; and finally the failure of the Irish potato crop in the autumn of 1845, with its profound social and political effects on both sides of the Irish Sea. Peel's Irish policy combined firmness in defence of the union with boldness in conciliation elsewhere. It was a policy which at times attracted much resistance, but which also achieved some success; and which might have achieved much more, if Peel had remained in office to develop it after 1846.[102]

O'Connell's agitation had at first posed no threat; but during 1843 a surge of support, which included that of most of Ireland's Roman Catholic priests, suddenly made it formidable. Mass meetings worked up excitement. Graham feared that the movement would culminate in at least a mass refusal to pay rents, which might then be followed by widespread violence. Landlords were everywhere reviled, reported *The Times* (1 August 1843); 'a rancorous and revengeful hatred' was developing among the Irish peasantry, which threatened 'to effect the wildest schemes without incurring the dangers or facing the difficulties of revolution'. Such a social climate, *The Times* concluded, could not be left unchanged. Peel was of the same mind. In a debate on the state of Ireland on 11 July he explained why he considered repeal of the union 'tantamount to a dismemberment of the empire'. He refused to contemplate disestablishment of the Irish Church, even though it served only a Protestant minority. But he also emphasized his determination to administer the law impartially between Protestants and Catholics; to ensure complete equality in civil rights for Catholics; and to give them substantial equality with regard to the franchise. He promised 'most deliberate consideration' of the key question of relations between landlords and tenants. A Royal Commission, chaired by the Earl of Devon, was appointed to enquire into the law and practice of land occupation.[103]

---

[101] Rev. N. Moule to Peel, 5, 13 June 1844; Peel to Moule, 7 June 1844 (Add. MSS. 40546, ff. 133, 135); T. Ashton to Peel, 25 June 1844; Peel to Ashton, 26 June 1844 (Add. MSS 40547, ff. 214, 216); Ashley to Bonham, 22 June 1844 (Add. MSS 40617, f. 159); *Parliamentary Debates*, third series, 75 (1844), pp. 383–9; Machin, *Politics and the Churches*, pp. 165–6.

[102] See K. B. Nolan, *The Politics of Repeal* (1965); and D. A. Kerr, *Peel, Priests and Politics: Sir Robert Peel's Administration and the Roman Catholics in Ireland, 1841–1846* (1982).

[103] Peel, *Speeches*, IV, pp. 282–3.

In February 1844 Peel wrote three memoranda on Ireland for his Cabinet colleagues.[104] He felt Irish reform to be the more necessary and urgent because of the persistent risk of war with France or the United States. He had come to know the Irish situation from the inside during his time as Chief Secretary (1812–18); and he had been the responsible Minister in Whitehall while Home Secretary during the 1820s. A running theme within his three memoranda was the need to detach the moderate Catholic clergy from the repeal movement. Only thus, argued Peel, could the Church of Ireland hope to retain its privileges. Except with regard to the Irish Church, Peel's sense of realism was strong. He reminded Lady de Grey, wife of the Irish Viceroy, how the Roman Catholic religion of Ireland was that of over half of Christendom: 'that it has therefore, as it exists in Ireland, the sympathies of many powerful Countries, that it is therefore equally consistent with the precepts of our own Religion, and with the dictates of justice and sound policy, not to presume too much upon our own infallibility.'[105]

Peel realized that the repeal movement could not be permanently checked by force alone, since this would leave five-sixths of the Irish people 'united, Rich and Poor, Lay and spiritual, in a confederacy of jealous, hostile feeling towards the Government and the Law'. But limits must be set to agitation. After enduring months of clamour, the Government at last intervened strongly. A massive repeal gathering called by O'Connell at Clontarf for 8 October 1843 was banned, with the authorities visibly making ready to disperse it by force. O'Connell cancelled the meeting. He was ageing and losing his grip. Nevertheless, he still found himself prosecuted for conspiracy. Peel had seized the initiative with regard to Ireland, which he was to retain for the rest of his time in office.[106]

Peel's February memoranda had identified charitable endowment as a field for reform which would benefit the Irish Catholics. The purpose of the Charitable Bequests Act of 1844 was to remove obstacles which had previously discouraged endowment of the Catholic Church in Ireland. A supervisory board was created with Catholic members; but this was contrived without directly recognizing the Roman Catholic hierarchy. The Act was indeed not immediately welcomed by many Catholic bishops and clergy; but in the end it found wide acceptance as a working solution, the more welcome because it came to be understood as only a first gesture of conciliation. When a new Lord Lieutenant, Lord Heytesbury, took over in the summer of 1844 Peel reiterated his hopes 'of weaning from the cause of Repeal the great body of wealthy and intelligent Roman Catholics by the steady manifestation of a desire to act with impartiality'.[107]

[104]   Add. MSS 40540, ff. 19, 26, 40.
[105]   Peel to Lady de Grey, 29 February 1844 (Add. MSS 40540, f. 383).
[106]   Peel to Hardinge, 27 May 1845 (Hardinge MSS U2348); Peel, *Speeches*, IV, pp. 316–41.
[107]   Peel to Heytesbury, 1 August 1844 (Add. MSS 40479, f. 15).

In 1845 Peel turned to Irish education, both to the creation of improved higher educational facilities and to the better training of the Catholic priesthood at Maynooth College, near Dublin. Each proposal ran into strong, prejudiced opposition. The Academic Institutions (Ireland) Act was intended to improve the instruction of the Irish middle classes, in the hope that this would make them more resistant to clerical influence or to political extremism. Peel was unimpressed by cries from Anglican ultras against his plan for establishing what they called 'Godless colleges'. He pointed out sharply how such people had not been previously interested in the religious welfare of Irish middle-class youths, leaving them to lead lives of idleness. Only now, when the Government was trying 'to substitute knowledge for idleness and profligacy, but cannot at the same time compel them to forswear their own religious faith and be good Protestants', was religious concern being paraded. Non-denominational university colleges were proposed for Cork, Galway and Belfast. But soon after Peel left office, the Vatican decided in July 1846 that such institutions would be harmful to the Catholic faith, and Peel's promising plan failed to come to fruition.[108]

His proposals for Maynooth did take effect; but only after an uproar which revealed the great depth of anti-Catholic feeling in Britain. The training college for Catholic priests at Maynooth had received a small grant from the state since 1795. This grant of less than £9,000 had soon proved to be seriously inadequate. Peel summed up the 'practical effect' in a memorandum of 11 February 1844. 'The State gets no credit for indulgence or liberality. The style of living, the habits engendered at the College, the acquirements probably of the Tutors and professors bearing a relation to the stipends provided for them, all combine to send forth a Priesthood embittered, rather than conciliated by the aid granted.' Another memorandum concluded that 'the wit of man could not devise a more effectual method for converting them into sour, malignant demagogues.' Peel therefore wanted to increase the grant so as to raise the social and intellectual level of the priesthood, in the hope that this would make the priests more inclined to moderate politics. In Cabinet Peel found that Gladstone was his chief critic. Gladstone doubted whether the priests were open to influence; he also feared that the gesture would increase pressure for disestablishment and disendowment of the Church of Ireland. Finally, he was sure that to increase the Maynooth grant went against the spirit of his 1838 book, and that therefore he must resign from Peel's Government. Peel only added to Gladstone's determination when he remarked in conversation that 'no one could remember' what Gladstone was pledged to. Gladstone therefore resigned in February 1845. But he then felt free to vote for the increase.[109]

Peel introduced his Maynooth Bill on 3 April 1845. Prolonged and

---

[108] Peel to H. L. Bulwer, 12 May 1845 (Add. MSS 40566, f. 344); Peel, *Speeches*, IV, pp. 521–7.
[109] Brooke and Sorensen, *W. E. Gladstone II*, pp. 238–41; Shannon, *Gladstone*, pp. 147–9.

contentious debate followed at every stage of its passage during the rest of April and into May. In moving the second reading, Peel explained the wide context of his proposals:

> you must break up, in some way or other, that formidable confederacy which exists in that country against the British government and the British connection. I do not believe you can break it up by force. You can do much, consistently with the principles you avow as to the maintenance of the union and the Protestant church. You can do much to break it up by acting in a spirit of kindliness, forbearance, and generosity.

The aim, reiterated in the peroration to his speech on the third reading, was 'to engender a kindly feeling between Ireland and Great Britain'.[110]

The Government therefore proposed to raise the Maynooth grant to £26,360 annually, with a single further payment of £30,000 for buildings. The old grant had been given as an act of grace reviewed each year. Now there was to be a steady commitment. This proved to be as alarming to many as the increase itself. Anglican ultras in England and Ireland saw such a commitment as implying official recognition of the Roman Catholic Church, and therefore as a challenge to the position of the Church of Ireland as the established body. Nonconformist 'voluntaries', for their part, opposed the payments because they disliked links between the state and any Christian sect. Anglicans and Nonconformists thus came from opposite directions to find common ground in opposition to the Maynooth grant; and this was reflected in the formation of a joint Anti-Maynooth Committee. Peel admitted to the Commons that he was surprised by the intensity of hostility. A grant had been paid for fifty years: 'We introduce no new principle.'[111]

Peel pressed his Maynooth plan through the Commons, well aware that many of his own backbenchers and the greater part of expressed opinion from the country stood against him. John Young, his Chief Whip, had warned of numerous likely defections in the Commons from those with 'many Dissenters' in their constituencies; from those of 'ultra opinions'; and from those with marginal seats eager 'to earn any popularity they can'. On the third reading of the Maynooth Bill, according to one calculation, 150 Conservatives voted for and the same number against. Altogether, 166 Conservatives recorded hostile votes in at least one major division. Peel's manner was said by one Irish backbench opponent to have reflected his sense of exposure: 'No turning round now behind the Treasury Bench, not a cheer from thence.'[112]

---

[110] Peel, *Speeches*, IV, pp. 497, 521.

[111] Ibid., pp. 489, 508.

[112] Young to Peel, 25 March 1845; Peel to Young, 25 March 1845 (Add. MSS 40563, ff. 275, 281); Sir W. Gregory, *An Autobiography* (1894), pp. 125–6; Fisher, 'Opposition to Sir Robert Peel', ch. 5.

Peel therefore won his majorities thanks more to Whig votes than to Conservative ones. Yet he was made to pay a price for this Whig support. In the debate on the second reading Macaulay delivered one of his great set orations. Among Peel's private papers has survived a newspaper report of part of this speech, pasted on a piece of paper, with passages marked in the margin. These passages expressed Macaulay's agreement with Peel that no change of principle underlay the increase in grant. But Peel did not keep a cutting of the latter part of the speech, which scathingly attacked him for exploiting religious passions when in opposition only to repudiate them when in office, thereby betraying the 'hotheaded Protestants' for a second time. 'Explain to us why, after having goaded Ireland to madness for the purpose of ingratiating yourselves with the English, you are now setting England on fire for the purpose of ingratiating yourselves with the Irish.' Macaulay concluded, however, that he would vote for the Bill; that he would not act factiously with Disraeli. The fate of the measure lay in Whig hands; and if both main parties in the state seemed willing to swing back and forth as Peel had done, there would be 'one vast shipwreck of all the public character in this country'.[113]

The Whig *Morning Chronicle* of 16 April took up the same line – offering support for the measure but not for the man. Peel had sat white-faced through Macaulay's attack; but in an answering speech on 18 April he prudently declined to discuss all 'taunts' of inconsistency. Instead, he contended temperately that, even if reproaches were due to the authors of the Bill, this should not affect support for the measure itself. Peel assured Croker, in a letter which reflected some discomfiture despite its bold tone, that he had won the support of 'almost all the youth, Talent and real influence' in the Commons. Many Members were merely yielding to pressure from Nonconformist constituents. 'Tariffs – Drought – 46 shillings a quarter for wheat, quicken the religious apprehensions of some, disappointed ambition and the rejection of applications for office others.' Here was a reference to Disraeli. 'All this raises a storm at which I look with indifference, being resolved to carry the Bill, and being very careless as to the consequences which may follow its passing so far as they concern me & my position.'[114]

Opinion within the Church of England was divided over Maynooth. Low Churchmen feared that further encouragement would be given to 'Romanizing' tendencies; but broad and high Churchmen wrote to Peel with expressions of support. 'The Low Church Party alarmed by Puseyism, the Dissenters hating all Establishments, and the Wesleyan Methodists are the parties who have combined.' Such was Peel's own assessment. The Wesleyan Committee of Privileges told Peel that, because Roman Catholicism was intolerant and persecuting, Wesleyans were opposed to state support for Catholics even while

---

[113] Add. MSS 40565, f. 430; Trevelyan, *Macaulay*, II, pp. 103–4.
[114] Peel to Croker, 6 April 1845 (Add. MSS 40565, f. 9).

themselves in favour of toleration. The Protestant Dissenting Deputies of London – representing Presbyterians, Independents and Baptists – reminded Peel that they had always opposed even the small grant to Maynooth because of their hostility towards state involvement.[115]

During the four months from February to May 1845 the House of Commons received 10,204 petitions with 1,284,296 signatures against the Maynooth Bill, only 90 with 17,482 signatures in favour.[116] Hostile petitions were promoted by the Central Anti-Maynooth Committee, which circulated a standard petition form. Thirty-nine Anglicans served on this committee, nineteen Congregationalists, nine Wesleyans and four Presbyterians. Their connection was, however, a precarious one, for motivation varied between Anglicans and Nonconformists, and even among the Nonconformists. In the end, the extreme Nonconformist 'voluntaries' decided that Anglicans could hardly be true opponents of a measure allegedly intended to secure the Anglican establishment. The anti-Maynooth movement therefore split at a crucial moment in late April into two wings, which subsequently spent as much time attacking each other as in opposing the third reading of the Maynooth Bill. This gave the Government a good excuse for ignoring all petitions.

Not that Peel admitted any need for such an excuse. He treated the Central Anti-Maynooth Committee with disdain, unsympathetic as ever towards 'pressure from without'. At the end of April he refused to meet delegates 'to discuss in personal conferences out of Parliament the merits of measures of general public policy specially affecting particular or local interests'. In the same spirit, Peel was explicit in refusing to bow to mass petitioning. The very strength of outside feeling, he argued awkwardly but firmly:

> will only impose an additional obligation on me to persevere steadily in the course I have adopted – I do not say in violation and opposition to popular opinion, for I have no desire to run counter to it; but this I feel, it is absolutely necessary to prove to the Roman Catholics of Ireland that the manifestation of that feeling should not induce public men to swerve from the course which, at any rate, appears to have produced kindly feelings among those in whose favour it is to be given.[117]

The greater part of the press came out against Peel over Maynooth. It was hardly surprising that the *Nonconformist* (9 April 1845), with its strong

---

[115] Add. MSS 40564, f. 20; Add MSS 40612, f. 168; T. A. Green to Peel, 9 April 1845 (Add. MSS 40564, f. 209); W. P. Houston to Peel, 9 April 1845 (Add. MSS 40564, f. 215); Rev. T. Lathbury to Peel, 18 April 1845 (Add. MSS 40564, f. 456); Rev. R. Parkinson to Peel (Add. MSS 40565, f. 166); T. Baines to Peel, 26 April 1845 (Add. MSS 40565, f. 208); Peel to Hardinge, 4 May 1845 (Hardinge MSS U2348).

[116] See G. I. T. Machin, 'The Maynooth Grant, the Dissenters and Disestablishment, 1845–1847', *English Historical Review*, 82 (1967), pp. 61–85.

[117] Sir C. Eardley Smith to Peel, 28, 30 April 1845; Peel to Eardley Smith, 29 April 1845 (Add. MSS 40565, ff. 272, 275, 277); Peel, *Speeches*, IV, p. 508).

commitment against religious establishments, should have called for Peel's declared objective of 'conciliation' to be secured not by increased payments to Maynooth but by disestablishment of the Church of Ireland. But which way would *The Times* go? It began cautiously. Then, 'with one of its accustomed gyrations' (as the *Norfolk News* of 29 March noted), it finally came out firmly against the proposals, after the strength of hostility in the country had become apparent. 'When Peel is on one side, and the people on another,' *The Times* of 19 April smugly proclaimed it was 'almost content .. to resign to him that monopoly of wisdom and virtue which he so sufficiently appreciates'. If the Maynooth measure really was 'so healing, so necessary', why had Peel not taken greater pains to prepare the public for it? 'As it is, the majority is Ministerial, not popular.' In the view of the people, and of *The Times* (17 April), here was 'not Liberalism but Romanism which Peel is forcing on the nation'. It mattered much more that British statesmen could be trusted, 'than that the Maynooth students should sleep one in a bed' (14 April). Peel's party, and the country, complained the paper, never knew what he would suggest next. Regardless of the merits of his measures, this unpredictability was undermining confidence in the whole system of government. *The Times* of 11 June defended itself for supporting Peel against O'Connell's agitation, while yet opposing reform of Maynooth. 'We cannot move quite fast enough for the versatile, not to say volatile Premier ... Under Peel's fatherly tuition we learned to suspect, to watch, to control, to limit Maynooth.' *The Times* predicted that Peel would soon be advocating open endowment of the Roman Catholic Church in Ireland.

So only months before the great Corn Law crisis, during which *The Times* was to lend Peel at least qualified support, it was still expressing fundamental doubts about him as a politician. Conversely, the *Standard*, which was to separate from Peel over Corn Law repeal, was still his steady supporter over Maynooth. Giffard, its editor, had written to Peel on 21 March warning him to expect 'angry opposition', and asking for an authoritative statement about Government policy which could be published in the *Standard*. Giffard reminded Peel of the 'good effect' achieved ten years earlier, when an outline of Peel's plan of ecclesiastical reform had been published in the paper before presentation to Parliament. This time, however, Graham advised Peel that such preference would be more likely to upset than to conciliate opinion in the press or in Parliament. Peel therefore replied to Giffard on 23 March in complimentary terms, but declining to issue a statement. Peel obviously still hoped for editorial support from the *Standard*. 'Could you not without any reference to a particular plan satisfy many that any course is better than a parsimonious niggardly grant that we have not the courage to withold?'[118]

---

[118] Giffard to Peel, 21 March 1845; Peel to Giffard, 23 March 1845 (Add. MSS 40563, ff. 135, 138).

In response to this prompting, two days later appeared a leading article which advocated a liberal Maynooth policy in terms cleverly calculated to appeal to non-liberal minds. The article suggested to Anglicans that the prominence of Nonconformists in the anti-Maynooth agitation ought to be taken as a warning. Moreover, the principle of a grant had been conceded when it was first made. Readers' belief in Catholic bigotry was then adroitly made into a reason for backing a generous policy. Those who believed that Catholic priests would be more 'obstinately bigoted, more bitterly hostile to England' if better educated, would do well to oppose an increased grant. Those who thought the opposite, as did the *Standard*, 'will look with complacency upon an experiment, the worst effect of which will be, merely, to throw away some money'. Later editorials emphasized how the *Standard* would still have resisted Catholic Emancipation in 1845, as it had done in 1829; but the Maynooth scheme was to be judged as an educational reform which (taking Catholic bigotry as a fact) would reduce 'the power of ignorance and of rudeness' (4 April). The *Standard* accepted Peel's assurance that the increase in grant did not imply any prospect of endowment for the Roman Catholic Church. The paper gave this point a reassuring twist by suggesting (19 April) that the 'rabid clamour' from the Nonconformists may have largely resulted from Peel's reiterated firmness in favour of the establishment of the Church of Ireland. The *Standard*'s companion, the *Morning Herald*, adopted a similar line. It turned round the very strength of the anti-Maynooth clamour by remarking (5 April) that this demonstrated the underlying strength of Protestantism, which meant that Protestants had nothing to fear 'from a dozen Maynooths'.

At the other end of the political spectrum Radical *Punch* (3 May) also supported the increased grant, but in terms which remained contemptuous of Peel personally:

> How wonderful is Peel!
>   He changes with the time;
> Turning and twisting like an eel,
>   Ascending through the slime.
> He gives whate'er they want.
>   To them who ask with zeal,
> He yields the Maynooth grant
>   To the clamour for repeal.

*   *   *

> 'Tis true he is a rat,
> But what of that?
> Tory he used to be,
> But now a Liberal he!

Shall we for soaring high
The altered Premier snub?
Who in the butterfly
Would recollect the grub?

The Liberal Unitarian *Manchester Guardian* (19 April) backed Peel's Maynooth policy; but it went further by recommending state endowment of the Roman Catholic Church in Ireland. The Liberal *Norwich Mercury* of 3 May was glad to support the increased grant explicitly because it regarded the increase as a preliminary step towards endowment. In the same city, on the other hand, the *Norfolk News* of 10 May attacked Peel, partly because it opposed state interference in religion, but also because it thought the Maynooth measure only a decoy to conceal Peel's unwillingness to propose 'a large and comprehensive measure of justice to Ireland'.

The Sunday newspapers offered a variety of reactions. The *Weekly Dispatch* (20, 27 April) accepted that Peel's Maynooth plan was part of a programme of 'justice'; but a plan which did not threaten the Church of Ireland establishment. *The Sunday Times* (13, 20 April) also welcomed the plan, even in the expectation that it would lead to the endowment of the Catholic majority church. *Lloyd's Weekly* (6 April) anticipated the same consequence, 'whatever Sir Plausible may say to the contrary'; but for that reason took the side of opposition. The *News of the World* (6 April) emphasized that it opposed the increase not because of anti-Catholic prejudice, but because it disapproved of all state support for religion.

Protectionist provincial papers tended to be strongly anti-Maynooth. The *Blackburn Standard* of 23 April disliked 'endowing a creed so full of monstrous errors as that of Rome'; and it deplored Peel's readiness to ignore the opinion of the constituencies. This last complaint was widely voiced. The *Derby Mercury* (9 April) characterized Peel's reasoning as: 'the nation has for a number of years done wrong, therefore it is now incumbent on it to do worse.' Payment of the Roman Catholic priesthood was to be expected soon. Peel seemed determined to break up his party: 'if it is to become a question whether we must sacrifice our principles or the Minister, there will be no hesitating in the matter.'

In the event, such resistance could not stop Peel. The Maynooth Bill was opposed by 149 Conservatives on its third reading, one more than voted for it. Nevertheless, it passed with Whig support. The Conservative Party, in the country and at Westminster, remained intact, still accepting Peel as its leader. The Government Chief Whip reported on 14 June that confidence in Peel was 'unabated and universal'.[119] The Liberal *Liverpool Journal* (19 April) claimed that much 'seeming opposition' had been dictated by half-hearted 'conscience

---

[119] Young to Peel, 14 June 1845 (Add. MSS 40569, f. 62).

and appearance'. Certainly, the *Norfolk News* of 7 June acquiesced with surprising calm. 'Our efforts have been directed not so much against the endowment of a college, as against the principle of State interference in matters of religion.' Lord Ashley expressed surprise in his diary on 18 August that Peel's Ministry appeared to be enjoying continued public favour despite Maynooth, for it was still winning by-elections. Between April and October Conservatives lost only one out of thirteen contests for Conservative-held seats, and gained four other seats.[120] Right in the middle of the crisis, the *Spectator* of 19 April shrewdly suggested that it was significant how all extremes of religious and political opinion were crying out against Peel. Rather than being damaged by this diverse opposition, he was able to draw strength from it, since it highlighted his affinity with usually silent, middle opinion, which disliked extremism and clamour. Even Disraeli was later to admit that Ministers 'had succeeded in appropriating a mass of loose, superficial opinion, not trammelled by party ties', which was ready to accept a policy of moderate reform in church and state. 'Peel is, in fact,' concluded the *Spectator*, 'the embodied reflex of the public mind of England.'[121]

What then did the public make of Disraeli and his attacks upon Peel? The Young England group had split over Maynooth. Its concern for social harmony could easily have justified Disraeli in offering eloquent support for the increased grant. Instead, he chose to voice scathing opposition directed at Peel personally, summed up in memorable phrases which may have been unfair but which were not entirely untrue. Thus on 11 April Disraeli portrayed Peel as 'a great Parliamentary middleman . . . who bamboozles one party and plunders the other, till, having obtained a position to which he is not entitled, he cries out, "Let us have no party questions, but fixity of tenure".' In 1845 such brilliant sallies gained Disraeli a hearing from the Conservative backbenches, but not yet a following. Peel's disaffected backbenchers were still not ready to accept such a strange leader. Disraeli knew that what was wanted from him was not constructive leadership but destructive criticism. *The Times* of 14 April praised him for consecrating himself to the revelation of Peel 'for the warning of the present age, and the instruction of posterity'. Once a week Peel was being 'cut up, laid open, and exposed, every sinew and nerve, to the curious eyes of a nation'. *The Times* was glad that Peel's shortcomings as a party leader were being ruthlessly displayed. 'It cannot be consistent that the country was to be saved by creating a party ten years since, and by confounding and smashing all parties, especially that saviour party, now.' *The Times* suggested two days later that this attitude reflected Peel's underlying lack of respect for public opinion. 'The Premier has exactly the same respect for his countrymen as the hunter has for the elk.'

---

120 Stewart, *Foundation of the Conservative Party*, pp. 193, 199, n. 62.
121 Disraeli, *Bentinck*, p. 8.

A London correspondent of the *Liverpool Journal* (19 April) recognized that readers in the country might not understand why Disraeli's speeches were so successful in the Commons. His mimickry of Peel's manner, 'the voice, the attitude, the look, almost the very thought of the premier', gained extra effect from the way Disraeli never laughed at his own shafts, and also from 'the desperately futile efforts of Peel to appear insensible to what is going on'. That such an explanation was thought to be necessary may have meant that Disraeli's speeches were found less persuasive in the constituencies than at Westminster. This certainly seems to have been the case with Disraeli's novels. *Coningsby* (1844) and *Sybil* (1845) were eagerly read in London society and parliamentary circles, but not by the middle-class reading public.[122]

IX

The year 1845 saw Peel's second great budget. Not all had gone as anticipated in the 1842 budget; but this was hardly noticed by the general public because the policy of shifting from indirect to direct taxation was found to have worked well overall, both in terms of public finance and of public psychology. In May 1845 Peel compared the atmosphere of 'profound tranquillity' in the North of England with the turmoil of 1842. Peel noted with satisfaction and relief how 'True Conservative Policy' had visibly succeeded.[123] He was ready by 1845 for another round of measures, similar to those of 1842, designed to stimulate trade. This meant renewing the income tax, which (as Peel said in his budget speech) had become 'the foundation of the commercial policy of the country'. Such words seemed to be threatening a permanent tax, even though Peel was proposing renewal only for three more years. He was certainly not seeking easy popularity, and he took particular credit in the peroration to his budget speech for not choosing tariff reductions under the influence of lobbying: 'we have not acted in deference to popular clamour, for we have selected taxes for reduction and abolition against which there has been no agitation.' He proposed a revision of the sugar duties to bring the colonial duty down to 14s and the foreign free-grown duty down to 23s 4d. Import duties were to be completely abolished on 430 of the remaining 813 articles subject to tariff, the abolitions applying especially to raw materials used by industry. For example, the raw cotton duty was removed, as were the excise duties on glass and on auctions. The estimated revenue loss of £3,338,000 was expected to absorb almost the whole forecast surplus for 1845–6; and Peel anticipated a deficit by 1846–7. Prudence therefore suggested a continuation of the income tax. Peel conceded that the principles upon which he was acting would have justified

---

[122] Blake, *Disraeli*, chs. 8, 9.
[123] Peel to Hardinge, 4 May 1845 (Hardinge MSS U2348).

even more free trade measures: 'but it is our object, while we establish good principles, to allow for the present state of society.' Trade and industry must not be too much disturbed. Peel, in short, was being characteristically practical in his response to the urgings of free-trade theory.[124]

Only the proposals with regard to sugar provoked much open dispute. *The Times* of 17 February described the budget as 'decidedly popular in tendency; for, except in the matter of the income-tax, it emancipates commerce at the expense of property, and ostentatiously favours the poor.' The *Manchester Guardian* of 19 February found the budget 'highly satisfactory'. It was glad to notice that Peel had pointed the way towards even more measures of free trade. Peel's presentation had been skilfully contrived to carry majority opinion with him, both in the Commons and in the country. By 24 March he was able to write exultantly to Hardinge in India that he had 'repeated the Coup d'Etat of 1842'; the House of Commons 'was taken by surprise'.[125] *The Times* of 17 February had noticed how such 'surprise' was most apparent on the Ministerial side, where the budget had been heard 'in comparative silence'. It had been received by the Opposition with hearty cheers; 'and by the people generally with satisfaction. The walls of the metropolis are placarded with Sir Robert's "Free Trade Budget".'[125]

Agriculturalists, in and out of Parliament, had complained that the land was not mentioned in Peel's budget speech. 'The truth is,' remarked the protectionist *Derby Mercury* (5 February), even before the budget was known, 'the Cabinet is essentially a commercial Cabinet.' The *Mercury* still praised Peel as one of the greatest statesmen ever to rule the country, who had given 'solid security' to property, and the death blow to agitation. But it warned Peel to guard himself against showing 'undue preference'. In this same spirit the *Mercury*'s budget editorial of 19 February, although it found Peel's proposals commendable, expressed concern that agriculturalists seemed to be 'completely erased from his recollection'. Peel responded to such complaints, in and out of Parliament, by arguing that farmers and agricultural labourers would benefit from any expansion of industry, which would increase the demand for agricultural produce. A correspondent from Fife assured him that this connection was well understood there, and that his budget had met with 'universal approval'.[126]

The *Morning Post* had welcomed the budget of 1842; but since then its chief proprietor and editor, C. Eastland Michele, had deliberately hardened his protectionist line, after buying out several less committed shareholders. The *Post* strongly attacked the budget of 1845 by taking the criticisms of the *Derby*

[124] Peel, *Speeches*, IV, pp. 436–57.
[125] Peel to Hardinge, 24 March 1845 (Hardinge MSS U2348).
[126] Col. J. Lindsay to Peel, 25 February 1845; Peel to Lindsay, 28 February 1845 (Add. MSS 40561, ff. 70, 72).

Mercury much further. It contended that the budget favoured merchants and manufacturers who deserved no new help, and forgot about agriculturalists or about the poor. The *Post* complained (19 March) that since taking office Peel had been 'almost exclusively a mercantile Minister'. On 28 February 1845 it looked back disapprovingly over the main measures of his Government, and noted how he had worn down opposition. 'Since the prospects of the landed interest were blighted by the passing of the New Corn Law, the Canada Corn Bill, the Tariff, and the Bank Charter Bill, a sort of apathy appeared to come over the agricultural body.' However, the *Morning Post* was glad to notice that agricultural opposition to Peel was now beginning to organize itself. In February 1845 the paper was still suggesting that the Premier might be open to persuasion; but by 17 April it was declaring that he 'must soon cease to be the head of a Government styling itself "Agricultural and Conservative"'. He had destroyed the Tory party in 1829, and since 1841 he had been busily destroying the Conservative party. Peel seemed:

> really to imagine that the more widely his measures differ from the principles which he professed when he was raised to office, the more imperatively is he called on to disparage the principles in question, and to promote the success of schemes which war with all his previous convictions. Never, assuredly, was there devised a moral code more favourable to the growth of habits of rascality in public men.

Conservative critics in Parliament and in the press were left grumbling but wrong-footed, as Peel pointed out to Hardinge in May 1845:

> You will see by the Papers what is the notion that the Conservative party take of the functions and duties of a Conservative Government.
>
> They cannot deny that Trade is prosperous, That the people are contented, That the Labourer has a greater Command than he ever had over the Necessaries and Comforts of Life.
>
> That Chartism is extinguished, or at least fast asleep.
>
> That the Church is stronger than ever it was except for its own internal stupid differences & Controversies.
>
> That any wish for organic Change in the Constitution, for addition to popular privileges, is dormant.
>
> That the Revenue is so prosperous that our calculations of deficiency are certainly baffled.
>
> That our monetary system is sounder than it has ever been, and yet that there has been boundless activity in commerce and in all speculations of gain.
>
> That even Land is increasing in value in consequence of the prosperity of Commerce.
>
> But we have Reduced protection of agriculture, and tried to lay the

foundation of Peace in Ireland, and these are offences for which nothing can atone.[127]

Peel was certainly entitled to indulge in such private self-congratulation about the success of many of his policies. Yet at this same period he was pursuing an indecisive railway policy, which had lasting bad effects. Goldwin Smith, in his generally favourable 1858 *Encyclopaedia Britannica* article on Peel, was to deplore his failure to control the railway mania 'by promptly laying down the lines of a Government plan'.

During 1845 railway speculation had grown as never before. *The Times* warned repeatedly against 'railway gambling', but to no effect. 'This un-precedented mass of speculation . . . is not the folly or the wickedness of a few, but a national act – the wide-spread mania of numerous classes' (17 November). Railway shares were being bought by people of small means simply by putting down their names, or by paying a 10 per cent deposit. Many of them expected to make a quick re-sale and profit before the full cost had to be met. In April 1846 Peel told the Commons that 519 railway Bills were under parliamentary consideration, not counting the many which had not got so far. The problem for Ministers was obvious – should Government intervene? There was much uncertainty in the contemporary mind whether railways should be treated as partly public or wholly private enterprises. *The Times* (9 June 1847) drew attention to this uncertainty, but came out firmly in favour of state intervention. The state authorized the railway companies 'to spoil the face of the country, and pump the money market, the corn market, the coal market, the wine market, the provision market all dry for the purpose'. The state remained therefore under an obligation 'to secure the greatest possible benefit to all classes' by controlling the companies. But how? Peel's Ministers were reluctant to attempt close supervision. Gladstone's 1844 Railway Act had been weakened under pressure from the railway interest. Peel himself had thought the measure 'a precedent dangerous to the security of all property'.[128] A Railway Board was created in August 1844 to vet proposals for new lines. Lord Dalhousie, the responsible Minister, wanted its reports to be given Govern-ment backing; but Peel refused this, on the ground that the discretion of the House of Commons must not be undermined, nor the 'neutrality' of Govern-ment compromised. When in June 1845 Peel and four other Ministers voted to reject one Railway Board report, Dalhousie protested that the reports had better be stopped. Peel agreed, and the Railway Board was dissolved.[129]

Peel eventually came to recognize that such a detached attitude by Government could not be maintained, as the railway mania intensified during the second half of 1845. But he remained slow to act. His tone to the Commons

---

[127] Peel to Hardinge, 27 May 1845 (Hardinge MSS U2348).
[128] Peel to Gladstone, 18 May 1844 (Add. MSS 44650, f. 202).
[129] See H. Parris, *Government and the Railways in Nineteenth-Century Britain* (1965), ch. 2.

on 6 April 1846 was unusually defensive. 'He thought the Government ought not to be blamed for not interfering before with the spirit of railway speculation. The right time for interfering was the great point. The House should be sure that they had public feeling with them.' On 23 April he claimed that only now were investors ready to tolerate interference. He proposed a plan to reduce the number of railway Bills accepted for third reading. A certificate was to be required confirming that at least three-fifths of shareholders wished to proceed. But this restriction had come much too late to check the railway mania. The *Illustrated London News* of 11 April explained how the Government had missed the chance to render a great national service by supervising railway development. It should have selected the lines for construction. If this had been done in time, intervention could have both created the best network, and checked speculation: 'as all schemes had the same chance of succeeding, speculation increased to a dangerous extent.' This charge seems to have been just. Disraeli even claimed in the April debates that Peel's 'dramatic performance' at the gathering to mark the start of work upon the Trent Valley Railway in the previous November had added to railway speculation. This was unfair. But the enthusiasm for railway development which Peel had voiced on that occasion did not seem to include any sense of a major directing role for the state. Some of the consequent weaknesses in the railway network have continued even to the present day.

X

The Peel Government's foreign policy was fortunately much more successful than its railway policy, even though at times war seemed close either with France or the United States, or with both. This danger was not the result of British bellicosity. Indeed, the quiet style of Lord Aberdeen, the Foreign Secretary, even led the Liberal *Daily News* to claim at the end of the Peel administration (2 July 1846) that it had pursued 'no foreign policy at all'; that it had dealt with issues simply as they had arisen. This had kept the peace, admitted the *News*, but at a price in lost prestige. Foreigners had been given the impression that England was slipping into quiet old age. 'And they look upon our political economic struggles, our commercial and financial changes, as so many nostrums which age loves to employ, for the maintenance of tottering health.'

In reality, although Aberdeen's style certainly contrasted with that of his extrovert predecessor, Lord Palmerston, Peel saw to it that British policy was quietly purposeful; and that British interests were always protected, although he put the preservation of an honourable peace prominent among such interests.[130] This firm but fair dealing with foreigners came to be understood by

---

[130] See Muriel Chamberlain, *Lord Aberdeen* (1983), chs 18–23.

the British public, which trusted Peel's judgement even though necessarily unaware of the details of diplomacy. *Chambers's Papers for the People* remembered, after Peel's death in 1850, how he had 'conciliated the good-will of other nations', but never by 'unworthy truckling'. Notably, he had shown firmness during the Tahiti dispute with France (1844) and the Oregon crisis with the United States (1845–6). But he was at all times temperate, well aware that 'words from one in his position were to a great extent equivalent to deeds'. John Bright recollected at the time of the Crimean War in 1854 how, when in the 1840s conflict had threatened with the Americans, the solemnity of Peel's manner had shown 'that he felt in his soul the responsibility'. This sense of responsibility carried with it a decided claim to the last word. Peel told Gladstone in 1850 that although newspapers served a purpose in expressing 'national Feelings', feelings must not be allowed to run counter to national interests, and the assessment of such interests must be the prerogative of Ministers.[131]

The Times was particularly interested in foreign affairs. Delane, its editor, kept in close touch with Aberdeen, who was willing to supply the paper with inside information. In return, *The Times* usually supported his policies. Peel was at first content with this arrangement, although (as already noticed) he later became irritated over Aberdeen's connection with *The Times* because of its hostility on major matters of domestic policy.[132]

The *Morning Chronicle* was Palmerston's organ, for which he wrote anonymously. In the autumn of 1842 he tried through the *Chronicle* to discredit the Ashburton Treaty, by which the long-standing dispute with the United States over its north-eastern frontier with Canada was finally settled. Greville (24 September) noticed how Palmerston's attacks were well answered by *The Times* which had started cool but warmed up in defence of the treaty; also by the *Standard*, and best of all by the two leading weeklies, the *Examiner* and *Spectator*. 'He ought to have felt the public pulse,' concluded Greville; 'he will not carry the public nor even his own party with him.' *The Times* of 16 September concluded that the treaty had brought a 'permanent boon' by avoiding an unnecessary war. Peel himself had seen no reason to fight, as he made clear to Aberdeen: 'seeing that the Boundary Question involves no Principle, I would go as far as we safely can go.'[133]

Relations with France were thought to have improved to such an extent from 1841 that contemporaries began to speak of an *entente cordiale*; with Aberdeen on the one side, and Guizot on the other, known to be on friendly personal terms. Yet the word *entente* was really too strong a description of the temper of Anglo-French relations during these years. Conflicting interests in

---

[131] Peel to Gladstone, 14 August 1840 (Add. MSS 44275, f. 30); J. Bright, *Speeches on Questions of Public Policy* (1869), p. 245.

[132] *History of The Times*, II, ch. V.

[133] Peel to Aberdeen, 16 May 1842 (Add. MSS 43062, f. 48).

many parts of the world made a real *entente* unattainable; on the other hand, they made the achievement of a spirit of understanding highly desirable, if peace was to be preserved. And indeed, Aberdeen's words in a letter to the French Foreign Minister, which the French had translated as '*entente cordiale*', had spoken only of 'a cordial good understanding'. Peel, as much as Aberdeen, accepted the need for harmony between the two countries in the interests of world peace. If Britain and France were not agreed, Peel told the Commons in 1844, 'our disagreement must influence the policy of every country'. If differences between them created English and French parties in every state, 'I can only say that England and France will be the curses of the world.' But Peel never let such awareness soften his assessment of the realities of French policy; and he became increasingly more guarded towards Guizot.[134]

The French were busily developing a colonial empire, which was likely to bring them into conflict with the British in distant parts of the globe. Britain would have preferred to remain the only world imperial power. In 1844 a major dispute occurred over French activity in Tahiti. A French admiral proclaimed a protectorate over the Society Islands, and imprisoned the British consul, George Pritchard. This represented a direct and aggravated challenge to Britain's 'open door' policy in the Pacific. Fortunately, both Governments were less militant than their local representatives or much newspaper opinion at home. But Peel denounced the 'gross outrage' in the Commons (31 July), and wrote and spoke angrily to his Cabinet colleagues. He told Aberdeen that the possibility of war must be accepted. 'Matters are in that state that the interval of 24 hours, some act of violence for which the French ministry is not strong enough to make representation or disavowal, may not only dissipate the shadows of the *Entente Cordiale* but change our relations from Peace to War. Let us be prepared for War.' The French were 'much more likely to presume upon our weakness than to take offence at our Strength'. It was essential, in Peel's view, to ensure victory in any first naval encounter so as to discourage an American declaration of support for the French.[135]

The crisis had been intensified when on 6 August the French had bombarded Tangier. This emphasized their expansionist intentions in North Africa, which was becoming the centre of their empire. Eventually they made half a concession by offering financial compensation for Pritchard's expulsion, even while insisting upon their right to remove him. The policy of peace, desired by both Governments, had held – but only just.

The Times of 28 August had been undisturbed by the prospect of war, and had felt patronizing towards the French navy. 'It is no fault of theirs that they are not born sailors . . . Their genius loves the land. With us – but why repeat

[134] Peel, *Speeches*, IV, pp. 302–4. See A. B. Cunningham, 'Peel, Aberdeen and the entente cordiale', *Bulletin of the Institute of Historical Research*, 30 (1957), pp. 189–206.

[135] Peel to Aberdeen, 21 August 1844 (Add. MSS 43063, f. 324).

the familiar boast.' *The Times* even anticipated the 'jingo' song of a generation later. 'Our men, our ships, and our skill, are as they were in the best days of our history.' Lord Francis Egerton reported to Peel that support for war was 'very prevalent among all ranks' except 'the regular Irish traitors & the Chartist Socialists'.[136]

After this episode, Peel and Wellington determined to put the army and navy upon a stronger footing. The budget of 1845 increased the naval estimates, and Wellington occupied himself with plans for the defence of the British Isles against sudden French attack. A letter from Peel to Wellington at the end of 1844 discussed defence problems with characteristic balance. Financial constraints, Peel began, meant that priorities must be agreed. Only a continuation of the income tax could ensure sufficient revenue for defence improvements. Yet naval and military changes should not be made so dramatically as to cause foreign powers to fear aggressive intent: 'or lead other powers to think that we are so defenceless that it is a good policy to precipitate hostilities'.[137]

Aberdeen disliked this new defence policy, despite Peel's care not to present it as provocative. In September 1845 the Foreign Secretary offered his resignation, but he was firmly persuaded by Peel to remain in office. A month later Peel spelt out for Aberdeen's benefit his basic thinking on defence. Even in peacetime, wrote Peel, Britain ought to feel 'at ease upon vital points', ought to be able to maintain her rights in any crisis without having necessarily to take extraordinary steps. 'There is a medium which we ought to observe between preparation for War, and the defenceless state in which we might be content to remain if we could have entire confidence in peace.' The whole history of France, awareness of 'the military genius and recklessness and want of principle of the people of that Country', ought to set a limit to confidence in the maintenance of peace.[138] After his departure from office in 1846, opportunist French action with regard to the Spanish marriages question confirmed Peel in the view that his guarded attitude had been right. '*The Entente Cordiale* is blown to the winds. I have not a word to say in favour either of the King of the French or Guizot.'[139]

Peel intervened in matters of colonial policy less readily than in matters of foreign policy; but the affairs of India, which were administered separately, took up much of his attention early and late in his administration.[140] Peel was not an imperial expansionist. He regarded acquisition of territory as 'a serious affair', which was to be discouraged both because it would incur expense and because it brought the probability of conflict with other powers. On taking

---

[136] Egerton to Peel, 9 September 1844 (Add. MSS 40550, f. 316).

[137] Peel to Wellington, 26 December 1844 (Add. MSS 40460, f. 322).

[138] Aberdeen to Peel, 18 September 1845; Peel to Aberdeen, 20 September 1845 (Add. MSS 43064, ff. 337, 349); Peel to Aberdeen, 17 October 1845 (Add. MSS 43065, f. 43).

[139] Peel to Goulburn, 17 October 1846 (Goulburn Papers).

[140] See W. P. Morrell, *British Colonial Policy in the Age of Peel and Russell* (1930), chs. 1–8.

office in 1841 he acted in this spirit with regard to the Afghan crisis, inherited from the Whigs: 'the most absurd and insane project that was ever undertaken in the wantonness of Power'.[141] He wished to avenge the recent British disasters and to ensure the safety of India, but he did not seek to annexe any part of Afghanistan. He believed this to be not only the prudent course, but also what the British public wanted. He elaborated his understanding of public expectations about imperial policy in a letter to Hardinge, who went out to India as Governor-General in 1844:

> If you can keep Peace, reduce expense, extend Commerce, and strengthen our hold on India by Confidence in our justice and kindness and wisdom, you will be received on your Return with acclamations a thousand times louder and a welcome infinitely more cordial than if you have a dozen victories to boast of, and annexe the Punjaub to the overgrown Empire of India.[142]

The previous Governor-General, Lord Ellenborough, sent out by Peel in 1841, had seen British prestige restored in Afghanistan; but had then become increasingly grandiose in his conceptions, much to Peel's discomfort. 'He will not infect the people of this Country with the Love of military glory.'

Relations with Canada – where both French-speaking Quebec, and English-speaking Ontario had rebelled during 1837 – continued to be difficult during the years of Peel's Government. The Canada Act of 1840 had united Quebec and Ontario; but it had said nothing about responsible government. Such government nevertheless came into being, as successive Governors-General began to appoint Ministers who could command popular majorities. Peel and Stanley, the Colonial Secretary, did nothing to encourage this; for Peel was as suspicious of 'democracy' in the colonies as at home. At times he grew impatient with the Canadians and talked of separation, especially as boundary problems, first in the north-east and then in the north-west, brought serious risk of war with the United States. In addition, the Canada Corn Act of 1843 exposed the Government to attack (as already noticed) from its own protectionist backbenchers, even though Stanley tried to present it as a measure not of free trade but of colonial preference. Repeal of the Corn Laws in 1846 drew protests from the Canadians themselves because of their loss of such preference. The Peel Government's Canadian policy, in short, continued uncomfortable throughout. But in 1849 Peel was to come forward with a new confidence. His speech on the Canada Rebellion Losses Bill (15 June) not only looked forward to a continuing imperial connection, but also accepted the right of the Canadians to fully responsible self-government. Peel had been slow to see the right way ahead; but he had come to see and to speak clearly in the end.

[141] Peel to Egerton, 30 May 1846 (Add. MSS 40592, f. 361); Peel to H. St G. Tucker, 26 March 1842 (Add. MSS 40504, f. 339).
[142] Peel to Hardinge, 6 November 1844 (Hardinge MSS U2348).

XI

The Times of 24 February 1846 described the new affluence which had begun to spread among the lower middle classes. As background, it listed the statistics of increased imports for 1845. But it suggested that the growing prosperity of 'the great family of the nation' was best pictured within individual homes:

We appeal to a small tradesman, or a small clergyman, or a small clerk in a counting-house, or any other small person, with not a small family . . . He has two or three joints a week, instead of only one. He sometimes sees a sirloin on his table. Once a month or so fish is substituted or preferred. Instead of the everlasting 'light' dumplings, and suet dumplings, and batter puddings with which he was compelled to satisfy or deaden the hunger of his children, he can afford an occasional plum pudding, and is not deterred from rice or fruit tarts by the expensive appendage of sugar. The batter betrays a little more of the egg, and winter is beguiled with jam and preserves. Cheese comes in after dinner . . . After that, also, now and then there is a dessert. Oranges, almonds and raisins, figs and prunes, are either spread out in state, or made the subject of an agreeable surprise at some less solemn hour of the day. The young gentlemen and ladies are earlier delivered from the bondage of milk and water, and made free of tea and coffee. It is no longer a rule that the third cup shall be without sugar, and the presiding matron has not quite so anxious an eye on the butter pot. There are two candles instead of one on the table, and if any of the family should be discovered reading, or talking, or playing by candlelight in another room, it is not thought as bad as schism or rebellion. Then the children do not go so long out at the elbows, or knees, or toes, or heels, or other salient points of their structure. New kid gloves and new silk pocket handkerchiefs oftener remind the elders of their first infantine delight at 'new clothes.' When the family becomes a little too large for the home, and the crowded population of the nursery begins to emigrate into separate bedrooms, the father either himself builds another 'room below and room above,' or gets his landlord to build them with a rise of rent. As the furniture has then to be rearranged, the mistress of the house takes the opportunity of dignifying herself with a new mahogany wardrobe, and perhaps a new drawing-room table.

Such was the lower middle-class domestic scene after four years of Peel's economic reforms. And some at least of this improvement, concluded *The Times*, had reached down to the working classes.

Not that Peel ever claimed that this pleasing tendency was entirely a result of his policies. During the 1845 budget debates he spoke of 'many causes combining to increase the prosperity of the country' – the spread of railways;

ample capital in search of investment; the growth of population. But Peel did claim that his policies were well designed to give room for such influences to operate with maximum advantage. And his two great budgets had been widely noticed. Non-partisan, middle opinion – including many among the lower middle classes who were living more comfortably – felt at ease with Peel in charge of the national economy.

So explained *The Times* on 23 December 1845. The paper itself, however, had continued ambivalent towards Peel even into the Corn Law crisis which had first become public knowledge a fortnight earlier. On 13 October a retrospective editorial cheerfully surveyed the many changes which had occurred since the end of the Napoleonic Wars, 'greater changes in the actual state of the nation than the boldest astrologer would have dared to predict in 1815'. Currency reform, repeal of the Test and Corporation Acts, Catholic Emancipation, the Reform Act, the New Poor Law, the abolition of slavery, the Ecclesiastical Commission, the income tax, the Maynooth grant, Game Law reform, the Charity Commission, Church Building Acts, 'the alteration of the Corn Laws', prohibition of female labour in mines, Dissenters' Marriage and Registration Acts, abolition of imprisonment for debt, tariff reform. 'We are engaged as a nation, in something very like a remodelling of our national and social condition.' Other changes, large and small, were operating alongside changes brought about by legislation – lucifer matches, the electric telegraph, penny postage, railway trains at seventy-five miles per hour, the spread of popular literacy.

Peel had been connected with most of these reforms and advances. Yet *The Times* in 1845 was still not prepared to call him a great Minister. Its lament in the same issue of 13 October, about the lack of a national political hero, and its dismissal of Peel as merely a man of expediency, has already been noticed. It returned to the same theme on 17 November. Peel's very capacity to relate to the prevailing state of the public mind was taken as disqualifying him from greatness; for the public mind was materialistic and self-interested, not high principled and detached: 'the Minister who avails himself of such a tone in the public mind is not a great Minister. He may be a cautious, a dextrous, a *clever* Minister; but a great Minister he certainly is not. For he is breaking down a strong bulwark of public honesty.'

During the summer of 1845 *The Times*, and many other newspapers, began to predict the ending of the Corn Laws. The logic of free trade was becoming irresistible, even before the Irish potato blight added a new dimension to the argument. The London correspondent of the Liberal *Norwich Mercury* reported on 1 November that 'the whole current of the public mind in the metropolis, the decided and unanimous tone of the daily press, and the private opinions of well informed politicians', all assumed that the Corn Laws had reached the beginning of the end. Agriculturalists should brace themselves for change, whether they liked it or not. 'Such a paper therefore as the *Norwich*

Mercury, established for such a long period in the capital of the finest of England's agricultural districts, cannot too soon or too forcibly prepare its many readers for a change in which they must feel a deep interest.' A week later *The Times* remarked how unusually few Members of Parliament had been addressing their constituents during the recess. 'There is a growing distance between county members and their country friends, between statesmen and their provincial allies. "Least said, soonest mended," is the feeling of the day.' Such silence could not last much longer. What would Peel do? *Punch* of 3 May had carried a striking cartoon entitled 'Papa Cobden Taking Master Robert A Free Trade Walk':

Papa Cobden. – 'Come along, Master Robert, do step out.'
Master Robert. – 'That's all very well, but you know I cannot go as fast as you do.'

By 6 November *The Times* was arguing that Peel could no longer hold back:

The present corn laws are doomed. It is for the Premier to decide whether he will sign the warrant for their execution . . . the most prudish of Premiers may hesitate before he condemns what he has sanctioned, and sanctions what he has strenuously denounced. If this be so, there is only one course for him to take – to abstain from taking an open part in this important discussion – to leave to others the merit of settling the question – and to RESIGN.

4

Repeal of the Corn Laws: 1845–6

I

In the space of a few months between the end of 1845 and the middle of 1846 Peel was transformed in the eyes of many Victorians from a 'Knave of Spades' (as *Punch* was still portraying him on 29 November 1845) into a widely admired King of Hearts. Over this period of the great Corn Law crisis Peel's appeal to middle opinion, which had already met with considerable success, was to become almost irresistible. He now ceased to be (what he had remained to the end of 1845) a party leader who had been appealing for support irrespective of party, and became even more charismatic as a leader who was making his appeal from a position of self-sacrifice *above* party, in order to carry repeal of the Corn Laws.

Peel's growing magnetism was well reflected in *Punch*. The splendid 'Knave of Spades' cartoon on 29 November still treated him as an opportunist, who might indeed introduce reforms, but not because he was trustworthy as a reformer. He was a great political survivor, not a great statesman. Then the political crisis of December led to a conscious change of attitude by *Punch*; a change made in the expectation that Peel was now committed to dealing boldly with the Corn Laws, a commitment for which he was beginning to be abused by the protectionist press. An open letter '*Punch* to Peel' in the Christmas number began: 'Beloved Peel, – When you were popular in Downing Street I never spared you.' But now, 'it shall not be said that in this, the day of your tribulation, you have not a friend. *Punch* slaps you on the shoulder, and cries "be of good heart".' *Punch* was appalled by the venom of attacks from protectionist papers such as the *Morning Post*. 'Can men have no compassion?':

> Because so many other pens are piercing you, we would fain let fall from our quill some few drops of balm. Therefore, good Sir Robert do we hope that – for Christmas, at least, you will be tranquil – happy. And to that end may your beef sit lightly on your stomach; may your plum-pudding melt deliciously in your mouth; your mince-pies dissolve like honey dew!

THE KNAVE OF SPADES.

'The Knave of Spades': *Punch*, 29 November 1845

On 24 January 1846, after Peel had outlined his intentions to Parliament, a cartoon appeared entitled 'Peel's Cheap Bread Shop, Opened January 22 1846'. As yet, however, *Punch* was still giving more credit to Cobden than to Peel. A fortnight later 'The Man Who Works The Automation' showed Cobden starting the moves from below the political chessboard, even though Peel was holding the pieces. In the same number appeared 'The British Lion in 1850; Or The Effects Of Free Trade'. This pictured a well-fed lion at ease with the world. By the time of Peel's retirement after the enactment of repeal in the summer of 1846, *Punch* had made the final shift. Its admiration for Peel personally was summed up on 11 July in a cartoon called 'Manager Peel Taking His Farewell Benefit'. This showed the audience (including Mr Punch himself) warmly applauding Peel as he bowed on stage, with only Disraeli dissenting and being taken away by a policeman. There was now no suggestion of Peel being manipulated by Cobden; he was accepted as the man who had carried through repeal.

R. W. Emerson, the American writer, was to remark in his *English Traits* (1856) how both *Punch* and *The Times* were mouthpieces of the same English good sense. Many *Punch* cartoons, wrote Emerson, were as influential as the best pamphlets; 'and will convey to the eye in an instant the popular view which was taken of each turn of public affairs'. This had become increasingly true of *Punch* as it softened its early Radicalism and moved towards the middle ground, a shift strikingly reflected in its change of tone towards Peel.

II

The *Colonial Gazette* of 16 August 1845 reported that at the prorogation of Parliament the Duke of Argyle, walking backwards, had stumbled and dropped the crown. 'Foreboders of evil infer from this either that "repeal" is to be carried, or Oregon given up to Janathan.' Certainly, even before the Irish crisis had become apparent, Peel was showing himself to be moving too far and too fast for his old protectionist friend, J. W. Croker. On the last day of August he told his friend that, although Croker's views about the importance of the agricultural interest were sound enough in a short view, 'the question at issue is, what will induce to the real Welfare of that interest'. Peel emphasized the importance of manufacturing prosperity, which he linked with agricultural prosperity. He was implying that he could not guarantee to continue protection for agriculture if depression returned to industry. 'I should shudder at the recurrence of such a winter and Spring as those of 1841–2.'[1]

Reports of the failure of the Irish potato crop came in with increasing certainty during the autumn of 1845. By 13 October both Peel and Graham

---

[1] Peel to Croker, 31 August 1845 (Add. MSS 40573, f. 160).

MANAGER PEEL TAKING HIS FAREWELL BENEFIT.

'Manager Peel': *Punch*, 11 July 1846

simultaneously and independently had made up their minds that Ireland was likely soon to be facing economic and social disaster. Four years later Graham was to remember this 'remarkable coincidence' in their reactions. Both had received gloomy reports from Ireland. Ways and means must be found, wrote Graham to Peel, to mitigate the prospective calamity: 'if we opened the Ports to Maize duty free, most popular and irresistible arguments present themselves why Flour and Oat-meal, the staple Food of Man, should not be restricted in its Supply . . . Can these duties, once remitted by Act of Parliament, be again reimposed?' Peel had written that, although reports from Ireland were often exaggerated, he foresaw the early necessity 'of considering whether there is not that well grounded apprehension of actual scarcity that justifies and compels the adoption of every means of relief which the exercise of the Prerogative and Legislation might afford'. Minor relaxations would not suffice. 'The removal of impediments to import is the only effectual remedy.'[2]

A potato famine would not become fully felt in Ireland until the spring. Time was therefore in hand, but action must be taken within a few weeks. An estimated three to four million Irish peasants depended upon potatoes as their basic food; and the British potato crop was only slightly less affected than the Irish. The Cabinet met on the last day of October, then again next day. But it could not agree what to do. Goulburn and others still believed that it would be morally wrong for a Conservative Ministry to propose repeal. He told Peel on 30 November that 'an abandonment of your former opinions now would, I think, prejudice your and our characters as public men'.[3] For Peel, however, the first consideration was the national interest as he saw it as a Minister of the Crown. Petitions for an opening of the ports began to flood in, encouraged by the Anti-Corn Law League. Then on 22 November Lord John Russell, the Whig leader, issued from Edinburgh a 'Letter to the Electors of the City of London', which announced his abandonment of support for a fixed corn duty and his conversion to advocacy of total repeal. This was a well-timed party move. Any Government action would now seem to be a response to Russell's letter. Peel felt annoyed that the Cabinet's long hesitation had left him exposed. He was not used to being outmanoeuvred by Russell.

In a Cabinet memorandum of 29 November Peel pressed the now un-avoidable question – were the Corn Laws to be maintained, modified or suspended? Peel recommended suspension, to be followed by consideration of 'the principle and degree of protection to agriculture'. He did not mention total repeal as such, but his mind was clearly running that way. Wellington replied with a short memorandum in favour of the Corn Laws; but still more in favour of any course of action which Peel deemed to be necessary. Peel submitted a

---

[2] Graham to Peel, 13 October 1845 (Add. MSS 40451, f. 376); Peel to Graham, 13, 15 October 1845 (Add. MSS 40451, ff. 380, 384); Graham to Peel, 8 August 1849 (Add. MSS 40452, f. 341).
[3] Peel, *Memoirs*, II, p. 201; and part III.

further memorandum to his colleagues on 2 December. He now stated plainly that he had become persuaded in favour of repeal in principle. 'I think, quite independent of present circumstances, that it would be true policy to relax protective duties, and that the experience of the past four years is decisively in favour of that policy.' He therefore proposed a plan for the gradual removal of all corn duties over an eight-year period. Only on 4 December did Lord Stanley and the Duke of Buccleugh declare their preference for resignation rather than support such a complete change of policy. That same morning *The Times* had published a sensational report which claimed that the Cabinet had agreed to call Parliament early in January to announce proposals for the total repeal of the Corn Laws.

Obviously, the crisis was now urgent. The public expected a statement from Peel. But what could he say? He had no time and no room for further manoeuvre. Resignation was the only course left. He had only just failed to carry an initially reluctant Cabinet with him. Reluctance had been strong because the famine in Ireland was not yet a visible fact, and because of doubts about the morality of a Conservative Government suddenly acting against the Corn Laws, at least so long as Russell and the Whigs were available to form an alternative Ministry. Peel claimed to be glad to resign from a 'thankless and dangerous Post', so as to leave the Whigs free to do what was necessary. He was tired, he told Fremantle on 19 December, of being tied 'to certain party Doctrines to be blindly followed whatever new circumstances may arise'.[4]

Peel had begun to argue for repeal of the Corn Laws as desirable in principle, even without reference to the prospective potato famine in Ireland. But a worrying link between the repeal question and the Irish crisis arose because of the existence of the Anti-Corn Law League, with its highly organized machinery for agitation. Peel and Graham were agreed that to ask Parliament for a million or more of taxpayers' money to feed Ireland, while still trying to retain the Corn Laws, would produce a clamour from the industrial districts orchestrated by the League which would threaten the whole social and political predominance of the landed aristocracy. 'The worst ground on which we can *now* fight the battle for institutions, for the just privileges of Monarchy and Landed Aristocracy, is on a question of food.' Promotion in the army, the Game Laws, the Church were already 'getting attacked with the aid of the league'.[5]

The revelation by *The Times* on 4 December was one of the most daring initiatives in Victorian journalism, long admired more than condemned even though it partly misled the public.[6] It was still remembered forty years later when George Meredith made his novel, *Diana of the Crossways*, turn upon a

---

[4] Peel to Fremantle, 19 December 1845 (Add. MSS 40476, f. 508).
[5] Peel to E. B. Denison, 7 January 1846 (Add. MSS 40532, f. 89).
[6] Sir E. Cook, *Delane of 'The Times'* (1916), pp. 20–30; *History of The Times*, II, pp. 12–14.

romantic but untrue explanation of how *The Times* had secured its information. This explanation, which enjoyed wide circulation in 1845–6, was that the leak had been sold to the editor by Mrs Norton, who was attached to a young Cabinet Minister, Sidney Herbert. *The Times* editorial made its dramatic announcement plainly in its opening sentences: 'The decision of the Cabinet is no longer a secret. Parliament, it is confidently reported, is to be summoned for the first week in January; and the Royal Speech will, it is added, recommend an immediate consideration of the Corn Laws, preparatory to their total repeal.' 'The thing must be done,' the article concluded, 'and it is Sir Robert Peel's common-sense and convenient view of the case that he is the actual Premier, and therefore bound to do it.' An angry Peel had forthwith to write to the Queen that the report was 'quite without foundation'. But no official contradiction appeared; and the reputation of *The Times* meant that its forecast was soon widely believed. This was reinforced when the *Standard*, which was regarded as the mouthpiece of Peel's Government, did not next day contradict *The Times* totally. On the evening of 4 December it did indeed dismiss the report as either a falsehood or a guess. '*We do not believe a word of it.*' And next day it came out with the headline 'ATROCIOUS FABRICATION BY THE "TIMES" ': 'THE CABINET HAS COME TO NO DECISION WHATEVER UPON THE SUBJECT OF THE CORN-LAWS.' But the *Standard* weakened the effect of its emphasis by making a point of explaining that it was not the Government's mouthpiece. It admitted that, with regard to what the Cabinet might come to decide, it could not therefore 'contradict the statement with truth'. It could only contradict from general confidence in Peel. 'The foul breath of the *Times* ought not to shake any one's confidence in an administration so well proved as that of Sir Robert Peel.'

Some official hint, however, does seem to have been made to the *Standard* at this time; for three months later (5 March) – when Peel's commitment to repeal was long known, and the *Standard* had separated from him – it complained how it had been duped in December: 'we contradicted *by authority*, being instructed (unconsciously on our part) to "tell a lie in the words of truth," an insult and an injury which we must ever remember.' Next day *The Times* gloated over this admission. The *Morning Herald* of 7 March then came to the aid of its companion paper by suggesting what *The Times* had actually done in December. The *Herald* argued that *The Times* had discovered only that Peel had proposed to his colleagues *some* change in the Corn Laws; how much change, it had only guessed at. It had then published 'a truth in the words of falsehood'.

The Times had indeed been guessing. But not about Peel's conversion; only about the Cabinet's solidarity. Delane, the editor of *The Times*, had been misled by Aberdeen, who had told him only half the truth – that there was now a strong repeal party within the Cabinet. He may or may not have expected Delane to risk announcing as an accomplished fact what seemed likely to happen, and what would have happened but for Stanley's and Buccleugh's late refusals. How *The Times* never knew as much as it pretended at this time was well illustrated by its prolonged ignorance, along with the rest of the press, of the fact that Peel had decided to resign after the Cabinet breakdown of 4 December. Aberdeen never told Delane, and the news did not come out for a whole week. Meanwhile, *The Times* stuck to its story. 'The Ministerial decision is by this time universally received not merely as a fact, but as the only thing that could have been done.' Such was the confident assertion on 9 December. The following day came the suggestion that the Privy Council to be held at Osborne might 'remove all doubt of the Ministerial determination in favour of an entire repeal of the Corn Laws'. Then on 11 December *The Times* had suddenly to admit that Ministers had visited Osborne only to resign. To justify its own earlier report, it claimed that a last-minute change of mind by the Duke of Wellington, who had gone back to defending the Corn Laws, was the reason for the unexpected fall of the Government. This was untrue, but it gave *The Times* the cover of a plausible explanation.

III

The Times went on to assert that although Wellington would not associate himself with repeal if introduced by Peel, he would not risk the survival of the House of Lords by organizing a majority there against a repeal measure proposed by Russell. It was certainly the case that the Whig leader now held the initiative, as Peel himself explained to the Queen and Prince Albert at an interview on 7 December. Peel regretted that his colleagues had been unwilling to suspend the Corn Laws early in November: 'there had been no agitation, everybody looking to the Government; as soon as they saw this wavering and hesitating, the country decided for itself, and Lord John has the merit, owing to his most dexterous move and our want of unanimity.'[7]

On 8 December Peel gave the Queen a promise, for communication to Russell, that he would support 'in a private capacity' any Whig proposal for gradual repeal of the Corn Laws. In this knowledge Russell set about trying to form a Cabinet, although he did so without enthusiasm. He feared fierce opposition to repeal from the House of Lords. He also wanted Peel to promise support not merely in general but in particular, to a finished measure which would be shown to him in advance. Peel refused to do this, on the ground that it would seem to verge upon concerted dictation to Parliament, and might actually reduce the chances of success. Under backbench pressure, Russell next began to argue for total and immediate repeal after a period of suspension. Peel told the Queen firmly that he was not willing to commit himself to this extreme

---

[7] A. C. Benson and Lord Esher (eds), *Letters of Queen Victoria* (1908), II, pp. 48–51.

version of repeal, the demand of the Anti-Corn Law League. There may have been a misunderstanding here, for Russell was later to tell the Commons that he had not required a positive pledge from Peel, only an assurance that he did not feel precluded in advance from supporting immediate repeal if it were to be proposed. Russell decided to act on the assumption that Peel's support in Parliament would be forthcoming, and the Whig leader entered into what was expected to be the final stage of Cabinet-making. But he then found that Lord Grey refused to join any Cabinet in which Palmerston was again to be Foreign Secretary. This personality clash proved too much for Russell, who had never been eager to face the crisis as Prime Minister. He refused to attempt to carry a contentious measure through Parliament with a weakened Cabinet, and so belatedly he told the Queen that he must give up.

Peel believed that Russell had been brought to failure by his procrastination. He deplored the Whig leader's refusal to serve his Sovereign at a difficult time. Peel's own reaction was now as swift and positive as Russell's had been hesitant. Upon seeing the Queen on 20 December, he offered to resume office forthwith, without waiting to discuss the situation with his former colleagues. In the national interest he was convinced that the Corn Law question must be resolved, and he was now sure that he was the only politician who could achieve this. In Peel's mind such considerations overrode any arguments claiming that he was bound to sustain the Corn Laws for party reasons, or for reasons of consistency. In his *Memoirs* he explained that he was acting in the same spirit as he had done in 1834, when William IV had called for his assistance even though Peel had recently opposed the Reform Act. He had not then felt inhibited by his past views; similarly, he did not now feel constrained by his previous support for the Corn Laws. He therefore returned from the Queen to his colleagues 'for the purpose of announcing to them that he was Her Majesty's Minister, and whether supported or not, was firmly resolved to meet Parliament as Her Majesty's Minister, and to propose such measures as the public exigencies required'.

With this high purpose before him, Peel's mood became suddenly buoyant. He was well aware that his position was now stronger than if he had simply stayed in office. Lord Stanley still refused to act with him; but the Duke of Buccleugh decided that in the new circumstances he could return to the Cabinet: 'recent events have rendered the measure proposed by you one of necessity, and no longer one of expediency'.[8]

How far would Peel go? For a month until Parliament met, speculation abounded. The staunchly protectionist *Morning Post* of 23 December forecast a compromise 10s duty, falling by 1s per year until a permanent duty of 5s was reached; it expected also reductions in county rates. The *Post* thought that such a change would satisfy no party; but described it as 'very like a Peel

---

[8] Buccleugh to Peel, 22 December 1845 (Add. MSS 40581, f. 196).

scheme'. This article was copied into the *Manchester Guardian* of 24 December, as was a contrasting article from the free-trade *Economist* a week later. This argued that Peel would not opt for compromise at all, but would go for repeal, in order to settle the corn question finally. Peel kept silent, as he nearly always did while maturing his great schemes, until the time came for presentation to Parliament. This reserve did not offend public opinion, rather the contrary. 'It was this solitary retentativeness, this determined reserve, that first procured him recognition as a master by the nation.' So wrote *Fraser's Magazine*, looking back from November 1846. The public welcomed Peel's silent acceptance of responsibility.

Some guesses, and some advice, accurately anticipated the spirit of Peel's eventual proposals. Sir Thomas Lethbridge, a Somerset landowner but a high farmer and keen free trader, wrote to Peel on 10 January 1846 to assure him that the yeomen and farmers of that county were ready to accept an opening of the ports; '& few ever *expect to see them closed again*.' Steadily growing population, continued Lethbridge, justified such action, provided that at the same time taxation was equalized between the various interests, so that land was not left overburdened. '*Land*, *Money* & *Trade*, all are *calling* upon you . . . The great body of the People are ready for this Immense Change, and you are the only *Person* in Existence that can do it.'[9]

Peel was indeed maturing just such a general plan. Simple suspension of the Corn Laws was now rejected, as was an eight-year timetable for gradual repeal. Peel decided instead to advance upon a broad front and to place the speedy, although not immediate removal of the corn duties within the context of a further round of tariff reform. This was an appropriate framework if repeal of the Corn Laws were to be justified as an application of free trade ideas; but it did seem to diminish the justification for repeal as a response to the Irish emergency.[10]

IV

Parliament met on 22 January 1846. Peel delivered his first big speech on the Corn Laws that same day; five other major Corn Law speeches followed on 27 January, 16 February, 27 March, 4 May, and 15 May.[11] In these orations Peel expounded and defended his case not only to the Members of Parliament in front of him but also to the public outside, where (as already noticed) his words were given unprecedentedly rapid and full publicity through the London and provincial newspapers.

[9] Lethbridge to Peel, 10 January 1846 (Add. MSS 40582, f. 208).
[10] Peel to Goulburn, 27 December 1845 (Add. MSS 40445, f. 286).
[11] See T. L. Fernandez, 'The speeches of Sir Robert Peel on the repeal of the Corn Laws'. Unpublished Ph.D thesis, Ann Arbor University, Michigan, USA, 1960.

Peel's speech on the Address described the December political crisis, 'the immediate cause' of which he identified as the Irish potato disease. But he freely admitted that this was not the main reason for his changed attitude towards the Corn Laws. 'I will not withold the homage which is due to the progress of reason and to truth, by denying that my opinions on the subject of protection have undergone a change.' He emphasized, however, that while others may have been persuaded by theoretical arguments alone, he had waited for theory to be borne out by observation. 'I have had the means and opportunity of comparing the results of periods of abundance and low prices with periods of scarcity and high prices.' He had found, first, that the free-trade policy inaugurated in 1842 had led to a drop in the cost of living, and to an increase in earnings. Secondly, that contrary to the doctrine of economists who favoured the Corn Laws, the level of wages did not rise and fall with the price of corn. Prices could be high even while wages remained low, thereby causing distress. Finally, he had been impressed by the way low prices and comparative abundance had brought a reduction in crime and disorder. All this had occurred while the level of protection was being reduced. Yet agriculture had not suffered. If the land bore particular burdens, as protectionists claimed, such burdens did not automatically justify a continuation of protection, for compensation could be arranged. Peel admitted that he would have preferred the next Parliament to take up the Corn Law question. But alarming reports from Ireland during the autumn of 1845, of which he gave long examples, had forced the issue forward. 'I must, for the public interest, claim for myself the unfettered power of judging.'[12]

Next day The Times remarked how Peel 'almost threw himself into the arena' by the urgency and frankness of his language. 'His case was plain. All theory, all reason, all instinct was against protection.' Such indeed was his theme; and John Blackwood, a hostile listener in the public gallery, noticed the 'gloomy silence' among the protectionist backbenchers behind Peel. Not a single cheer came from them.[13]

On 27 January Peel revealed his proposals in detail. Prince Albert was present in the gallery, which was rightly taken as a sign of royal support. This time Peel delayed discussion of the corn question until halfway through his speech. He began with a long list of articles for which he proposed the removal or reduction of duties, so continuing his programme of tariff reform. Disraeli was to describe later how Peel built up frustrated excitement among his hearers by going through this catalogue and by talking of manufactures before agriculture. While agriculturalists waited to hear the worst, Peel 'pursued at considerable length to the wondering assembly, an elaborate and argumenta-

---

[12] Peel, *Speeches*, IV, pp. 567–81.

[13] J. Blackwood to R. Blackwood, 23 January 1846 (National Library of Scotland, MS 4077, f. 286). Transcript kindly supplied by Dr Maurice Milne.

tive statement, the object of which was to reconcile the manufacturers to the deprival of protection'.[14] But if he addressed the manufacturers in general terms, he spoke to their workpeople by offering specific benefits. He proposed to reduce the cost of living through cuts in duties upon such items of everyday consumption as soap, candles, boots, shoes, butter, cheese, hops, and 'the clothing of the great body of the people'.

Disraeli recollected how 'with imperturbable gravity' Peel even read to the Commons a passage from Adam Smith, which asserted that country gentlemen and farmers were 'to their great honour, of all people the least subject to the wretched spirit of monopoly'. When interrupted at one point by a laugh of derision, Peel cleverly chose (as Disraeli noticed) to treat this as impatience with his businesslike methods; and so obtained a cheer of encouragement from the Opposition benches. As Disraeli said in his long-remembered phrase, Peel was playing upon the House as upon an old fiddle. Peel's purpose in taking this circuitous route was presumably to create a pent-up atmosphere in which his Corn Law proposals – however contentious – would be received with relief. Turning to the Corn Laws at last, he proposed a final settlement of the question; but not total and immediate repeal. To give time for agriculture to adjust, he recommended reduced duties upon foreign corn for three more years, with all protection to be removed on 1 February 1849. The duty upon wheat was to reach 10s when the domestic price stood below 48s, dropping to 4s, when the price touched 53s and above. Other cereals were to be treated comparably; and colonial corn was to be admitted at a nominal duty.

Peel then turned to his proposals intended to compensate and to assist agriculture, compensation which was to become effective ahead of repeal. These measures sought not only to remove burdens but also to encourage more efficient farming. He recommended a reduction of the seed duties, and free importation of maize and buckwheat. This last reduction was intended to lower the cost of fattening cattle, not least with an eye to one very material benefit of increased numbers; for Peel remarked that the best fertilizer for improved agriculture was still manure. Helped in this way, Peel argued that up-to-date farmers would be able to withstand any increased foreign competition under free trade. Peel also proposed improved rural highway administration; abolition of the law of settlement, which unfairly allowed town authorities to return rural immigrants to their country parishes; public loans for land drainage; removal from the counties of costs of prosecutions and custody; and the assumption of central financial responsibility for Poor Law medical officers and school teachers.

Disraeli remembered how this compensation was immediately felt to be inadequate by the protectionists. But Peel in his peroration declared that he was moved by a higher purpose than keeping his backbenchers in good

[14] Disraeli, *Bentinck*, pp. 66–75.

humour. He wanted to maintain social peace in the manufacturing districts. There would be, he admitted, no great present danger to the public peace if the Corn Laws were continued. Agitation against them was certainly growing, for there had been 'a great change in the opinion of the great mass of the community'. This included the working classes. But the masses were not yet agitating violently. Yet they might do so if trade depression were to return. Peel wanted to act before this happened. He had been particularly impressed by the way class cleavage in the manufacturing districts was now being bridged by a shared desire for repeal of the Corn Laws. 'There is between the master manufacturers and the operative classes a common conviction that did not prevail in 1842 or at a former period – that it will be for the public advantage that these laws should be repealed.' Middle and working-class people were alike expecting Parliament to respond, and it would be a serious mistake in social and political psychology for Parliament to refuse to do so.[15]

Politicians and the public were now left to digest Peel's plan until 9 February, when the first great Commons debate opened. If the unexpected construction of Peel's speech had been intended to blunt protectionist resistance, it failed to do so. Charles Greville suggested (28 January) that even moderate Conservatives had been insufficiently rallied by its deliberately unrhetorical tone. A comprehensive plan had been revealed, but it remained in need of forceful exposition. This it started to receive when Peel made his next speech on 16 February. Peel had by this time begun to understand not only the bitterness of the hostility among the protectionists, but also that the Conservative party was becoming permanently split. Over a hundred backbenchers spoke against their leader during this first debate, which extended from 9 to 27 February. Paradoxically, the emergence of this irreconcilable opposition from his own side gave Peel a new freedom. He now began to sound like a statesman who was not merely acting apart from his own party, but who was making an appeal above all party. His speeches from 16 February onwards were straightforwardly in favour of repeal and free trade. And so was his private correspondence. He wrote in March to Sir Henry Bunbury, a large Suffolk and Cheshire landowner who supported repeal, about the misrepresentation and obloquy heaped upon him by those 'whom I verily believe I am protecting from Evils and dangers of which they seem little aware'. But he emphasized his indifference to party consequences, so long as his measures passed first the Commons and then the Lords. 'This Country is now very quiescent, but the calm is the consequence of full reliance that the Measures must speedily pass.'[16]

Peel's speech of 16 February was therefore much sharper than his speech of 27 January, more incisive in argument and more pointed against the protectionists. He dismissed the idea that he should have raised a cry of

[15] Peel, *Speeches*, IV, pp. 582–604.
[16] Peel to Bunbury, 12 March 1846 (Add. MSS 40585, f. 351).

protection for native industry 'to animate and please a party'. By May this would have left Ireland in famine. Nor should the Corn Laws be merely suspended: 'the fact of suspension would be a condemnation of the law.' He recommended high farming to increase yields and to increase the demand for agricultural labour. Nevertheless, he emphasized how he was looking beyond agriculture by proposing a programme of tariff reform which treated repeal of the Corn Laws within a broad economic and social context. His peroration left no doubt that he believed the protectionists to be not merely wrong but reactionary. 'This night you will select the motto which is to indicate the commercial policy of England. Shall it be "advance" or "recede"?'[17]

The vote at the end of the debate on 27 February revealed the extent of the Conservative split. Two-thirds of Peel's party had turned from him: 231 voted against, only 112 for. It was Opposition votes, added to those of the Peelites, which gave Peel his majority of 97.

The Anti-Corn Law League remained very much in the background throughout these weeks. C. P. Villiers's annual Commons motion for total and immediate repeal, introduced on 2 March, was voted down by 265 to 78. Peel refused to support immediate repeal, for he was sure that it could not hope to pass. Moreover, despite the claim that surprisingly many protectionists preferred a sudden ending of the Corn Laws to a drawn-out process, Peel favoured gradualism even in the application of right policy: 'great public measures cannot be carried by the influence of mere reason.'[18]

On 27 March Peel spoke on the second reading of the Corn Importation Bill. He was met with ironical cheers from the protectionist ranks when he claimed attachment to the prosperity of agriculture and the 'just influence' of the landed interest. He argued that his measures were designed to promote such prosperity and influence. But he made plain that his first concern was for the working classes. He spelt out in detail and by example the relief which his tariff changes, including Corn Law repeal, would bring to working-class budgets. 'This is by far the most important aspect under which you can view the question.' Peel's peroration anticipated his own fall once repeal had been passed. 'When I do fall, I shall have the satisfaction of reflecting that I do not fall because I have shown subservience to a party. I shall not fall because I preferred the interests of party to the general interests of the community.'[19]

Peel's fifth major Corn Law speech on 4 May did admit that the adjustment process might bring 'some temporary suffering' to those upon the land. But under free trade combined with high farming, agriculture would soon find a

---

[17] Peel, *Speeches*, IV, pp. 605–26.

[18] Lord Radnor to Peel, 2 February 1846; Peel to Radnor, 4 February 1846 (Add. MSS 40584, ff. 48, 50); Wynn to Peel, 16 February 1846; Peel to Wynn, 17 February 1846 (Add. MSS 40585, ff. 99, 101); Peel, *Speeches*, IV, pp. 634–7; McCord, *Anti-Corn Law League*, pp. 200–4.

[19] Peel, *Speeches*, IV, pp. 637–55.

sound prosperity which would sustain 'the legitimate influence and authority of a territorial aristocracy'.[20] In his last Corn Law speech on 15 May Peel boldly based his argument not simply on the ground of temporary scarcity in Ireland, but also upon his belief in the need to make 'a permanent adjustment'.[21] He presented this as the true 'conservative' policy. This adjective was printed without a capital 'C', a reflection of how it now mattered much more to him in qualitative than in party terms:

> if I look to the prerogative of the Crown – if I look to the position of the Church – if I look to the influence of the aristocracy – I cannot charge myself with having taken any course inconsistent with conservative principles, calculated to endanger the privileges of any branch of the legislature, or of any of the institutions of the country.

Peel's peroration closed with a passage which emphasized the psychological importance of repeal, in showing non-electors that the system of government had their interests at heart, even though they possessed no votes:

> My earnest wish has been, during my tenure of power, to impress the people of this country with a belief that the legislature was animated by a sincere desire to frame its legislation upon the principles of equity and justice. I have a strong belief that the greatest object which we or any other government can contemplate should be to elevate the social condition of that class of the people with whom we are brought into no direct relationship by the exercise of the elective franchise. I wish to convince them that our object has been so to apportion taxation, that we shall relieve industry and labour from any undue burden, and transfer it, so far as is consistent with the public good, to those who are better enabled to bear it ... I look to the increased and growing public confidence on account of the course you have taken in relieving trade from restrictions, and industry from unjust burdens; and where there was dissatisfaction I see contentment; where there was turbulence I see there is peace; where there was disloyalty I see there is loyalty; I see a disposition to confide in you, and not to agitate questions that are at the foundations of your institutions.

Peel, in short, was presenting himself more deliberately than ever before as a Prime Minister who cared; who (to repeat the phrase which was first attached to him by the ten-hours delegates in 1841) indeed 'had a heart'.

Peel thus made an effective ending to his speech of 15 May. Yet at first he had almost broken down under a storm of jeers from his own side of the House. A few minutes earlier Disraeli had delivered one of his most scathing personal

---

[20] Ibid., pp. 679–87.
[21] Ibid., pp. 687–96.

attacks, in which he had described Peel's whole career as 'a great appropriation clause. He is a burglar of other's intellect . . . all confidence in public men is lost.' Peel could just about bear Disraeli's barbs in themselves; and indeed he dismissed his enemy in a few sentences at the beginning of his speech. But the audible contempt of his former followers was hard to absorb over the weeks, as the protectionists succeeded in drawing out the debates to the maximum extent. At the close of Peel's speech, Disraeli sprang up to deny that he had ever solicited office or favours as Peel had briefly indicated. Yet Disraeli had certainly done so; and it remains a mystery why, then or later, Peel did not produce the evidence which would have discredited his tormentor. But Disraeli's modern biographer has suggested that, even so, many contemporaries probably believed Peel rather than Disraeli.[22]

The third reading was finally carried by a majority of 98, with 106 Conservatives voting for the Government and 222 against. Peel's Chief Whip reported that the Peelite faithful numbered 117 in all. Five Conservatives who had previously voted against repeal had deliberately absented themselves from this vote. Such late conversions were never going to be many. On the other hand, the rallying effect of Peel's speeches kept the more than one hundred open Peelites behind their leader through each major division. In the country the Peelites were proportionately much greater in numbers than at Westminster. The free-trade *Liverpool Mercury* (30 January) claimed that Peel's speech of 27 January would change the opinions of thousands of influential people, 'for thousands will read it with respectful attention who would not so read any other free-trade speech'. A Bedfordshire magistrate explained to Peel how 'before your exposition, I was what is termed a Protectionist. Your speech and Prepositions have converted me.'[23]

V

The protectionist case against Peel and repeal rested partly on reasoned argument, partly on emotional reaction. Peel was resisted, first, on grounds of economic principle; secondly, on the ground that he was capitulating to Anti-Corn Law League clamour; thirdly, on the ground that the compensation offered to agriculture was inadequate; fourthly, on the ground that his change of mind over the Corn Laws was an act of treachery, made worse by his willingness to remain as Prime Minister in order to manoeuvre through the new policy.[24]

No fresh economic arguments in favour of the Corn Laws were now

[22] Blake, *Disraeli*, pp. 237–9.
[23] T. A. Green to Peel, 31 January 1846 (Add. MSS 40583, f. 400).
[24] Fisher, 'Opposition to Sir Robert Peel', ch. VII; R. Stewart, *The Politics of Protection* (1971), ch. 2.

advanced. All possible points had been made long since. Many of them had been elaborated in articles in *Blackwood's Magazine* down the years. Four main arguments in defence of the Corn Laws have been found in its pages. That a transfer of resources from agriculture to industry would be socially disruptive; that foreigners would not necessarily buy more British goods in return for increased grain imports, and so there might be no new industrial jobs for displaced agricultural workers; also that additional foreign grain would be expensive to grow, and consequently any increased importation would lead to rising prices; and finally, that foreign grain supplies were uncertain and liable to be cut off in time of war.[25]

The charge that Peel was capitulating to clamour from the Anti-Corn Law League was widely made in 1846. It directly rejected Peel's claim that repeal was a conservative measure, well designed to maintain as much as possible of the status quo. Many of the League leaders were known to want radical political reform. The Duke of Richmond told the Central Agricultural Protection Society on 12 January 1846 that repeal was but a first step for the Leaguers: 'they feel that it is the yeomanry of England that stand between them and the democratic principles which they wish to carry out.' Peel countered by also referring to the bogy of democracy. He argued that the decision of the Protection Society to fight the League with its own weapons by intervening in by-elections would 'tell ultimately in favour of democracy when the excitement of the moment shall have subsided'.[26]

Although complaint about the inadequacy of the proposed compensation for agriculture did not constitute opposition in principle, in practice it justified firm resistance to repeal, since the help demanded far outran what Peel was offering. In effect, the expectation was for continued special treatment for the landed interest. The demand was for a sweeping away of burdens imposed by rates, taxes, tithes and the malt tax. Instead of abolishing the malt tax or transferring local rates into general taxation, Peel promised only small direct reliefs, plus the prospect of greater competitiveness through high farming. Experience was indeed to show that Peel's reliefs brought only limited benefit over the next few years. High farming required more free capital and individual initiative than many small landlords or tenants could command. They might try new fertilizers, but they were less likely to risk the long-term commitment required for drainage or use of new machinery. Some landowners were reluctant to relax control of their estates by granting the long leases necessary to justify tenants in making improvements. Conversely, many tenant farmers did not wish to bind themselves through long leases, a reluctance which Peel himself encountered on his Drayton estate.[27]

[25] F. W. Fetter, 'The economic articles in *Blackwood's Edinburgh Magazine*, and their authors, 1817–1853', *Scottish Journal of Political Economy*, 7 (1960), pp. 98–9.

[26] *Morning Herald*, 13 January 1846; Peel, *Memoirs*, II, p. 265.

It was widely said, both at the time and later, that Peel had mishandled the presentation of his case for repeal of the Corn Laws. Greville (16 February) argued that Peel's step-by-step progress in favour of free trade had made his speeches misleading. 'He was so afraid of saying too much at first, and of prematurely frightening his friends, that he ran into the opposite danger of confirming them in the convictions and expectations which it was his object to loosen.' Lytton Bulwer's poem, *The New Timon*, published during the Corn Law crisis and claimed by its publisher to be the best-selling poem since Byron's day, pictured Peel as slyly cautious:

> Sir Robert rides – he never rides at speed –
> Careful his seat, and circumspect his gaze;
> And still the cautious trot the cautious mind betrays.
> Wise is thy heed! – how stout soe'er his back,
> Thy weight has oft proved fatal to thy hack!

Lytton Bulwer was well-disposed towards Russell, but not towards Peel. 'This stupendous treachery of Peel's excites my gall.'[28]

Such a charge of treachery was the predominant cry from the protectionist ranks, both inside and outside Parliament. The kindest thing that some protectionist Members could say about Peel was that he had gone mad. Colonel Sibthorp, a diehard Tory, expressed himself on 2 March: 'sorry to see the Treasury benches so infested with the noxious animals called rats'. The same charge was put with more restraint by C. N. Newdegate, who represented Warwickshire, on 20 February: 'such conduct as that of the right hon. Baronet, overbearing the opinion of his Colleagues; concealing his principles, to take the country by surprise; working by force upon those who had long followed him, until he had overborne their better judgment; and then going over to their adversaries, and adopting their policy – such conduct was not the conduct of a constitutional Minister.'

Greville at the time (16 February), and Guizot later, pointed out how especial emphasis was given in the speeches of the protectionists to the charge of treachery: 'bitter lamentations and reproaches, and quotations from former speeches or addresses of the Ministers who are now abandoning them'. Disraeli and Lord George Bentinck gave the lead here. Bentinck delivered his first speech against Peel on 27 February. His assaults laboriously deployed economic facts and figures, but it was (as Guizot noted) 'always with considerations of honour and political fidelity that he commences and

---

[27] D. C. Moore, 'The Corn Laws and high farming', *Economic History Review*, second series, 18 (1965), pp. 544–61; E. L. Jones, *The Development of English Agriculture, 1815–1873* (1968), pp. 27–30; T. L. Crosby, *English Farmers and the Politics of Protection 1815–1852* (1977), ch. 5.

[28] Lord Lytton, *Life of Edward Bulwer, First Lord Lytton* (1913) II, pp. 69–76, 82, 501.

terminates his attacks'.[29] Disraeli adroitly emphasized on 20 February how the protectionists did not complain because Peel had changed his opinions: 'but that he has outraged public opinion – that he has prevented its legitimate action in the settlement of questions by the aid of party, or embodied public opinion'. For Russell to propose free trade in corn was legitimate. Yet Peel, who had promised to uphold the Corn Laws, was himself leading the way in their repeal, and without even consulting the electorate.

Personal attacks upon Peel may have satisfied the feelings of protectionists inside and outside Parliament, but they were unlikely to sway non-party opinion. The Whig *Globe*, quoted by *The Times* of 4 February, suggested why they were counter-productive, even helpful to Peel's reputation as a statesman moving above party:

> the English people will hardly be satisfied to be told that their Minister was elevated to his post to be the tool of a faction; nor will they accept these wretched *argumenta ad hominem* as a substitute for sound logic and common sense. We seek to get a repeal of the Corn Law. It is no answer to tell us that Peel is a shuffler or a traitor. Abuse of the individual is no reason against the measure which he brings forward; if anything, it is an argument against the Tories themselves, for having so long employed as their factotum a man who now deserts their cause because it is utterly incapable of support.

In the same spirit, Sidney Herbert hoped on 15 February that the public would be 'rather disgusted to see a debate on such a subject as this occupied almost exclusively by personal & party crimination'.[30]

Peel had expected more rational argument in debate. He wrote on 7 January how he had persuaded Members from South Lancashire and the West Riding (Lord Francis Egerton and Becket Denison) to propose and to second the Address. He thought that such a choice of representatives from two major industrial counties 'should have great weight with the Rational and prudent'. He expressed confidence that he would carry his measures, including repeal, because he was seeking only to extend policies which had already proved successful:

> I can demonstrate that every thing that has been done has been for the benefit not merely of the Community at large but of the Agricultural Interest. Wool bears a higher price than it did before the reduction of the duty on foreign Wool. So does Meat. So do Bullocks and Cows, and Sheep about which there was such absurd panic. The Agricultural labourers have been better off this Winter and the last than they were before.[31]

[29] Guizot, *Peel*, pp. 272–3.
[30] Herbert to Lincoln, 15 February 1846 (NeC 11930).
[31] Peel to Arbuthnot, 7 January 1846 (Add. MSS 40484, f. 263).

Such economic points took no account of the charge that Peel had shown disregard for his Conservative followers in Parliament by failing to call a party meeting to explain his intentions. In debate on 9 February A. J. B. Hope, a protectionist Member for Maidstone, remembered how in 1842 Peel's followers had been primed about the spirit of the Address in advance of the opening of Parliament. But 'a total change in the whole commercial system of the empire' was now brought forward without prior warning or discussion. Peel was tired and over-strained, and this may have been the reason why he made no gesture of consultation towards his backbenchers. But he later sought to justify his apparent negligence by claiming that there was no time when he could have consulted his backbenchers to his or to their satisfaction. He used this explanation in a letter to Lord Aberdeen in 1847, which he reprinted in his *Memoirs*. By 1847 Peel was claiming that he had realized how he could not both carry repeal and keep his party united; and that he was prepared to sacrifice the latter 'subordinate object' in the public interest. Peel claimed that private lobbying of individual Members, or the calling of a party meeting would have changed very few minds. 'I should have appeared to have been flying in the face of a whole party, contumaciously disregarding their opinions and advice after I had professed to consult them.' Peel was determined to carry repeal, and he believed that purposeful disregard of his party was necessary to such an end. He told the King of the Belgians on the first day of 1846 that it had ceased to be possible to take the easy course of governing according to the old opinions of the Conservative majority. Such opinions were 'no safe guide' for the good government of Ireland or for commercial policy. Parliamentary parties were not so well informed as Ministers, who must retain the right to decide.[32]

In his *Memoirs* Peel answered the charge that his sudden change was damaging to trust in public men. He admitted the risk; but he believed that it would become apparent that he was acting honourably by putting the national interest before party interest, or before his own continuation in office.[33] Obviously, Peel would have preferred not to have hurried forward before he had prepared his party to accept the case for repeal as part of overall free trade. Just when he intended to reveal himself is not certain. He gave Prince Albert the impression in December 1845 that he had planned to tell his party of his changed attitude towards the Corn Laws in advance of a general election in 1847. In this same spirit he told the Commons on 22 January that in normal circumstances 'another Parliament' would have been left to consider the Corn Laws. In his *Memoirs*, however, Peel wrote that it had been his intention 'to enter into that friendly communication, the omission of which is blamed and

[32] Peel to the King of the Belgians, 1 January 1846 (Add. MSS 40581, f. 327); Peel to Aberdeen, 19 August 1847 (Add. MSS 43065, f. 322); Peel, *Memoirs*, II, pp. 322–4.

[33] Peel, *Memoirs*, II, pp. 167–9.

lamented, to apprise the Conservative party, before the Corn Law could be discussed in the Session of 1846'.[34]

Although Peel had probably anticipated repeal being an issue at the next general election, he had no desire for a general election to be called in 1846 to secure a majority for his measures. He regarded this as a 'democratic' course, such as the Whigs had followed during the Reform Bill crisis, which should be avoided except as a last resort. He was determined to collect, if possible, a majority within the existing House of Commons, even if it comprised more Opposition than Conservative votes. The protectionists cried out for a dissolution of Parliament; but Peel was eager to emphasize that it was the responsibility of the two Houses of Parliament to decide matters of policy, not the responsibility of the electorate directly. Moreover, as he explained in his *Memoirs*, a general election dominated by the repeal question would have produced a bad House of Commons, whose Members would have lacked independence because they were tied by pledges. Finally, and not least, such an appeal to the constituencies 'would ensure a bitter conflict between different classes of society'.[35]

Peel would have sought a dissolution only if his Corn Bill had been defeated in either the Commons or the Lords. Croker, in the *Quarterly Review* for March, hoped that the peers would indeed reject the measure and so force a dissolution. The protectionists professed to believe that they would win a majority in a general election. But while they were strong in the counties, many Peelites were well entrenched in small borough constituencies. It has been estimated by two modern historians that the outcome of a general election called in 1846 would have been similar to the result of the 1847 election, when a clear majority of free traders (Peelite, Whig, Liberal and Radical) was returned. This was also the opinion of Peel's contemporary biographer, J. C. Symons. He contended, however, that this likely outcome made Peel's refusal to recommend a dissolution indefensible. 'The course he took was to induce his followers in Parliament to break faith with their constituents, instead of announcing his change of policy and dissolving Parliament.' Defeat in a few constituencies, continued Symons, would have helped to reconcile the protectionists to the ending of the Corn Laws. Conversely, victories for Peelites in their constituencies would have maintained the political honour of converts to repeal.[36]

---

[34] Peel, *Speeches*, IV, p. 572; Peel, *Memoirs*, II, p. 318; Queen Victoria, *Letters*, II, pp. 65–6.

[35] Peel to the King of the Belgians, 19 December 1845 (Add. MSS 40581, f. 170); Peel to Arbuthnot, 24 April 1846 (Add. MSS 40484, f. 309); Peel, *Memoirs*, II. p. 166. See also Betty Kemp, 'Reflections on repeal of the Corn Laws', *Victorian Studies*, 5 (1962), pp. 189–204.

[36] J. C. Symons, *Sir Robert Peel As a Type of Statesmanship* (1856), pp. 164–5; W. D. Jones and A. B. Erickson, *The Peelites, 1846–1857* (1972), pp. 22–3.

VI

Admittedly, the by-elections of early 1846 ran in favour of the protectionists, by sixteen victories to eight. But the protectionist successes had come mainly in county seats where sitting Members had resigned because they felt unable to vote against Peel's scheme. Uncertainty persisted for several weeks about possible resignations over repeal. For example, Lord Mahon contemplated retiring, not from Parliament, but from his junior office in Peel's Government. He wrote to the Premier on 22 December 1845 that he 'could be no party' to repeal. Peel answered that he could not reveal details of his plan, and would leave it to Mahon to decide whether to resign now or to wait until he knew what was proposed. Mahon decided to wait; and in the end, after hearing Peel speak on 27 January and sounding opinion in his Hertford constituency, he became a reluctant convert. He had noticed, he told Peel, how every Member who held, or had ever held Cabinet office, as well as such respected back-benchers as Lords Ashley, Sandon and Francis Egerton, were all prepared 'to agree with, or to acquiesce in, the measures you propose'. Out of doors he observed not only the agitation of the Anti-Corn Law League, which might have been withstood; 'but also some doubt & uncertainty amongst the Conservatives, arising from your speech on the first day of the Session'. Many of Mahon's leading constituents in Hertford had urged him to support Peel. 'Under all these circumstances of public feeling within & without the House of Commons,' Mahon had decided, 'very reluctantly but decidedly' to vote with the Government because maintenance of the Corn Laws had become impossible. Peel answered that Mahon was taking 'the manly & honourable course'.[37]

Here, therefore, was clear evidence of constituency pressure in support of Peel. Mahon's agent, Philip Longmore, had been sounding out Hertford opinion. The feeling among leading local Conservatives was that the 'cheap bread' cry would become irresistible. Also the local leaders themselves liked Peel's plan. Mahon frankly admitted that he was acting under the influence of such constituency opinion. 'Had my Constituents seemed in general to take another course from that which your letter shows I doubt very much whether I should have felt justified in receding from the opinions in favor of the Corn Laws which I expressed at my Election & which I still retain.' Mahon was also aware that if he and others had helped to vote down Peel's plan, the protectionists would have been unable to form a stable Government. So

[37] Mahon to Peel, 22, 25 December 1845; Peel to Mahon, 24 December 1845 (Add. MSS 40581, ff. 240, 242, 301); Peel to Queen Victoria, 26 December 1845 (Add. MSS 40440, f. 460); Mahon to Peel, 29 January 1846; Peel to Mahon, 30 January 1846 (Add. MSS 40583, ff. 267, 269); Peel, *Memoirs*, II, pp. 260–3.

support for Peel was the sensible course. Lord Salisbury, who possessed the greatest influence in the constituency, supported Mahon's action on the ground that if Cabinet Ministers were willing to sacrifice their opinions for Peel, it was justifiable for a junior Minister to follow suit. None the less, Mahon exclaimed to Bonham on the same day as he sent his final decision to Peel, how he had never before felt so much perplexity. At the 1847 general election he felt it necessary fully to explain his decision in his published election address.[38]

Lord Mahon does not seem, however, to have explained himself in the Commons in 1846. Perhaps he felt it imprudent for a Minister to reveal the qualified nature of his support for official policy. But Lord Sandon, one of the Members for Liverpool, who seems to have held similar views to Mahon but who was not in the Government, did speak out in the Commons on 9 February. He declared that he remained unconvinced by Peel's arguments against the Corn Laws. What would happen to tenant farmers when the corn price fell, or to agricultural labourers who would then be laid off? Yet Sandon accepted that the country must be governed; and (like Mahon) he had noticed how all those who were qualified to govern had come out against protection. It could not stand 'when unsupported by the authority of great names'. The protectionist *Liverpool Courier* (18 February) noted this speech from its local Member of Parliament, and answered that the proper course was to call a general election. If a free-trade House of Commons were returned, 'then Lord Sandon and such as he might with character give way to necessity, but only after doing their best against the measure.'

One Member who came under constituency pressure to resign, but who manoeuvred successfully not to do so, was Wilson Patten from North Lancashire. He issued an ambiguous address to his constituents, and then claimed that hundreds had responded by urging him to stay in order to vote for repeal. Like Lord Mahon, Wilson Patten explained himself at the 1847 general election. He was then returned without a contest because, as he reported to Peel, 'notwithstanding the dissatisfaction which prevailed respecting my corn law & Maynooth votes' nearly all his former supporters had promised their votes again.[39]

Peel himself never had any intention of resigning his Tamworth seat because of his change of policy. When told in February 1846 that moves were afoot in the constituency to ask for this, he remarked that Tamworth had 'not flourished much' under protection. He also adopted the high line that he was not 'a local delegate' but 'an independent member of a great legislative

[38] Longmore to Mahon, 25, 31 January 1846; Mahon to Longmore, 29 January 1846; Mahon to Bonham, 29 January 1846; Salisbury to Mahon, n.d. (Stanhope MSS); A. Newman, *The Stanhopes of Chevening* (1969), pp. 264–5.

[39] Patten to Peel, 6 August 1847 (Add. MSS 40599, f. 108); D. Foster, 'The politics of uncontested elections: North Lancashire, 1832–1865', *Northern History*, 13 (1977), pp. 240–1.

Council'.[40] On this same ground he tried to discourage others from resigning their seats because he had persuaded them of the need for repeal. Nevertheless, Lord Ashley and H. C. Sturt both insisted upon retiring from Dorsetshire, as did Lord Henniker from East Suffolk, W. H. Dawnay from Rutland, F. Charteris from East Gloucestershire, Lord Arthur Lennox from Chichester and Sir Thomas Fremantle from Buckingham.

Lord Ashley was determined to resign; but he had at first been willing to stand again. He pointed out in a speech on nomination day how in a letter to his constituents in the previous October he had noticed that Peel and Russell were both moving towards repeal; and how he had himself advocated 'gradual abolition'. He was therefore no sudden convert. He had found, however, that the by-election contest would be fierce and expensive. He could not afford to stand. He felt unable to accept £2,000 collected by Bonham, a collection which had included contributions from Peel and Graham. Ashley feared that to do so would limit his independence if elected. In consequence, with Sturt also declining to stand again, two protectionists were returned unopposed in February to vote against repeal.[41]

Another uncontested by-election occurred in January 1846 at Newark. Gladstone, the sitting Member, had been required to vacate the seat on appointment as Colonial Secretary in Peel's reconstructed Cabinet. The Duke of Newcastle was a staunch protectionist, and his influence in the constituency was sufficient to make it difficult for Gladstone to stand again, even though some local Conservatives remained well disposed towards him. Embarrassing offers of support from Liberals and Leaguers only confirmed Gladstone in his decision to withdraw. As a result, he was to remain frustratedly out of Parliament throughout the rest of Peel's time in office.[42]

The Duke of Newcastle was even more influential in South Nottinghamshire, where in February his estranged son, Lord Lincoln, stood for re-election upon appointment as Chief Secretary for Ireland. Lincoln believed that, even if only after strenuous canvassing, he might retain the seat against the influence of his father. In this hope, Peel took a close interest in the contest. He concluded that not only would victory provide a great boost to the cause of repeal, but that it would constitute a desirable rebuff for what he regarded as improper interference in freedom of election, either by individuals such as the Duke of Newcastle or by outside organizations such as the protection societies.

---

[40] S. Palmer to Peel, 4 February 1846; Peel to Palmer, 5 February 1846 (Add. MSS 40584, ff. 178, 180).

[41] Ashley to Peel, 31 January, 5 February 1846; Peel to Ashley, 1 February 1846 (Add. MSS 40583, ff. 365, 367, 368); *The Times*, 20 October 1845, 10, 16, 20 February 1846; E. Hodder, *Life and Work of the Seventh Earl of Shaftesbury* (1887), pp. 338–41; G. B. Finlayson, *The Seventh Earl of Shaftesbury* (1981), pp. 242–8.

[42] Shannon, *Gladstone*, pp. 189–90.

Peel told the Queen that 'dictation' to Members of Parliament had reached 'dangerous lengths'.

Peel assisted Lincoln with his election address. It attacked the Central Protection Society for allegedly attempting to dictate to constituency opinion. Lincoln accepted the right of constituents to be told his opinions in full, but he repudiated the idea that a Member of Parliament should be regarded as a delegate. He explained how his views on the Corn Laws had been gradually changing. 'Three years ago my confidence in the principles of Protection was shaken – last year I felt they had become indefensible.' He had hoped, however, that the 'inevitable change' could have been delayed until the meeting of a new Parliament. This would have avoided 'violent shock to party attachment'.

Lincoln wrote to Peel almost every day during the by-election campaign. By 18 February Lincoln was admitting that the odds were against him. It was not, however, a matter of all the local influence, or of influence alone, being wielded against him. Most farmers, both owner–occupiers and tenants, were genuinely opposed to Corn Law repeal. On the other hand, Lincoln did win over some landowners, and these brought the votes of their tenants more or less willingly with them. So freedom of election was not wholly practised on the Peelite side, any more than on the protectionist side. Lincoln noted how his prospects were injured by the accident that as Irish Chief Secretary he was Visitor of Maynooth College. 'It is placarded all over the County . . . the damage it will do is not to be told.' Memories of the Maynooth episode were to remain strong in many constituencies into the 1847 general election. One Nottinghamshire rector wrote to explain why, after first promising his vote to Lincoln, he had eventually abstained, because he had been reminded of Lincoln's support for the increased Maynooth grant. A farmer wrote to say that although he admired Lincoln's election address, he remembered the surrender of Wellington and Peel to Catholic clamour in 1829; now they were about to surrender to the clamour of the Anti-Corn Law League. After repeal, claimed the farmer, prices would fall so low that tenants would be unable to pay their rents.[43]

Lincoln's father, the Duke of Newcastle, took the unusual step for a peer of intervening directly in the election proceedings. He issued an 'Address to the Inhabitants of South Nottinghamshire'. This attempted to turn round Peel's attack on 'dictation' by asking 'why should any one from authority be sent as a Government Emissary to force upon us opinions which we hate?' *The Times* (21 February) wondered sympathetically why Lincoln had thought it 'worthwhile' to put his father in such a 'cruel and embarrassing position'. Five days

---

[43] Peel to Queen Victoria, 4 February 1846 (Add. MSS 40441, f. 76); Lincoln to Peel, 6, 7, 10, 12, 15, 24, 25 February 1846 (NeC 12109, 12110a, 12111, 12115, 12157/5); G. Barron to Lincoln, 18 February 1846 (NeC 4619); Lincoln to ?, 26 February 1846 (NeC 4597). Rev. T. White to Lincoln, 24 March 1846 (NeC 4600); Election expenses statement (NeC 4643b). See also J. R. Fisher, 'Issues and influence: two by-elections in South Nottinghamshire in the mid-nineteenth century', *Historical Journal*, 24 (1981), pp. 155–65.

later, after Lincoln's defeat, *The Times* blamed Peel for driving Lincoln to act in public against his father. Lincoln's failure was decisive. He polled only 1,049 votes, against 1,736 for the protectionist candidate, T. B. T. Hildyard. The by-election cost Lincoln £1,281 9s 10d, all of it borrowed.

'The risk is great but there are times when it is politic to incur great risks.' So Peel had written of the South Nottinghamshire contest. While that campaign was proceeding, the excitement of contest had led him to countenance a second risky by-election, in hopes of endorsement for his new Corn Law policy. 'I have thoughts of vacating Westminster,' he told Lincoln on 10 February, 'and fighting a battle at the door of Parliament.' By this Peel meant that he was offering office to Captain H. J. Rous, the sitting Member for Westminster. The seat was traditionally Radical; but Rous had won it as a Conservative in 1841, and now assured Peel that he could hold it at the necessary by-election. Few informed observers agreed with Rous. Sir John Cam Hobhouse, who had himself once represented the constituency as a Liberal Radical, deplored the forcing of an unnecessary contest, for which his party would feel bound to field a candidate who would defeat Rous: 'a very foolish move on the part of Peel'. The Liberal candidate, Sir De Lacy Evans, was a long-standing free-trader, which could not be said of Rous, a recent convert. Many prominent politicians had votes in the constituency. Peel himself cast the second vote for Rous; but Russell and others of his party polled for Evans. So did Disraeli, along with perhaps a hundred Conservative protectionists engaged in tactical voting. Evans won on 18 February by 3,843 votes to 2,906.[44]

Rous blamed the combination of parties for his defeat. Peel answered tartly that he had expected Rous to have allowed for this in his calculations. *The Times*, on the day after the election, made the perceptive point that 'Conservative apostates' could not expect to share 'the condonation that is awarded, for the sake of his individual importance, to the leader of the great apostasy'. Peel at least had the consolation of knowing that Evans would vote as readily for repeal as Rous would have done. But the Westminster episode showed that party loyalty among free traders in the constituencies was not to be ignored.[45]

VII

The enduring strength of feeling among the protectionist minority both in the Commons and in the country quickly became clear during February 1846. The

---

[44] Rous to Peel, 28 January 1846 (Add. MSS 40583, f. 229); Hobhouse's Diary, 11, 12, 14, 15, 16, 18 February 1846 (Add. MSS 43748, ff. 41–9).

[45] Rous to Peel, 19 February 1846; Peel to Rous, 19 February 1846 (Add. MSS 40585, ff. 142, 144); Queen Victoria to Peel, 15, 19 February 1846 (Add. MSS 40441, ff. 98, 106).

protectionists were now well organized inside and outside Parliament, a development which Peel had not anticipated. Sidney Herbert was admitting by 11 February that the breach between the Peelites and the protectionists was irreconcilable. 'Nothing could be more hostile than the House last night.' The worst construction, complained Herbert, was being put upon the motives of the Peelites by their former party associates. Once repeal had been carried, he felt that the sooner the Government resigned the better.[46]

Peel was to keep the allegiance of only one-third of the parliamentary Conservative party. Four categories of opinion have been identified among the 112 Peelites who voted for repeal on 27 February.[47] First, enthusiastic free traders; secondly, those who emphasized the need to end a controversy between agriculture and industry which had become dangerous to society; thirdly, those (such as Lord Sandon) who wanted Peel as Prime Minister, even though they had doubts about his Corn Law scheme; and fourthly, a category with miscellaneous and even idiosyncratic reasons for following Peel. These Peelites included many landowners. It has been calculated that 97 Conservatives with landed connections voted for the third reading of the Corn Bill on 15 May, and 215 against. Repeal would never have passed but for the support of Liberal and Peelite landowners in a predominantly landed House of Commons and a still more predominantly landed House of Lords. Admittedly, 86 per cent of Conservative English county Members voted against repeal, whereas only 54 per cent of Conservative English borough Members did so. But the social backgrounds of most county and borough representatives were equally agricultural. Constituency opinion, expressed in the same way as to Lord Mahon at Hertford, helped to decide which way these Members voted. Representatives of the larger and more urban boroughs (those with over 500 electors) were more likely to follow Peel than those from smaller, rural boroughs.[48]

In the countryside, larger landowners who had capital to spare, and who were perhaps already committed to high farming, were more inclined to favour repeal than country gentlemen. Small owner–occupiers and tenant farmers were (as in South Nottinghamshire) the most solidly hostile. A. S. O'Brien, a Member for North Northamptonshire, made on 10 February one of the best speeches from the protectionist side while arguing that protection was largely a tenants' question. 'We will not aid you in your triumph over these poor men,' he told Peel. Such tenants formed the bulk of the membership of the county protection societies which sprang into activity during December, January and February. Pressure from these angry farmers kept many protectionist Members

---

[46] Herbert to Lincoln, 11 February 1846 (NeC 11929).

[47] Jones and Erickson, *The Peelites*, ch. 6.

[48] W. O. Aydelotte, 'The country gentlemen and the repeal of the Corn Law', *English Historical Review*, 82 (1967), pp. 47–60; Fisher, 'Opposition to Sir Robert Peel', ch. 7.

of Parliament up to the mark, against repeal and in favour of a dissolution. What had been only a tendency towards separation from Peel, even after the Maynooth crisis a year earlier, now became a reality. Maynooth voting by Conservatives was mirrored in Corn Law voting. Of 162 Conservatives who voted against the increased Maynooth grant, only 20 supported Corn Law repeal, and 133 voted against.[49]

Bentinck and Disraeli did not themselves cause the split in the Conservative party. They simply consolidated it by articulating the complaints against Peel. At a meeting of the Central Protection Society on 28 January, the day after Peel had revealed his plan, Bentinck made his first appearance among the protectionists. This meeting established, as Disraeli remembered, 'a third political party'. Lists of debaters were drawn up; a party committee was appointed; a party office was opened; and the form of the protectionist amendment to set off the first Commons debate was settled.[50]

Had Peel initially expected to keep his party united? Did he hope to persuade most of his backbenchers of the need to accept repeal? Or if not, did he at least expect, after he had carried repeal with Opposition votes, that his back-benchers would relapse into acceptance of his continued leadership? Such a relapse had occurred after the Maynooth crisis. The evidence about Peel's thinking is contradictory. Gladstone was to claim six years later that on returning to office in December 1845 Peel had spoken confidently, as if he had expected to carry his party with him. It may be, however, that this confidence referred only to carrying the repeal measure, regardless of any party split. On 5 February 1846, after his plan was known but before the Commons debates began, Peel was still writing hopefully. He forecast that when 'passion, prejudice and mistaken views of self-interest' had dissipated, there would be 'a very general and cordial approbation' of his policy. If this meant that Peel was still expecting to convert most of his party, the hostile temper of the debate which opened four days later quickly disabused him. By 11 February he was already admitting to the Queen that 197 Conservative Members were expected to vote against him, and not more than 123 for him. 'This is of course a very heavy blow to the Government.'[51]

Peel was now resigning himself to dependence upon well over 200 Opposition votes to make up his Commons majorities. He hoped that this would still enable him to outvote the protectionists by the comfortable margin of about 100, 'in order that the Peers may not be encouraged to resistance'. It was partly with the Lords in mind that he had proposed gradual repeal. Peel

---

[49] Stewart, *Foundation of the Conservative Party*, pp. 194–5.

[50] Disraeli, *Bentinck*, pp. 56–7.

[51] Peel to C. Harding, 5 February 1846 (Add. MSS 40584, f. 159); Peel to Queen Victoria, 11 February 1846 (Add. MSS 40441, f. 86); Brooke and Sorensen, *W. E. Gladstone III*, p. 79; Gash, *Peel*, II, p. 567, n. 1.

was eager to get his measure smoothly and quickly through the Lords, not only for the national good, but also for the sake of the upper house itself. He believed that rejection by the peers, perhaps forcing a dissolution of Parliament, would put the whole future of the second chamber in question. He did not wish to upset the balanced constitution of Queen, Lords and Commons. Nor did the Duke of Wellington. His dragooning of Conservative peers, plus pressure from Russell upon reluctant Whig peers, induced a majority to acquiesce in repeal. The Corn Importation Bill, which had finally passed the Commons in the early hours of 16 May by a majority of 98 (327 to 229), passed the Lords on 25 June. On the same day Peel's Government was defeated in the Commons on its Irish Coercion Bill.

VIII

Whatever might be happening to his party, Peel's popularity was extending rapidly during these months. The more he was attacked in the Commons, the more his appeal from above party drew a favourable response from all but firm protectionists outside Parliament. He was regarded by middle opinion not as a politician to be blamed for betraying his party, but as a statesman who was sacrificing himself in the national interest. The Times of 6 July 1846, writing after Peel's resignation, summed up 'the one great cause for this general and intense apprehension of Sir Robert Peel's merits'. It was not merely that he had carried his Bills: 'the singular merit of the statesman in the popular eyes is his unprecedented sacrifice to attain a good for his country.' He had given up place, power and show of consistency; he had braved all abuse; he had fully admitted his past errors of judgement. 'In a word he sacrificed the individual to the nation. All is paid, with interest.'

Popular willingness to support Peel in 1846 was reinforced by his already established reputation as a financial expert; and also by the complexity of the Corn Law question. The Wakefield Journal (12 June 1846), a moderate protectionist paper, noticed how the Corn Laws were 'at all times a most perplexing subject' because the public was 'only half informed. It is impossible to listen to a discussion on these laws in the most enlightened assembly without at once perceiving that many important elements relating thereto are omitted or unknown.' In such circumstances very many people were prepared to trust Peel's judgement. Thus the Chartist Northern Star of 31 January welcomed 'the ALL-MIGHTY measures of this mental Hercules'. J.G. Lockhart, editor of the Tory Quarterly Review, remarked that Peel's speech on the Address had 'if possible raised the general notion of his capacity'. Lockhart found even 'in quarters not at all kindly to him, a sort of vague feeling that somehow or other he must govern England while his vigour lasts'. Peel himself was told how eight out of the ten Bedfordshire magistrates were ready to welcome his proposals, 'not so much from a *knowledge* of their probable effects, as from their great confidence in your judgment & integrity'.[52]

The growth of trust in free trade was reflected by the calm way in which various industries received the prospect of tariff changes designed to remove or reduce their own protection. A *Morning Chronicle* (9 February) survey of Midland opinion reported such acceptance among the Birmingham metal trades, the Nottingham lace trade and the Northampton boot and shoe trade. Paradoxically, prosperity under the Corn Laws was said to have led Lincolnshire farmers to view repeal with '*comparative indifference*'. This seems to have been the case even though all the Lincolnshire county Members voted against the third reading of the Corn Bill.[53]

Peel himself was satisfied that opinion was proportionately much more in his favour outside Parliament than inside. He told the Queen in February that 'the Country generally, as distinguished from mere party is in favour of the measures proposed.' Prince Albert noticed in a letter to Peel on 1 March how Members of Parliament seemed to be 'less open to reason than the mass of the People'.[54] While the protectionists continued their delaying tactics at Westminster into the summer, Peel remained keen to hear about the state of outside opinion. In June Charles Arbuthnot passed on a letter in which Lady Westmoreland had reported the views of Charles Villiers, the League leader. Villiers had apparently remarked that if a general election were called, all the towns would return Peelites. The City of London, for which Russell sat, would much prefer Peel. City businessmen reasoned that upon a question 'where so much is said on both sides, & upon which our own minds are not made up, we feel that the safest course is to trust to him who has proved himself the greatest financier of the day'. Peel answered Arbuthnot that his accounts of public opinion 'tally with mine, but it is very important to me to have a confirmation from other sources of the intelligence I receive'.[55]

Peel may have sensed that a majority of newspapers, London and provincial, had declared in favour of repeal of the Corn Laws, even though no one in his circle seems to have analysed press reaction. But Peel and his colleagues certainly read the chief London publications. And at least some of the younger ones saw *Punch*; on Christmas Day 1845 Sidney Herbert was asking Lord Lincoln if he had seen the latest number. In 1848 this same pair were to be prominent in buying the *Morning Chronicle* for transformation into a Peelite mouthpiece. Between 1846 and 1848 there was no daily paper committed to

[52] T. A. Green to Peel, 31 January 1846 (Add. MSS 40583, f. 400); *Notes and Queries*, 189 (1945), p. 124.

[53] R. J. Olney, *Lincolnshire Politics 1832–1885* (1973), pp. 117–19.

[54] Peel to Queen Victoria, 11 February 1846; Prince Albert to Peel, 1 March 1846 (Add. MSS 40441, ff. 86, 120).

[55] Arbuthnot to Peel, 8 June 1846, enclosing Lady Westmoreland to Arbuthnot, 8 June 1846; Peel to Arbuthnot, 8 June 1846 (Add. MSS 40484, ff. 321, 323, 327).

Peel, once the *Morning Herald* and *Standard* had refused to follow him over repeal. It was a reflection of the above-party nature of Peel's growing popularity that the lack of a mouthpiece hardly mattered in 1846. His reputation seemed to rise almost regardless, independently not only of abuse from the protectionist papers but even of the varying degrees of support, from tepid to warm, expressed by the rest of the press.

Peel did not convince Croker and the *Quarterly Review* of the need for Corn Law repeal. Croker had written to Peel on 28 November 1845, after publication of Russell's Edinburgh letter, to emphasize that any change in the Corn Laws would be 'the ruin of the Monarchical party'. Yet he had heard rumours that some members of the Government favoured modification. Croker explained that he did not wish to act without receiving Peel's advice, 'if you think it proper & worth while to give it'. But Croker made it clear that he felt bound by what the *Quarterly* had said in defence of the Corn Laws in articles published during Peel's Ministry. All these articles, remembered Croker, had been given Peel's approval before or after publication, including the one as recent as September 1843. 'It may happen that you should have some difficulty in answering this, or you may be willing to let the press take its own unbiased line. In either case you will take no notice of this letter.' And that was what seems to have happened; for by 17 December Croker was warning Peel that he had written an article without having received any inside information, an article which defended the Corn Law sliding scale 'and our doctrine of 1841–2'.[56]

This piece in the December *Quarterly* marked the beginning of a permanent breach between Peel and Croker, after a political and personal friendship which had lasted almost forty years. Further articles from Croker appeared in the March and September 1846 numbers. These included regretful attacks upon Peel personally. 'We speak of Sir Robert Peel's share in the whole of this unhappy affair with the deepest pain.' Croker blamed Peel not merely for changing his policy, but for doing so disingenuously and damagingly, since (as Croker saw it) Peel was using the Irish potato famine as an excuse to bow before the clamour of the Anti-Corn Law League. This put in danger such national institutions as the Church of England, the monarchy, the House of Lords and primogeniture, all of which were under threat in the programme of the League Radicals. The breach between the two men, which had been tacit, became open after an exchange of letters in January 1847. In the June 1847 number of the *Quarterly* a final article by Croker appeared on 'Peel Policy'. Peel himself was seen by Samuel Wilberforce as he read this article while travelling back from Cambridge: 'peeping into its uncut leaves with intense interest, and yet not liking to show that interest by cutting'. The article accused

---

[56] Croker to Peel, 28 November 1845 (Add. MSS 40580, f. 5); Croker to Peel, 17 December 1845 (Add. MSS 40581, f. 126); Jennings, *Croker*, III, pp. 40–73.

Peel of a 'secret design' to repeal the Corn Laws. 'But the difficulty was to find a practical excuse and opportunity.' This attack was said to have enraged Peel, and to have provoked the writing of the self-defence which he published soon afterwards as his 1847 election address.[57]

Like the *Quarterly Review*, *Blackwood's Magazine* refused to follow Peel. An article on 'Ministerial Measures' in the March 1846 issue could find no new grounds for abandoning its belief in the Corn Laws. But *Blackwood's*, unlike the *Quarterly*, made a point of saying that it did not believe that Peel had succumbed to fear of the Anti-Corn Law League. It confessed that it could find no explanation at all for Peel's change. In the same month, *Fraser's Magazine* was accepting that only Peel could carry repeal. It drew, however, an unexpected conclusion from the fact of Peel's unique position. *Fraser's* felt that this did not give Peel a good reason for pressing forward, since it meant that the time was not right for change. If repeal did pass, Peel ought certainly to retire straight afterwards. 'For, whether the country thrive or not under the new system which he has devised for it, in him no human being can hereafter repose confidence.' Peel's views were too liable to alteration: 'he claims for himself the privilege of changing his opinions whenever he chooses, and insists that others shall change theirs in like manner.'

Among the weeklies, the *Spectator*, which had backed Peel strongly throughout his Ministry, stayed with him over Corn Law repeal. It noticed approvingly (24 January 1846) how, while a demagogue Minister might have used the people's fear of famine to ride roughshod over opposition, Peel was presenting a reasoned argument for a coherent 'revolution in commercial policy'. Six months later the *Spectator* (13 July) was left with one regret: 'The Corn Laws are abolished – but so is Peel.' From being the leader of a clique, he had become 'the leader of a nation . . . There must be something rotten in the thing called Party which can force from office the very man whom the country would choose, at the very height of his popularity and power.'

The Liberal *Examiner* welcomed repeal as a policy; but, like *Fraser's* and unlike the *Spectator*, it was doubtful about Peel's position in politics as a result of his action. When he returned to office with acclamation, the *Examiner* (27 December 1845) remarked unsympathetically that there was always 'a great liking for the roguish servant who tricked everybody'. It complained (24 January) that Peel's first statement to Parliament of his new views assumed too readily that his own course had been the best way. 'Other men who had before come to the same conclusion, were mere abstract reasoners, it seems, and had none of those practical lights that had guided him.' In fact, explained the *Examiner*, the Leaguers had long based their arguments upon experience. But by 31 January it was ready to admit that Peel's 'great scheme' had far exceeded its expectations, even though it would have preferred total and immediate repeal. Why delay such a benefit for three years, and risk continuous protectionist agitation?

Despite such questioning, by 1 March the *Examiner* was describing Peel's policy as indispensable, although it remained unenthusiastic about Peel himself. 'Peelservatism has attained a frantic pitch. Mr. Hume will soon give notice of motion to vote the Premier divine honours – Janus's of course.' With the enactment of repeal in sight, the *Examiner* of 20 June was still refusing to join unreservedly in the popular admiration of Peel.

> The popularity of what at best is next to a death-bed repentance is only the express sign of the demoralization . . . A portion of the public is becoming of opinion that honesty is not the best policy . . . Both the hatred and the popularity that follow Sir Robert are in bad extremes and of evil tendencies. He makes the worst enemies and not the most principled friends.

After Peel's defeat, the *Examiner* (27 June) took the line that his conduct out of office would settle the doubts about his character, 'whether politics with him is a game, or a high patriotic duty'.

The *Illustrated London News* started in December 1845 with as much reserve towards Peel as the *Examiner*, but it was to end much warmer. It was glad (13 December) to see him retire because his administration had continued too long as 'a Conservative Ministry governing upon Opposition principles', which amounted to 'political immorality'. But a fortnight later the *Illustrated London News* was describing the general satisfaction at Peel's return to office, because he was accepted as the only man able to conduct an effective Government. It listed some of the reasons for this sense of relief. The railway interest was glad not to lose its bills because of a dissolution; the friends of peace were glad to escape from Palmerston as Foreign Secretary; the landed interest had decided that only Peel could continue the system of protection, even if reducing it: 'and make terms in case even he finds it impossible to preserve the system'. The *News* itself hoped for the introduction of a corn duty which would diminish year by year. Its number for 3 January 1846 dwelt upon the growth of urban population, and the attendant risk of a mass food shortage. 'To govern such masses is an awful responsibility.' The issue of 31 January complained that Peel's repeal plan followed too much of a middle course. The *News* assumed, however, that a general election would be called, when 'the verdict of the people' would decide. By 30 May its attitude towards Peel had softened considerably. Too much virtue could be claimed for political consistency, it wrote, in answer to its own argument of 13 December. 'To-day is not as yesterday.' A month later (27 June) it was explaining away Peel's past career, and regretting his present fall. Peel had been misplaced first among the

Tories, then among the Conservatives: 'his mind, on every question, appears to have been always advancing.' This was to be an often repeated argument in Peel's favour, both in 1846 and at his death four years later.

The *League*, the official organ of the Anti-Corn Law League, was predicting on 1 November 1845 that Parliament would be recalled to suspend the Corn Laws, without prospect of restoration. It seems to have known that Peel was wanting decisive action, and that he was being frustrated by his Cabinet; for in its next number on 8 November it reported that 'the landlord faction has triumphed . . . The ports are not open – Parliament is not summoned – Sir Robert Peel does not resign. Of the "three courses" which, as the premier is so fond of saying, were "open to him," he has chosen neither.' The *League* emphasized that Peel would therefore be personally responsible for the forthcoming famine. '*He* is the Ministry.' On 15 November it carried quotations from newspapers in favour of opening the ports, adding a week later that over fifty leading provincial papers favoured such action. When *The Times* made its revelations, the *League* (6 December) advised that if, 'after all', Peel was to be 'the Free Trade Minister', he should be supported. When Peel eventually revealed his plan, he was criticized (31 January) for not proposing total and immediate repeal, as demanded by the League. Five days after Peel's speech of 16 February, however, he was being praised for his 'new heart, energy and eloquence . . . since he has sunk the party politician in the statesman'. Similarly, Peel's speech of 27 March was welcomed for its evidence of careful enquiry into the details of working-class life. 'Our poor man's financier dwells with kind-hearted satisfaction on those alleviations of the burden which his own policy has effected, and appeals to the human sympathies of his auditors, to include further among the exempted the chief article of all . . . We feel deeply grateful to Sir Robert Peel for this speech.'

If the Lords were to reject the Corn Bill, the *League* of 23 May felt sure that 'the people's Minister' would call a general election, with a cry for total and immediate repeal. Yet the *League* accepted that Peel had been right not to make an early appeal to the electors. It was to his credit that he had taken his bill to the existing Parliament, 'which involved the *minimum* of eclat, and the *maximum* of odium and unpleasantness for himself individually'. When Peel resigned, the *League* (27 June) praised him for understanding how 'self-sacrifice' would be necessary to ensure the prosperity of his country. 'He descends from power just as he had attained the summit of popularity.'

The *League* does not seem to have been aware of the paradox that the official organ of the Anti-Corn Law League, a body which Peel still regarded with deep distrust, should by its writing have helped to boost his popularity. *The Struggle*, the lively anti-Corn Law publication from Preston, came to a similarly favourable conclusion about Peel. Its proprietor, Joseph Livesey, wrote in its final June number how Peel's adoption of free trade was 'one of the most discreet, sagacious, and dignified acts of statesmanship the world ever witnessed'. Peel was pictured as 'one who gratefully received enlightenment from the people, and gave the people in return the copious blessings of trade, peace, and plenty'. Peel himself would have been dismayed to notice such a ready assumption that he had been directly influenced by 'the people' through the Anti-Corn Law League.

IX

How did *The Times* – which to Peel's annoyance had in 1843 accepted the League as a 'great fact', and which also to his annoyance had heightened the political atmosphere by its revelations on 4 December 1845 – how did the most widely read newspaper react during the final Corn Law crisis? Its revelations had been made in dramatic rather than friendly terms. Thereafter, it supported the policy of repeal, but it was to remain at best tepid in its assessment of Peel himself. When on 22 December *The Times* wrote that it was now for Peel to make plain that he had finally shaken off party constraints, Lord Lincoln wondered if this meant that 'amicable relations' could be established between the paper and the Ministry.[58] *The Times* had written how Peel had resumed office 'certainly not as a Tory Premier – that he never was – but not even as a Conservative. He must now be the *popular* Premier.' Lincoln tried to use J. D. Cook as an intermediary with Delane, the editor. But Delane went his own way, unwilling to qualify the independence of his paper. He was reported to be confident that Peel would propose a bold measure.[59] And the paper was not disappointed when Peel's scheme was at last revealed. *The Times* of 28 January welcomed the plan as 'a microcosm of commerce and finance. Like as in a gothic building, its multiplicity of parts and exactness of proportion are as much its merits as the greatness of the whole.' Farmers, according to the paper, would not suffer as much as they feared; manufacturers did not want any protection; dying trades, such as handloom weaving, were beyond saving, so that all the state could do was to encourage the prosperity of alternative occupations through free trade. *The Times* did suggest that the compensation proposals were over-generous, and it regretted the three-year delay in repeal; but its general tone was decidedly favourable. It was much less sympathetic, however, towards the man behind the measures. It discussed Peel's personal position after he had made his major speech of 16 February. It found this speech 'only too successful . . . He has crushed all objections, but they were his own; he has demolished a party, but he was once its leader; he has revealed a great crisis, but that crisis is the catastrophe of his own life's drama' (18 February).

---

[58] Lincoln to Cook, 22 December 1845 (NeC 12169).
[59] J. Blackwood to R. Blackwood, 14 January 1846 (NLS MS 4077, f. 280).

On the previous day *The Times* had picked out three shades of right-wing opinion in the Commons. Old Tories were appalled at Peel's apostasy; unthinking Conservatives, who had not understood 'that the fruits of the Reform Bill were yet to be put forth', were angry at the prospect of losing influence and favours; other Conservatives defended Peel only at the expense either of his judgement or his integrity. 'They applaud the policy, but denounce its author.' *The Times* then emphasized why public opinion was right to be unafraid of repeal:

> history should also record a fact more striking than the present collision of parties in Parliament, or of opinions in the clubs. Whilst the Carlton is indignant, the Conservative pettish, and many boudoirs plaintive, there is a slow and gradual mutation taking place in the minds of the community . . . men do not augur any evil from the proposed changes. Previous experience has taught them that great changes can be effected in England without damaging the character or safety of our institutions.

By 5 March *The Times* was accepting the three-year delay cheerfully enough, albeit still in barbed terms with regard to Peel. 'It would be too much – a transcendant, superhuman, and dangerous success – for Sir Robert Peel to carry immediate and entire abolition.' When a dissolution of Parliament was rumoured, *The Times* of 22 April saw little sense in the protectionists forcing such a confrontation in the constituencies. The paper was sure that they would lose, especially in the boroughs.

On 30 May *The Times* discussed Peel's handling of his party. It claimed that his method had been to drive his backbenchers 'into a cul de sac, of which he should himself retain the key'. Such had been his way over Catholic Emancipation; and he would have repeated it over parliamentary reform if the Whigs had not managed for once to snatch the initiative. During thirty years, the editorial concluded, the Peel method had produced 'much essential good, but not without considerable detriment to the credit of statesmen and parties'. By 10 June *The Times* was forecasting the formation of new parties to do the political work of the next generation. The condition of England question would require more positive state intervention than the existing parties contemplated. So would legal reform and charity reform. 'Who has heart, or nerve, or sinew, to grapple with the Irish landlord?' The great problems of the day were everywhere discussed, 'and receive every other than a Parliamentary solution'.

By the third week in June the likelihood was that Corn Law repeal would pass the Lords, but that Peel would be defeated in the Commons over his Irish Coercion Bill. Even if not so defeated, *The Times* of 24 June was arguing that Peel must resign because of the sugar question. The sugar duties must now be removed, and Peel himself seemed to have become persuaded of the need. But

The Times was sure that he ought not to undertake for a second time to propose as Prime Minister what he had previously opposed.

Peel duly resigned, although not at the prompting of *The Times*. Its commendation was still muted, notwithstanding Peel's great popularity in the country. *The Times* of 30 June conceded that, except in Ireland, the Peel administration had done well since 1841. It had brought commercial prosperity, and also 'the palms of peace and the laurels of war'. Peel had been lucky as well as skilful, with the result that he was now popular. 'Unquestionably with those whose favour is called popularity, he is more popular just now than he has ever been.' Yet how much smoother would have been the path for both Peel and his country if he had seen the right way ahead much sooner:

> How long was it urged as a solemn obligation on all devout Conservatives to abhor the League, and anathematize Cobden? Popular movements of all sorts were denounced as injurious to good order . . . Now, from the lips of the Premier, we are told that the name of Richard Cobden is associated with one of the greatest measures of social reform known to modern times.

Such was 'the fallibility of party'.

Given that party was so fallible, Peel's new stance above party might have been expected to earn him the endorsement of *The Times*, which had always emphasized its independence from party attitudes. Instead, *The Times* chose to continue to emphasize its distance from Peel as well as from party. In this important instance, it declined to endorse fully that middle-class majority opinion which it usually humoured and rarely contradicted. It admitted and described the enthusiasm of the majority for Peel; but its retrospect of 1846 remained unadmiring in its explanation of how he had gained his great popularity. *The Times* (1 January 1847) praised the victories in India, and the Oregon settlement with the United States. It also welcomed repeal of the Corn Laws. But it described repeal as a victory achieved by 'a powerful combination and the vindictive treachery of a self-confiding egotism' – in other words, by the Anti-Corn Law League and Peel together. Peel was remembered as having cunningly contrived to outmanoeuvre both protectionists and free traders. 'He filched from the latter a prize which he could not have won without their aid, and from the former a *prestige* which they had gained only through his own.'

It might have seemed unlikely that the *Morning Chronicle*, long an Opposition critic of Peel, would have ended up better disposed towards him than *The Times*, with its reputation for independence. Yet the unlikely gradually happened. In November 1845 the *Chronicle* was already pressing hard for repeal of the Corn Laws, even before publication of Russell's Edinburgh letter. It denounced Peel's Government for its apparent reluctance to act in the face of prospective famine. 'Indignation is, for the moment, lost in astonishment' (11 November). 'That "Sir Robert Peel has a heart, after all," we did not take it on ourselves to affirm very positively; but we certainly never supposed him to have the nerves of iron which he will need between now and next February.' The *Chronicle* was certain that the Corn Laws could not last many months longer. 'Public opinion has doomed them' (18 November). Peel must be forced into action, notably by the Anti-Corn Law League, which the *Chronicle* of 20 November refused to fear as 'Jacobin or Destructive'. There was 'a law of free countries' that a feeling of great grievance produced 'an association of the many'.

The *Morning Chronicle* of 26 November naturally welcomed Russell's Edinburgh letter. It pointed out on 2 December that the Whig leader had now made it easy for Peel to come out in favour of repeal, since he would have the votes of a large part of the Opposition to outweigh those of his own protectionist diehards. The *Chronicle* of 6 December was dismissive about the accuracy or otherwise of *The Times* revelations over Peel's Corn Law intentions, for it was convinced that 'the public mind' would insist upon repeal. Perhaps surprisingly, the *Morning Chronicle* was not especially encouraging towards Russell during the December political uncertainty. It felt that he should only take office if he was sure of being able to carry repeal. Repeal would pass more easily if Peel remained in charge. By 17 December the *Chronicle* was accurately reporting that Peel had now become a total, even though not an immediate, repealer. Peel's resumption of power was therefore welcomed. 'He possesses certain extraordinary and valuable faculties for undoing his own work' (22 December).

Underlying fears that Peel would lapse into compromise were removed by his speech on the Address, which the *Chronicle* of 24 January praised as the speech 'of a statesman and a man', because it revealed a new naturalness and earnestness. Peel's detailed plan was welcomed four days later. It went as far as the *Chronicle* had dared to hope, even though the paper would have preferred immediate repeal. Protectionists blamed Peel, noticed the *Chronicle* of 17 February, for arousing feeling in favour of repeal. 'They make a personal affair of it.' But the free-trade movement had been 'quite independent of him'. Nevertheless, the *Chronicle* was now prepared to give Peel steady support for rising above party constraints. 'He has lost with his party, but he has gained with the country' (15 March). When the protectionist *Morning Herald* charged the *Morning Chronicle* with whitewashing Peel, the *Chronicle* (7 May) answered that it praised Peel's present policy, not his past conduct. An overall judgement of Peel as a politician had better be postponed until repeal had passed. Yet even with the Corn Laws abolished, the *Chronicle* still delayed committing itself. Peel's career after resignation would eventually decide his reputation in history – whether he was a statesman or not. In this context, the *Chronicle* found his resignation speech a hopeful omen. Peel's tone suggested 'that the moral aspects of the new epoch of the late Premier's life which is to explain and redeem everything' would be 'such as to place him finally right with his country' (30 June).

The *Morning Chronicle* had therefore moved some way towards Peel: the *Morning Advertiser* moved further. As the organ of the licensed victuallers, it always claimed to stand above party, and this helped it to soften towards Peel during 1846. As early as 3 November 1845 the *Advertiser* was accurately reporting divisions in the Cabinet over the Corn Laws; and it published 'A Threnody on the Approaching Demise of Old Mother Corn-law' by Tom Moore. Wellington was reported on 11 November to have gained 'a triumph over the Premier'; but Peel was described as still determined to repeal the Corn Laws. Nevertheless, his slowness in following 'the bold and manly course' was portrayed as likely to cost large numbers of Irish lives. 'Such a man can have no pretensions to statesmanship' (17 November). The *Advertiser* of 6 December accepted *The Times* revelations about Peel's intentions as substantially correct. When, however, Peel had resumed office, the *Advertiser* (30 December) feared that he would settle for half measures. 'His name will go down to posterity as the Medium Minister.' On 1 January, though, the *Advertiser* reacted in the same spirit as *Punch* to the extreme attacks being made upon Peel by some protectionist papers. 'Englishmen love justice. Why deny it to Sir Robert Peel? Give even *him* praise where he deserves it . . . Who could have imagined in July 1841 that we should begin the year 1846 with a vindication of Sir Robert Peel from Tory assailants?'

Peel's speech on the Address was praised in the *Advertiser* of 24 January for its 'manliness'. Whereas Peel's conversion in favour of Catholic Emancipation had been a case of 'expediency', he was now acting from 'conviction'. Peel's detailed proposals were welcomed overall, although the *Advertiser* of 31 January would have preferred immediate repeal, and also equalization and reduction of the sugar duties. By 2 March the *Advertiser* was even wondering if, having turned round on the Corn Laws, Peel would go further. 'Will they believe it, that Sir Robert is already understood to have some predilections for the ballot? Let not this be dismissed as a joke.' With so much left in need of reform, the *Advertiser* argued on 27 March that the country could not do without Peel. His departure from office would be 'a great public calamity'. If defeated in the Commons, Peel should not resign but should appeal to the people, who would make him their Minister (10 June). The *Advertiser*'s thinking here was very much like Cobden's in his letter of a fortnight later to Peel; and Peel's eulogy of Cobden in his resignation speech was warmly received by the *Advertiser* (1 July) as an indication of Peel's supposed new reformist leanings.

The first number of the new *Daily News* on 21 January 1846 carried a leading article which demanded repeal of the Corn Laws. The paper wanted its support for the Anti-Corn Law League to be clearly understood. On 23 January it welcomed Peel's speech on the Address as evidence that the free-trade principle was about to be fully recognized, as demanded by the people and their teachers. The *News* of 29 January praised Peel's tariff proposals, but it did not think that his compensation measures would disarm the protectionists; nor would free traders be satisfied with less than immediate repeal. A general election was expected, and the *News* of 2 February regretted that Peel's 'compound of complication and compromise' would not provide a good election cry. Soon after this, John Forster took over from Charles Dickens as editor. Forster's *News* praised Peel on 10 February for deciding to concentrate upon the corn duties. 'We have not been lavish of praise on the Premier's manner of introducing his improvements, however much we rejoice in the improvements themselves. But in this instance he has well earned a lively expression of gratitude.' Peel's speech of 16 February was highly commended next day:

> It is seldom that statesmen or orators, on the Tory side of politics, can draw from that great source of inspiration – the feeling that they struggle for popular rights, and minister to the necessities of the people. Sir Robert Peel seemed, however, to have felt the charm and the power of that inspiration, and felt it the more from its being new.

Peel's speech of 27 March was, however, criticized next day by the *News* for giving too much attention to self-justification. On 23 April the Premier was described as a tactician, not a statesman. 'He wants the simplicity and determination of true greatness. He strives for good objects by petty means.' He had wasted time over the Corn Bill, and he had gone wrong by introducing the Irish Coercion Bill. The *News* of 1 May concluded that Peel had 'two souls': 'the partisan and the patriot, the sophist and the statesman'. In the same spirit, by 12 June the *News* was describing Peel as running into imminent danger of becoming known to posterity as a Minister who narrowly missed greatness. Yet ten days later the paper was hoping that Peel would stay in office, even though it also hoped that his Coercion Bill would be defeated. The *News* believed that Peel could find a majority for further reform. To throw up office because the Commons refused to sanction 'his paltry and peevish Curfew Bill' would show him to be less of a statesman than even his enemies conceded. The *News* of 27 June claimed that Peel would himself have been willing to ally with the Whigs and Liberals to promote further commercial reform and conciliatory measures for Ireland; but that Goulburn and Gladstone had raised difficulties over the sugar duties, on grounds of 'personal consistency'. So at the last Peel ceased to be the object of even selective complaint by the *News*. Indeed, his resignation speech drew high praise. His willing personal sacrifices for a great object were now accepted as ennobling, leaving 'no room for pity, none for contempt. They silence hatred and redeem many faults.' And what of the future? 'Commercial freedom and Irish equality will make the late Premier, without a party, a party in himself. We had almost said, the people's party.

Relinquishing office, he enters on a power and dignity above those of office' (3 July).

In Norwich, too, a new and successful paper had appeared, which shared the enthusiasm of the *Daily News* for the Anti-Corn Law League. This was the *Norfolk News*, which began publication on 4 January 1845. It proclaimed in its opening address that the victory of the League was certain, and that this would pave the way for parliamentary reform and abolition of tithe. As a Nonconformist paper, the *Norfolk News* opposed Peel over the increased Maynooth grant; but it praised his steering of business through Parliament during 1845. 'It must be admitted that he keeps his team in capital order' (14 June). By 6 December the *Norfolk News* was assuring its readers that Peel had resolved 'absolutely to repeal the Corn Laws'. But a week later, after Peel's resignation, it felt less sure how far he wanted to go. The next issue on 20 December declared that 'Sir Robert's course is mysterious'; but it also claimed that 'an aroused people' had now broken down the constraints of party. What would Peel do? 'As usual there are three courses open to Sir Robert Peel – the right one – the wrong one – and the half-way between' (3 January). When Peel had made his plan known, the *Norfolk News* of 31 January concluded that he had taken the halfway course. 'Crablike, he cannot go straight.' He had proposed compensation and delay. And yet a degree of appreciation broke through the paper's complaints. 'The very greatness of the scheme makes its absurdities the more painfully obstructive. We hardly know which most to wonder at, the courage which dared to devise the plan, or the timidity which flinched from its completion.' These mixed feelings about Peel persisted in the columns of the *Norfolk News* through to his fall. It was seen as poetic justice that a Minister who had long held office by serving the selfishness of his followers, should finally lose it 'on account of the good service he has rendered to his country' (13 June).

The *Norfolk News* cannot therefore be said to have become a Peelite newspaper in 1846, even though it was no longer so suspicious of Peel's intentions. But what of the Chartist *Northern Star*, which headed its editorial for 31 January, 'ALL-MIGHTY PEEL'? This article may well have been written by Feargus O'Connor himself, for it referred in passing to complaints about Irish policy which 'we' had made 'twenty years and more since'. Peel's 'gigantic scheme' was praised as likely to stimulate agriculture and to increase the demand for labour, at the same time as it lowered the cost of food and other necessaries. Beyond this, however, the *Star* foresaw consequences from repeal which Peel did not intend, and which indeed he positively hoped to avoid: 'the working of the new State machinery must, as surely as effect follows cause, lead to the no distant acceptation of Chartist principles.' By 22 May, however, the *Northern Star* was no longer so enthusiastic about Peel. It now claimed that its first comments upon his proposals had drawn a distinction 'between the measures and their proposer'. It described Peel's speech of 15 May as 'a mere heckling', whereas Disraeli's attack was printed in full and praised as the best speech 'we' ever heard in the House. 'However, we hail the repeal of the Corn Laws, not for the substantive or immediate benefit that the change will confer upon the labouring classes, but for the many collateral issues that will arise from the experiment.' This was expecting much less from repeal than had been anticipated in January, although the implication was still that Chartist reforms would follow. By the time of Peel's resignation, the *Northern Star* (4 July) had moved some way back towards clear praise both of repeal and of Peel himself. The Chartist paper admitted that during his five years in office 'there has been more of steady prosperity and constant progress at home, more of dignified, peaceful, and conciliatory policy abroad, than ever distinguished the career of any previous administration'.

If the *Northern Star*'s praise for Peel was too uncertain and too idiosyncratic for the paper to be called a convert to Peelite opinions, a number of provincial newspapers have been found which made this transition; just three or four from the Conservative side, and more from the Opposition side. They reflected at its clearest the persuasive impact of Peel and his policies upon contemporary opinion. Other such newspaper conversions could no doubt be found in other places.

The *Bolton Chronicle*, the *Manchester Courier* and the *Nottingham Journal* were all papers which moved strikingly from protectionist to Peelite positions. As late as 13 December 1845, the *Bolton Chronicle* was declaring that even if Peel chose to join the ranks of 'that revolutionary faction known as the League', there was no reason for protectionists to despair. Conservatism was not 'another name for Sir Robert Peel'. Yet when Peel's plan was revealed, the *Chronicle* noted how several Conservative papers had followed him, including the *Manchester Courier*. Suddenly, on 28 February it followed suit. It declared itself 'weary' of writing about the Corn Laws. Great and good men differed on the question. Peel was widely supported, and his detractors 'are not of the people' (21 March). By 27 June the *Bolton Chronicle* was pressing Peel to remain in office. And at the end of the year it was declaring that a protectionist Cabinet was 'an egregious exaggeration of fancy'. This transformation in attitude seems to have paid off in terms of circulation; for the paper was selling an average of less than 800 copies weekly in 1845, whereas it averaged more than 1,300 for 1846.

The *Manchester Courier* was the best-selling provincial Conservative newspaper, with weekly totals approaching 5,400 throughout 1845 and 1846. This steadiness in circulation reflected the *Courier*'s success in adjusting its opinions to suit the local situation. It could hardly forget that it was published within the free-trade stronghold of Manchester; and when Peel announced his conversion to full repeal, the issue of 28 January 1846 accepted that this was 'a naturally flowing consequence' of his previous free-trade measures, which Conservatives had accepted. This gloss enabled the *Courier* to move with the

Premier. The agricultural interest had not opposed Peel's application of free-trade principles since 1842, and therefore agriculturalists could not consistently oppose Peel now. The very success of his earlier measures made a sufficient case for now introducing free trade in corn (14 February): 'Are men who have witnessed, in common with all others, the fair and luxurious growth of that policy, to be ashamed because the fruit is finer than they anticipated, and because on that account, and urged on by popular desire, they are disposed still more to promote the growth of it?' When repeal had passed, and Peel was about to resign, the *Manchester Courier* of 27 June almost matched its free-trade rival, the *Manchester Guardian*, in the warmth of its eulogy. In 'pre-eminently a *practical* age', Peel was known as the most practical statesman of the day. He had given commerce *'steadiness* and *security* – the two things chiefly needful to mercantile prosperity. Every man sleeps soundly whilst he has charge of the watch.'

The *Nottingham Journal* was to follow a similar course of conversion, and was likewise to end by praising Peel for his 'practical' qualities. As late as 16 January the *Journal* had been expressing its dread of repeal of the Corn Laws. Yet two weeks later it was receiving Peel's plan favourably, and recommending agriculturalists to make the sacrifice, 'if it should turn out to be one'. This change of view arose explicitly from confidence in Peel's judgement. Peel alone, declared the *Journal* on 3 April, deserved the thanks of the nation. Lord John Russell was described (17 July) as 'a pretender to statesmanship'. Early in 1847 the *Journal* summed up the Corn Law crisis in terms which would have much pleased Peel. It remarked (8 January) how he had 'succeeded in convincing the people that there is a practical desire at work in the mind of government to minister as far as legislation can do to the wants and promote the comforts of the masses'. Some Nottinghamshire agriculturalists were shocked by the *Journal*'s volte-face. They started a new protectionist paper in May 1846 – the *Nottinghamshire Guardian*. On 2 October it described the *Journal* as 'Peel's candle holder'.[60]

The *Nottingham Journal* eventually lost nearly 900 readers, apparently to the *Guardian*. The *Journal*'s average weekly circulation had been 2,230 copies in 1845, but was down to 1,346 for 1847. The *Guardian*'s new sale made up the difference. The *Nottingham Review* now became the largest-selling Nottingham newspaper, with a steady circulation of about 2,000. The *Review* was a Radical paper, which (like the *Journal*) swung behind Peel. It was easier for papers of Radical or Liberal opinions to do this than for Conservative papers, since Radical and Liberal readers were probably already free traders. That the Peelite *Nottingham Journal* lost so many readers was less striking than that it retained so many more.

[60] D. Fraser, 'Newspapers and opinion in three Midland cities 1800–1850'. Unpublished MA thesis, Leeds University, 1962, pp. 373–5, 476.

As early as 20 June 1845, the Radical *Nottingham Review* had forecast that Peel and Cobden would soon be 'arm in arm together'. During the December uncertainty it preferred Peel to Russell as the Minister to carry repeal. The *Review* of 19 December thought it fitting for a cotton-spinner's son to emancipate the industry which had made his father's wealth. The paper showed its Radicalism by claiming on 9 January that Corn Law repeal would open the way for parliamentary reform. Peel's repeal plan was described on 30 January as 'MAGNIFICENT'. The *Review* even conceded that immediate repeal was not practicable. Peel had lost a party but gained the nation. There was a 'vast majority' for repeal within all classes – 'trading, agricultural, moneyed, aristocratical, and working. This majority has created, and now upholds a public opinion – a pressure from without, which for power and determination has never been surpassed.' When Peel resigned, the *Nottingham Review* of 3 July emphasized that he had done more for 'Liberalism' than all the Whigs put together.

The Radical *Leeds Times* reached a similar conclusion. In the summer of 1845 (9 August) it was still complaining that Peel 'seems to regard principles as mere articles of commerce'. But after his repeal plan had been announced, the issue of 31 January 1846 spoke very differently. 'We count Peel emphatically as a man of progress.' And after his fall he was praised on 4 July for his 'regard for truth, right, and justice, which will stand as an example to statesmen for all time coming'. The paper chose to forget that this was in flat contradiction to its assessment of a year earlier.

In Leeds, as in Manchester, the climate of opinion was overwhelmingly in favour of free trade. Like the Conservative *Manchester Courier*, the Conservative *Leeds Intelligencer* convinced itself that, despite its previous support for the Corn Laws, it could not now resist their removal. In December 1845 the *Intelligencer* was still saying that Peel could not in honour propose repeal; but by 31 January it was admitting that feeling was widespread for ending the Corn Laws. And so the paper did not oppose Peel's scheme: 'the experiment of Free Trade must be tried.' By 27 June the *Intelligencer* was recognizing the virtue and strength of Peel's new position above party: 'it is this very superiority to the conventional ties of party, this easy sacrifice of power to public duty, which places him in affinity to the nascent spirit of the times.'

In Liverpool, unlike Leeds or Manchester, the local press did retain a protectionist newspaper voice through the Corn Law crisis. The *Liverpool Courier* refused to follow Peel. But most Liverpool newspaper readers subscribed to titles which supported repeal. The *Liverpool Albion* made a considerable progression from Whig to Peelite. As late as 24 November 1845 it was emphasizing how it did not place 'a shadow of hope upon the treachery of Sir Robert Peel'. On 15 December it was declaring Russell to be its preferred Prime Minister, and it expressed bafflement a week later at the Whig retreat from office. It anticipated only 'some bungling piece of patchwork' from Peel

(29 December). But by 26 January the *Albion* was beginning to admit to a sense of pleasant anticipation with regard to Peel's intentions. It felt, however, that it must remain vigilant: 'we have not yet learned to repose confidence in one who has so frequently given instances of his fondness for *finesse*.' When the detailed repeal plan was announced, the *Albion* expressed satisfaction. But the issue for 6 March was still declaring trust in Russell and distrust of Peel. 'It is not free trade he worships, but himself.' In the end, however, such suspicion was to be completely abandoned. By 15 June Peel was being described, in contrast to the comment of 6 March, as 'far above suspicion of selfishness'. He had demonstrated that he was prepared to sacrifice himself and his party for the sake of genuine conviction. When Russell succeeded as Prime Minister, the *Albion* of 6 July was now much less enthusiastic than earlier. Russell's aristocratic Ministry was criticized for lack of 'popular' membership.

The free-trade Liberal *Liverpool Journal* followed a similar course to the *Liverpool Albion*, from suspicion of Peel to acceptance. By 24 January 1846 it had only reached the point of describing Peel as 'the Minister best calculated to advance the immediate interests of the country'. But by 27 June such short-term support had been transformed into a strong desire for Peel to retain office. 'Parliament at this moment is not the country.' Each week the *Journal* carried a lively report about local opinion called 'Talk on "Change"'. That for 31 January had described the reception of Peel's plan among the city's commercial community:

> People got up much earlier than usual on Wednesday morning. A dense, dull fog was succeeded by a thick, heavy rain, but still the streets were in a comparative bustle, and the Exchange Rooms filled rapidly on being opened. The news they expected was up all night, to be there before them. It flowed through twelve lengthy columns in the *Daily News*, the *Standard*, and the *Sun*, and the excitement of the moment privileged every one to inquire and tell what Sir Robert Peel had said a few hours before in the House of Commons.
>
> The first talk was, that the measure was a bold one, an admirable one, and that Sir Robert Peel was a wise minister – a great man. There was no qualification in people's praise – admiration; every one seemed satisfied – and everybody said so; but anon, one doubted, and then another doubted, and, ultimately, several doubted. A few venerable protectionists compressed their eyebrows, to show what they thought, and then their lips, to prevent, no doubt, unseemly verbal explosions. Curses, not loud, but deep, were a consolation to their mortified spirits, but the general cheerfulness soon operated on them, for the many seemed to rejoice in the fulness of conviction that great good had been accomplished.
>
> The most ardent free-traders hesitated approbation; they did not like

the sliding scale even for a period, and the talk was, that a better measure was desirable – possible. That the people would not – ought not, to be satisfied with anything less than total and immediate repeal, and that, to obtain this, the manufacturers should give up, at once, and for ever, every remnant of protection.

The general talk, however, was a good one; the conservatives tacitly assented to it as a matter of prudence, if not of wisdom, and the liberals thought it so good that they were not without apprehension that it would not pass; and the talk was that a dissolution of Parliament was not an impossibility . . .

The general talk is that this is unprofitable gossip; that there will be no dissolution; that Sir Robert Peel is safe in a majority of 90, at least, in the Commons, and that the Duke has the Lords in his pocket. That the scheme is laid with consummate art; that needy landowners will swallow the bait of borrowed money from the state Treasury; and that Cobden has alarmed the Lord Charleses, who find it convenient to represent counties. Another registration would hand their hereditary seats over to the master manufacturers, and they know full well that the question once settled, a lull will follow. The talk is that exhaustion succeeded the Reform Bill; that exhaustion will follow the corn-freeing bill, and that registration will fall into comparative neglect.

Here was much shrewd comment and anticipation, a reflection of how intelligently early Victorian public opinion could respond to major political developments. This newspaper report was privately confirmed by Liverpool's Commissioner of Bankruptcy who, in a letter to Brougham passed on to Peel, wrote of the 'universal satisfaction' on 'change; the only 'murmur' came from the Brazilian merchants, over the question of slave sugar. The *Journal*'s own comment summed up in a few words the essence of Peel's successful national appeal to middle opinion. 'His measure satisfies only moderate men – that is, the many.'[61]

The leading Liverpool newspaper was the *Liverpool Mercury*. This was one of a trinity of powerful North of England Liberal organs. It had itself been modelled (1811) upon the *Leeds Mercury* (1801), and both had served as models for the *Manchester Guardian* (1821). The *Liverpool Mercury*'s stated circulation (15 May 1846) rose from 7,840 copies per week during the last quarter of 1845 to 8,275 during the first quarter of 1846.

The *Mercury* of 21 November 1845 had described Peel's manner at the inauguration of the Trent Valley Railway as characteristic, 'large pretensions and small performance'. It noticed how Peel had not turned over the turf as expected of him even though the ground had been loosened by labourers, 'the Cobdens and Brights of railway-making'. No allowance was made for the

[61] C. Phillips to Brougham, February 1846 (Add. MSS 40482, f. 253).

attack of gout from which he was suffering. The *Mercury* of 12 December dismissed speculation over *The Times* leak by saying that it was for the country 'to MAKE it true'. By 19 December, however, its line towards Peel was softening. 'He has done his best to undo his own wrong . . . It is about the sincerest thing that any public man ever did.' Yet a week later the *Mercury* was still fearing that Peel back in office might prepare only a compromise Corn Law measure: 'the cunning man's cunning policy'. Then, after announcement of the full plan, the editorial of 30 January was enthusiastic: 'he may be, if you will, the falsest of men breathing, in all other matters; but he is most certainly sincere *now*, in *this* matter.' Peel's speech was proclaimed as 'DECISIVE', even though the *Mercury* regretted the absence of immediate repeal. 'But it is not in his nature to do a great work in a great spirit.' A week later such asides were being submerged in praise of Peel's application of Adam Smith's principles: 'the first Minister who has given a full and unqualified application'.

After Peel's speech of 16 February the *Mercury* wished four days later that it could have written an unqualified eulogy. 'Pity! that there should be a fatal moral flaw in the life and character of our Free Trade Premier, that checks eulogy and chills enthusiasm.' Otherwise, Peel's speech could have been hailed as the words of 'the man whom God and nature have made to bear chief rule over a country whose power is in its industry'. When by 5 June Peel was visibly preparing to be turned out, the *Liverpool Mercury* deplored the prospect. It now felt able to support a Conservative Premier without hesitation, not because its own opinions had changed but because Peel's had. Let him be 'England's Minister as long as he please'. Although opposed to the Irish Coercion Bill, this remained the *Mercury*'s line until Peel insisted upon retirement. The paper recognized that Peel was no longer ambitious for power. He now stood above party: 'his functions become almost paternal' (5 July). If he avoided all factious opposition while out of office, he would confirm himself as one of the greatest statesmen ever to rule his country.

Across the Pennines, the opinions of the *Leeds Mercury* (with its circulation steady at about 9,000 weekly) followed a somewhat similar course to that of its Liverpool namesake. At first the *Leeds Mercury* was not impressed by Peel's willingness to deal with the Corn Laws himself, regardless of the personal consequences. He was described (6 December) as a man who cared 'more for fame than for place. He would any day quit Downing-street for a niche in history.' But Peel's repeal plan was admitted on 31 January to equal Russell's Reform Bill in its 'boldness, grandeur, and true wisdom'. The *Leeds Mercury* now had to make a conscious effort to avoid speaking approvingly of the Premier. 'Not that we are to give to Sir Robert Peel the honour that is due to consistent politicians.' Then after Peel's speech of 27 March, the *Mercury* (4 April) withdrew most of its reservations. 'We feel that we are actually in danger of becoming Peelites: but if so, it is because Peel has become a Whig, and a martyr to Free Trade. Hurrah for the Truth, whoever speaks it!' And in this spirit the *Leeds Mercury* continued until Peel's resignation.

The *Manchester Guardian* came by the summer of 1846 to an even more approving view. Although published from the home town of the Anti-Corn Law League, and itself always a free-trade paper, the *Guardian*, like the *Leeds Mercury*, had always been careful not to be mistaken for a mere mouthpiece of the League. It reiterated its independence as late as 31 December 1845, after the *League* had four days previously described the *Guardian*'s opinions as 'too unstable'. Yet as early as 22 March 1845 the *Guardian* was anticipating that Peel might himself give the lead for repeal, and so become 'one of the greatest benefactors that England has ever known'. By 10 December it was claiming that Peel was about to propose total and immediate repeal. After he had eventually proposed a more gradual process, the *Guardian* of 31 January welcomed Peel's plan as still sufficient; for it demonstrated that he 'would not tarnish his reputation as a statesman by bringing in any measure which would not *finally* settle the question'. At the time of Peel's retirement, the *Guardian* of 27 June emphasized how 'in the eyes of the intelligent portion of the public' he had reached a level of popularity 'to which no minister has attained during the present century'. The paper regretted that Peel had insisted upon resigning, rather than call a general election. If, however, a Whig Ministry had become inevitable, it should be supported by the people. 'Let them not forget, in their admiration of Sir Robert Peel, for how many great reforms the country is indebted to the whigs.'

These pro-Peel but not anti-Russell opinions seem to have well satisfied *Manchester Guardian* readers. Its circulation continued to rise steadily, averaging 8,914 bi-weekly for the second half of 1845, 9,482 for the first half of 1846, and 9,750 for the second half; its Saturday edition was selling above these averages, and its Wednesday number below. A Cobdenite paper, the *Manchester Examiner*, was started in the city at the beginning of 1846. With even the Conservative *Manchester Courier* in favour of Corn Law repeal, there can therefore have been few protectionist newspaper readers left in the Manchester area. The same seems to have been the case around Leeds, which likewise had no local protectionist paper once the *Leeds Intelligencer* had accepted repeal. In Sheffield, however, the *Sheffield Mercury* remained staunchly protectionist. As for the *Sheffield Independent*, the leading local paper, and a long-standing advocate of free trade, it still refused to praise Peel in 1846. He might be honest now; but he had been dishonest in the past while opposing Corn Law repeal for party ends. He should have proposed repeal in response to the distress of 1841–2. 'Of his great offence, we can say nothing in extenuation . . . he has made bread dear and life cheap' (6 June).

The *Nottingham Mercury* was, like the *Manchester Guardian* and the *Leeds Mercury*, a paper which favoured free trade first and the Anti-Corn Law League only second. The *Nottingham Mercury* pointed out on 19 December that the demand for repeal was not the creation of the League alone. Here was 'no creature of mere out-of-doors agitation' but 'a cause sanctioned by the property, probity, and intelligence of the kingdom'. By 30 January the *Nottingham Mercury* was ready to place Peel above the League. 'Talk of "great facts!" This Minister of ours is the great fact of this age . . . he contains within himself, and is conscious of it, – the wants and wishes of the English people.' In East Anglia, the *Norwich Mercury* was likewise a free-trade paper without being an Anti-Corn Law League organ. By 27 December it was expecting that Peel would introduce repeal, 'liked or disliked, trusted or distrusted'. It countenanced the cautious elaboration of Peel's speech on 27 January, and it positively welcomed that of 16 February as a turning point. But as late as 7 June it was remembering how Peel had resisted 'every advance' until the last minute. He could not, therefore, be accepted as a man of high principle. Like the *Sheffield Independent*, the *Norwich Mercury* of 4 July declined to join in the eulogies after Peel's retirement. The congratulatory addresses sent to him were described as encouragements to dishonesty in public life. 'It is a course which is calculated to undermine and weaken the power public opinion possesses over the acts of our representatives.' Here, therefore, was a conclusion hostile to Peel from the free-trade side. Interestingly, it mirrored the charge made by protectionists; that in overriding party constraints Peel was, in Disraeli's phrase already quoted, repudiating 'embodied public opinion'.

X

The evening *Standard*, which had been Peel's most reliable supporter in the daily press, now became one of his foremost opponents, albeit reluctantly. As late as 12 December 1845 it was forecasting that there would be no split in the Conservative ranks. Although Peel wanted relaxation of the Corn Laws, he was described as also wanting adequate compensation for agriculture. By 18 December, however, the *Standard* was warning the party to be ready to 'act without' Peel, if his proposals proved to be unacceptable. The paper encouraged the calling of protectionist meetings in the country. Yet Peel's speech on the Address was still not treated as conclusive; agriculturalists were urged to wait for the details of compensation. But finally on 28 January the *Standard* had to face the fact that Peel had proposed complete repeal: 'we cannot believe that we rightly understood a change proposed by one whom we have been accustomed to regard as a statesman of the first order.' If Peel now spoke rightly, then the Conservative party had been wrong for thirty years. Longer than the proposed three years would be needed for British agriculture to be able to compete in the open market. Next day the *Standard* announced with 'deep regret' that it must oppose 'the best and most successful minister that this country has possessed for many years'. It promised to avoid personalities.

Peel's measure must be attacked, not the man. If defeated, he would probably retire. This would be a great loss, but it remained a price worth paying for the creation of 'a powerful party of liberal and moderate but firm Conservatives', not influenced by 'mob power'.

The *Standard* of 2 February argued for a dissolution of Parliament, to provide a proper test for Members who had changed their minds with Peel. His speech of 16 February was dismissed next day as merely an admission that he had ruined his party for the sake of expediency. Peel's tone was growing sharper, and so was the *Standard*'s. By 25 February, the Premier was being described as a man of great talents, but not a wise man or an original mind. His function should be 'not to contrive but to criticise – his proper place is that of a senator without office'. Peel's majority of 97 was described on 28 February as equalling the exact number of the Peelite 'apostates'; men who had trampled on their pledges, infected by 'moral phthisis'. The threat of famine in Ireland was dismissed on 14 March as exaggerated; partial famine there was '*perennial*'. Graham was blamed for misleading Peel. During April the *Standard* began to speak of the beginning of the end for the Government. The issue for 3 June deplored Peel's 'systematic succession of treacheries'. It could not find in the history of any country, not even of revolutionary France, 'any prototype, at least among statesmen, to Sir Robert Peel; for even Talleyrand did not *himself contrive* the treasons by which he was led away.' Peel must go. 'A moral people will not forgive the use of base and wicked means to compass even the best ends.'

The *Morning Herald*, the *Standard*'s companion paper, took a similar line. During December it was urging its readers to wait for details before making up their minds, although by 12 January it was wondering if Peel would adopt the same tone of regretful concession as he had used to justify Catholic Emancipation. 'He will assert it to be his duty as Prime Minister, to reconcile, if he can, the jarring interests of the country.' After Peel's plan had been announced, the *Herald* took several days to digest it, especially its compensation proposals. Not until 2 February did the paper finally announce its refusal to follow Peel. His speech of 16 February was dismissed as good but bad: 'good indeed as a summary of "the League" arguments – good as a collection of sarcasms upon his deserted friends.' Peel had shown himself to be 'the ambidextrous orator' (21 February), able to argue any way, and not to be trusted. 'If we are to have *Cobdenisms*, let us have them from Cobden's own lips' (31 March). After the *Morning Chronicle* had charged the *Herald* with attacking Peel with 'more than mere party hostility', the *Herald* of 26 May readily accepted the point. It felt 'a duty to entertain a very different feeling towards a mere opponent and a perfidious deserter'. It noted how the *Chronicle* had moved in the opposite direction to itself with regard to Peel. At the time of his fall, the *Herald* of 27 June claimed that he would never have proposed repeal if he could have foreseen his 'disgraceful expulsion'; for Peel loved power more than any principle. The paper rejoiced three days later that he would never again speak as a Minister. 'His is an offence not merely against party but *against morals*.'

The most bitter of all the protectionist denunciations of Peel in the London papers were delivered by the *Morning Post*. Their virulence provoked *Punch*'s sudden and surprising Christmas gesture of sympathy towards the Prime Minister. When *The Times* made its revelations, the *Morning Post* of 6 December had immediately admitted that they might be true. It reminded its readers how it had long since lost all respect for Peel. Two days later the *Post* concluded that 'something strange' was going on. Otherwise, why had not the *Standard* or *Morning Herald* been authorized to publish clear denials? The *Post* expressed satisfaction that the protectionist societies were stirring. When Peel resigned, the paper of 12 December looked critically over his time in office:

> His whole career since 1842 has been one of insanity or treachery. We have done all in our power to expose him. He has not (since 1842) deceived *us*. We regard him as the most loathsome of public men. His abilities (which are unquestionable) only add to his odiousness. He prostitutes to the meanest purposes the talents which God has given him. We hope there can now be no doubt of his joining the Whigs. That the Tories should ever again have anything to do with him, we can not suppose.

Peel, said the *Post*, had betrayed his party over the Test and Corporation Acts, over Catholic Emancipation, over 'the odious Poor Law', and now over agricultural protection. 'We do not say that none of these things should have been done, but they should not have been so done as to bring disgrace and dishonour upon the Tory party.' Peel had shown no care for the way he left his party exposed. 'First he subjects it to the charge of injustice and bigotry, and then, when the clamour excited by his false advocacy is at the highest, he gets frightened and takes to his heels.' He seemed to have no views of his own on the Poor Law question, which he had handed over to Graham, who had done nothing 'to reconcile the poor of England to their superiors in station'. The *Post* of 24 December copied from Lytton Bulwer's *The New Timon* the lines already quoted about Peel's untrustworthiness (p. 175).

Three days later an editorial emphasized that although the Peel Government had been reconstructed, the Peel party had not. It forecast that the Ministry would be short-lived. Peel's speech on the Address confirmed the *Morning Post*'s worst fears. It welcomed Disraeli's quick response, which had laid bare 'the vanity, the egotism, the tyranny and the inconsistency of the Premier'. When Peel's detailed plan was revealed, the *Post* began to press for a dissolution of Parliament. The paper was appalled that Peel, of all people, should be taking the lead in proposing repeal: 'if the revolution he proposes were as full of good, as we believe it to be full of evil, we should revolt from such a proposition at *his* hands.' Repeal was Cobden's policy, not Peel's.

'The Farmers' Lament' appeared in the *Post* of 17 February. It began:

> When first we met thee, warm and young,
> There shone such truth about thee.
> And on thy lip such promise hung,
> We did not dare to doubt thee.

It ended:

> Go–go– 'tis vain to curse,
> 'Tis weakness to upbraid thee –
> Hate cannot wish thee worse
> Than guilt and shame have made thee.

When Peel finally resigned, the *Morning Post* of 27 June rejoiced. Better the Whigs, 'an open foe', in office. The paper described Peel's resignation speech as an admission that he had been forced by Cobden to concede repeal. The *Post* then returned with vigour to the underlying protectionist charge of treachery. It deplored Peel's actions even more because they had undermined proper constitutional practice, than because of their social and economic consequences:

> Waiving the question of the national effects of his policy, we hold that his cold deceit – his treachery to those who trusted him – is far too palpable to be denied by any honest and observing man; and this offence, now committed for the second time, deserves every public reproach and public disgrace that can befall him. His position in history, if he hold any position at all, ought, in our judgment, to be among the infamous. If yesterday evening he had made anything like a fitting apology, we might have thought it our duty to refrain from language so harsh as this; but as it is, we see no reason why we should not say as we think, that the conduct of Sir Robert Peel is the greatest disgrace to England which has occurred in the nineteenth century.

Peel had destroyed the party which he had himself built up with ability and energy. There was 'nothing so reckless' in all the history of party. His appeal for remembrance by the masses was dismissed in a letter published in the *Morning Post* of 6 July as 'hypocrisy and impudence unparalleled'. If the Corn Laws were as unjust as Peel was now claiming, were the poor 'likely to respect the man who for thirty years has taxed their bread, and only now withdraws the impost when compelled to do so by the Anti-Corn Law League?' An editorial on 1 July had forecast no benefits from repeal for such depressed groups as Spitalfields weavers, shirt makers and rural husbandmen.

Although Peel was increasingly denounced by the protectionist press, Disraeli had been only reluctantly accepted. Thus his attack on Peel during the debate on the Address was described by the *Standard* of 26 January as motivated by 'private spleen'. 'Nothing could be in worse taste.' 'Respectable' protectionists did not relish association with such an unusual personality. John Blackwood, who had heard this philippic, exclaimed how 'nothing could more completely prove the prostration of the Conservative and Agricultural party than such a swab as Disraeli being the first to rise from among them'.[62] Blackwood had to admit, however, that if Disraeli's speech had not gone too far, and had not lasted so long, it would have been 'very effective'. The scathing brilliance of Disraeli's contributions won him an increasing hearing, both in the Commons and in the country. The *Morning Post* led the way in giving Disraeli recognition. While the *Standard* was still expressing distaste about his motives, the *Post* (24 January) was welcoming his readiness to stand up to Peel.

> The friends of Conservative policy in this country are under great obligations to Mr. Disraeli for the promptitude of his criticism of Sir R. Peel's speech of Thursday night. But for him, that heap of fraudulent plausibility and vulgar egotism would have gone forth to the world without any evidence that its meanness and untruth were seen through in the House of Commons.

Protectionist provincial newspapers, which often had started by noticing Disraeli's attacks only briefly, were soon reporting him at length; and even pro-Peel papers could not ignore him. 'A three hours speech from Disraeli on consistency,' joked the *Weekly Dispatch* of 1 March, '– is it not fit to make society grin?'

As early as 16 December 1845 the *Maidstone Journal*, a typical county protectionist paper, with a circulation of just over 1,000 weekly, had explained what it believed would result from repeal. Two-thirds of the soil would go out of cultivation; a large part of the farming class would be extinguished; two-thirds of the agricultural labourers would starve; manufacturers would be ruined: 'in short, a social revolution, the consequences of which are too frightful to contemplate'. Peel's speech on the Address was reported by the *Journal* of 27 January in the first person over three columns, whereas Disraeli's answer was given only ten inches in the third person. Disraeli was, however, awkwardly commended for 'a speech of considerable ability and replete with personal acerbities towards Sir Robert Peel'.

Another protectionist county paper was the *Derby Mercury*, which sold about 1,500 copies each week. On 10 December 1845 it was dismissing *The Times* revelations as 'utterly worthless'. It refused to believe that Peel could 'be guilty of the tremendous inconsistency imputed to him'. The *Mercury* of 31 December noted that his return to office had restored confidence 'in an especial manner'. But a week later the paper was expressing satisfaction that farmers were meeting to demonstrate their refusal to be 'hunted down' by the League,

---

[62] J. Blackwood to R. Blackwood, 23 January 1846 (NLS MS 4077, f. 286).

'nor sacrificed by ministers'. By 21 January the *Mercury* was arguing that Peel was not the right man to propose repeal of the Corn Laws, even if it could be proved to be necessary. When Peel's plan was revealed, he was denounced for inconsistency, and his compensation proposals were dismissed as inadequate. Corn would sink to 35s per quarter in three years. 'Wheat, to be grown and sold in England at the continental price with all the various burdens which are peculiar to this country affecting the land, and with labour on the continent at 6d. per day and with us at 2s., will, we fancy, very sorely puzzle the British agriculturists should Sir Robert's plan succeed.' By 6 May the *Derby Mercury* was asking to be shown the Irish famine forecast by Peel in January. It noted how Peel had shifted his ground, and now justified repeal because the Corn Laws were said to be unjust. In reality, continued the *Mercury* of 3 June, this was class legislation, surrender to the Anti-Corn Law League. 'Government living upon concession' would soon be forced to concede endowment of the Irish Roman Catholic clergy, Irish Church disestablishment, abolition of tithes, and an extension of the franchise. And yet, the *Mercury* of 1 July had to admit that in Derby town 'a very large number' of 'most respectable supporters' of the sitting Liberal Members, Edward Strutt and Viscount Duncannon, had followed them as 'ardent admirers of the Peel policy'.

The *Lincolnshire Chronicle* was a similar protectionist county paper, circulating some 1,300 weekly. As early as 26 December 1845 it was remembering that the example of the Maynooth agitation had shown that Peel was not amenable to pressure through petitioning. The issue for 30 January was unimpressed by Peel's repeal plan, and found his compensation proposals insufficient. Corn was forecast to fall to 25s. or 30s. per quarter. Disraeli's speeches were not yet reported in the *Chronicle*'s columns; but he was given brief mention for 'a speech of considerable ability, and replete with personal acerbities towards Sir R. Peel for having, as he (Mr. D'Israeli) alleged, betrayed those who had placed him in power'. This same formulation had appeared, as already quoted, in the *Maidstone Journal*, and no doubt in other protectionist prints. During the next weeks the *Lincolnshire Chronicle* looked back not only to Catholic Emancipation but also to Peel's introduction of an income tax. Its resignation assessment of Peel on 3 July was unyielding. 'He leaves behind him an ugly remembrance of his free-trade predilections in an income tax of six millions per annum, retained for the aggrandisement of the league manufacturers.'

The *Liverpool Courier* had not waited for the worst to happen over the Corn Laws before looking to Peel's past record. As early as 10 December 1845 it was admitting to regret that Peel did not possess a greater character for consistency, so that it could be sure of the error of *The Times* revelations. By 31 December, with Peel back in office, the *Courier* was already forecasting 'a fixed duty, gradually to diminish down to nothing'. After Peel had begun to reveal himself, the issue of 28 January concluded that he had sold out to the League, the manufacturers' pressure group. And yet, argued the protectionist press, industry as well as agriculture would be shattered by Corn Law repeal. Thus the *Kentish Gazette* of 2 June forecast not only 'hard, brown or black bread' as eaten by Russian serfs; but also that 'the productions of the British loom' would not be able to compete 'with the untaxed merchandize of the continental artizan'; and that shopkeepers would soon be overwhelmed by much higher rates and taxes.

But what was the reaction to the Corn Law crisis of the *Stamford Mercury*? Its circulation of over 10,000 copies per week was the largest of any provincial paper, spread throughout a mainly agricultural area of eastern England. It concentrated upon news and advertisements, and did not carry leading articles. On the other hand, it did print letters to the editor, some of which he may have written to himself.[63] And the way it reported, or failed to report, national and local political news, and how it summarized or selected for quotation the opinions of London and other newspapers did give a colour to its columns. For example, on 12 December 1845 it reported *The Times* leak as follows:

> The *Times* of Monday affords no indication of diminished confidence in its information; but, on the contrary, comments upon it as an incontrovertible fact. The *Herald* of that day, though insisting upon the falsity of the *Times* statement, nevertheless betrays a doubt, and speaks in a tone implying that great danger of the existing Corn-Laws is at least apprehended.

The *Stamford Mercury*'s weekly article on the 'Spirit of the Public Journals' was an important feature. On 2 January 1846 it quoted from the *Examiner*. 'The beauty of the present juncture is that nobody knows what Sir Robert Peel is going to do, and yet everybody is satisfied that he is the man to do nobody knows what.'

A protectionist meeting at Grantham was reported over three columns in the *Mercury* of 16 January; but a week later another meeting at Stamford was covered only briefly, and the attendance was said to have been less than expected. Most Lincolnshire farmers were not so strongly against repeal as many farmers elsewhere. They wanted above all a quick and final settlement which would bring calm to the markets.[64] This made it easier for the *Stamford Mercury* quietly to incline towards repeal. Thus its report on 30 January of Peel's speech three days earlier was accompanied by a three-quarter column comment from *The Times*, which argued in favour of Peel's plan on the ground that no 'avalanche of corn' would pour into the country. On 6 March the *Mercury* published a letter from a tenant farmer which asked, 'does Sir Robert Peel wish to ruin the tenant farmer? I say, he does not: but he says to the tenant-

---

[63] Olney, *Lincolnshire Politics*, pp. 85–6.
[64] Ibid., p. 119.

farmer, you must no longer depend on a monopoly, you must depend on your landlord . . . he must meet you by allowing you to make a fair bargain as between man and man.' On 3 April the paper printed Lord Mount Edgcumbe's letter to his tenants, 'the first Peer who has publicly announced his intention of yielding to the arguments of Sir R. Peel'. When the Corn Bill had finally passed the Commons, the *Mercury*'s 'Spirit of the Public Journals' gave first place on 22 May to an article from the *Morning Chronicle*. This described the event as 'memorable as the national realization of a great error . . . the assertion of principles of policy and morality which must, at no distant date, become part and parcel of the public opinion and law of civilised nations.' Without itself ever directly praising Peel during the Corn Law crisis, the *Stamford Mercury* had gently encouraged its perhaps 100,000 readers to look on his new policy with favour, or at least without hostility.

XI

Among the Sunday newspapers, *Lloyd's Weekly* was read especially by artisans and shopkeepers, with a first edition published on Friday afternoon for distribution from London to distant parts. The paper's attitude towards Peel at the start of the crisis (9 November 1845) was critical yet not hostile. 'It is hard and ungracious to impute to one who, in the main, wishes well to his country, the misery about to fall upon us; but it would be harder to deny that it is to him we are indebted for it.' *Lloyd's* deplored the long delay in responding to prospective famine. On 23 November it called Peel 'this dumb waiter upon Providence'. His achievement was not yet secure. 'He cannot afford to sport with his reputation.' By 7 December *Lloyd's* was accepting *The Times* revelations. Firm pressure from public opinion, rather than clamour from the Anti-Corn Law League, had driven Peel and Russell forward. 'Was the country ever more peaceable? . . . No, public opinion has brought these men to their senses.' As already indicated, Peel had certainly become persuaded by this time that the restraint of the current demand for Corn Law repeal was itself a reason for concession, to prevent a build-up of violent agitation for wider reform.

When Peel resumed power, *Lloyd's* of 28 December recommended a continuation of peaceful pressure, even though its retrospect of 1845 recognized in the next number how Peel's Maynooth and other Irish measures had shown that he had 'grown wiser' during the year. When his repeal plan became known, the paper welcomed it. Other papers were busy dwelling upon Peel's inconsistencies; but to *Lloyd's Weekly*, with its motto of 'Measures not Men', this seemed pointless. The paper accepted Peel's argument that immediate repeal would not pass. It noticed (15 February) how the Spitalfields silk weavers were the only working men not to support repeal. *Lloyd's* answer was that if they could not survive even with the 15 per cent protective duty which Peel was leaving them, then they should emigrate or change trades. When the correspondence relating to the December political manoeuvres was published, *Lloyd's* of 22 February was impressed by the evidence of Peel's sympathy for the suffering poor. This would 'obliterate the memory of many a past error'. *Lloyd's* of 28 June was still inclined to regard Peel's fall 'as a punishment for the sins by which his administration has been characterised'. But his resignation speech totally transformed the paper's view. Peel was next week described as 'fairly and fully committed to the cause of the people', entitled 'not only to the present gratitude, but to the enduring affection of the country'. Peel's abandonment of his party was counted among his greatest services; for party had enabled 'a luxurious aristocracy' to plunder 'the productive classes'. The paper's final attitude was summed up in verse:

> Who is the King of the Commons?
> The chief with the heart true and great,
> The sire of the poor and the humble,
> The monarch without any state.
>
>   *   *   *
>
> God save the King of the Commons!
> He's sheathing the warrior's sword,
> He's catching the dewdrops from Heaven,
> He's carving at Plenty's own board.

The *Weekly Dispatch*, read mainly by operatives and artisans, came to almost as favourable a conclusion as *Lloyd's Weekly*, even though it began (16 November) by asserting that 'Sir Robert Peel wants bravery'; and by wrongly claiming (7 December) that his Government had been lavish in awarding places and pensions. Already by 21 December the *Dispatch* was preferring Peel to Russell as Prime Minister, since Peel had 'given us more'. When his Corn Law plan was published, the *Dispatch* of 1 February 1846 regretted the refusal of immediate repeal, but welcomed the 'noble and expansive tariff'. The absence of immediate repeal led to the complaint on 15 February that 'the character of the Minister greatly injures every cause he espouses'. Peel was portrayed as believing in immediate repeal, while yet refusing to act upon his belief. A fortnight later the question was being asked whether he had deliberately slowed down the passage of the Corn Bill. The delay might or might not be 'treachery'. 'With every party he has played some slippery trick.' By 5 April the *Dispatch* was hoping that Peel would go on from Corn Law repeal to Poor Law reform. Repeal would do much to empty the workhouses; but there would still be the aged, the young and the infirm, against whom the existing law was 'most vindictive' (12 April).

By 14 June sympathy for Peel was becoming uppermost in the *Dispatch*, with only residual reservations. 'We are no supporters of Sir Robert Peel, and we have already expressed, with sufficient emphasis, our opinion of his stupid

Irish Coercion Bill. But the way he has been basted, night after night, with the lowest personalities, by men utterly incapable of one generous impulse' was deplorable coming from so-called gentlemen. A discerning article, entitled 'A Word for Peel', described his December resignation as 'a receipt in full of party demands upon him'. He had been subsequently 'forced' back into office, but upon his own new terms. 'Party obligations are at all times subordinate to the higher obligations of patriotism and political morality. But even the technical case against Peel is not made out.' Here was clear acceptance of the propriety of Peel's above-party stance. The *Dispatch* of 21 June could find no good reason for wanting to replace Peel by Russell, who had only promised what Peel had performed. He would win a general election, if he chose to call one. Finally, Peel's resignation speech impressed the *Weekly Dispatch* of 5 July as much as it had impressed *Lloyd's Weekly*. 'With all our hostility to the party which chose him as its leader, and to the general policy with which that party has been identified, we feel bound honestly to declare our conviction, that he does not lay claim to a single merit which he has not conspicuously displayed.'

The *News of the World*, described by Mitchell's *Newspaper Press Directory* for 1846 as written for 'respectable tradesmen' and the like, remained Cobdenite throughout the Corn Law crisis. It claimed on 25 October 1845 that Peel would keep the Corn Law 'as long as it will bring a shilling to his clients – the landlords – but that Sir Robert is attached to the Corn Law *on principle*, we do not believe.' For Peel had no principles. Russell, by contrast, was described a fortnight later as 'honest and consistent'. Adversity had now caught up with 'the boastful, braggart Administration of Sir Robert Peel' (16 November); and his inadequacy was being demonstrated by his inaction in the face of the potato blight. He would go down to posterity as '"Pecksniff" Peel'. Russell's Edinburgh Letter was welcomed, and so was Peel's resignation. On the other hand, argued the *News of the World* (14 December), the country did not want too aristocratic a Whig administration. 'We have had enough of Lords.' But Peel's resumption of office demonstrated to the paper (28 December) how privilege and oligarchy still ruled. Peel was expected (4 January) to offer 'some alteration' of the Corn Laws, with compensation to landlords; but what right had they to any compensation when land ownership was based upon 'robbery'?

The *News of the World* of 18 January discussed Peel's attitude to news-papers and to extra-parliamentary opinion. Whether or not he had actually said that he never read newspapers, he had always acted as if he did not read them; he remained 'superior to democratic influence'. He was only interested in parliamentary opinion:

The conscience and conviction of Sir Robert Peel up to this time have been the opinion and the inclination of the majority of the House of Commons – not the majority of his own party – but of *the House altogether*; and his art consists as a Minister in forming measures which will secure *that majority* – at one time defeating the Whigs with the aid of the ultra Tories, at another outvoting the ultra Tories by the support given to him by the Whigs.

In other words, Peel's above-party stance was solely a parliamentary manoeuvre, aloof from outside opinion.

The *News of the World* forecast that Peel's Corn Law plan would be complicated and many-sided, designed 'to catch the majority' by offering something to as many interests as possible. 'Again he will endeavour in Parliament, by the members there, to bribe them by benefits to the peculiar cliques to which they belong, into becoming his allies, in adding to the burthens of those who are not represented.' When Peel's plan was known, the *News of the World* of 1 February thought it characteristic, 'a great plan, overladen with pettiness'. Its greatness was Cobden's: 'the dirty, little, fiddling work is Peel's.' But the paper half hoped for its rejection 'by the oligarchy', since the people would then take the business into their own hands. This was, of course, precisely what Peel wanted to avoid. His first majority of ninety-seven was hailed by the *News of the World* of 8 March as a victory for Cobden. Delay in passing the Corn Bill was described (5 April) as resulting from Peel's Machiavellian plotting to retain power. The paper of 19 April gave its readers an unsympathetic pen portrait of the Premier at work in the Commons:

> a gentleman of a remarkably bland and open countenance. He is tall and well proportioned, but rather inclining to corpulency . . . he is dressed with scrupulous care – even nicety. A snow-white cambric neckcloth and collar surmounts a white waistcoat and blue frock coat; and nether garments of the same colour, which cover ill-formed lower extremities, complete his costume . . . his mind is busily working, but not a wheel of the machinery is to be seen. He rises, the very personification of candour – the incarnation of courtesy – he speaks, and his persuasive, plausible tones allure your attention and almost win your confidence – and you admire the colour of the fish which you think you have caught – but while gazing, it slips through your fingers – you have *not* made anything out of Sir Robert.

In the same spirit, an editorial on 21 June described Peel's ends as good, but his means as bad. He had avoided a general election: 'he has excluded a popular measure from a popular discussion.' Repeal of the Corn Laws had been passed in precisely the same way as the Six Acts. Peel was no friend to public opinion. Cobden remained the paper's hero: 'if the people of England had not been led by Richard Cobden, they never could have enlisted a Prime Minister under their banner' (5 July).

The Sunday Times was a middle-class paper (at 6d twice the price of *Lloyd's*

Weekly or the *News of the World*) strongly in favour of free trade, but more inclined towards the Whigs than towards the Anti-Corn Law League. An editorial of 9 November 1845 dismissed the whole foreign and colonial policy of Peel's Government as a failure. 'We believe him to be a very good man. We dare say he is an extremely hospitable host, and we make no doubt of his being favourable to the railway system; but we fear we must grant him to be a very bad minister, and to have the misfortune of having worse colleagues.' A week later Peel's political character was analysed: 'neither Whig, nor Tory, nor Radical. He is merely Sir Robert Peel. He cares very little for party.' Yet he was distrusted by the people. 'He pleases, but just as a consummate actor does.' Russell was much to be preferred because of his sincerity. Nevertheless, when Peel resigned he was accused on 14 December of cravenly abandoning his post. On his return to office, he was described as likely to produce only a trimming Corn Law measure. His speech on the Address was viewed with continuing suspicion. 'He threatens more than he performs.' But *The Sunday Times* of 1 February found itself welcoming Peel's detailed proposals as Whig and 'something more'. Peel was now praised as 'the benefactor of his country'. Past differences should be forgotten. He had been prepared to give way to Russell and even to support his rival, 'not the actions of a vulgar man'. The paper accepted the need for a three-year delay, and even for 'compensation for relinquishing the right to rob'. By 28 June it was exclaiming how 'the good wishes of all honest men' went with Peel into retirement. Whether some words in this editorial may have influenced a famous passage in Peel's resignation speech will be discussed at the end of this chapter. Although Peel's domestic policy had ended in success, *The Sunday Times* continued to believe that there had been too much concession in his Government's foreign policy, and also weakness shown in India. On balance, therefore, it did not regret Peel's departure, which would be 'a great advantage to the public'.

Other Sunday reading was provided by family and religious journals. Because the penny weekly *London Journal* was avowedly non-party, it was able to become quietly Peelite when Peel placed himself above party in 1846. Its sale each week to a lower middle-class and superior working-class readership, especially of women, exceeded the daily sale of *The Times*. G. W. M. Reynolds, the editor of the *London Journal* from its first number in March 1845 until November 1846, did not intrude his ultra-Radical views into its columns. Its readers have been characterized as against the aristocracy, but also afraid of the mob; as not entirely ignorant of politics, but without a sustained interest.[65] Such people were likely to respond to Peel in 1846, and the *London Journal* realized this. It began a series of 'Political Sketches' on 16 May with

[65] L. James, 'The trouble with Betsy: periodicals and the common reader in mid-nineteenth century England', in Joanne Shattock and N. Wolff (eds), *The Victorian Periodical Press* (1982), pp. 364–5.

'Sir Robert Peel and His Free-Trade Measures'. This article's first paragraph contrived to praise Peel in carefully disarming terms:

> Start not, reader! We are not about to inflict upon you a political article, nor to attempt by the aid of our immense circulation to encourage the animosities now existing between Free-Traders and Protectionists. Our intention is entirely innocent, and yet, we believe, very useful. We purpose to give you an account of the various grains which constitute so large a portion of human food; and this narrative we shall precede with a brief sketch of Sir Robert Peel, the present Prime Minister of England, – inasmuch as to the policy of this illustrious statesman, aided by the wisdom of his colleagues, Graham, Goulburn, Clerk, Lincoln, Herbert, Aberdeen, &c., will the country be shortly indebted for a more adequate supply and a far more varied assortment of cereals than it has ever yet known.

The next three paragraphs then described a Peel speech in the House of Commons. 'Peel has been speaking two hours – and it does not seem as if he had been on his legs more than one third of that time!' The article then moved into a discussion of 'the real nature of the food of man'. It came to the free-trade conclusion that there would be no benefit to British consumers from growing all their grain at home, since this would mean using marginal land and so forcing up prices. Disraeli was not profiled until 14 November 1846, and then his attacks upon Peel were dismissed as 'froth on the top of the beer-pot'. The Commons listened to him, but only as a performer. Wellington, by contrast, had been praised on 6 June for supporting Peel over repeal, even against his own convictions. This partly compensated, in the eyes of the *London Journal*, for Wellington's hostility to the Reform Bill.

The *Journal*'s rival, the *Family Herald*, was free-trade in its inclinations, as a paragraph on 4 September 1847 was to illustrate:

> Using only such letters as occur in the sentence, 'Richard Cobden, M.P.
> for Stockport,' we may construct the following lines: –
> The champion of free trade!
> The poor man's best friend!
> Cheap corn and bread!

Nevertheless, an article of 4 December 1847 on 'Heroes; or Popular Men' did not rate their influence highly. 'In our days, we have no instance of a single individual impassioning a people upon any subject. There are many men who can impassion a party of chartists, socialists, methodists, free-traders, or protectionists; but of men who can impassion a people we know not one.' Peel was therefore not regarded by the *Family Herald* as such a transcending figure.

Among the religious journals, the *Nonconformist* was almost as interested in free trade as in religious questions; and indeed it regarded repeal of the Corn

Laws and international free trade as Christian causes. Its headline for 24 December 1845, after Peel had resumed office, was 'THE DEMISE OF PARTY'. 'Peel, the Conservative minister, is no more – Peel, the minister of an irresistible public opinion is but newly-borne.' The *Nonconformist* of 28 January welcomed Peel's repeal plan for its 'manliness of tone never before exhibited by Sir R. Peel', based upon sound free-trade reasoning. The paper admitted, however, that Disraeli had put Peel 'to the torture for the delusions which he had practised upon his too-confiding followers'. But Disraeli's 'malignity' had lessened the moral force of his argument. By 11 February the *Nonconformist* was accepting that Peel had probably proposed 'as much as he is able to carry'. As late as 20 May the paper was still accepting Disraeli's charge that Peel had practised deceit upon his party. 'We take the gift, and despise the giver.' Peel's fate would be 'a useful warning to future statesmen'. And yet after Peel's fall, the *Nonconformist* of 1 July was describing his last act as 'gloriously redeeming – great, just, difficult, successful, and fatal. Perhaps no political passage of modern times has so closely approached the heroic.' Nevertheless, Peel's fall was a just conclusion, for he had created a party and then repudiated it. The *Nonconformist* hoped that this episode would mark the end of rule by party, that politicians would in future be willingly guided by public opinion.

The Baptists had long pressed for repeal, in part because they believed that the existence of the Corn Laws helped the continuation of American slavery.[66] The Baptist *Eclectic Review* had been highly critical of Peel's party at the 1841 general election; but by July 1847 it was praising Peel both for 'keeping in a proper working order the machinery of the state fabric', and for ending 'the aristocratic privilege of starving the people'. Peel would not have liked the phrasing of the latter point; but he would have been glad to notice how the Baptists understood that in proposing and carrying repeal he was demonstrating the responsiveness of the existing system of government.

At the other end of the English religious spectrum, the Tractarian *English Churchman* of 24 December 1845 complained that Cobden and the cotton lords only wanted repeal in order to reduce wages. Repeal would cut corn prices to only 30s or 40s per quarter, which would ruin British agriculture. Foreigners would then be able to force up prices again. 'Should we not be in great danger through popular commotions?' And would Britain not be at the mercy of its main foreign supplier? Would she not need a large army and fleet so that, in the last resort, she might 'take food by force'? And yet, the *English Churchman* accepted that a change was needed. 'With the debt and the Corn Law, manufacturers cannot go on. Without the Corn Law, the landlords cannot pay the debt and live, under Peel's currency system.' Whatever was

---

[66] See K. R. M. Short, 'English Baptists and the Corn Laws', *Baptist Quarterly*, 21 (1965–6), pp. 309–20.

proposed, however, must involve equal sacrifice. And the *English Churchman* of 29 January accepted that, 'whatever Sir Robert Peel's real convictions are, or whether he has any', his plan was fair. It did call for equality of sacrifice, 'and this ostensibly at least for the sake of the million'. The *English Churchman* never came to praise Peel personally. It simply ended by grumbling (2 July) that he was retiring at a time when the application of his free-trade measures would require his skills as a financier.

XII

Thirty pamphlet titles are listed for the year 1846 under the heading of 'Corn Laws' in the *Catalogue of the Goldsmiths' Library of Economic Literature*. But this is still a far from complete list. Probably the year's most-noticed pamphlet was Charles Greville's *Sir Robert Peel and the Corn Law Crisis*. This was published anonymously, but without any attempt by Greville to keep his authorship secret. Peel read it on publication, and wrote to Graham on 17 January that he had 'rarely seen within the same number of pages so much truth told with so much ability'.[67] Graham passed this letter on to Greville himself, as he noted in his diary five days later. The pamphlet emphasized how Peel had reached the point where he was closer to the Whigs on the Corn Law question than to the majority of his own party, with which he had 'little agreement, less sympathy, and no cordiality'. But this separation, claimed Greville, had ceased to matter to Peel, because his strength now lay 'neither in the support of the aristocracy, nor in any personal popularity; but in the sober dispassionate opinion of the middle classes that he is the fittest man to govern the country'. Here was 'an immense body of persons, neither Whigs nor Tories, and free from party prejudices and connections'. Greville was identifying and describing that middle opinion from which Peel was more than ever seeking support. Those whose interests were identified with the prosperity of the country, wrote Greville:

> care only for having the management of public affairs committed to the ablest public men. Sir Robert Peel enjoys the reputation of being sagacious, prudent, and experienced, and therefore thousands of practical men, who may be indifferent to his person, and perhaps dislike many of his measures, are well contented to see him the Minister of the Crown. This may not be a glittering, but it is a noted sort of popularity.

Greville's analysis becomes, of course, the more interesting because Peel in his letter to Graham seems to have endorsed it. Greville felt bound to add that the

---

[67] Peel to Graham, 17 January 1846 (Add. MSS 40452, f. 102).

John Bull and the Corn Bill

Says old John Bull, here is a job!
Shiver me tight and break my nob,
The Waterloo Cock and little Bob,
  Has carried the cursed Corn Bill,
They have set the nation in a blaze,
They have killed the farmers with amaze;
They have drove poor R——nearly mad,
And B——k and B——m they are sad,
There never was such times says Bob,
Since old King Jonah swallowed the cod,
Cries old John Bull a glorious job,
  It is to bury the Corn Bill.
      CHORUS.
Flare up you British ladies all,
Duchess and Countess, great and small,
You shall have a petticoat gown & shawl,
  Made nicely out of the Corn Bill.

On Monday last you know it's true,
In Hyde Park there was a grand review,
And the great big hero of Waterloo,
  Let fly and shot the Corn Bill ;
The soldiers they did sweat and run,
Prime and load, and follow the drum,
Pipe clay and powder blazing hot,
A penny a bottle ginger pop,
And then the ladies all in bloom,
Did bolt away in the afternoon,
To see Green go up in his great balloon,
  They swore 'twas made of the Corn Bill.

Ibrahim Pacha in the Lords that night,
Pulled out a great tobacco pipe,
And then to get himself a light,
  He took a piece of the Corn Bill ;
The Corn Bill they are going to use,
To make soldiers breeches, boots & shoes,
Sausages and German clocks,
Tailors shirts, and ladies smocks,
Oh ! won't it be a funny rig,
Rifum, tifum jigglem jig,
To see oh dear ! the Lord Mayor's wig,
  Made out of a piece of the Corn Bill.

The last little boy Victoria got,
And happy yet may be his lot,
Was marked upon a certain spot,
  With Bobby Peel and the Corn Bill ;
Oh ! what advantage we shall reap,
Penny loaves and butter cheap,
Puddings in country, pies in town,
And apple dumplings six for a brown,

And the Queen declares if time should come
That she should have another son,
Stamped in gold should be upon his b—
  Sir Robert Peel and the Corn Bill.

You would laugh to hear O'Brien & Dan,
The Patriots of Paddy's land,
Sing tunder and turf Peel is the man,
  To massacre the Corn Bill ;
And since he has done the trick so glad,
We will make him Duke of Ballinafad.
And he shall happily pass his days,
In a mansion made of turf and clay,
He shall have lots of buttermilk, meal & figs
A cow and a goat, a bull and a pig,
And we will make him a breeches, shirt
      and wig,
  And stockings out of the Corn Bill.

This Bill will reach the people say,
From John O'Groat's to Botany Bay,
And ten times farther than that hurrah !
  Oh ! what a flashing Corn Bill :
It will cover Asia and Africa.
Europe and America.
It will make the ladies some handsome
      gowns,
With their fine fandangas hanging down,
Like pheasants they'll turn the corners
      round,
With their-deckers dangling to the ground
Each flounce will weigh near 90 pounds,
  So what do you think of the Corn Bill.

Now Bobby will resign you see,
And then to have a glorious spree,
He will take a trip to Germany,
  In a ship made out of the Corn Bill ;
Prince Albert and his lady sweet,
Are going to have a pair of sheets,
A blanket, pillow case, and quilt,
And counterpane as white as milk,
The Prince of Wales will have some pap,
Sir Robert Peel will make a trap,
And nosey will have a three cocked hat,
  Made out of a piece of the Corn Bill.
      CHORUS.
May nothing old John Bull annoy,
All Victoria's little girls and boys,
Are going to have some handsome togs,
  Manufactured out of toe Corn Bill.

BIRT, Printer, 39, Great St. Andrew Street, Seven Dials, London.

'John Bull': street ballad, 1846

same 'might possibly' be said about Russell 'and his able colleagues', indulgent words which he probably felt bound to add about his Whig friends.

At the other end of the range of occasional printed comment came the street ballads. Their overall tone showed how well the broad and good intentions of Peel's plan were being understood at a lowly social level. 'John Bull and the Corn Bill', sent by Brougham to Peel, has already been mentioned. This was published in London; but a particularly prolific publisher of widely circulated ballads was John Harkness of Preston. One of his titles, 'A New Song on the Repeal of the Corn Laws', began with a promise of cheap bread:

> Come every heart rejoice with me,
> We soon shall have a glorious spree,
> Cheap food once more we soon shall see.[68]

Harkness's publications usually inclined to the Radical side; but now he was prepared to half-praise even Wellington, as well as Peel:

> The van was led by Bobby Blue
> And the boasting cock of Waterloo,
> For a Revolution would not do,
> They dread its desperation.

The cheap bread theme came through strongly in most of the ballads, as in 'A New Song On The Corn Bill':

> Cheap food from every foreign shore,
> In shiploads will sail in galore,
> The landlords now are wounded sore.
>
> *   *   *
>
> The landlords cry, Oh, Bobby P–l,
> You have a heart as hard as any steel.
>
> *   *   *
>
> The bread will shortly get a fall,
> The bakers will go to the wall,
> No 'taters they must use at all,
> But all the best and cheapest.[69]

'The Landowners Thrown Overboard; Or Bob Peel Coming to His Senses', printed in Norwich, began with an appreciation of Peel's intention to lower the cost of working-class living:

> Well done Robert Peel! you may say what you will,
> There are many worse Trumps than our friend Robert Peel;
> To lessen the Tories Bob Shews that he is willing,
> Which will do good to all that work for a Shilling.[70]

The following benevolent words were put into Peel's mouth:

> I must think of the Poor Man, the Man that is willing,
> To maintain his Family and Toil for a Shilling;
> No more shall his Children be crying for Bread,
> To Pamper you Landowners, I say 'tis too bad.

How Peel was seeking much more than cheap bread was clearly expressed:

---

[68] C. Hindley, *Curiosities of Street Literature* (1871), p. 95.
[69] J. Ashton, *Modern Street Ballads* (1888), pp. 327–30.
[70] Goldsmiths' Library, London University, collection of broadsides, VI, p. 613.

Cheap Bread and cheap Meat, cheap Clothes and cheap Shoes,
Cheap Tobacco for chewing and cheap Snuff for the Nose.
Cheap Tea and cheap Sugar, oh you grumbling old women
Tis odd if the News won't set you a grinning;
Cheap Soap and cheap Candles, why you'll gossip all night,
And a cheap Drop of Brandy!!! won't that be all right?

* * *

And Plenty once more Bless the Home of a Weaver;
And our own native City have cause to rejoice,
That the Free Traders spoke and that Peel heard the voice.

The street ballads regularly praised 'the people' for their wisdom:

And if Bob hadn't granted what the People demanded,
Instead of begging for it they would soon have commanded;
So Bob wisely submitted, spite of all opposition,
That the People should no longer be kept in Starvation.

'Free Trade; or The Coalition', published by Ryan of London, commended the harmonization of interests, an emphasis very important to Peel:

The Plough and the Loom, the Mill and the Mine
Shall have interest the same, & together combine,
And their taxes be less, – and their comforts be more,
And men shall not be punished because they are poor.[71]

'A Political Parody on Tubal Cain', also from Ryan, obviously feared that mass enthusiasm for Peel might be leading to underestimation of the League:

And sing, Hurrah for Robert Peel,
    For a staunch friend proveth he,
And for the repeal of the Corn Law Bill
    To him our praise shall be.
But if e'er protection lifts its head,
    Or for mischief should intrigue,
Though we may thank him for Repeal
    We'll not forget the League.[72]

Verse circulated not only on the streets but in the newspapers. The lines already quoted from *Lloyd's Weekly* of 28 June were typical. The *Spectator* of 4 July remarked how 'a curious flood of Peel poetry pours in upon us'. The paper explicitly recognized the significance of this flood as a mirror of public opinion: 'the fact that the versifiers, who, as a body, reflect prevalent notions

[71] Ibid., p. 614.
[72] Ibid., p. 615.

and feelings, should have adopted the late Premier so warmly, is not without its value as a proof of the juster estimate to which the public opinion has arrived.'

This middle-class newspaper verse rarely rose above the stilted. The *Spectator* of the same day published two effusions in praise of Peel. Nineteen lines 'To Sir Robert Peel, On His Resignation' took up the theme of Peel as the poor man's friend, yet without the crude freshness of the better street ballads:

> Thou claim'st from us, and from posterity
>   Undying laurels: yet high Poetry
> Tells what they are, – the poor man's blessing thine!
>   Thou like a light before his path dost shine
>   Sole watcher over his humanities.

'The Leader of the Millions' compared Peel and Disraeli:

> [Disraeli]
> What to the fleshly novelist,
>   The orator, the wit,
> Who raked up bygone grievances,
>   And was the biter bit?
>   *   *   *
> [Peel]
> Who legislates for future years;
>   Who, conscience-led, in spite
> Of enemy or partisan,
>   Does simply what is right.
>   *   *   *
> He to whose suasive accents
>   The crowded Senate bends,
> Who turns it from each selfish plan
>   To his more glorious ends.

XIII

One street ballad already quoted, 'Free Trade; or The Coalition', referred with relief to the ending of the long-standing Oregon boundary dispute with the United States. Negotiations were completed just as Corn Law repeal was finally passing:

> Now the Oregon's settled we shan't go very far
> In saying we want no more rows with America,
> But we'll trade, and we'll write, until every Yankee
> To our 'how d'ye do?' will say, 'very well, thank-ye.'

The British public had strongly desired peace with the United States. Public opinion had none the less been too much distracted by the domestic political crisis to give foreign affairs continuous attention, as *Lloyd's Weekly* remarked on 1 February, 'however interesting and important they may be'. The *News of the World* suggested three weeks later that the wish for peace with America was so general among all classes that people would be willing to consent 'to what may almost be termed an unjust peace; at least, a peace which will entail upon us loss in lands, and even in subjects'. Certainly, Peel was much more praised than blamed for a settlement which overall favoured the United States.[73]

Peel and Aberdeen had been influenced towards concession by three main considerations – by impatience with the Canadians; by a sense of the especial need to act in a spirit of free-trade internationalism at such a time; and by awareness of the strong feeling for peace in financial and commercial circles, especially among holders of American state bonds. The protectionist *Quarterly Review* did not subscribe to free-trade internationalism; but in its March issue Croker explained that the protectionists were too patriotic to wish to embarrass the Government on a matter of foreign policy. Most of the press welcomed the Oregon agreement. *The Times* of 30 June concluded that honour and interest had been satisfied, and concessions made from strength not weakness.

Peel had announced the good news as part of his resignation speech to the Commons on the previous day. That the information had been received from Washington only just in time for inclusion helped him to present it with maximum effect. 'From the importance of the subject, and considering that this is the last day I shall have to address the House as a minister of the Crown', Peel had felt justified in going into considerable detail about the negotiations. The two Governments, he concluded, 'impelled, I believe, by the public opinion of each country in favour of peace – by that opinion which ought to guide and influence statesmen – have, by moderation, by mutual compromise, averted the calamity of a war between two nations of kindred origin and common language, the breaking out of which might have involved the civilized world in general conflict'.[74] This happy outcome added to the impact of Peel's famous speech. The *Manchester Guardian* of 1 July exclaimed that never since its establishment a quarter of a century earlier had the paper been able to congratulate its readers 'on two events of such mighty import to the best interests of humanity' as the passing of the Corn Bill and the consolidation of peaceful relations with America.

---

[73] Chamberlain, *Lord Aberdeen*, ch. 20. See also F. Merk, 'British party politics and the Oregon Treaty', *American Historical Review*, 37 (1931), pp. 653–77; and 'British government propaganda and the Oregon Treaty', *American Historical Review*, 40 (1934–5), pp. 38–62.

[74] Peel, *Speeches*, IV, pp. 714–16.

Peace successfully preserved with America had been complemented by war successfully conducted in India. This had likewise benefited the final reputation of the Peel Government. Peel himself emphasized the connection between the two episodes. He had written in April to Sir Henry Hardinge, the Governor-General, that the victories on the banks of the Sutlej in India would exert an influence far away on the banks of the Oregon. These battles and their aftermath demonstrated that Britain was ready to fight but also ready to be conciliatory.[75] Peel was certain that it was right to respond decisively in India because the Sikhs had been the aggressors by crossing the Sutlej in December 1845. Three British victories had followed, leading to the treaty of Lahore on 11 March by which the Punjab became a British protectorate. Both the Government and the public felt justified in celebrating the brilliant triumph of British arms. Walter Bagehot noted in a private letter at this time how the English people tended to forget about their colonial wars until some big battle led to high casualties. Then explanations were asked for. 'We generally acquiesce pretty easily in the doctrine that we have the right on our side.' As the Indians knew nothing of European international law, wrote Bagehot, it was easy to put them in the wrong. In proposing thanks to the army in India on 2 March, Peel had vividly described the first British victory at Forezeshah, quoting effectively from a letter written by Hardinge to his family. Peel concluded that the night of 21 December 'was one of the most memorable in the military annals of the British Empire'. The parliamentary reporter noticed how Peel's speech had been punctuated by 'great and enthusiastic cheering' from all sides of the House.[76]

On 2 April Peel was back before the Commons to report the victory of Aliwal. His tone was buoyant, as he recollected that on five occasions since February 1843 it had been his good fortune to propose the thanks of the Commons to the armies of India. 'National gratitude must keep pace with national glory.' Peel wrote to Hardinge two days later that 'we have thought so much of you and of the Sutlej for some days past that we have almost forgotten domestic Conflicts.' On the Conservative benches, noted Peel gladly but sadly, 'the protection of National Honour seemed for a moment to outweigh Protection of national wheat.'[77] On 4 May Peel proposed pensions to the Commons for Hardinge, and for Sir Hugh Gough, the Commander-in-Chief in India, in recognition of their services.[78] These patriotic diversions came at intervals during the protracted Corn Law debates, and served to increase the sense of Peel's omnicompetence as a Minister. Peel himself described the Indian

---

[75] Peel to Hardinge, 22 April 1846 (Hardinge MSS U2348).

[76] Peel, *Speeches*, IV, pp. 626–34; N. St John-Stevas (ed.), *Collected Works of Walter Bagehot*, XII (1986), pp. 208–9.

[77] Peel, *Speeches*, IV, pp. 655–62; Peel to Hardinge, 4 April 1846 (Hardinge MSS U2348).

[78] Peel, *Speeches*, IV, pp. 675–8.

victories to the Archbishop of Canterbury as 'the more glorious from the justice and moderation which have directed our Councils'. A correspondent told Peel that the victories were 'a subject of great national congratulation & an element of power placed in *your* hands'.[79]

While America and India helped the growth of Peel's reputation during 1846, Ireland hindered it. Peel insisted upon promoting an Irish Coercion Bill to put down agrarian outrages. In normal circumstances he could have expected the Conservative majority in the Commons to pass such a law without much hesitation. But these were not normal times. Moreover, Peel added to his difficulties by the slowness with which he moved. The bill was not introduced into the Lords until 24 February, and not into the Commons until 30 March. Given such delay, it could reasonably be asked if the situation were sufficiently serious to require coercion at all. Many Liberal Members of Parliament were always going to vote against the bill. But would the protectionists, who now so despised Peel, necessarily vote *for* his measure? As early as 10 March the *Standard* was saying that the bill was of little value, since it gave the authorities no penal powers not already available. Most protectionist Members did vote for the first reading on 1 May, including Lord George Bentinck, but Disraeli abstained.

Henceforth there was a risk that defeat in the Commons on the Coercion Bill would bring down the Government before the Corn Bill had passed both Houses. H. B.'s cartoon, 'A Dangerous Situation', published on 27 April, showed Peel falling between two stools. Most newspapers could find little sense in this timetable, especially as a majority of them opposed Peel as firmly over coercion as they supported him over repeal. The *Morning Advertiser* of 4 April complained of the 'gratuitous odium' brought upon the Government by the Coercion Bill. *The Sunday Times* (19 April) argued that the widespread benefits expected from Corn Law repeal should have been given priority, especially as the Irish were not to be blamed for resorting to crime in desperation. By June it was becoming apparent that protectionists and Liberals might well combine to throw out the bill. The Whig *Morning Chronicle* claimed on 11 June that Peel even wanted this to happen, so that he could retire in an atmosphere of martyrdom. 'He has courted and planned a defeat which will count in his calculations for a triumph.' In reality, this was not so. Peel sincerely believed in the need for short-term coercion.

Many otherwise firmly Peelite papers insisted upon maintaining their opposition to the Coercion Bill; but they urged Peel not to resign even if defeated on the measure. The *Morning Advertiser* (17 June) advised him to abandon the bill in committee. The one qualification to *Punch*'s new enthusiasm for Peel related to his coercion policy. A cartoon on 18 April,

[79] Peel to Archbishop of Canterbury, 3 April 1846; T. Ensor to Peel, 25 April 1846 (Add. MSS 40590, ff. 46, 260).

entitled 'Justice to Ireland', showed the Premier as Old Mother Hubbard wielding a broom marked 'Coercion Bill' to sweep Irish peasants into a hovel:

> She gave them some Broth without any Bread,
> Then whipp'd them all Round, and sent them to Bed.

The Times of 15 June hedged. It recognized a case for the bill, as explained by Peel in his speech of 12 June. But this left the Irish question unresolved. 'Is a Minister's "going out on an Irish question" all that he can do for that country?'

Peel never claimed that coercion was the whole answer for Ireland. Quite the contrary. The Government had introduced during the session a whole series of relief and improvement measures. These dealt with public works, county administration, drainage, and fishery piers and harbours. But Peel regarded the re-establishment of social peace as an essential preliminary to further long-term reform. He told the Commons loftily on 28 April that, although more popularity might be gained by withdrawing the Coercion Bill, 'that popularity would be gained at a costly sacrifice, if it were obtained by the sacrifice of the duty of those who are responsible for maintaining the public peace'. Here was striking evidence of how, even though Peel's reputation stood higher than ever before as a result of his Corn Law policy, he was never prepared to bid for popularity by abandoning any course which he judged to be necessary.[80]

Not content with announcing that the protectionists would combine with the Opposition in the hope of defeating Peel's Irish measure, Lord George Bentinck made a final attempt to destroy Peel's character for political honesty. He told the Commons on 8 June that in 1827 Peel had refused to serve in Canning's Ministry because of supposed differences over Catholic Emancipation, when in reality Peel had already privately changed his mind in favour of emancipation as early as 1825. Peel had 'chased and hunted' Canning to his early death later in that year in order to gain personal political advantage. And now, added Bentinck, 'A second time has the right hon. Baronet insulted the honour of Parliament and of the country.'

The whole charge turned upon words alleged to have been used by Peel in the Commons in 1829. Bentinck had found reports which said that Peel had in that year admitted telling Lord Liverpool in 1825 that 'something respecting the Catholics ought to be done'. Here was a slender enough basis for Bentinck's charge, even if Peel's speech had been accurately reported. But it soon transpired that the key words had not been given in *Hansard*, only in *The Times* and in the *Mirror of Parliament*. Nevertheless, the feverish political atmosphere of 1846 ensured that Bentinck's charge was taken seriously, both inside and outside Parliament; and not least by Peel, who had always been sensitive about his honour. Only with difficulty was he dissuaded from challenging Bentinck to a duel. Peel heard that an associated rumour was circu-

[80] Peel, *Speeches*, IV, pp. 662–75.

lating, which said that he had encouraged anonymous newspaper attacks upon Canning in 1827, some of them written by his brother and brother-in-law; and that Giffard of the *Standard* had expressed reservations about inserting such smears. Peel correctly summed up the whole episode as 'a foul and malignant attack, made in the hope that I might not have the means of repelling it'. Bentinck's assault was repeated by Disraeli in a speech on 15 June.[81]

At Lord Aberdeen's request, Delane, the editor of *The Times*, initiated enquiries about reporting practice in the 1820s. Delane found that the *Mirror of Parliament* was not an independent source, but depended upon material supplied by the parliamentary reporters for the daily newspapers, including *The Times*. Several reporters wrote directly to Peel himself to the same effect. The *Mirror*'s version had clearly been taken from *The Times* reporter, whose text therefore stood uncorroborated. On the other hand, the parliamentary reports in the *Morning Chronicle*, *Morning Herald* and *Morning Post*, all confirmed the *Hansard* version by not including the allegedly damaging words. This information, plus contemporary letters retrieved from his private papers, enabled Peel to make a detailed and effective refutation in the Commons on 19 June. Delane had drawn attention in particular to the *Morning Journal* which, although very hostile to Peel in 1829, had not carried the damaging words now discovered by Bentinck. Peel duly quoted from the *Journal*'s report with good effect. Delane had asked, however, that his assistance should not be mentioned.[82]

He had good reason to do so; for *The Times* was moving carefully day by day. It had begun by arguing on 17 June that even if accurately reported, Peel's words did not commit Peel himself to taking action on behalf of the Catholics. Bentinck's charge was therefore 'not proven'. After Peel's explanation to the Commons, *The Times* of 20 June conceded that there was no substance in the precise charge at all. This was hardly surprising, since Delane had provided Peel with some of his best evidence. But *The Times* set tight limits to its acceptance of Peel's innocence, which helps to explain why Delane had not wanted to be publicly thanked. His paper was still steering a course between Peel, on the one hand, and Bentinck and Disraeli, on the other. 'In their larger, more comprehensive, and, we will add, rather more candid views of the career of our great Minister, there is much that commands our assent.' Why, continued *The Times* of 23 June, had suspicion lasted for twenty years about Peel's dealings with Canning? Because Peel was too secretive. This was bad enough even when a party's policy was clear; but it was worse when, as over Catholic Emancipation and Corn Law repeal, Peel wished to change that policy. 'On each the

---

[81] Add. MSS 40593, ff. 166–75; Peel to Lord Dunsandle, 20 June 1846 (Add. MSS 40593, f. 461); Add. MSS 40594, ff. 161–4.

[82] Graham to Peel, 18 June 1846 (Add. MSS 40452, f. 118); Aberdeen to Peel, 19 June 1846; Delane to Aberdeen, 18, 19 June 1846 (Add. MSS 40455, ff. 361, 362, 370); Peel, *Speeches*, IV, pp. 697–709.

apostasy was beneficial to the country. But, admitting this, what can be said for the judgment which undergoes such mutations.' Peel's integrity had been confirmed, but at the expense of his reputation for frankness and foresight.

Nevertheless, the final protectionist attempt at denigration had failed. The Queen wrote to Peel that the Commons 'ought to be ashamed of having such Members as Lord G. Bentinck & that detestable Mr. D'Israeli. They ruin their cause – the Queen feels sure that Sir Robert will only stand higher in the country.' And so he did. Peel was told by a Birkenhead correspondent that the Canning charge was 'rallying around you the sympathy of all high-minded and honourable men'. Greville noted how the Whigs at Westminster had at first been quietly pleased by the attack; but how Peel's 'very triumphant' speech had changed the atmosphere. 'The abortive attempt to ruin his character . . . has gathered round him feelings of sympathy which will find a loud and general echo in the country' (20 June).[83] Many of the addresses sent to Peel after his resignation referred approvingly to his refutation of Bentinck's claims. Peel none the less never forgot the affair. Shortly before his death he left a note in his private papers which drew attention to letters received in January 1850 from Canning's son. These showed, wrote Peel, that Stratford Canning did not regard him as 'a Maligner of his father's Character'.[84]

XIV

On 25 June the Corn Importation Bill passed the Lords, and received the royal assent. Later the same evening the Protection of Life (Ireland) Bill was defeated in the Commons by 73 votes, 292 to 219. The Peelites had voted nearly unanimously for coercion, whereas less than one-third (74) of Bentinck's 241 Conservative protectionists had followed him factiously into the hostile lobby. As many as 116 Conservative protectionists voted for the bill, while 51 abstained. These figures made it plain that Peel was not ejected by a solid phalanx of enraged country gentlemen. The gentry in Parliament were divided, both over Corn Law repeal itself and over whether those opposed to repeal should follow Bentinck to the extent of allowing their hostility to Peel to decide their voting on the coercion question. Nevertheless, the 74 Conservatives who voted with Bentinck alongside the Liberals and Radicals were enough to make the difference between victory and defeat for Peel.[85]

This defeat, regardless of the motley make-up of the majority, convinced Peel that he must resign forthwith. In a memorandum of 21 June, published in

---

[83] Queen Victoria to Peel, 21 June 1846 (Add. MSS 40441, f. 272); W. Fisher to Peel, 26 June 1846 (Add. MSS 40594, f. 296).

[84] Add. MSS 40603, f. 48.

[85] Aydelotte, 'Country gentlemen and the repeal of the Corn Law', pp. 55–9.

his *Memoirs*, he had already discussed what he regarded as the unpromising prospects for his administration, even if it survived the Irish vote four days later. He did not expect to carry the Irish Bill in its later stages. In the meantime, other important Government business would be delayed. After defeat, whenever it might come, should he ask for a dissolution rather than resign? Peel deplored the prospect of a general election which would turn 'on a question between Great Britain and Ireland'. This would be alarmingly divisive. Resignation was 'a better and safer course than an appeal to the constituencies of Great Britain against the constituencies of Ireland', with discordant cries across the Irish Sea of 'Coercion for Ireland' and 'Equal Law. No coercion.' Should a dissolution be sought on some other ground? The natural cry would be 'Free Trade and the destruction of Protection'. But this implied coalition with the Whigs and Radicals. Yet true harmony would be unattainable. Were Peelite candidates to oppose Russell or Cobden? 'Are we to be fighting under the same banner against Protectionists in half of the counties and small towns of England, and in the other half, although fighting under the same banner of public principle, to have a battle between the Government and the Liberal candidate on some narrow party ground?' How would Peelite candidates speak on the sugar question? Peel refused to support the free admission of slave-grown sugar. But a Peelite cry of 'Free Trade but not in Sugar' would sound disharmonious alongside a Liberal cry of 'Free Trade without Restriction'. If, despite all these difficulties, a majority of Members came back prepared to support a Peel Government, the favour of the non-Peelites would reflect only 'short-lived sympathy' generated by repeal and recent commercial policy. Moreover, asked Peel finally, what hope would there be in such circumstances of reconstructing a Conservative party in the House of Lords?[86]

At a brief Cabinet meeting on 26 June no one dissented from Peel's view that Ministers must resign. On Monday, 29 June, Peel went down to the House of Commons to deliver his resignation speech. Cheering crowds lined his route from Whitehall Gardens. 'It was something more than a mere *temporary huzza*,' explained the *Nottingham Review* (3 July); 'it was the utterance of emotions in no sense confined to a *London* crowd.' Certainly, Peel's speech was destined to be the best-remembered (even though not the best in quality) of all his orations.[87]

Peel arrived in the Commons at 5.30; and after pausing a few moments to compose himself, he began his speech by explaining why he had not asked for a dissolution of Parliament. He would certainly have recommended calling a general election if this had become necessary to carry his commercial measures. But to propose a dissolution at the present moment would be unwise, since

---

[86] Add. MSS 40594, f. 89; Peel, *Memoirs*, II, pp. 288–97.

[87] Peel, *Speeches*, IV, pp. 709–17; Fernandez, 'Speeches of Sir Robert Peel', ch. 6.

Ministers could not be certain of winning a firm majority. 'I do not mean a support founded upon mere temporary sympathy, or a support founded upon concurrence in a great question of domestic policy, however important.' Peel insisted that a Government needed steady backing based upon general agreement over principles and purpose. After recent excitement, the country would benefit from a period of political tranquillity.

Peel then turned to Ireland. He emphasized how he would have built upon the restoration of law and order by offering further positive and conciliatory measures in the spirit of the Maynooth and Charitable Bequests Acts. He looked forward to the establishment of 'a complete equality of municipal, civil and political rights'. Roman Catholics should be brought into Irish administration on equal terms with Protestants. Difficult problems of tenure between landlords and tenants deserved 'immediate though most cautious consideration'; and he held out the possibility of his personal support for any Irish land legislation which the new Whig Government might propose.

The three paragraphs on Ireland in Peel's resignation speech, hinting at what he might have done if he had remained in office, made a notable impression upon politicians on both sides of the Irish Sea. Daniel O'Connell even wondered if Peel contemplated repeal of the Union. Of course, he did not.[88] The *Daily News* of 30 June abandoned its last qualifications about Peel when it heard about his wishes for Ireland. 'Let him sit for his portrait now, his hand upon the Corn Bill, whilst, in lieu of that very stupid, untoward, and prepense Coercion Bill, let him have limned his declaration of last night.' It seems likely, however, that Peel's liberal intentions towards Ireland contributed much less to his popularity in Britain than his free-trade measures. Conversely, his coercion policy probably did him little harm with the British public. 'The country has manifested no interest in it, either one way or the other.' So admitted the protectionist *John Bull* on 27 June, even after the ultra-protectionists whom the paper favoured had achieved their revenge through the Irish vote.

Moving on from Ireland, Peel continued his resignation speech by commending a free-trade commercial policy to the next Government. Characteristically, however, he warned against 'abrupt and sudden application' such as would risk 'derangement of the social system'. Peel regretted that he was leaving behind a smaller financial surplus than was desirable. But, in general, he looked back over his five years of rule with satisfaction. At least in Great Britain, there had been 'obedience and submission to the law', encouraged by confidence in its just administration and by awareness of the good intentions of Parliament, all against a background of 'greater command over the necessaries and minor luxuries of life'. Peace had been maintained with the powers of Europe on terms consistent with national honour. The stability of the Indian Empire had been assured, as had the reputation of British arms. Peace with the

---

[88] Kerr, *Peel, Priests and Politics*, pp. 350–1.

United States had just been confirmed by the Oregon settlement. As already noticed, Peel was able to report this American good news with both satisfaction and effect, obviously conscious that it would be regarded as rounding off his achievement. 'Sir, I do cordially rejoice, that, in surrendering power at the feet of a majority of this House, I have the opportunity of giving them the official assurance that every cause of quarrel with that great country on the other side of the Atlantic is amicably terminated.'

There were only two paragraphs of Peel's speech left. But these were to be the passages which made the greatest impact, both upon the audience before him and upon opinion outside. Peel's penultimate paragraph spoke of Richard Cobden; and his final paragraph referred to himself.

Peel and Cobden had never met privately. Moreover, since the altercation between them in February 1843 Cobden had harboured a sense of grievance for what he thought had been an unscrupulous personal attack upon him by Peel, for which there had been only an inadequate apology at the time. This led Cobden into some over-strong language about Peel in December 1845, first at a League meeting in Stockport and then at Covent Garden. Cobden remembered at Stockport how Peel had seemed to writhe physically when in 1842 the League leader had told the Commons of the suffering in the town. But, claimed Cobden in 1845, Peel's feeling had not been for the suffering people, but for the threat to his own tenure of power. 'Sir R. Peel felt for Sir R. Peel, and not for you.' At Covent Garden a few days later, Cobden exclaimed that Peel was the only man in the Commons to whom he would never be able to talk in private 'without forfeiting his own respect'.[89] Even Cobden's friends regretted such exaggerated language. Remonstrances from some of them, and a letter of explanation to Charles Buller, were eventually communicated to Graham, who was even able to pass a copy of Cobden's apologetic letter on to Peel. The Prime Minister expressed surprise that Cobden still felt aggrieved about exchanges in 1843. Peel drily left it to others, in the light especially of Cobden's recent outbursts, to decide which of them had since been the more successful in avoiding personalities in their speeches.[90]

One of those who had complained to Cobden was Harriet Martineau, the Radical writer. A month later, greatly daring, she sent Peel a persuasive letter which urged him to make a gesture towards Cobden. 'For many years past, I have trusted you, & hoped from you that which too many are now receiving from you with an amazed gratitude which I think might & ought to have less of surprise in it.' She referred back to the clash between Peel and Cobden, which she mis-dated to 1842. Cobden had been deeply offended. 'You are a great doer of the impossible,' wrote Miss Martineau temptingly, ' – in the government of yourself, as well as in the government of the country.' She hoped

[89] *The Times*, 13, 18 December 1845.
[90] Graham to Peel, 24 January 1846; Peel to Graham, 25 January 1846 (Add. MSS 40452, ff. 104, 108).

that Peel would do the bold thing in this instance. He replied by return that he had never realized that Cobden had not been satisfied by the way the episode had ended, when he had accepted Cobden's gloss upon the sharp words with which he had blamed Peel for the distress of the time. Miss Martineau answered that Cobden regretted the attack, and she promised to pass on Peel's comments. A lucky chance a few days later gave Peel an early opportunity to explain himself publicly. Disraeli had claimed in debate that Peel had once accused Cobden of abetting assassination. Peel seized this opening to answer that he wished to remove the impression of any such imputation about Cobden, 'thrown out in the heat of debate under an erroneous impression of his meaning'. Cobden then rose to express his satisfaction at Peel's remarks, and also his regret for his recent attacks upon Peel.[91]

Miss Martineau's part in removing all tension between the two great figures on the side of repeal was not known at the time; but the friendly exchanges in the House of Commons were, of course, widely publicised. There was, however, to be an epilogue which few knew about, not even Cobden himself. In May 1846 Prince Albert passed to Peel a copy of a private letter which Cobden had written on 29 December to his friend George Combe, the phrenologist. Combe had given it to Sir James Clark to read, who had copied it to Baron Stockmar, Albert's mentor. Albert sent a copy of the copy to Peel on 29 May, with the comment: 'it confirms very much the opinion which you seem to have of the man's character and motives.' In the letter Cobden had regretted his virulent attack upon Peel at Stockport. He asked not to be judged by what he said at tumultuous public meetings, where his efforts to work up feeling ran the risk of degenerating into 'flattery, vindictiveness, and grossness'.

Peel carefully had his own copy taken of Cobden's letter. As a high politician, he was himself clear of such temptations. He remained still suspicious, or at least disdainful, of all extra-parliamentary agitation. His tart comment to Prince Albert was that 'it would have been more generous and just to appease an excited mob rejoicing in the fall of a Minister, or at least to be neutral rather than to inflame their passions by a reference to forgotten events.' Yet the distress of 1841–2 in Stockport and elsewhere could not be forgotten. Its memory explicitly formed part of Peel's own case for repeal of the Corn Laws. Cobden may have been over-excited; but he was not wrong when he remembered that Peel had earlier denied the existence of any link between distress and the workings of the Corn Laws. By the end of 1845 Peel was using his discovery of just such a link as a key part of his case for repeal.[92]

---

[91] Harriet Martineau to Peel, 22, 24 February 1846; Peel to Harriet Martineau, 23 February 1846 (Add. MSS 40585, ff. 287, 291, 293); Harriet Martineau, *Autobiography* (1877), II, pp. 259–64; Morley, *Cobden*, pp. 350–4.

[92] Prince Albert to Peel, 29 May 1846; Peel to Prince Albert, 30 May 1846; Cobden to Combe (copy), 29 December 1845 (Add. MSS 40441, ff. 241, 245, 247); Morley, *Cobden*, pp. 207–8, 352.

A month later the relationship between Peel and Cobden developed further, even though the two men had still not met privately. On 23 June, when the defeat of Peel's Government was only two days off, Cobden wrote to Peel a private letter. Peel replied next day in a letter penned from his seat in the House of Commons. Cobden began by emphasizing how he would keep his communication with Peel entirely secret. His object in writing was to ask Peel if he understood the strength of his position in the country. 'If so, why bow to a chance medley of factions in the legislature, with a nation ready and waiting to be called to your rescue?' 'The populace' was solidly behind Peel; while among 'the active and intelligent middle classes', Peel had won a sympathy greater than ever before possessed by a Minister. Enthusiasm for the Reform Bill had been even greater than it was for repeal, but it had been less rational and less enduring. It had also been directed towards several popular heroes. 'Now, the whole interest centres in yourself. You represent the *Idea* of the age.' The word 'Idea' was double-underlined by Cobden. Why not call a general election? There were no substantial differences in the country between Peelites, Whigs and Liberals. 'Do you shrink from the post of governing through the *bona fide* representatives of the middle class?' Constitutional changes were not expected by the electorate. The condition of England question and Irish reforms would provide a programme. 'Practical reforms are the order of the day, and you are by common consent the practical reformer.'[93]

Peel sent back a friendly but discouraging answer, in the spirit of his Cabinet memorandum of 21 June. He began by expressing the hope that he would soon make Cobden's personal acquaintance. 'If you were aware of the opinions I have been expressing during the last two years to my most intimate friends with regard to the purity of your motives, your intellectual power, and ability to give effect to it by real eloquence – you would share in my surprise that all this time I was supposed to harbour some hostile personal feeling towards you.' Peel did not believe that a union of Peelites, Liberals and Radicals would work, especially as he was not prepared to give up his Irish Coercion Bill. Nor did he wish to lead a Government attached to one social class. Moreover, he thought that the country needed a period of repose, not exposure to a contentious general election. He touched only lightly upon these aspects; but he did emphasize one point. If, as Cobden said, he had come to represent 'a prevailing and magnificent conception of the public mind', he must be the more careful not to give 'the suspicion even' of holding on to office for personal gratification.[94]

This exchange of letters did not become known to the public until John Morley published his life of Cobden a generation later. But the letters, and the earlier public agreement between Peel and Cobden to forget their 1843 clash,

[93] Cobden to Peel, 23 June 1846 (Add. MSS 40594, f. 123); Morley, *Cobden*, pp. 390–7.
[94] Peel to Cobden, 24 June 1846 (Add. MSS 40594, f. 135); Morley, *Cobden*, pp. 397–401.

were part of the background to Peel's high praise of Cobden in his resignation speech. Desire to be friendly may have lured Peel into speaking in what even many of his close associates thought to be exaggerated terms. On the other hand, it was characteristic of Peel, when making proposals after changing his own mind, to commend those who had advocated a policy which he had previously opposed. In 1819 in recommending currency reform, he remembered that eight years earlier he had voted against Francis Horner's resolutions which he now thought well founded. In 1829 while proposing Catholic Emancipation he gave chief credit to Fox, Grattan, Plunket and Canning. And now in 1846 he remembered Richard Cobden:

> There has been a combination of parties, generally opposed to each other, and that combination, and the influence of government, have led to their ultimate success; but the name which ought to be associated with the success of those measures is not the name of the noble lord, the organ of the party of which he is the leader, nor is it mine. The name which ought to be, and will be associated with the success of those measures, is the name of one who, acting, I believe, from pure and disinterested motives, has, with untiring eloquence the more to be admired because it was unaffected and unadorned: the name which ought to be chiefly associated with the success of those measures, is the name of RICHARD COBDEN.

Then came the long last sentence:

> In relinquishing power, I shall leave a name severely censured I fear by many who, on public grounds, deeply regret the severance of party ties – deeply regret that severance, not from interested or personal motives, but from the firm conviction that fidelity to party engagements – the existence and maintenance of a great party – constitutes a powerful instrument of government: I shall surrender power severely censured also, by others who, from no interested motive, adhere to the principle of protection, considering the maintenance of it to be essential to the welfare and interests of the country: I shall leave a name execrated by every monopolist who, from less honourable motives, clamours for protection because it conduces to his own individual benefit; but it may be that I shall leave a name sometimes remembered with expressions of good will in the abodes of those whose lot it is to labour, and to earn their daily bread by the sweat of their brow, when they shall recruit their exhausted strength with abundant and untaxed food, the sweeter because it is no longer leavened by a sense of injustice.

When Peel left the Palace of Westminster soon after 7 p.m., *The Times* (30 June) reported how he had been cheered and followed home by a large crowd, 'which included many well-dressed persons'. Peel, the reporter noticed, 'seemed much gratified by his reception, notwithstanding the somewhat rude and inconvenient pressure'.

The content of Peel's resignation speech, and especially of its last two paragraphs, came everywhere under discussion during the next few hours and days. Greville (4 July) wrote that Peel was 'very generally condemned . . . his unnecessary panegyric of Cobden, his allusion to the selfish monopolists, and his clap-trap about cheap bread in the peroration, exasperated to the last degree his former friends and adherents, were unpalatable to those he has kept, were condemned by all parties indiscriminately, and above all deeply offended the Duke of Wellington'. This was a view from Westminster, where the speech seems to have been less well received by many of the few hundred who had heard it at first hand than by many of the hundreds of thousands who read reports in their newspapers. The praise bestowed upon Cobden seemed excessive to House of Commons Peelites who had put their parliamentary seats at risk by following Peel; and also to many Liberals who had provided the greater part of the repeal majority. These points were made by J. C. Hobhouse in his diary: 'by his eulogy of *Richard Cobden* by name he endeavoured to deprive all other free traders of their due credit.' Admittedly this was a view from the Opposition side; but Aberdeen, Herbert and Gladstone were all upset by Peel's exclusive praise of Cobden, which ignored his denunciations of landowners to League audiences as plunderers of the people. Gladstone noted these doubting Peelite responses in his diary. Aberdeen and Herbert suggested that the speech was deliberately intended to make it impossible for Peel ever again to work with 'the Conservative party as a party'.[95]

Peel never explained himself in public. Brougham wrote to tell him that he wished two or three sentences had been omitted, 'especially about Cobden, & also monopolists'. In Brougham's view, the League's contribution had been 'utterly unimportant'. Repeal was Peel's doing alone; '& with my anti-mob views', Brougham welcomed this. Peel answered that he did not wish to be drawn into controversy. 'I said it deliberately and meant what I said to apply to his Speeches and Conduct in the House of Commons.' He reminded Brougham of his publicly expressed disapproval of Anti-Corn Law League meddling with the franchise through the systematic creation of freeholder votes.[96]

The non-party *Morning Advertiser* of 30 June described the whole speech as 'triumphant', and next day it particularly praised the Cobden eulogy, which would be 'hereafter quoted by the historians of England'. The *Daily News* of 1 July welcomed 'a just, bold, and graceful tribute to the name of Richard Cobden'. The *Manchester Guardian* of the same day found the speech

[95] Hobhouse Diary, 29 June 1846 (Add. MSS 43748, f. 151); Jennings, *Croker*, III, pp. 69–70; Gladstone, *Diaries*, III, pp. 547, 553–4.

[96] Brougham to Peel, 30 June 1846; Peel to Brougham, 10 July 1846 (Add. MSS 40482, ff. 307, 325).

'admirable' in its above-party emphasis. The Chartist *Northern Star* (4 July) described the praise of Cobden as evidence of 'a great revolution in our political and social system'. Other Richard Cobdens would arise to voice the wants of the people. The *Spectator* (4 July) believed that it was Peel's honesty, his wish to give 'plain truth a crowning avowal', which had led him to praise Cobden. Cobden had organized opinion, but Peel himself had been needed to translate it into legislation. The *Examiner* (4 July) welcomed the recognition of Cobden, but thought that Peel's final appeal to the people had introduced a note of conflicting egoism. 'So, after all, it is not to be Richard Cobden's name that is to be remembered with good will when the daily bread of labour is eaten, but Sir Robert Peel's!'

Peel's appeal to those who sweated and laboured was certainly novel coming from a Prime Minister, both in the fact of its being made at all and in its plainness of expression. Hobhouse underlined the key phrase in his diary as if it were demagoguery. 'His speech was egotistical in the highest sense, and he told us he should leave a name execrated by monopolists but dear to the humble tenant of the *cottage who earns his bread by the sweat of his brow*, or some such language a la Hunt.'

It may be that Peel's choice of words was influenced by his newspaper reading over the weekend while he was composing the speech. *The Sunday Times* of 28 June was far from being unreservedly favourable towards Peel. It anticipated that the Whigs would do better. But it forecast that honest men would wish Peel well in his retirement:

> When the poor in millions of cottages, are enjoying the blessings of untaxed bread – when our numerous colonies are found springing into immensely-increasing importance through having the shackles of monopoly removed from their exertions, the name of Sir Robert Peel will be remembered and respected with gratitude and honour.

The paper itself reported that Peel was at home in Whitehall Gardens on the morning of Sunday 28 June, before leaving for Osborne to see the Queen. He could have read this passage that morning, or perhaps in an early edition on Saturday. Whether or not Peel's famous words were coloured by such reading is, however, less important than the evidence here of how the idea was circulating that Peel deserved grateful remembrance in humble homes. He was asking in his resignation speech for a popular endorsement which was already becoming audible.

Yet *The Times* of 1 July was carping. It had expected a great speech, but Peel had preferred to include 'unnecessary and rather irrelevant matter'. In view of what had happened, he ought to have discussed the relationship between a Prime Minister and his party. Was there a 'compact' between them? 'He may perhaps be unwilling to admit that there had been any compact. He said first and last, and that often many times, that he never would be a Minister on sufferance, the slave of a party.' His party had certainly been given plenty of warning. 'More than five years since it was the joke of the enemy that the Conservatives followed the leader and cried "Stop thief" at the same time.' And what was now Peel's attitude to extra-parliamentary agitations such as the Anti-Corn Law League? 'How will Sir Robert explain his act of submission? True, he has not joined the League, but he has taken its place, and pledged his whole self to its merits.' Had such bodies become respectable channels of political action? Were people 'to hate leagues, or to join them?' Peel had given no proper answer. 'A great agitator is not only triumphant but glorified.'

The protectionist *Standard* of 30 June had taken this point to its extreme hostile conclusion. Praise of Cobden meant praise of the League, which meant praise of a 'seditious conspiracy'. The *Morning Post* of 2 July quoted from *The Times* editorial of the previous day, and asked if submission by Ministers to extra-parliamentary pressure was to become normal practice. 'Is this to be the statesmanship for the future?' If middle-class capitalists were to dictate the political agenda, what chance was there for the interests of the working classes? As for Peel's appeal for remembrance by such working people, this was dismissed by the *Standard* as 'stark nonsense', since the masses would soon have little bread to thank him for. In the same spirit, the protectionist *Liverpool Courier* (1 July) wrote of 'a jacobin speech'. Peel's 'effort at pathos' was described as 'exquisitely ludicrous were it not so absolutely disgusting'. The Whig free-trade *Preston Chronicle* (4 July) was equally dismissive. 'Is not this the very clap-trap of a melo-dramatic popularity hunter?' How could Peel be 'venerated' by working people, when he had merely succumbed to necessity?

Newspaper response to Peel's resignation speech was thus mixed. Not only were the protectionist papers hostile, but so were some free-trade papers, led by *The Times*. Yet the words of Peel's parting appeal were to be long remembered with satisfaction by many Victorians. G. A. Sala recollected in his auto-biography half a century later how at Peel's death in 1850 there was scarcely a schoolboy who had not got by heart his 'pathetic expression of his hopes'.[97] Peel's words may have offended many high politicians and some newspaper editors; but they did not offend non-party opinion, either among the middle classes or among working people. One working man had written to Peel from Nottingham to thank him 'for unfettering the Staf [sic] of Life to the poore man'. He told Peel explicitly that his appeal for remembrance had been heard. 'Be assured that you do dwell in the Hearts of Thousands for ever utering [sic] those memerable [sic] words.' There then followed a garbled version of the famous last paragraph:

> But it may be that I shall leave a name Sometimes remembered with expressions of goodwill in those places which are the abodes of men whose Lot is to labour and earn there [sic] daily bread by the sweat of

[97] G. A. Sala, *Life and Adventures* (1896), pp. 221–2.

there daily brow a name remembered with expressions of good will when they shall reacreate [sic] there exhausted strength with abundant and untaxed Food the sweeter because it is no longer leavened by a sence [sic] of injustice.[98]

A letter from a Hull man to Peel was the same in spirit, but much briefer:

> To Sir Robert Peel
>
> For his Boldness and Perseverance in bringing forward his great Free Trade Measures.
>
> A Working Man
>
> P.S. If it ever should happen that I visit London I shall try to get a glance of that Great Man.[99]

Here was what Carlyle called 'the Dumb Heart of England' responding to Peel. A 'great veracity' had been done in Parliament, for which Peel had sacrificed himself. 'Let this merit never be forgotten in Sir Rt., that he could do without articulate backing and depend upon the inarticulate; which indeed argues a strong man.'[100]

What of the middle classes? John Hope, the Lord Justice Clerk, reported from Ayrshire on 31 July 'the nearly universal wish of the middling classes' for Peel to come back as Minister, in confidence that he would undertake necessary improvements without disturbing the social system or interfering with prosperity. Peel answered that although he knew something of the opinions of the middle classes, he had been surprised by the strength of feeling against the Corn Laws in Scotland, as revealed in the addresses of support sent to him from numerous large and small towns. He had made the same point a month earlier in conversation with John Bright. He had also told Bright that 'he felt great pleasure at the satisfaction evident among the working classes'. Bright replied that no Minister had retired more universally regretted. To which Peel responded by repeating words from his own peroration: ' "or more execrated by the Monopolists," and laughed with the consciousness of the victory which had been won'.[101]

A. P. Stanley, the future Dean of Westminster, described Peel's resignation speech as 'the most affecting public event I ever remember'; the great Minister was retiring after having bequeathed to the world 'free trade with one hand, and universal peace with the other, and casting under foot the miserable factions which had dethroned him'.[102] Free trade (including cheap bread);

---

[98] F. Snelson to Peel, 8 July 1846 (Add. MSS 40595, f. 306).

[99] Add. MSS 40597, f. 48.

[100] J. Seigel, 'Carlyle and Peel', *Victorian Studies*, 26 (1983), p. 193.

[101] Hope to Peel, 31 July 1846 (Add. MSS 40596, f. 407); Peel, *Private Letters*, pp. 280–2; R. A. J. Walling (ed.), *Diaries of John Bright* (1930), pp. 80–1.

[102] Gregory, *Autobiography*, p. 131.

peace with foreign powers; self-sacrifice for the sake of politics above party – such were the benefits with which Peel's name was triumphantly linked, not just in Stanley's mind but in the minds of people of all classes. Arthur Helps's *Claims of Labour* (1844) had noticed 'a great distrust' of public men among working people, distrust stimulated by the extremism of rival election candidates and of party attitudes in general. Peel soared above party and overcame distrust. This was confirmed by the many public addresses sent to him. At first these urged him not to retire; and then, when he had done so, they thanked him warmly for his services. Peel himself told Graham that the address from Bradford was 'not a bad specimen of the feeling'.[103] This was given national publicity in *The Times* of 3 July. It was signed by over a thousand merchants, bankers, professional men, worsted spinners, manufacturers, shopkeepers and other tradesmen. It began by deploring the way, while piloting his great measures of commercial reform through Parliament, Peel had been assailed 'even to the detriment of life'. It expressed particular distaste for the slanderous attacks made upon him for his alleged dishonesty towards Canning; 'but which you so ably expelled'. It assured Peel that his measures 'for the relief of trade, and the comfort of the industrial classes' were considered 'by men of all parties here as among the greatest and most beneficial ever proposed by any Minister'. Peel was particularly thanked for 'the manifest sacrifices, both private and public' which he had made in the national interest. Finally, the address hoped that Peel would be spared in health and happiness for further service to his country.

But Peel was tired in body and mind; if not tired of all politics, he was at least tired of involvement in party politics. Yet he recognized the need for division into parties to make the system of parliamentary government work. He admitted this in his resignation speech and in his Cabinet memorandum of 21 June. 'A Government ought to have a *natural* support. A Conservative Government should be supported by a Conservative party.' Nevertheless, he himself no longer wanted to be involved at this level. He wished to stay where the Corn Law crisis had placed him, acting not merely apart from party but above party. And there he was to remain, in a uniquely influential position as an elder statesman, for the last four years of his life.

[103] Peel to Graham, 3 July 1846 (Add. MSS 40452, f. 142).

5

Peel in Retirement: 1846–50

I

Peel's reputation was significantly strengthened even before repeal of the Corn Laws by his support for the arts and sciences, an interest which had become increasingly well publicised. He was a discriminating patron, both in his official and private capacities.[1] The link between Peel, the patron, and Peel, the politician, was explicitly made just after his resignation in 1846 by 'Alfred' (Samuel Kydd, a Chartist lawyer and friend of Richard Oastler) in the *Morning Advertiser* for 4 July: 'Had not Sir Robert Peel been a minister he would have been a Maecenas. Had he not been Sir Robert Peel the Premier, he would have been the modern Lorenzo de Medici, the patron. His tastes are only second to that virtuous ambition which has saved his country by a self-sacrifice unparalleled.'

The range of Peel's cultural interests was well reflected in his official commitments over the years – as an active trustee of the National Gallery from 1827; as the moving spirit behind the Fine Arts Commission of 1841, which had been appointed to supervise the decoration of the new Houses of Parliament; as an advocate for the Royal Academy against Radical critics in the Commons; as a leading patron of the Artists' Benevolent Fund; and at the very end of his life as an enthusiastic supporter of the Great Exhibition project.

Peel's interest in architecture was expressed, not entirely successfully, through the care and money which he lavished upon the building of his two houses, both designed by Robert Smirke: first in the 1820s, 4 Whitehall Gardens, London, and then, during the 1830s, Drayton Manor in Staffordshire. The former was built in an unexceptionable Greek revival style; the latter ended up with a confused Elizabethan exterior, but with a splendidly comfortable interior. Each contained a picture gallery. Drayton came to house Peel's notable array of commissioned portraits of leading contemporaries,

---

[1] See J. Mordaunt Crook, 'Sir Robert Peel: patron of the arts', *History Today*, 16 (1966), pp. 3–11.

fifteen of them by Lawrence. Anna Jameson's *Companion to the Most Celebrated Galleries of Art in London* (1844) was dedicated to Peel, and made known in detail the contents of his collection to that date. His most outstanding picture was *Le Chapeau de Paille* by Rubens. The largest category consisted of seventeenth-century Dutch and Flemish work. Many of the best pictures at Whitehall Gardens were deliberately kept in the family sitting-room.[2] Requests from artists to copy *Le Chapeau de Paille* were frequent, as were requests from strangers to view the pictures. All had to be rejected, to protect the privacy of the family. But Peel delighted in exhibiting his collection to friends and acquaintances, as was illustrated in Jemima Wedderburn's 1844 drawing of *Sir Robert Peel Shewing His Pictures*. He strongly advocated making the national art collections, and places of national interest such as Westminster Abbey, readily open to the general public.[3]

Brief descriptions of Peel's art collection appeared at intervals in the press. *Bentley's Miscellany* for February 1838 contained (along with episode twelve of *Oliver Twist*) an admiring account taken from a book by Dr G. F. Waagen of Berlin. The *Kentish Gazette* of 20 January 1846 copied an enthusiastic description by the physician to the King of Saxony of a visit to Peel's London home in June 1844. Although fresh from defeat in the Commons on the sugar question, Peel was said to have exuded his 'usual prudent serenity' as he took diplomats and leading literary men round his pictures. This sympathetic view of Peel was the more striking for being published in a protectionist county newspaper in the middle of the Corn Law crisis. Four months later, the *Art Union* for May 1846 published not only a leading article in which it deliberately abandoned its political neutrality – on the ground that 'every great patron and every distinguished amateur of Art' favoured free trade – but also carried a description of Peel's art collection. 'Proud and earnest gratification' was expressed that the Premier was both a connoisseur and a patron of the arts.

The Times of 26 April 1847 reported approvingly that Peel had opened his London mansion to an especially large number of men of letters and science along with peers and Members of Parliament. The party had included Dickens, Thackeray, Turner, Landseer, Westmacott, Faraday and Lyon Playfair. Lord John Russell, the Whig Prime Minister, was also present; and the genial meeting of host and guest was welcomed by one gentleman present for making 'as pleasing a picture as any which adorned the walls'. So Peel's political above-party image was given further support even within favourable publicity for his cultural leadership.

[2] Anna Jameson to Peel, 13 August 1843; Peel to Anna Jameson, 14 August 1843 (Add. MSS 40532, ff. 168, 170); Anna Jameson to Peel, 22 March 1844; Peel to Anna Jameson, 26 March 1844 (Add. MSS 40541, ff. 338–49); Peel, *Private Letters*, pp. 214–15.

[3] C. J. Palmer to Peel, 21 April 1842 (Add. MSS 40507, f. 20); E. Everitt to Peel, 1 November 1842; Peel to Everitt, 2 November 1842 (Add. MSS 40518, ff. 13, 15); Ormond, *Early Victorian Portraits*, p. 370, plate 728.

Peel remained characteristically 'practical' in his encouragement of the arts and sciences. As a British Museum trustee, he was pressing in 1843 for 'very cheap' guidebooks to the collections, and also for 'necessary *Conveniences*' for the crowds of visitors.[4] As Prime Minister in 1834–5 it fell to him to offer pensions out of the £1,200 made available from the Civil List thanks to an initiative taken by the Whig Government in February 1834. Recipients included Faraday (recommended to Peel by Lord Ashley); Airy, the Cambridge astronomer; and Southey and James Montgomery, poets.[5] The son of Mrs Hemans ('The boy stood on the burning deck' was her best-known line) was given a clerkship, and she herself a gift of £100 because of distressed circumstances. Lord Sandon, who had written on her behalf, was told by Peel that such an application was 'precisely of the class which I prefer to every other, prefer in every sense'. Peel's kindness to Mrs Hemans was revealed in *The Times* of 7 April 1835. But Peel was responsible for many unofficial acts of generosity out of his own pocket which passed unnoticed.[6]

Yet on one occasion a correspondent threatened to damage Peel's good name both as a politician and as a patron of the arts by claiming that he had shown ingratitude by failing to help 'a distressed Literary gentleman (a Protestant)', who had been an active Conservative in Ireland. This man was Henry Bayly, the author of *A Topographical and Historical Account of Lisburn* (1834), the only one of his publications to appear in the British Library catalogue. Contact between Bayly and Peel began in 1835 with the presentation of a copy of this book to Peel. Three years later Bayly complained that Peel had not paid for his copy. 'You form a miserable living monument of that despicable and damnable hard-heartedness which so frequently characterizes the possessors of enormous wealth.' Peel wrote a soothing reply, which seems to have been sent before he received another letter in which Bayly threatened to publicise his alleged grievances. However, when Bayly received Peel's reply to the earlier letter, he changed in a further letter to a tone of contrition. At the same time he told Peel of his political work in preparing addresses, speaking at public meetings, and in journalism. Peel answered soothingly a second time, expressing sorrow at Bayly's distress and enclosing £5. So the episode might have ended, with Peel showing in practical form his respect for a hard-pressed writer who remained none the less an independent gentleman. But three

---

[4] Peel to Rev. J. Forshall, 11 April 1843 (Add. MSS 40527, f. 185); Peel to Hume, 1 June 1843 (Add. MSS 40529, ff. 146, 303).

[5] Peel to Ashley, 17 February 1835 (Add. MSS 40414, f. 369); Ashley to Peel, 18 February 1835; Peel to Ashley, 19 February 1835 (Add. MSS 40415, ff. 1, 3); Ashley to Peel, 4 April 1835 (Add. MSS 40419, f. 292). See R. Macleod, 'Science and the Civil List, 1824–1914', *Technology and Society*, 6 (1970), pp. 47–55.

[6] Sandon to Peel, 5 February 1835; Peel to Sandon, 7 February 1835; Peel to Mrs Hemans, 7 February 1835 (Add. MSS 40413, ff. 205, 267, 291); Mrs Hemans to Peel, 10 February 1835 (Add. MSS 40414, f. 74).

months later Bayly surfaced again. He now abandoned all pretensions by asking for employment 'in the *Household*' of a Conservative peer or commoner, with a strong hint of preference for service with Peel. No reply was sent to this very different approach.[7]

Peel's great art collection was, of course, made possible by his large personal fortune, as were also his many acts of private benevolence. His wealth seems to have aroused no great resentment, although Bayly mentioned it, and one frustrated poet, Richard Wemyss, complained in 1843 when Peel refused to meet the cost of printing his poem, 'Hood'. 'God, who is no respecter of persons, I flatter myself meant some share of these revenues for me.' The compiler of Peel's collected speeches contrived to set up a contrast which turned Peel's possession of wealth to advantage. 'Peel was rich and suffered – persecuted and generous.'[8]

Two particularly noteworthy examples of Peel's kindness were his attempts to help Tom Hood, the poet, and B. R. Haydon, the artist, in their last days. Harriet Martineau wrote in her contemporary history that Peel's letters to Hood, announcing the grant of a state pension, remained 'one of the chief honours of the great statesman'. The facts first became known through the *Literary Gazette* of 10 May 1845, where it was explained how Peel's letters had given solace to Hood on his deathbed. Hood's pension was transferred to his widow; and when she also died soon afterwards, provision was made for their children.[9]

A year later a crisis occurred in the affairs of Haydon, which ended with his suicide. The fact that in June 1846 the Premier had quickly responded to Haydon's last call for help, even while himself under pressure from the Canning charges, contributed perceptibly towards the growth of his reputation. Peel had helped to get Haydon out of a debtor's prison as early as 1830; and he had commissioned a large portrait of Napoleon. In February 1846 Haydon had asked to draw a chalk study of the Prime Minister, but not surprisingly Peel had declined owing to pressure of public business. By June, overwhelmed with debt, Haydon was sending despairing letters to Peel, Brougham, the Duke of Buccleugh and others, asking for help. Peel responded with £50. Brougham and Buccleugh ignored the cry. 'And this Peel,' exclaimed Haydon in his diary, 'is the man who has *no heart*!' But despair prevailed. On 22 June Haydon killed himself. Peel's responsiveness quickly became public knowledge through the

---

[7] Bayly to Peel, 28 January, 8, 10, 11 February 1838; Peel to Bayly, 8, 14 February 1838 (Add. MSS 40424, ff. 307, 308, 328, 330, 332, 334); Bayly to Peel, 24 May 1838 (Add. MSS 40425, f. 101).

[8] Wemyss to G. Arbuthnot, 3 July 1843 (Add. MSS 40530, f. 158); Peel, *Speeches*, I, p. 4.

[9] Hood to Peel, 17 February 1845; Peel to Hood, 18 February 1845 (Add. MSS 40560, ff. 100, 101); W. Jordan to Peel, 10 May 1845 (Add. MSS 40566, f. 295); Peel to Mrs Hood, 24 May 1845; Mrs Hood to Peel, 27 May 1845 (Add. MSS 40567, ff. 348, 389); Martineau, *Thirty Years' Peace*, IV, pp. 425–6.

national publicity given to the inquest, at which Peel's letter and extracts from the diary were read out. The inquest was also told that immediately after Haydon's death Peel had sent £200 from the Royal Bounty Fund to tide the family over. The coroner remarked that these kindnesses 'must speak to the heart of a great many thousand persons'. *The Times* published a two-column report on 25 June, the very day that the Corn Bill finally passed.[10]

> Who, listening to his own good heart,
>   Amid the cares of state
> And venom'd maledictions
>   Of disappointed hate,
>
> Can find the time and find the will
>   To do a kindly deed,
> To help the artist in despair
>   The widow in her need.

Thus was Peel eulogized in the *Spectator* of 4 July. Nearly every journal seems to have complimented him over the Haydon affair. The *Art Union* exclaimed in its July number how 'the glory of this one act – which he little dreamed the world would ever hear of – is a set-off against a score of party-victories and a hundred arena-defeats'. But one unwanted effect of the favourable national publicity was to increase the number of begging letters in Peel's incoming post.

Peel was active in support of science as well as of the arts, especially of applied science. He liked to mix men of science and men of affairs socially to the benefit of both. He held one such 'select philosophico/Agricultural party' at Drayton in October 1845. It was attended by Josiah Parkes, consulting engineer to the Royal Agricultural Society; Lyon Playfair, the chemist; William Buckland, the clerical geologist; Lord Talbot; and the Earl of Aylesford. Peel described this group as 'fair representatives of the feelings and unbiassed sentiments of two powerful classes in England. Men of Rank and Property, and Men of Science and practical Philosophy.' A year earlier he had been characteristically urging upon Buckland the need for an up-to-date account of geology intelligible to laymen: 'science should remove the prejudices of the unlearned as well as satisfy the Cravings of the learned for new knowledge.'[11]

Peel was particularly interested in the application of science to agricultural improvement. In 1847 he was reported by *The Times* of 1 October, in an article copied from the *Worcester Chronicle*, as having brought to Drayton in late September 'a party of scientific and practical agriculturists, geologists, botanists, etc.' for 'animated discussion' of such matters as cattle feeding and

---

[10] Haydon to Peel, 3 February 1846 (Add. MSS 40584, f. 101); Add. MSS 40593, ff. 308–31; W. B. Pope (ed.), *Diary of Benjamin Robert Haydon* (1963), V, pp. 551–2.

[11] Peel to Buckland, 27 December 1844 (Add. MSS 40556, f. 296); Peel to E. Everitt, 16 October 1845 (Add. MSS 40574, f. 382).

field drainage. Next day, *The Times* reported the holding in Drayton picture gallery of a dinner for farmers and freeholders of the neighbourhood, 'irrespective of party', attended also by Lyon Playfair, George Stephenson, the railway engineer, and others. Agricultural topics were discussed, and speeches made 'irrespective of all political, protective, or free trade opinions'. Peel had been commended by the *Worcester Chronicle* for fulfilling in retirement the important duty of encouraging country gentlemen to improve their estates 'to meet the altered spirit of the times'.

In other words, Peel's interest in the latest developments both in the arts and the sciences showed him to be well in touch with the mood of the 1830s and 1840s quite apart from politics. Gladstone remarked in 1840 that there was 'a manifest and peculiar adaptation in Peel's mind to the age in which he lives and its exigencies and to the position he holds as a public man'.[12] His commitment to the central contemporary gospel of work was obvious. Appropriately, the Peel family success story occupied four pages in Samuel Smiles's *Self-Help* (1859). After Peel's death, *The Times* (5 July 1850) emphasized how 'in a country where labour is the condition of happiness and honour', his example had not been lost, 'either in Parliament or with the people'. Yet although he was hard working and his family was self-made, Peel was also rich and titled. This mixture gave him a double appeal. In his own person he was able to exploit both the Victorian tendency towards social deference and the contrasting desire to find evidence of opportunities for social rising. In Peel's later years the story spread that at the time of his birth the family home, Chamber Hall, near Bury, had been under repair, and that he was born in an estate cottage. This story was probably mistaken. The reason for its wide circulation and acceptance was shrewdly noticed in Sir Lawrence Peel's 1860 sketch of his cousin's career; how the man who 'was to take the tax from the poor man's food, was to be born under a poor man's roof'.[13]

II

The frequent use of the adjective 'practical' by and about Peel has already been mentioned. This quality constituted the popular test for literature as well as for statesmanship. J. R. McCulloch's *Dictionary, Geographical, Statistical and Historical* (new edition 1852, first edition 1841) suggested that 'the practical, common-sense character of the philosophy and literature of England' was probably caused by its being centred not in Oxbridge but in London. Writers mixed with the world, and so were discouraged from favouring 'over-refined theories and fanciful distractions'. It was certainly the case that leading early

[12] Add. MSS 44819, f. 50.
[13] Sir L. Peel, *Sketch of the Life of Sir Robert Peel* (1860), p. 43.

Victorian writers regarded themselves as belonging to society in general, not as living in a separate literary environment. They readily addressed themselves to contemporary problems. This was conspicuously true of four writers who were prominent during Peel's later years – Carlyle, Dickens, Thackeray and Tennyson. How much affinity may be found then between Peel and these great Victorian men of letters?

The sympathy shown by Carlyle for Peel has already been discussed. But Peel matched not only Carlyle's high ideal hero; he seems also to have matched the typical heroes of the popular novelists who contributed to such publications as the *London Journal* and the *Family Herald*. These fictional heroes have been found to share a range of characteristics. Although some of them might have wasted time in youth, they were usually portrayed as later becoming responsible social leaders. Most of them were depicted as careful landowners, and many were shown as entering Parliament. They were usually revealed as staying faithful in love each to one woman, and they were frequently described as quiet but committed Christians. They were expected to possess underlying fortitude, but they were allowed to reveal emotion and even to shed tears. It is striking how Peel in his real-life experience satisfied this fictional formula for admiration, excepting only that he had never wasted time in his youth.[14]

Dickens was not the author of popular novels of this sort, but he became the most popular novelist of the age. His aim as a novelist was avowedly to influence his readers for good, even while he entertained them. Thackeray pursued the same objective. 'Our profession seems to me,' he wrote in 1847, 'to be as serious as the Parson's own.'[15] Thackeray had sprung into the first rank of novelists with *Vanity Fair*, which appeared in monthly parts between January 1847 and July 1848. Dickens had already been ten years at the top; but *Dombey and Son*, which ran from October 1846 to April 1848, was one of his less popular novels. When, however, during most of 1849–50 *David Copperfield* and *Pendennis* were appearing side by side, the *Weekly Chronicle* complained that Thackeray seemed to be losing his way whereas Dickens was bringing *Copperfield* to a triumphant conclusion.[16] 'We may fairly presume,' decided the Chartist *Northern Star* on 27 December 1850, 'that everybody has read *David Copperfield*, and as naturally conclude that everybody has been delighted with it.' Every page gave 'a lesson in self-denial, in the patient endurance of unavoidable ills, in strenuous effort against such as are remediable, and in that virtuous aspiration after the pure heart and unselfish will'. *Copperfield*, in short, pleasingly reflected Victorian ideal standards of

[14] Margaret Dalziel, *Popular Fiction 100 Years Ago* (1957), ch. 10.

[15] G. N. Ray (ed.), *Letters and Private Papers of William Makepeace Thackeray* (1945), II, p.282. See also Janice Carlisle, *The Sense of an Audience, Dickens, Thackeray, and George Eliot at Mid-Century* (1982).

[16] Rebecca Rodolff, 'The *Weekly Chronicle*'s month-by-month reception of *Pendennis* and *David Copperfield*', *Victorian Periodicals Review*, 14 (1981), pp. 101–11.

attitude and behaviour. And these standards were presented and tested not as abstractions but in their everyday application. In this same temper, R. H. Horne's *The Spirit of the Age* (1844) had noticed how Dickens's early work was dominated by 'a practical tendency. His universality does not extend beyond the verge of the actual and concrete.'

Dickens and Thackeray both became personal friends of Lord John Russell, the Whig Prime Minister; but Peel's personal contact with the two authors was only occasional. Dickens inclined to be suspicious of all rulers, assuming that society's problems persisted because they would not use their power to solve them. He had not been impressed by what he had seen and heard while a parliamentary reporter in the 1830s. Well into the next decade he shared *Punch*'s dislike of Peel, as did Thackeray, who was a regular contributor. Nevertheless, like *Punch*, Dickens found his assessment changing rapidly during the Corn Law crisis. 'I little thought, once upon a time,' he admitted just after Peel's fall, 'that I should ever live to praise Peel. But d'Israeli and that Dunghill Lord have so disgusted me, that I feel disposed to champion him – and should have done so even if he hadn't shewn a starving artist such delicate attention and compassion as he shewed to Haydon.' At Peel's death in 1850 Dickens mourned 'a man of merit who could ill be spared from the Great Dust Heap down at Westminster'.[17]

Thackeray responded to the same pull, but even more reluctantly. He noted in October 1846 how *Punch* had gone over to Peel, 'with the rest of the well thinking part of the nation. What a pity he's such a dem Humbug.' Thackeray was invited to the view of Peel's pictures in April 1847 which Dickens also attended. Peel told Thackeray there that he had read 'with delight *every line you ever wrote*'. Thackeray was not yet famous, but he was unimpressed by such well-meant hyperbole. In April 1850 he chanced to meet Peel at the Water Colour Society. 'Sir Robert Peel elaborately gracious.' The outcome was that Thackeray went to dinner chez Peel on the following Saturday.[18]

The political opinions of Dickens and Thackeray now had much in common with those of Peel, but they did not coincide entirely. The two novelists wanted further social reform to improve conditions for the masses. On the other hand, their Radicalism had limits. They did not challenge the social order. It is noticeable how the working classes in Dickens's writings always know their place. This was assumed, for example, even in the circumstances of rapid economic change portrayed in *Dombey and Son*. Dickens had begun to write this novel in August 1846, just after repeal of the Corn Laws. In the final chapter Mr Dombey, old Sol, Captain Cuttle and Toots join in drinking the last

---

[17] E. Johnson, *Charles Dickens* (1953), pp. 597, 709; Tillotson, *Letters of Charles Dickens*, vol. 4, pp. 576–7.

[18] Ray, *Letters and Papers of Thackeray*, II, pp. 251, 664; G. N. Ray, *Thackeray: The Age of Wisdom* (1958), p. 40.

bottle of old Madeira, to toast Walter and Florence. This coming together was intended to show how the classes might achieve harmony; but Dickens was not claiming that class differences could be removed. The same benevolent but not levelling spirit underlay his opening addresses as editor first of the *Daily News* (21 January 1846) and then of *Household Words* (30 March 1850). *Punch* followed the same line, and it is interesting how one cartoon (28 August 1847), entitled 'Dombey and Son', even portrayed Peel as Mr Dombey. Dombey had made a difficult but successful progress towards understanding the need for sympathy in dealings between men; and the same was felt by middle-class Radicals to have been the case with Peel. The similarity might have been heightened if, as Dickens seems to have originally intended, Dombey had entered Parliament. George Orwell was to point out how Dickens always liked rich men if they were also good; how they recurred in his novels from Pickwick through to Boffin.[19]

This dream of harmony through contact between classes was so powerful a middle-class aspiration of the time that Mrs Gaskell risked weakening two of her novels, *Mary Barton* (1848) and *North and South* (1855), in order to make room for the idea of reconciliation. Perhaps under the influence of this climate of opinion, even novels published in Chartist journals about 1850, although they still emphasized the need for working-class solidarity, seem to have become increasingly hesitant about advocating class hostility. T. M. Wheeler's *Sunshine and Shadow*, which finished serialization in the *Northern Star* in January 1850, reflected this sense of hesitation. And six months later the *Star* was telling the readers of the novel to mourn Peel as 'the right hand of the country'.[20]

Thackeray's *Vanity Fair* claimed in its subtitle to be a novel without a hero. But, as John Forster pointed out in the *Examiner* of 22 July 1848, it none the less acquired a hero in the worthy Dobbin. Thackeray's heroes were ordinary people for most of the time, becoming heroic only in the presence of great occasions. Thackeray, indeed, seems to have believed that heroes never could be otherwise. He remarked that Napoleon and Nelson 'in their common life' were as frail and mean as ordinary men. R. S. Rintoul in the *Spectator* of 21 December 1850, while discussing the character of George Warrington in *Pendennis*, argued that the 'natural ideal' preferred strength to refinement, sense rather than learning, kindness of heart before elaborate polish; 'and many a man eminent for social and political success, might have supplied the oddest

[19] J. Butt and Kathleen Tillotson, 'Dickens at work on *Dombey and Son*', *Essays and Studies 1951*, pp. 70–93; M. Engel, 'The politics of Dickens' novels', *Publications of the Modern Language Association of America*, 71 (1956), pp. 945–74; D. Donaghue, 'The English Dickens and *Dombey and Son*', *Nineteenth-Century Fiction*, 24 (1969–70), pp. 383–403; G. Orwell, *Collected Essays, Journalism and Letters* (1970), I, pp. 458–9.

[20] Martha Vicinus, *The Industrial Muse* (1974), pp. 122–34; J. Lucas, *The Literature of Change* (1977), pp. 1–2.

as well as the noblest traits of Warrington's character.' Among this number of plain yet admirable models, Peel must surely have figured prominently.[21]

Thackeray's religious doubt tending to scepticism underlay *Pendennis*. The same *Spectator* article described chapter 61 of the novel as 'a prose echo of *In Memoriam*'. This was the poem, published on 1 June 1850, which finally established Tennyson's reputation as a great poet, and which led to his appointment as Poet Laureate later in the year. Gladstone had recommended Tennyson to Peel for a pension as early as 1845, with the imperceptive remark that although 'a true and even a great poet he can hardly become popular'. Peel had already begun to admire Tennyson's work, and eventually the poet was prevailed upon to accept a pension of £200 a year.[22] Some 60,000 copies of 'In Memoriam' were sold during the period which included the death of Peel and its aftermath. The poem appropriately surveyed the problems of the day in relation to death and religion. Its grief for Arthur Hallam came close to presenting him as a Christ-like figure. At the least, he was lamented as a lost statesman, very much in the Peel mould:

> A life in civic action warm,
> A soul on highest mission sent,
> A potent voice of Parliament,
> A pillar steadfast in the storm.

Tennyson published nothing directly to mourn Peel; but two years later he composed his 'Ode on the Death of the Duke of Wellington', with its affirmation:

> On God and Godlike men we build our trust.

It seems likely that Tennyson had Peel in mind among others in making this affirmation.[23]

III

During the years 1847–9 Peel ventured upon several distant visits outside London and Drayton. Such trips had now been made much easier by the spread of the railway network. All Peel's journeys were well publicised in *The Times*

[21] M. Praz, *The Hero in Eclipse in Victorian Fiction* (1956), pp. 224–33.

[22] Henry Hallam to Peel, 11, 22 February 1845; Peel to Hallam, 15 February 1845; Gladstone to Peel, 24 February 1845 (Add. MSS 40559, ff. 310, 312, 317, 319); Peel to Hallam, 21 September 1845; Hallam to Peel, 22 September 1845; Tennyson to Peel, 29 September, 3 October 1845; Peel to Tennyson, 1 October 1845 (Add. MSS 40574, ff. 201, 203, 205, 206, 207).

[23] J. D. Hunt (ed.), *Tennyson: In Memoriam* (1970); I. Jack, 'Tennyson, the poet and his audience', *Times Higher Educational Supplement*, 11 June 1982.

and other newspapers. The mood of these occasions was uniformly congratulatory, both towards Peel's policies and about Peel personally. In April
1847 he visited his properties in Lancashire. The *Manchester Guardian* of 17
April, copied into *The Times* five days later, reported how Peel on his tour met
with some adventures 'which will furnish materials for capital after dinner
stories'. The *Guardian* then told of an old woman's 'obstreperous invitation'
to enter her cottage, which Peel owned: 'coom an' look at th' heaven hoo it
rained ith' roof.' Peel duly did so, and gave instructions for repair. The old
woman had mistaken him for the head factor. Here was a human interest story,
trivial in itself, but making newspaper readers aware of Peel's human kindness.
But he was not expected to countenance familiarity. The *Manchester Guardian*
reported how when a man came to Peel's room at a Blackburn hotel and asked
the statesman to step downstairs so that the man's friends could see him, Peel
ordered 'that man' to be taken away. 'The affair has caused much annoyance to
the more respectable inhabitants.'

In September 1847 Peel stayed at Lord Londonderry's seat in County
Durham to attend the marriage of his daughter. Greville reported that Peel was
surrounded by protectionists, but still made himself affable. The protectionists,
however, 'made wry faces' at the congratulatory addresses which were offered
to him from local towns.[24] Peel's visit to Darlington to receive such an address
was reported in *The Times* of 3 September. 'Sir Robert's arrival at the railway
station was announced by the hoisting of the union jack on the top of the
Central-hall, and by a peel being rung on the church bells. The inhabitants, out
of respect, closed their shops at 4 o'clock.' Joseph Pease of the local Quaker
family presented the address in terms which gave explicit recognition to Peel's
above-party status. 'We ranged ourselves under different political leaders and
banners, but we are here as one man to pay honour where honour is due.' The
address praised Peel's enlightened policy of advancing the general well-being.
In reply he agreed that such advancement was his 'earnest desire'. Edward
Pease noted in his diary how formerly Peel 'was the object of dislike and hate by
those who now extol him'.[25]

A month later Peel was in Liverpool, his visit reported each day by *The
Times* (13–18 October). 'On Friday Sir R. Peel will walk through the town, sail
on the river, and chat on 'Change, and in the evening he will dine with the
Mayor.' In the event, he did not have time to go on 'change. The local
excitement was considerable: 'people of all grades are rushing about in every
direction endeavouring to catch a glimpse of Sir Robert.' His health was
proposed at an official dinner in above-party terms: 'although this was not a
political dinner, it was impossible in proposing the health of so eminent a
statesman to avoid acknowledging his great public services.'

---

[24] A. H. Johnson (ed.), *Letters of Charles Greville and Henry Reeve* (1924), p. 188.
[25] Sir A. E. Pease (ed.), *Diaries of Edward Pease* (1907), p. 245.

A Tamworth event attracted national notice in January 1849, when Peel addressed a meeting of subscribers to the public library. This was reported in *The Times* of 27 January. Peel remembered in his speech the fears expressed at its foundation eight years earlier that because of the library's lack of religious connection, infidelity would take root. 'I felt confident that the reverse would be the case; I knew that animosities, political and personal, would here be assuaged.' Once again Peel was emphasizing his above-party preference, to which he alluded revealingly at a dinner on the same evening: 'even at times when I have felt much deeper interest than I now do in party conflicts, I had always much greater pleasure in dwelling upon those topics on which we were all agreed than in referring to others which had a tendency to excite personal or party hostility.'

A visit to the Scottish highlands for shooting and sightseeing in the late summer and autumn of 1849 attracted great publicity for Peel's few public appearances. 'This has been a gala day in Aberdeen,' reported *The Times* of 15 October. Peel was given the freedom of the city at a dinner where the Lord Provost praised the purity of the new freeman's motives in a speech which tried but failed to be non-political. The Provost could not avoid congratulating Peel for putting 'the trade of this country in a solid and permanent position', although he did add a contradictory gloss, 'whatever be the ultimate result of these measures'. Peel responded amiably by welcoming the recognition of the purity of his motives even by those who did not approve of all his measures. On leaving the hall, he walked to his hotel 'with the burgess-ticket in his hat, and was loudly cheered by the multitude'. Here was Peel indulging in a rare populist gesture. That he was not uninterested in reading the newspaper reports is illustrated by a cutting in his archives from an Elgin newspaper of 12 October, which described his passage through that town. A highlander was reported as having forced his way to Peel's carriage, shouting excitedly: 'Will ye gie's a shak' o' your han', Sir?' The request was readily granted. The old man gave Peel's hand rather a rough shake with the exclamation, 'Leeng mat ye leeve, Sir.'[26]

So from 1846 Peel was attracting praise for his political achievements even on non-political occasions. This was permissible because he was widely accepted as having cast off party constraints. George Dawson, the Birmingham preacher and lecturer, argued in lectures 'On the characteristics and tendencies of the present age', delivered in Manchester while Corn Law repeal was passing in 1846, that great men should not be restricted by party considerations. 'Their parallel of sectarian or political latitude cannot be given; it is a shifting parallel. They are walking by an inner rule.' The applicability of this to Peel's career must have been obvious to Dawson's audience of eight or nine thousand.[27]

[26] Add. MSS 40602, f. 131.
[27] *Manchester Guardian*, 2, 6, 9, 30 May 1846.

If Peel's above-party stance was widely welcomed in 1846, he seems to have become still more popular during the next four years as he demonstrated his determination to remain above party. Harriet Martineau described Peel's situation in her contemporary history as 'the noblest that in our period of time, can be held by any man'.[28] The strength of his position was confirmed by the way it was recognized even by some who did not feel themselves to have benefited from his policies. Greville noted (22 July 1847) how Peel was 'very unpopular' in Liverpool because of losses during the commercial crisis of that year, which were attributed to his currency and banking reforms: 'but my informant added that nevertheless everybody, even those who were most angry with him on account of this Bill, would be glad to see him in office again.' An address of support for Peel from a group of Ulverston check factory workers in 1849 was the more striking for being sent even though they themselves had not yet felt much advantage from free trade. They welcomed the way Peel had increased both home and foreign commerce, 'as well also the great increase of labour for the people throughout the manufacturing districts, and accompanied too with the low price in bread'. This would 'forever endear' Peel's name to the working classes. 'The transition state, on account of the high rents paid for farms in this district which is almost purely agricultural, may for a short time be prejudicial to us in curtailing our local Home trade, but, confident in the soundness of Free trade principles, we will cheerfully bear a temporary inconvenience.' The address ended with the hope that 'whether in Office, or out of Office', Peel would promote other measures for the benefit of the people.[29]

Two months later, at the time of Peel's last birthday on 5 February 1850, he received a letter which voiced the support of that 'dumb heart of England' to which Carlyle had drawn attention. The writer was a working-class woman from Sheffield, whose husband had been born just four days before Peel in 1788:

> my Motive in Troubling the Hon[d] Gent is that the Fifth of Feb[r] is near. I hope that his lordship may be spared to his Dear Family a many more returns of the day. I must at the same time acquaint his Lordship that his Health has been drank this day at our Humble Table as my Dear Husband was Born the First of Feb 1788. Therefore is the Senior of his Lordship. It was last Friday but we have honor it to day with a good Dinner of beef Stake Dumpling and half a Pint of Ale in wich the Health of his lordship and my dear Husband was Drank and that the Almighty will prolong the Life of Both to a good Old Age. I ask Ten Thousand

---

[28] Martineau, *Thirty Years' Peace*, IV, pp. 410–11.
[29] T. F. Briggs to Peel, 28 November 1849 (Add. MSS 40602, f. 261).

Pardons for this Liberty but Gratitude I hope will plead my Excuse. I remain with all due Submission your Lordships Humble Servant,
Ann Watkinson.[30]

Peel's above-party stance was more praised in the country than in Parliament. Even his close supporters, 'the Peelites', hankered at times after active leadership, which Peel declined to give.[31] He was determined never to take office again, whereas at least the younger ones among his followers did not wish to exclude themselves permanently. Gladstone was particularly critical, at the time and in retrospect, of Peel's attitude during these final four years. The younger man disliked the steady support for Russell's weak Whig Government which Peel claimed to be necessary, in the belief that it was the best available shield against the formation of a protectionist Ministry. Gladstone wanted Peel to attempt to reunite the Conservative party. Peel seemed to Gladstone to have become preoccupied with his own fame as an above-party figure. If he did not wish to play an active part in the Commons, Gladstone believed that Peel should not have retained his seat there as an obstacle to others: 'the position of Sir Robert Peel for the last four years of his life was a thoroughly false position.'[32]

Peel refused to act as a party leader or to define a party programme. None the less, the Peelite group existed in the Commons both before and after the general election of 1847, and its members had certain political objectives in common. They were at one and the same time 'liberal' and 'conservative'. They believed in 'progress', both through private enterprise and by Government encouragement, but they were also strong advocates of 'economy' in expenditure. Although they wanted a peace-seeking foreign policy, they were not for peace at the price of national interest or honour. Over the question of further parliamentary reform, they were divided among themselves, except that all of them opposed the ballot. On religious liberty the group was likewise split, with its leaders more liberal than the rank and file. From February 1848, the *Morning Chronicle* was in Peelite hands, and it began to recommend a liberal line. Peel himself formed no connection with the paper; but Gladstone kept in close touch with J. D. Cook, its editor, and with Abraham Hayward, its chief leader writer. The *Chronicle* adopted a more critical attitude towards the Whig Government than Peel liked. Hayward even wrote privately that he found it 'impossible to *admire* Peel as a statesman or a man'. This was being more Gladstonian than Gladstone himself.[33]

---

[30] Ann Watkinson to Peel, February 1846 (Add. MSS 40603, f. 78).

[31] See Jones and Erickson, *The Peelites*, parts 1–2; and J. B. Conacher, *The Peelites and the Party System 1846–52* (1972), chs. 1–2.

[32] Add. MSS 44745, f. 190.

[33] H. E. Carlisle (ed.), *Selections from the Correspondence of Abraham Hayward* (1886), I, p. 135.

Some party organization was still available to assist Peelite candidates at the 1847 general election. Although Peel refused to act as a party leader, he did issue a long election address to his Tamworth constituents. This was clearly intended for national consumption, and was published in full in *The Times* of 17 July. It was framed, however, as a defence of his past foreign and domestic policies rather than as a call for the future. Bonham reported to Peel how their friends suffered more in the constituencies from memories of 'Maynooth' than from resentment against 'Free Trade'.[34]

During the months before the elections in July and August, corn prices had remained high. Even in the counties, the protectionists found it hard to arouse feeling against Corn Law repeal. As a result, and yet surprisingly in view of the high political temperature of the previous year, the 1847 general election became a lack-lustre contest overall. *The Times* of 11 June went so far as to claim that there was 'no controversy, no parties, no malice'. Fewer seats were contested than at any other nineteenth-century election. This unexcited atmosphere probably helped the Peelites. It has been found that of the 112 Conservatives who voted for repeal on 28 February 1846, sixty-nine were re-elected in 1847. Only ten were defeated. Another thirty-five Conservatives were returned who had not sat in Parliament during 1846–7, but who had expressed support for Peel's free-trade policies. This number included Gladstone, plus Lord Ashley and three others who had resigned in 1846. No pattern has been discovered with regard to types of constituency favouring Peelites; some were urbanized, others rural. The Peelites, in other words, represented a diversity of interests, a harmonizing spread which must have pleased Peel, if he noticed it. After the elections he was asked by Prince Albert to comment upon the outcome. Peel answered that there were signs of increased democratic leanings in some of the large urban constituencies, 'and many returns of busy enterprizing men, who must maintain themselves in popular favour by constant activity and constant display in debate'. Fortunately, repeal of the Corn Laws had removed the great spur to agitation. There was now little support in the country for parliamentary reform. If Governments pursued policies of rational improvement, Peel expressed confidence that the still aristocratic constitution would not be in danger, even from a House of Commons with too many restless Members of inferior talents and sectarian prejudices. 'The quiet good sense of the people of this Country will be a powerful instrument on which an Executive Government may rely for neutralizing the mischievous energies of the House of Commons.' So, if Peel was here allowing a reserve power to 'the people', it was as a moderating, conservative force. Public opinion was to be rallied by Ministers against extremism from both the Radical left and the protectionist right.[35]

---

[34] Bonham to Peel, 2 August 1847 (Add. MSS 40599, f. 122).
[35] Peel to Prince Albert, 11 August 1847 (RA/C45/23).

IV

The general election was hardly over before the great commercial crisis of 1847 came to a climax. Corn prices collapsed, with foreign supplies pouring in, and with a good home harvest in prospect. Business bankruptcies multiplied; credit was restricted, and there was a run on gold. Bank rate reached a crisis 8 per cent. Demands began to be heard for suspension of Peel's 1844 Bank Charter Act, especially from protectionists who tried to link it with repeal of the Corn Laws as causes of national misfortune. Peel would have none of this, defending the 1844 measure briefly in the Commons on 30 April, and at greater length in the new Parliament on 3 December. 'I do not in the slightest degree regret the course which was taken either in 1819 or 1844.' He argued that although the Bank Charter Act had not prevented the recurrence of financial crisis, it had stopped the unlimited issue of notes which would have made the crisis even worse. His December speech foreclosed debate, even though it was not a complete explanation. Lord Lincoln wrote that it 'appeared so to satisfy the House as to render it unwilling to hear anything more'.[36] An article in *Blackwood's* for July, arguing for repeal of the 1844 Act, had regretfully to admit that such difficult questions were 'the least palatable to the general reader'; there was an 'almost universal belief' in Peel's talents as a financier. *Punch* of 29 May had carried a cartoon entitled 'Robert the --- Paralysing John Bull With His Mystic Branch', the branch being marked 'Bank Charter'. The crisis was eventually ridden out, with the Bank Charter Act intact.

The repeal of the Navigation Acts in 1849 represented another landmark in the progress of free trade. They had been suspended by the Whig Government in January 1847, along with the residual Corn Laws, in order to assist the importation of food during the Irish famine. Ought they ever to be restored? Peel in an impressive speech on 9 June 1848 argued not. The Peelites were, however, divided among themselves about whether repeal should be unconditional, or should be made dependent (as Gladstone wanted) upon an equivalent response from each country. But under pressure from Peel, who urged support for the Whig Government because 'he saw a great battle coming on the question of reimposing protective duties', Gladstone eventually abandoned his resistance to complete repeal.[37]

By this date depression in agriculture had given renewed impetus to the

---

[36] Lincoln to Herbert, 4 December 1847 (NeC 11942); Peel, *Speeches*, IV, pp. 722–8, 733–44. See also C. N. Ward Perkins, 'The commercial crisis of 1847', in E. M. Carus-Wilson (ed.), *Essays in Economic History*, III (1962).

[37] Peel, *Speeches*, IV, pp. 761–70; Brooke and Sorensen, *W. E. Gladstone III*, pp. 35, 38–41. See also J. H. Clapham, 'The last years of the Navigation Acts', in Carus-Wilson, *Essays in Economic History*, III, pp. 144–78.

demand for protection.[38] Wheat prices dropped from a high of 70s per quarter early in 1847 to averages of only 44s 3d in 1849 and 40s 3d in 1850. The protectionist press blamed all this on Peel. *Punch* (18 December 1847) carried a mock article, supposedly from the *Morning Post*, attributing all calamities, great and small, to the 'Traitor of Tamworth'. 'Yesterday, a man walking in Downing Street suddenly slipt upon a piece of orange peel, and broke his leg. Poor victim! But what can now be hoped from Downing Street after the long tyranny of Peel?' A new protectionist organization, the National Association for the Protection of British Industry and Capital, was launched in May 1849. By-election victories encouraged a sense of protectionist revival, which tended to become exaggerated both by supporters and by opponents of protection. Almost all the by-elections occurred in English counties and in small boroughs across southern and south-western England, where protection was really doing no more than consolidate its hold.

Even free traders admitted the existence of agricultural depression alongside reviving industrial activity. *The Times* of Christmas Day 1849 described trade and industry as once again flourishing. In the towns, 'the pavement is crowded with comfortable people, who look as if they had not less than a week's wages in their pockets.' But the paper admitted that 'the majority of our agricultural readers' were not sharing in this prosperity. The protectionist *Dover Telegraph* claimed four days later that *The Times*, 'the head of the Free-trade press', had now abandoned the untenable cry of cheap bread 'as a panacea for all ills, social and political', and had resorted to abusing the advocates of a return to protection. The *Telegraph* called for a general election, which would shatter 'the traitorous Peel party'.

Peel had offered a major defence of free trade in the Commons on 6 June 1849. He admitted and regretted the prevalence of agricultural distress, but he pointed out how this had existed even under protection. Imports of articles of consumption, raw materials and manufactured goods had all risen, thanks to the tariff changes. 'Will any man tell me that he grudges the import of one single pound weight of those articles of consumption? What has become of them? They have been imported, they have been paid for, and they have been eaten.' The condition of the people in the towns and industrial districts was comfortable. This was an important psychological as well as material fact, for it meant 'that you have gained the confidence and goodwill of the labouring classes'. And this great conservative objective was all-important for Peel. He welcomed 'the resolution which pervaded this country to maintain its laws and constitution'; and he contrasted this pleasing acceptance with the state of turmoil in contemporary Europe.[39]

---

[38] Crosby, *English Farmers and the Politics of Protection*, ch. 6; Stewart, *Foundation of the Conservative Party*, ch. 11.

[39] Peel, *Speeches*, IV, pp. 804–22.

By 1851 one-quarter of the British people's bread was being made from foreign corn. The sheer size of the demand had justified repeal of the Corn Laws, and the population was still growing fast year by year. Peel also believed that increased corn importation would open the way for increased exports of manufactured goods by way of exchange. In the event, there was to be no great mid-Victorian jump in exports to the main foreign suppliers of corn; but there may have been indirect encouragement for British exports through the multilateral world trading network. Lower bread prices, Peel had contended, would leave more money in people's pockets to buy extra consumables; and certainly the statistics did show an early increase in tea and sugar consumption per head. With regard to compensation and encouragement for agriculture, however, Peel's 'general scheme' of 1846 was less successful. His various measures proved to be much less effective in helping hard-pressed farmers than he had promised.[40]

V

If the United Kingdom was finding a new prosperity, what of Ireland? Her problems were now compounded by the effects of the great famine, and consequent massive emigration. During his final years in office Peel had already been expressing a strong desire for major reforms in Ireland. The hopes for economic progress and religious reconciliation voiced in his 1846 resignation speech were linked in his mind to specific ideas. Graham assured Gladstone that these were 'not mere words'.[41] By 1848 Peel was apparently saying that he now favoured state endowment of the Catholic clergy in Ireland. On 30 March he spoke at length to the Commons about the problems of Ireland, and about possible remedies. The famine had not created the new situation, but it did provide a drastic opportunity for a new beginning. Poor Law reform, drainage loans, encouragement of fisheries, public works and assisted emigration would all be beneficial, suggested Peel. But the basic need was for land reform, to transform bankrupt and encumbered estates into efficient enterprises devoted to cereals and cattle instead of potatoes. This redevelopment could be supervised by a commission. If the break-up of great estates seemed daring, Peel reminded the Commons of the present state of Ireland. 'Let us . . . convert a grievous affliction into a means of future improvement.' This was one of Peel's greatest because most imaginative speeches; and it showed him taking full advantage of his now detached position in public life. *Fraser's Magazine* for April remarked that his proposals to introduce new proprietors into

---

[40] Jones, *English Agriculture 1815–1873*, pp. 27–9; F. Crouzet, *The Victorian Economy* (1982), pp. 121–8.
[41] Brooke and Sorensen, *W. E. Gladstone III*, p. 25.

impoverished districts had 'excited much attention'. The Whig Cabinet, however, proved to be unresponsive, although Peel did persuade the Lord Lieutenant, Lord Clarendon, to promote a modest Encumbered Estates Bill. A further generation was to pass before the Irish land question began to be tackled seriously.[42]

The state of the landed interest in England seemed to be problem enough for most British politicians in 1849–50. Protectionist complaints, inside and outside Parliament, reached a level reminiscent of 1846. The *Derby Mercury* of 2 January 1850 assured its readers that all classes, industrial as well as agricultural, wanted a return to protection. 'The matter has ceased to be one of abstract calculation. It is one which every man can judge by the simple process of examining his pocket or his till, his rick-yard or his rent-roll.' The difficulty was that the Whig Government, backed by Peel, stood in the way. During the first half of 1850 *Blackwood's Magazine* carried articles every month which argued the case for a return to protection. The June number contained a long report of a national delegate meeting called in London on 7 May by the National Association for the Protection of British Industry and Capital. Peel was referred to by one speaker as 'an individual whom he would not name, as his name appeared to grate upon the ears of every honest farmer in this country – (cheers) – but whom it was impossible to forget'.

Peel had caused additional irritation to protectionists at the end of 1849 by publishing a letter to his own tenant farmers, which contained proposals for countering the current 'undue depression'. He admitted that repeal of the Corn Laws was likely to mean low prices in average seasons, and prevent very high prices even in dearth. It was his 'firm persuasion' that no present or future Parliament would reimpose protection. How then might he help his tenants to face the future? Although unwilling to offer a general reduction in rents, he was willing to make reductions in deserving cases, and especially for 'an old and improving tenant'. But all tenants would need to compete with foreigners by becoming more efficient. Peel was prepared to offer an investment in improvement equal to 20 per cent of current rent. Preference would be given to schemes for improving drainage, for consolidating small fields and for facilitating collection of manure. Where drainage would cost more than this, he was prepared to finance it, provided tenants themselves met 4 per cent of the cost. Leases might be offered to those who preferred them to annual tenancies.

This letter received national publicity through *The Times* of 28 December 1849, and in many other newspapers, both protectionist and free trade. The free-trade papers welcomed it as pointing the way for agriculturalists to come to terms with the permanent reality of Corn Law repeal. Peel's letter was 'timely and good', concluded *The Times*. Peel had adroitly shown, claimed the *Manchester Guardian* (29 December), that 'the sluggish and ignorant farmer'

---

[42] Peel, *Speeches*, IV, pp. 788–804; Kerr, *Peel, Priests and Politics*, pp. 356–7.

would be driven out as much by efficient home producers 'as by those untaxed and naturally favoured foreigners, of whom we hear so much'. Peel had turned the protectionist argument on its head by 'converting the bugbear which paralyses the farmers into a stimulus to increased exertion'. But the protectionist press refused to accept that protection would never come back. The *Dover Telegraph* of 5 January 1850 suggested that farmers were too hard pressed to listen to Peel's 'plausibilities', while needing to pay wages, tithes, poor rates, highway rates, taxes, the costs of equipment, wear and tear, and interest on capital. The *Blackburn Standard* (2 January) noted that Peel's 20 per cent offer applied only when rent and arrears had been paid in full. So there was to be no easement for those of Peel's tenants already worn down by the effects of his national policy. A letter to *The Times* of 3 January from 'M. D.' of Lichfield likewise attacked Peel for allegedly exploiting his tenants. The tenants themselves, claimed the writer, resented such exploitation, but were frightened to speak out. Peel's scheme was really an attempt to bolster his rents, even though prices had fallen by nearly one-third.

Peel did not answer such misrepresentations in public; but in private correspondence he explained and defended himself. When criticized by J. A. Roebuck from the free-trade side for seeming to be willing to reduce rents to. meet lower prices, Peel admitted that he did not necessarily charge fully economic rents. He allowed sons on to land at the rents paid by their fathers. And he readily renewed tenancies, rather than put every farm up for auction every year. Commercial considerations could not override all social obligations.[43] Another correspondent, Henry Drummond, a former Member of Parliament, described to Peel the depression in agriculture as he saw it. 'Every estate that is mortgaged (i.e. three fourths of Great Britain) must be sold: every farmer who is farming with borrowed Capital (i.e. nine tenths of all farmers) must go to *jail*, or at least cease from farming. Their language is frantic.' Something had to be done for them, even if it must be less than they deserved: 'but the appearance of sympathy from you, more than from any other man, will do much: for they look on you as the author of all.' Peel answered that he did not see the force of Drummond's reasoning. If so many estates were mortgaged, and so many farmers were operating upon borrowed capital, 'What a cutting rebuke to Protection!' The price of corn had dropped even lower in 1836 under protection than it was now. 'Equalization of burdens', continued Peel, was a good cry at agricultural meetings. But what did it mean? He would like to see 'the practical details of the Plan'.[44]

Richard Lambert, a London attorney, pressed Peel in January 1850 by means

---

[43] Roebuck to Peel, 30 December 1849 (Add. MSS 40602, f. 394); Peel to Roebuck, 2 January 1850 (Add. MSS 40603, f. 1).

[44] Drummond to Peel, 28 December 1849 (Add. MSS 40602, f. 310); Peel to Drummond, 4 January 1850 (Add. MSS 40603, f. 11).

of an example. A few years earlier he had invested a considerable sum in a farm at Goudhurst in Kent. He had put it in good order. Yet his tenant was telling him that he 'cannot get on under the Free Trade System', even though Lambert had done some of the things recommended by Peel. He had remitted 20 per cent of rent, and he had given his tenant two tons of oilcake 'by way of encouragement'. The farm would have to go out of cultivation if present prices continued. Lambert concluded by hoping that Peel would not be '*too* confident' next session in Parliament. In May Lambert wrote again, saying that he had been a supporter of Peel's, but was now despairing at his neglect of the agricultural interest. 'The Indication of a Doubt by you on the past Policy, or if that cannot be, *by the Duke*, would, I sincerely believe be eagerly accepted by *all* Parties.' If not, Lambert threatened to emigrate with his nine children to 'another Hampshire', where he hoped not to live to hear of Peel repenting too late. This letter provoked Peel into a stiff reply, which emphasized that he entertained no doubts about free trade, and would do everything in his power to prevent the restoration of protection 'in any shape or any pretences whatever'. Lambert answered that he did not want a return to protection, but the placing of agriculture on the same footing as industry by the removal of its peculiar burdens. 'You are silent however, or perhaps I ought to say, pronounce *oracularly*.' In other words, Peel's record of changeability meant that even his seemingly total negative to Lambert was not necessarily accepted as his final position.[45]

Peel had spoken about agricultural distress in the Commons on 21 February 1850, and about taxation on 12 March. He admitted that the agricultural interest was suffering 'considerable distress', for which he expressed 'the warmest sympathy', not least because his personal fortunes were connected with the land. But low prices were to be found also in Europe. The distress was not exclusively a British problem. Moreover, Peel was encouraged by the great increase in the demand for food from the towns. This promised to bring 'ultimate prosperity' to home agriculture. Peel expressed great satisfaction that the Whig Government had adhered to the policies which he had introduced while in office. In 1846, under threat of 'a portentous and mysterious calamity', he had thought it to be his duty to God and country to counter the risk of famine by suspending the Corn Laws. 'I did conscientiously believe it would be most unwise to give a pledge, that after that suspension those duties should be renewed.' Protectionists were clamouring for a general election. Peel did not believe that they would win. The just influence of agriculture in Parliament would be best assured by ceasing to demand an increase in the price of food. There was now 'general contentment'. It was a pity that there was not to be some direct vote finally to decide for or against protection.[46]

[45] Lambert to Peel, 9 January, 8, 16 May 1850; Peel to Lambert, 16 May 1850 (Add. MSS 40603, ff.32, 225, 226, 227).

[46] Peel, *Speeches*, IV, pp. 822–38.

Peel insisted to the end that British agriculture would be well able to compete with foreign imports if it adopted modern farming methods. When *The Times* suggested sending James Caird on a tour of the agricultural districts, Caird wrote to Peel for his opinion of the venture. Peel replied encouragingly in a letter which was eventually published in Caird's book, *English Agriculture in 1850-51* (1852). Comparisons between different parts of the country, wrote Peel, might stimulate the spread of better farming. The need was for 'good farming under liberal covenants'. Peel was here echoing approvingly the title of a pamphlet of Caird's, *High Farming under Liberal Covenants the Best Substitute for Protection* (1849).

Acceptance by British agriculture of free trade along with modernization was not to be completed in Peel's lifetime, although there were encouraging signs in some places. 'I see a vast improvement in agriculture in this neighbourhood since Free Trade came in . . . Protection did but foster indolence.' So wrote one farmer on the edge of Dartmoor in his diary for 13 July 1851. Admittedly, he was a long-standing free trader. Eighteen months earlier (7 February 1850), at the height of the clamour for renewed protection, he had noted how there was 'no grumbling among the labourers, for now they have a cheap loaf, and are able to get a bit of meat to eat with it.' They could also get salt, sugar, tea and coffee cheaper than when their wages were only a half or one-third of present levels. From 1853 agricultural prices began to climb, especially for animal products, and this stimulated investment during the next twenty years. The basis here may not have been one of low prices matched by high farming, as assumed by Caird and Peel; but the fact of prosperity muted the call for a return to protection.[47]

VI

By the start of the 1850 session of Parliament the Peelites were growing increasingly restless over Peel's refusal to lead, while at the same time using his authority to maintain the weak Whig Government in office. Sir John Young pointed out how 'your friends' had split by twenty-eight to thirty-five for and against the Government over a proposal from Disraeli for consideration of the poor rate. Peel himself was in the minority of Peelites. Without their support, the Government would have been defeated. Young claimed, with some exaggeration, that as many as 160 Members of Parliament 'would rally round you personally, or any organization distinctly formed under your auspices and guided by your advice'. But these Members refused to sustain the Whigs year after year. They believed, wrote Young, that the only person who could provide an alternative to the eventual formation of a protectionist Government was

[47] Jones, *English Agriculture 1815–1873*, p. 29; C. Torr, *Small Talk at Wreyland* (1979), pp. 44–5.

Peel himself. It has been estimated that the number of Peelites willing still to vote regularly with Peel in support of the Whigs was down to forty-five by 1850.[48]

All the Peelites disliked Palmerston's abrasive conduct of foreign policy; but, even so, Peel refused to risk overthrowing the Whig Government because of it. However, in the famous Don Pacifico debate of June 1850 Peel had at last spoken and voted against Palmerston, secure in the knowledge that the Government would still win a majority. This debate was to be the very last in which Peel was involved. Disraeli, Gladstone and Cobden, as well as Peel, declaimed against the Government. Palmerston answered with his long-remembered *Civis Romanus Sum* oration. Peel rose on the last evening of debate, 28 June. His speech was not one of his best, being very loosely organized. It was deliberately unprovocative even in its strictures. Peel conceded that peace had been maintained, but relations with the leading Powers of Europe had been unnecessarily strained. Diplomatic channels had been used by Palmerston only to bluster, not to promote harmony. Don Pacifico's claims against the Greek Government were legitimate; but why had Palmerston resorted to threats so quickly? Peel went on to repudiate the doctrine that Britain's moral authority should be used to promote self-government in foreign states. Non-interference had been the rule of Pitt, Fox, Castlereagh and Canning. 'Constitutional liberty will be best worked out by those who aspire to freedom by their own efforts.'[49]

Peel had not missed the opportunity to emphasize the above-party character of the line-up against Palmerston. 'Is it not possible that, without reference to party or personal interests, men may decline to affirm a resolution which deals with principles of greater importance to the welfare of this country, for good or for evil, than have ever been under the consideration of the House?' Early in his speech Peel had briefly reminded the Commons how he had given the Whig Government his cordial support on home and Irish questions. 'I think that their policy in domestic affairs has been a liberal and conservative policy.' This was high praise in Peel's vocabulary. It was how he wanted his own policy to be remembered. He now much preferred 'liberal' and 'conservative' to be harmoniously used as balancing qualitative adjectives, rather than with capital letters as competing party labels.

The Times of 1 July 1850 praised the powerful exposition from Peel's side of the principles which ought to direct British foreign policy, exposition 'conducted without party concert or party objects'. By this date Peel was already lying fatally injured, and next day he died. On 9 July, the day of his funeral, *The Times* remembered how in office the dead statesman had

---

[48] Young to Peel, 22 February 1850 (Add. MSS 40603, f. 92); Conacher, *Peelites and the Party System*, p. 65.

[49] Peel, *Speeches*, IV, pp. 846–56.

successfully applied the moderate principles which he had commended in his last speech. Peel had won the respect of every power in Europe, and was even asked for his opinions on internal problems by more than one foreign state. 'He aimed not at the abasement of foreign nations, but at the growth of our own prosperity by their progress, not by their ruin.'

6

Death: 2 July 1850

I

Peel's death – the fact, reinforced by its manner – constituted his last lead to Victorian public opinion, the more powerful for being unanticipated either by Peel himself or by the public. Its impact was almost unbelievably strong, as *Fraser's Magazine* for August 1850 realized. 'Such an accumulation of eulogy on one whose lot it was to be reviled and lauded with a striking inconsistency by his countrymen, will be suspected by history.' Lord Campbell, the Liberal lawyer, was indeed to claim a few years later that Peel was especially fortunate in his death. 'If Peel had lived on in the common routine of parliamentary warfare, and died of old age, he would have had no statues erected to his memory.' But then the risk of being noticed in Campbell's reminiscences was said to have added a new terror to death.[1]

On the morning of Saturday 29 June, Peel attended a meeting of the Commissioners for the Great Exhibition, chaired by Prince Albert. In the afternoon he went out riding, on a horse still comparatively new to him and which, it transpired afterwards, had been known for its habit of kicking and bucking. Falls from horses were, of course, common enough; and it was a matter of chance whether serious injury resulted. Peel himself had described to his wife such accidents to the Duke of Wellington in 1828 ('not hurt, tho''') and to Queen Adelaide ('not hurt in the least') in 1842.[2] Peel proceeded to Buckingham Palace, where he signed the visitors' book. He then rode slowly to the top of Constitution Hill, where he exchanged greetings with two young ladies. Their groom's horse was restless, and Peel had barely finished making his gesture before his own mount threw him over its head. He fell face downwards, still holding the reins. His horse stumbled on top of him, striking

---

[1] Lord Campbell, *Lives of the Lord Chancellors*, VIII (1969), pp.543–4; Kitson Clark, *Life and Work of Sir Robert Peel*, p. 1.

[2] Peel, *Private Letters*, pp. 108, 212.

him with its knees in the back. This blow, rather than the fall itself, was probably what caused his fatal injuries.[3]

Dr Foucart, a Glasgow surgeon, had seen the accident, and ran up immediately; he was quickly joined by Sir James Clark, the royal physician. Peel was taken home, and laid down in the dining-room, where he was eventually placed upon a water mattress on the table. At some point, Wilkie's painting of *John Knox Preaching Before the Lords of the Congregation*, which was a favourite of Peel's, was set up beside him. A group of leading medical men, including Sir Benjamin Brodie, the foremost surgeon of the day, soon assembled round the stricken man. He was examined as far as possible; but Peel had always been acutely sensitive to pain, and this restricted examination, then and later. He himself told the doctors that his injuries were worse than they knew, and that he would not survive. Given the limitations of contemporary medical knowledge, a fatal conclusion was indeed probably unavoidable. But complaint was made after Peel's death that more might have been done to help him. An article in *The Lancet* of 6 July, reprinted in *The Times* a week later, explained how his 'excessive sensibility to pain had always been most remarkable. Like Cicero, Demosthenes, and other renowned orators, his nervous system was so finely and delicately wrought as to render him singularly impatient and sensitive under suffering.' Only a few weeks earlier, continued *The Lancet*, while visiting the zoo, Peel had fainted when a small monkey had jumped upon his hand. With such a sensitive patient, the article suggested that there was nothing surprising about the absence of the usual bandaging or manipulation. An account which Brodie wrote a year later for Peel's executors gave the zoo story differently. Brodie said that Peel's hand had been forced against some cage bars by the head of a goat which he was patting, and that even this slight injury had caused prolonged faintness. Whatever the precise nature of the zoo incident, it confirmed Peel's medical attendants in the belief that, in the words of *The Lancet*, 'with one of the most valuable lives in the kingdom under their hands they were not justified in incurring such additional risk and danger.'

Many of these details, plus some rumour and speculation, circulated to the public through the newspapers. The first of a series of bulletins was issued at 7 p.m. on the day of the accident: 'Sir Robert Peel has met with a severe accident by falling from his horse. There is severe injury of one shoulder, with a fracture of the left collar-bone. There is great reason to hope there is no internal injury.' This last hope was false, and Peel passed a restless night. It became apparent that there were serious internal injuries. Sunday's bulletins added greatly to public anxiety. But hope revived when on Monday morning a bulletin announced that the patient had passed a good night, 'and was on the

---

[3] Herbert to Lincoln, 6 July 1850 (NeC 11941); Sir B. Brodie to E. Cardwell, 2 June 1851 (Add. MSS 40608, f. 367); *The Times*, 4, 13 July 1850.

whole better'. Then optimism was deflated by a bulletin issued at 10 p.m. 'Since seven o'clock, Sir Robert Peel has been very restless, and his condition is less satisfactory than it was in the early part of the day.' Peel was now lapsing into periods of unconsciousness. He called for his friends Hardinge and Graham. Hardinge came from his house next door, and stayed all Monday night. There had been a stream of callers. Prince Albert had himself called on the first evening. But even more impressive than the comings and goings of the great was the crowd at the gates, which included many working people. They came and went, getting the latest news and looking up at the house. Carlyle found 'a great crowd of people, poor and rich, streaming about all day, and large placard-bulletins handed out to them'.[4] The *Illustrated London News* of 6 July published a drawing of the scene. 'Unknowing the significance of their own appearance, these poor folk were, in reality, the guard of honour accorded to the last hours of Sir Robert Peel – by the People.' Here was much more than simply Victorian fascination with a deathbed. Genuine concern transcended mere curiosity. The men and women of all types who crowded outside the house represented national middle opinion, which now revealed its sympathy for Peel more clearly than ever before. *Tait's Edinburgh Magazine* for August 1850 described this inarticulate affinity:

> The widespread reliance on his patriotism and practical wisdom, which was known to all who mixed in society beyond the range of mere professional politicians, had little opportunity of expressing itself in public, and little need of utterance ... Those who trusted him believed not that he would adopt this measure or that, but that he would judge of successive questions honestly and carefully, and, above all, that the country would be guided by his judgment. Such was the private or unexpressed opinion which has now almost for the first time made itself heard in the form of general regret for the loss which the country has suffered.

Peel slept from 4 to 8 a.m. on the morning of 2 July. He woke in less pain, took some tea and broth, and even walked round the room supported on each side. A bulletin at 1.30 p.m. reported the better news. This proved, however, to be the last rally. Early in the afternoon Peel became unconscious. At 6.30 p.m. hope was given up, and a bulletin warned that the patient was 'much exhausted, and altogether not so well as he was in the early part of the day'. Peel's friend, the Bishop of Gibraltar, administered the sacrament; and Peel revived just enough to take the hands of each in turn of his family and friends, and to whisper a blessing. His last words were to his youngest child, Eliza. Contemporaries were pleased to know that he had died with Christian

---

[4] E. W. Marrs (ed.), *Letters of Thomas Carlyle to His Brother Alexander* (1968), pp. 678–9.

Whitehall Gardens: rich and poor waiting for news: *Illustrated London News*, 6 July 1850

composure. Thus *The Times* of 5 July, while admitting that it was 'not the province of the journalist to violate the sanctity of a scene like this', did so to the extent of reporting how Peel had revived sufficiently 'to identify the features of those beloved ones surrounding his couch – towards whom he at length extended his faltering hand, and, in an attitude bespeaking the intensity of his feelings, whispered in a scarcely audible voice – "God bless you!" ' Peel breathed his last at nine minutes past eleven on the evening of Tuesday 2 July.

His agony had therefore been spread over four days. This chanced to be just about the right duration for maximizing concern in the public mind without risk of emotional exhaustion. And the suddenness of Peel's removal was the more striking for coming so soon after his well-publicised speech delivered in full health during the great Don Pacifico debate. He had been taken, complained *The Times* on 4 July, 'from his very seat in the Senate, with nothing to prepare us for his departure'.

The Times had given the whole sequence detailed coverage. The summaries in the weekly provincial papers were necessarily coloured by knowledge of the ending to come. But the London dailies were able to print running accounts of Peel's sufferings in their Monday and Tuesday issues, and to give late news of his death in the issues for Wednesday 3 July. 'Sir Robert Peel is no more,' announced *The Times*:

> After three days of excessive suffering, at a few minutes past eleven last night, the greatest statesman of his time quitted the scene in which he had performed so conspicuous a part. Even the anxiety and the rumours, which have penetrated every household since the first alarming intelligence will have failed to prepare the country for the deplorable result. Except, indeed, in the field of battle, never was the transition from life to death so marked and so touching.

The electric telegraph sent the news north in time for it to be reported in a black-edged paragraph in the Wednesday number of the *Manchester Guardian*. A full account of the whole sad story from first fall to last breath, much of it copied from *The Times*, appeared in the *Guardian*'s Saturday number on 6 July.

Peel was buried at Drayton Church on the afternoon of Tuesday 9 July. He had only recently confirmed to his wife that he wished to be buried there, beside his parents. The royal Duke of Cambridge had died six days after Peel, which meant a period of court mourning. But Baroness Bunsen wrote that it was Peel's death which remained 'the great event. All persons agree that there has never been an instance of such general gloom.' Only the protectionist ultras were not mourning the loss of a statesman 'towards it seems all looked, far more than they were aware'.[5] Certainly, 'all England' was said by the *Liverpool*

---

[5] A. J. C. Hare, *Life and Letters of Frances, Baroness Bunsen* (4th ed., 1894), II. p. 142.

Journal of 13 July to have been present in spirit at the funeral. Shops in the West End and City of London were closed. *The Times* listed the many provincial towns where business was suspended. At Birmingham and elsewhere muffled bells were tolled. 'No such universal recognition of the loss of a great man has ever before been made in this quarter of the country.' The *Manchester Guardian* (10 July) reported that 'one or two millowners' had shut their mills until after the funeral, 'paying their hands for the day as usual'.

Next day the *Morning Chronicle*, the Peelite organ, devoted four columns, and *The Times* two columns, to what the latter called 'the unostentatious obsequies of a country gentleman'. The *Spectator* of 13 July remarked more accurately that this was 'a plain interment after a somewhat sumptuous notion of plainness . . . It was a country-town public funeral.' Crowds had poured into Tamworth from a wide area to gather round the churchyard. The better-off wore full mourning; the working classes displayed bands of crape. A special train brought Peel's friends from London, although the Duke of Wellington could not come because of illness. Some of Peel's oldest political friends served as pallbearers, including Aberdeen, Bonham, Goulburn, Graham and Hardinge. Just as the mourning bell began to sound, a rainstorm started, but it eased as the funeral procession set off slowly down the drive of Drayton Manor. The hearse was covered with a rich pall, which displayed Peel's armorial bearings with their motto, 'Industria'. The *Illustrated London News* (13 July) noted how this appropriate motto 'was remarked and commented upon by many'. The cortège was joined at the lodge gates by Peel's principal tenants on horseback. The rain began again as the coffin was being borne into Drayton Bassett Church, and the *Illustrated London News* reported that many were moved to quote the old legend:

> Happy is the bride that the sun shines on!
> Happy are the dead that the rain rains on!

The *Morning Chronicle* briefly described the interment in the Peel family vault. 'In faltering tones the words of the sublime service were pronounced, amid choking sobs and many tears; and at the awful consignment of dust to dust and ashes to ashes, the mortal part of the great Sir Robert Peel was lowered into the tomb, to sleep beside the remains of the authors of his being.' The *Illustrated London News* ended its report with a description of the mourners coming red-eyed out of the church:

> leaving the famous dead, the great and good, the wise and patriotic Sir Robert Peel, to slumber peacefully with his fathers, his memory canonised, as it will be canonised by the people of Great Britain, and the story of his life handed down to all posterity in proof of the deathless honour in which a statesman should be held, who, when he sees the right,

has the moral courage and the moral steadfastness undauntedly to sacrifice every party claim, in order that he may pursue, may grasp, and may realize it to the people.

II

Peel was now above party for ever. The tributes in Parliament at his death had, of course, transcended party differences, except that Disraeli said nothing. 'He made no parade of regret, but seemed bewildered by the suddenness of the event, and the prospect which it offered of a new combination.' So noted Lord Stanley's son in his diary.[6] On the day after Peel's death, Wednesday 3 July, the House of Commons met at noon; and upon the motion of Joseph Hume, seconded by Gladstone, immediately adjourned as an exceptional token of mourning. Next day, with many Members in black and some taking their hats off as Russell began to speak, the Prime Minister paid tribute to his great rival. He emphasized especially the patriotic support which Peel had given to the Whig Governments after 1832. He offered a public funeral if Peel's family and friends desired it. Graham sat in tears unable to speak. Goulburn spoke simply and movingly on behalf of the family to decline the offer of a public ceremony because of Peel's express wish, given in writing in 1844 and repeated verbally to his wife only six weeks previously, to be buried in the family vault at Drayton, 'without ostentation or parade of any kind'.[7]

In the House of Lords, Lansdowne broke with precedent by making formal reference to the loss sustained by the other chamber. The Duke of Wellington's tribute was confused by emotion. He praised Peel's attachment to truth, by which presumably he meant that Peel's motivation in politics had always been pure. This was readily accepted by Lord Stanley, the protectionist leader, who was left to deliver the most balanced speech on the occasion in either House. He emphasized how he had never doubted Peel's motives; how 'that unflinching diligence' had always been at the service of the state, regardless of personal sacrifice. 'In some cases those sacrifices were so extensive that I hardly know whether the great and paramount object of his country's good was a sufficient reason to exact them from any public man.'

The tributes in the British Parliament were echoed in the French Assembly, where at the opening of the session on 5 July the President paid tribute to a statesman who in the course of his long career had expressed only 'kind feeling and justice' towards France. The Times of 6 July copied tributes from the French press, and its Paris correspondent noted with some surprise 'this general sympathy expressed by a rival people'. The Times of 9 July welcomed this

---

[6] J. Vincent (ed.), Disraeli, Derby and the Conservative Party (1968), p. 23.
[7] Add. MSS 43754, f. 93.

evidence of mutual respect and sympathy such as Peel had himself laboured to encourage. Peel's essential Englishness, the editorial concluded, had not prevented him from earning a European reputation.

Russell had been right to draw particular attention to Peel's services in the 1830s. He had not withdrawn in disgust after the passing of the Reform Act to leave 'a war of classes to be carried on . . . I consider Sir Robert Peel to have been the man who prevented such a contest from taking place.' He had built up a Conservative party to work within the reformed system, not against it, even though his party remained long in opposition. Sidney Herbert made the same point in a letter giving the news of Peel's death to Lord Lincoln, who was abroad: 'he represented to the nation that system of parliamentary government which he had himself established more than anyone else.'[8]

Since Peel had made the reformed system work, despite his dislike of the Reform Act itself, his resistance to its passing had within a few years come to be forgiven if not forgotten. Greville remembered in his diary (6 July 1850) how in the 1830s Peel had 'flung himself cheerfully and confidently into the new order of things, associated himself with the sentiments and the wants of the nation, and day by day saw his reputation increasing both in Parliament and throughout the country'. *The Times* of 5 July 1850 claimed that Peel had made the Commons into the predominant House of Parliament. Perhaps it would have been more accurate to say that the Reform Act had already made it so, but that Peel's influence had made it worthy of its new predominance. He had set an example to Members which had dispelled what *The Times* remembered as 'the Byronian fervour', with its 'contempt for labour and method':

> There now prevails a truer estimate of the means by which ability and distinction are acquired. In the House of Commons there can be no doubt that the example of the zealous and industrious member for Tamworth has contributed to this result; and when we read half a dozen excellent speeches in one night – when we find almost every Member, however young, able to instruct the country . . . we may recognise in those effects the model of Ministerial duty set by Sir Robert . . . in the Reformed House of Commons itself we beheld Sir Robert's most splendid and most significant memorial.

Constructive opposition in the 1830s; selfless dedication in shaping policy during five years as Prime Minister in the 1840s; and finally four years above party. Such had been the sequence of Peel's career, which the Victorians were now able to appreciate in its entirety for the first time. Sympathetic remembrance by his contemporaries and by posterity was the only recognition which Peel desired. He had left firm instructions, as Russell told the Commons on 12 July, that his wife and family were not to accept titles or rewards on

---

[8] Herbert to Lincoln, 6 July 1850 (NeC 11941).

account of his services. This refusal of all honours was immediately noticed in Peel's favour. His action, declared *Punch* (10 August), drawing a Radical conclusion which would have disconcerted Peel himself, 'repudiates the Peerage as a part of the Protective system which must fall one day as other Protective institutions have fallen'. But Peel knew that the 'honourable fame' which he had publicly admitted to be his goal was the highest reward of all.[9]

III

How did the press articulate and orchestrate the immediate reaction to Peel's death? The *Manchester Guardian*, which had become friendly towards Peel in 1846, was even more friendly by 1850. Its London correspondent explained on 6 July how during the last four years Peel had mellowed, become more genial, 'more of the man, and less of the politician'. His 'apparently untimely death' had shocked everyone. 'Though not exactly dying like Nelson in the hour of victory, the period and the manner of his sudden death have revealed the extent of his hold on the public mind.' His influence was the greater because 'he never rose much above what may be termed the average intellect of the community'. By 10 July the *Guardian* was already fearing political trouble, now that the 'great moral check' exercised by Peel had been removed. It reported, wrongly, that Gladstone, Herbert and other Peelites, even before Peel's death, 'had already entered into an understanding' with Disraeli and Lord John Manners to form a coalition in which free trade would be an open question.

The *Leeds Mercury* (6 July), which had become almost as sympathetic towards Peel in 1846 as the *Manchester Guardian*, now reported the 'most painful' sensation produced in the West Riding by the death of 'one of the first of his country's benefactors'. The *Liverpool Mercury*, the third of the trio of great northern Liberal newspapers, had been more guarded in 1846, arguing that Peel had still to prove his greatness. By the time of his death, however, the *Mercury* of 5 July 1850 felt certain that Peel had achieved greatness. No longer interested in party or office, within the House of Commons 'his functions became almost paternal'. Despite many superficial changes of policy he had retained one objective, 'the *progress of the British nation*'. He had made the reformed system work. On 9 July the *Liverpool Mercury* published 'Lines on the Death of Sir Robert Peel', which summed up the bases of his appeal to middle opinion:

> True to his God, his Queen, his country's cause,
> He won from all a well-deserv'd applause,
> Who did not view him as a partisan –
> Who know no party, but who know *the man*.

[9] Peel, *Speeches*, IV, p. 138.

The *Preston Chronicle* had likewise placed Peel upon probation for greatness in 1846. By 1850 it was accepting him as a man above party, 'something better than a functionary', who had never lost his warm Lancastrian heart: 'one of the people', who was well aware how 'his fortunes had grown from their prosperity'. The *Chronicle* (6 July) now placed the Whigs far beneath Peel, because they would never have dared to propose such a succession of reforms. The paper's end-of-year retrospect (4 January 1851) added that 'hundreds of thousands of working men were sanguine enough to believe that it was reserved to him to extend the elective franchise'. The careful choice of words suggested that the paper itself rightly had not expected this from Peel.

In 1846 the *Preston Chronicle* had quoted from the *Examiner*, the London weekly, in support of its wait-and-see view of Peel. By the time of Peel's death, the *Examiner* (6 July 1850), like the *Chronicle*, had become enthusiastic over the way since 1846 he had acted as 'moderator and guard'. He had willingly become a political lightning conductor, who drew attacks to himself personally and so screened 'the objects over which he extended his shield'. The *Examiner* believed that Peel had died before his work was completed, 'hardly less necessary for our future than he was instrumental to good in the past'. The *Spectator*, the *Examiner*'s rival, had strongly supported Peel throughout his great Ministry, as it reminded its readers at his death. It remembered (6 July) how its correct understanding of Peel's intentions had been wrongly attributed to possession of inside information. Peel's career had taught politicians 'that *courage* is *safe*, and that the courage which revises the convictions of youth and dictates an altered course will survive the hasty misconstruction of the day if it be steadfast in its purpose.'

The Times kept all politicians always on probation. But with Peel dead, it summed up his achievement on 4 July 1850 in warmer terms than it had used in life, although still with twists which set limits to praise. Posterity would ask whether Peel was right twice to break up his party – first over Catholic Emancipation, and then over repeal of the Corn Laws. 'Our own answer shall be without hesitation or reserve. They were among the most needful and salutary acts that man was given to do. Grant that Sir Robert compassed them unfairly, and it must at least be admitted that he had a fine taste for glory and prized the gifts of Heaven when he saw them. But is it possible that a man should do such deeds, and a whole life full of them, and yet do them basely?' Peel had sacrificed himself for the sake of repeal. 'His right is now proved, not by what he did, but by what he suffered, and he is the confessed author of free trade, because he has been a martyr to it.'

The Times went on to list with approval Peel's other main measures: currency reform, Catholic Emancipation, amelioration of the criminal code, reform of the police and improvements in administration. With such achievements behind him, there was no need to gloss over 'the ambiguities of this honourable career'. Peel remained open to the charge of double-dealing with regard to his party; but the ends which drew him on, sometimes suddenly, were always good ones. He was the great statesman of a period of transition. 'Undoubtedly the habit of political exhibition told on Sir Robert's manner and style, and even on his mind . . . His love of applause was closely allied to a still more dangerous appetite for national prosperity, without sufficient regard to its sources and permanence. It was this that induced him into encouraging, instead of controlling the railway mania.'

The other London dailies reacted to Peel's death along predictable lines. The Peelite *Morning Chronicle* mourned its hero with black-edged pages. It emphasized (3 July) his responsiveness. 'The English people felt this and knew it.' The people believed that he was in reserve for peacetime emergencies, just as Wellington was the leader for war. 'At the time of his last great speech on Irish affairs, men willingly recognized in him the only statesman possessing a mind capable of embracing a large and comprehensive policy.' The public admired too Peel's 'unspotted character', and his love of art and science. The *Morning Chronicle* for 5 July carried an anonymous article, written by Gladstone, which was designed (as he noted in his diary) 'to correct the *Times*' of 4 July, quoted above. Gladstone emphasized how it was entirely to Peel's credit that he had been taught by experience. 'No mind so great was ever so progressive':

> Without the contrasts he never could have made the sacrifices – without the sacrifices he never would have made the efforts and endured the agonies of the critical periods of his life – without the efforts and the agonies he never could have realized the growth – his understanding never could have been educated into the strength and the elasticity, the largeness and the fineness, for which it was alike marvellous.

The *Daily News* of 3 July 1850 remembered Peel as a model modern statesman. 'Prime Ministers used to be gay courtiers and boon companions. At present they are thinking and solitary men.' This left them at risk of running ahead of their parties, as Peel had done. The *Morning Advertiser* of the same day deplored Peel's 'premature demise'. His main shortcoming had been want of frankness, but there was no doubt about his honesty of purpose. Fortunately, the partisan personal assaults made upon him had left him untouched because he had risen above party. The *Advertiser* of 4 July repeated the peroration to the 1846 resignation speech, with the comment that Peel had been granted not simply his wish for remembrance, but 'an almost idolatrous respect'.

Among the Sunday newspapers, the *Weekly Dispatch*'s 'Estimate of Sir Robert Peel' on 7 July noticed the wide extent of mourning, especially among the middle classes. Peel's responsiveness to the need for change had overcome party restraints. 'His party was the nation.' *The Sunday Times* of the same day remembered Peel's willingness 'to yield to the mighty power of public opinion', which willingness had saved the constitution. The paper noticed how Peel had opposed the Reform Act, and yet had come to influence the reformed House of Commons much more than its unreformed predecessor. The *News of the World*, which was now claiming a weekly circulation of 60,000, noticed that Peel had received 'universal praise'. His merits had far outweighed his faults, not the least of his merits being his refusal of all honours for himself and his family. *Lloyd's Weekly*, which claimed a similar high circulation, remained more reserved in its editorial of 7 July. Peel had done much 'to blot out the remembrance of his earlier political career'; but his association with 'the persecution of George Canning' was still alleged, despite the 1846 explanation.

Lloyd's sympathy with popular Radicalism obviously held it back from unqualified admiration for Peel. Yet the Chartist *Northern Star* showed no hesitation. In 1846 it had argued that Peel's measures were steps towards acceptance of Chartist principles. Now at his death the *Star*'s editorial of 6 July 1850 was one of the most perceptive and appreciative. It explained how Peel was regretted 'by men of all classes and all parties. We believe that the great mass of the people, whose political predilections are of a moderate description, and who do not take any active part in political struggles, looked upon the deceased Statesman as the right hand of the country.' In other words, Peel had successfully appealed to middle opinion; and the *Northern Star* was implying that this included many working men as well as their social superiors. Peel 'knew how to solve that most difficult problem in Statesmanship, – how to reconcile Conservatism with progress'.

On 27 July, and for three months thereafter, an advertisement for an engraved portrait of Peel appeared in each issue of the *Star*, as one of the long-running series of political portraits offered by the paper to its readers. 'This splendid likeness, beautifully Engraved on Steel, of the deceased Statesman, is now ready, and may be had of any of the Agents, at the same price as the Portraits previously published.' So Peel joined the *Star*'s gallery of popular political figures. In life he would certainly have felt uncomfortable in such advanced company. It was a reflection of his popularity in death that working-class Radical reformers now wished to count him among their heroes. Less surprisingly, the Liberal *Preston Guardian*, owned by Joseph Livesey, the Anti-Corn Law Leaguer, gave purchasers of its number for 20 July a free engraved portrait of Peel.

Avowedly non-political publications for the working classes, such as the *Working Man's Friend* or the *London Journal*, contrived to encourage admiration for Peel. The *Working Man's Friend* had published a long and implicitly favourable sketch on 23 March 1850: 'we leave it to the reader to estimate the man from the facts we have detailed.' A week earlier it had not even pretended detachment in its sketch of Disraeli:

> A flux of sounds instead of sense,
> And, like his novels, all – a fiction.

The *London Journal* for 27 July 1850 carried a long factual account of Peel's career. It praised without hesitation his services to the arts, but held back until the last paragraph before hinting at a value judgement on Peel's political services: 'while the prominent facts and features of Sir Robert Peel's life and character took him out of that world within which it is our place to expatiate, he was yet linked to it by many a tie which will be long remembered; and for this sudden bereavement there are many mourners going about its streets.'

The London protectionist dailies received the news of Peel's death with varying degrees of regret. The *Standard* of 3 July preferred to dwell upon Peel's sincere religious belief, and upon 'the admirable tenor' of his private life in which 'there was no change'. Perhaps this last remark implied a comparison with the changes in his political career. Next day the *Standard* dismissed the whole contemporary age as one of 'littleness', without any great poets, philosophers – or statesmen. The *Morning Herald* was rather indulgent on 3 July, describing Peel as 'one of the ablest' of politicians. But next day, while admitting all his private qualities, it protested 'in the interests of history' against the 'unsparing eulogy' heaped upon Peel's political character in the previous day's morning press. He was not to be accepted as the greatest statesman of his time, even though he had possessed business habits and was 'occasionally eloquent'. He had kept his thoughts to himself, and yet 'expected his party to vote as he wished'. His currency policy had 'crippled the commerce and industry of his country'. As for 'so-called free trade', it had made both commerce and industry 'tributary to the foreigner without any reciprocity'.

The *Morning Post* had made the same point in an editorial on the very morning of Peel's death. But it had changed hands since 1846, and its language about Peel was now less abrasive. On 3 July it deplored his 'lamentable demise', even though it had differed from him in his later years. The *Post* now accepted that Peel's high administrative skill, his 'great political sagacity' and his irreproachable private character had placed him in the first rank of public men.

The provincial protectionist press ranged in its parting comments upon Peel from qualified regret to continuing hostility. The *Blackburn Standard* of 10 July, bearing in mind Peel's great changes of view, asked 'who can say how much of a free-trader Sir Robert would have been ten years hence?' The *Leeds Intelligencer* (6 July) had put the same point not questioningly but positively: 'if free trade proves unsatisfactory Peel would have been among the first to modify it.' The *Intelligencer* therefore felt able still to defend its acceptance of repeal at Peel's hands in 1846. The *Manchester Courier* had similarly accepted his proposals in 1846; but by 1850 it had slipped back into regretting repeal, at least in the sudden way it had been enacted. But the *Courier* recognized Peel's sincerity, and mourned 'in sackcloth the death of the Lancashire statesman'.

The *Hampshire Advertiser* of 6 July offered the thought that Peel was popular, and therefore must have been great. Here was a curiously democratic assumption to come from a protectionist county newspaper. 'He to whom such things happened must have been a great man.' The *Liverpool Courier* of 10 July argued that Peel had indeed encouraged 'democratic encroachment' by mistaking 'the voice of a clamorous faction for the will of the nation'. A *Dover Telegraph* correspondent complained on 20 July that Peel had been always demanding attention: 'and never more obtained it than by his death'. But in response to this last demand for notice, some protectionist papers simply declined to make any editorial comment at all, as did the *Kentish Gazette*; or kept comment to a minimum, as did the *Derby Mercury*, which on 10 July went no further than to acknowledge Peel's sincerity. The *Lincolnshire Chronicle* (5 July) briefly described Peel as 'a great statesman', but still emphasized in another editorial how free trade was 'ruining our farmers'. The *Preston Pilot* (27 July) in a late article on 'The Political Life and Character of Sir Robert Peel' rejected all fudging:

> Conservatives remember his long Conservative profession of political faith, and forget his abandonment of its stronghold; destructives forget all his opposition to their doctrines, and remember only his ultimate sweeping abolition of restrictions. Destructives are delighted to shake hands with Conservatives in honoring Sir R. Peel, because it sets the Conservative seal upon destructive doctrine in the most public and decisive manner, and displays an apparent unanimity of opinion in approbation of that doctrine. The hearts of Conservatives are better than their heads; their feeling blinds their judgment.

Yet such sharpness was rare in Lancashire. The *Bolton Chronicle*, which had become a Peelite paper in 1846, mourned its hero's death deeply. Its most interesting comment came in its retrospect of the year on 28 December 1850. Cobdenite peace meetings were being held on the one side and protectionist meetings on the other. Neither extreme, claimed the *Chronicle*, was widely supported. Peel's middle way was what most people wanted; he had been 'missed almost daily since'. Oddly, the *Chronicle* believed that Peel would have spoken out against the 'Papal aggression', which was dominating politics by the end of the year. The *Liverpool Journal* of 6 July 1850 had reported 'Talk on 'Change': 'if not the greatest statesman England ever produced, he was certainly the most remarkable.' He had shown 'a moral heroism perfectly unexampled'.

IV

One reader of *The Times* in 1850 was Emily Hall, a spinster of Ravenswood House, West Wickham, Kent. She recorded in her diary how *The Times* had said that Peel's speech in the Don Pacifico debate was a reminder of his youthful triumphs; and now, grieved Miss Hall, 'that busy thoughtful brain' was dead. Who could have imagined at the last Waterloo dinner that the old Duke of Wellington would outlast 'the young and vigorous Sir Robert'? This idea of Peel as still young, even though sixty-two, was widespread; young at least in the sense of dying before his time. Miss Hall agreed with *The Times* that it 'almost makes one question the dealings of the Almighty'.[10]

A youthful Quaker, Robert Fowler, a future banker and Member of Parliament, admitted in his diary that it was strange to be grieving deeply for someone whom he had never seen. Yet on hearing the news of Peel's death he had wept. Fowler noted that regret was widespread even among those who had not previously expressed admiration for Peel. One such was another Quaker, Samuel Tuke. 'Though not one of his admirers, I really feel as if I had lost something of value to me.' There was no one left to whom the country could turn in emergency.[11]

A third Quaker, Eliza Ellis, struggled while writing a letter to a favourable conclusion about Peel. When she had first heard the news of his death, it had seemed 'incredible'. She had found it difficult to make up her mind about him; but his exemplary private life, his refusal of honours for his family and his devotion to public duty had finally persuaded her that he was a great man. His changes of opinion over Catholic Emancipation and Corn Law repeal she found very difficult to understand, but she came up with an explanation. 'If he believed that the views he once held on these questions and the carrying out of these views would be at variance with the interests of the Country, might he not sacrifice them without sacrificing his own honesty?'[12] *Punch*'s poem called 'Our "In Memoriam"' (13 July) expressed this same point in verse:

> Of whom the worst his enemies can say
> Is, that he left the error of his way
> When Conscience told him he was in the wrong.

'Memorial Lines on Sir Robert Peel', by Joseph Arnauld, barrister of the Middle Temple, listed the bases of Peel's 'self-earned kingship'. These were, first, his sharp, laborious mind: 'That analysed all parts, yet grasped the whole.' Secondly, his eloquence: 'Clear to convince.' And, thirdly, his wisdom, achieved by abandoning false views:

> Glory to him who resolutely great
> Twice wrecked his Party and twice saved the State.

Martin Tupper, the popular rhymster whose *Proverbial Philosophy* was in its

---

[10] MSS Hall U923 F2/6, f. 249 (Kent Archives Office, Maidstone).

[11] J. S. Flynn, *Sir Robert N. Fowler* (1893), p. 46; C. Tylor (ed.), *Samuel Tuke* (1900), pp. 236–7.

[12] Margaret Ellis (ed.), *Letters and Memorials of Eliza Ellis* (1883), pp. 52–3.

tenth edition by 1850, dashed off a mourning sonnet, which was widely
reproduced in the press:

> Struck down at noon amid the startled throng,
>   An eagle shot while soaring to the sun:
> A wounded gladiator dying strong
>   As loth to leave the glories he had won:
>   A life-long patriot, with his work half-done, –
> Of thee, great statesman, shall my mourning song
>   Arise in dread solemnity! – of thee,
> Whom the wide world, so lately and so long
>   Thine acolyte, would crowd to hear and see
> Their intellectual Athlete, their high name
>   For eloquence and prudence, gifts, and powers:
> But lo! that starry mind, a heavenly flame,
>   Is well enfranchised from this evil of ours,
> Translated in the zenith of its fame.

Tupper, the versifier of the representative middle-class response, thus emphasized how Peel, the 'intellectual Athlete', had been trusted to act rightly on
issues hardly understood by ordinary minds. Tupper, hoping at this time to
succeed to the vacant Poet Laureateship, sent a handwritten copy of this poem
to Gladstone, whom he knew socially. 'I trust you may like it: if I had affected
to throw personal feeling into it, I should not have been as I always choose to be
– true; for I only knew Sir Robert Peel through the public papers.'[13]

So majority middle-class opinion mourned Peel in 1850 with even greater
intensity of feeling than it had shown in his support four years earlier. So also
did majority working-class opinion. *Chambers's Papers for the People* devoted
an issue to Peel. It explained how 'his humbler countrymen . . . felt instinctively
that he must be pure and single-minded, as he was intellectually vigorous and
great'. Street ballads assumed that he was everyone's hero. 'The Lamented Loss
and Death of the Right Honourable Sir Robert Peel, Bart. M.P.' was published
from Seven Dials, London, as a black-edged sheet with seven verses:

> The poor long has praised and bless'd him,
> Now tears wet each eye, while in sorrow they sigh,
> He is gone, is Sir Robert, God rest him.
>   *   *   *
> He'd by no one be led, he'd by no one be said,
>   No Government feared to trust him.
> In every way he carried the sway
>   For the good of his country, God rest him.

---

[13] Tupper to Gladstone, 4 July 1850 (Add. MSS 44336, f. 107).

The strength of Peel's popularity was reflected in the way one regular press advertiser felt it to be advantageous to express elaborate sympathy while offering mourning clothes for sale. Hyam's National Tailoring and Clothing Establishment had branches in most big towns. The *Manchester Guardian* of 6 July 1850 carried a quarter-page advertisement for the local branch, which also appeared in other cotton-district newspapers. It began with a verse of forty-four lines about Peel:

> When round the state's proud vessel foams each wave,
> And warring factions fiercely howl and wave,
> No more shall we behold the stately form,
> Which bore the good ship through the threat'ning storm.
> Who, with mild eloquence and lofty grace
> Shall now fill up thy proud and towering place?

The verse eventually descended from the high flown to the hard sell:

> No outward trappings truly can express
> A nation's sense of warm devotedness, –
> Yet such poor grief as sable garb will show,
> Is one small tribute we thy memory owe;
> This through the breadth of our now darken'd land,
> Thy fate and genius surely may command;
> And common sense at once points out the way
> Where to obtain the means without delay:
> A garb, which shows that we thy loss deplore,
> Is found at once in Hyam's ample store!

The *Manchester Guardian* of 14 September advertised for Hyam a new cloth specially patterned to suit Peel's admirers, 'singularly adapted for Shooting Coats (and shooting was one of Sir Robert's favourite pastimes)'. The advertisement quoted at length from the clothmaker's circular, where 'the object of the design' was described (with a revealing confusion between Peel's resignation and Don Pacifico speeches) as 'to carry out the last public expressed desire of the lamented statesman, that his name might be remembered amongst the sons of toil'. A sheaf of corn was placed at the centre of the pattern, and round the ribbon which tied it were inscribed the dates of Peel's birth and death; a 'never-setting sun' illustrated the extension of free trade over the whole globe.

Peel's name also seems to have been exploited at Blackpool, then in its early days as a popular seaside resort. A letter to the *Preston Pilot* of 27 July described how the town was claiming Peel as one of its own. The beach had been crowded on the previous Monday, and the *Pilot*'s correspondent had found 'a bevy of hale fellows discussing the merits of the late Sir Robert'. One 'respectable working man' had exclaimed:

Not go see, Will, the house Sir Robert slept in when he came to Blackpool? It deserves as much to be taken as a drawing as Chamber Hall. . . . Well, Sir Robert used, as a fisherman told me who had seen it, to walk to Blackpool with a knapsack on his back, and take up his abode in a little thatched house near the queer new building of Mr. Eastham.

Peel's sudden death naturally lent itself to discussion in sermons. Most of these, although not all, seem to have accepted that Peel had ended his career above party. This meant that pulpit enthusiasm could be freely expressed, in terms which went beyond merely not speaking ill of the dead. J. J. Tayler of Cross Street Unitarian Chapel, Manchester, noted approvingly in a sermon delivered on 29 December 1850 that between extremes of political opinion, 'there has ever existed a large and powerful middle party, adorned by our noblest historical names and associated with the remembrance of all our great constitutional struggles, which owns the claims at once of progress and of conservation.' Peel's affinity with this middle opinion was clearly in Tayler's mind when he emphasized how great changes 'have not hitherto been effected by men of extreme opinions on either side, but directly or indirectly through the moral force of the great intermediate party'. The 'cordial support' of middle opinion had carried Catholic Emancipation and Corn Law repeal, 'when introduced by their political opponents'.[14]

Yet in a sermon given just after Peel's death the incumbent of St James, Ryde, Isle of Wight, was still denouncing such responsiveness as mere expediency. 'The great mistake which this eminent and deeply-lamented statesman made, may be traced to this one fault, the yielding to a supposed expediency in his changes of policy, and the succumbing to a temporary pressure, through fear of rebellion, instead of a courageous resistance.'[15] But a mourning sermon on the text, 'How are the mighty fallen', preached at Uxbridge Church by the Reverend J. T. Brown, was much more enthusiastic. Peel's Don Pacifico speech was welcomed for being 'as free from partisanship as it was full of patriotism'. Moreover, Peel had gone from making this good speech to making a good deathbed. He had been honestly motivated in all his political shifts. 'Business was his congenial element. Practical result was his motto.' His attractive personal characteristics had added to his influence. 'Deeply beloved as a husband and father, faithful as a friend, kind to his domestics, considerate to his tenants, liberal yet discriminating in his charities, and a munificent patron of science, literature, and art, the esteem which his private life inspired, was the counterpart of the admiration commanded by his public career.'[16]

[14] J. J. Tayler, *Christian Aspects of Faith and Duty* (2nd ed., 1855), pp. 310–22.

[15] *A Sermon Upon the Death of the Rt. Hon. Sir Robert Peel, Bart. Preached in the Church of St. James, Ryde, Isle of Wight by the Incumbent* (1850).

[16] J. T. Brown, *Funeral Sermon for Sir Robert Peel, Bart. Preached at Uxbridge Church* (1850).

The Reverend J. S. M. Anderson of St George's, Brighton, likewise linked Peel's 'private virtue' with his 'public integrity'. Peel's wise generosity in the use of his wealth was commended. Anderson also remarked upon the significance of the way rich and poor had crowded together for news outside Peel's house; and of the emotion which almost choked the voice of 'the unconquered warrior of the age'. Such moving scenes highlighted the need for all men to live at peace with God. Another Brighton sermon, delivered by the Reverend F. W. Robertson of Trinity Chapel, one of the foremost Anglican preachers of the day, emphasized how the good done by men on earth constituted 'education for eternity'. Such good was therefore doubly important; for the benefit of others on earth, and for the sake of the doer himself in preparation for heaven. Peel's education on earth was now completed.[17]

The Reverend J. H. Gurney, Rector of St Mary's, Marylebone, took as his text, 'None of us liveth to himself, and no man dieth to himself'. Peel had patently not lived only for himself. 'He might have lived a life of luxurious ease, but he preferred a life of laborious usefulness.' He did not despair after the passing of the Reform Act, but worked instead to restore social and political harmony. After his resignation in 1846 he had continued to serve; 'and delivered, for his last effort, a speech from which, as a watchful listener told me, he would not have needed to blot one word, if he had known that his end was near.'[18]

The fact that Peel died within days of making this speech meant that its words were widely regarded as a last message, which deserved especial attention; 'a farewell to the nation', as The Times wrote on 4 July. Peel had recommended conciliation rather than confrontation between nations, an emphasis which suited well as a parting exhortation. Although in form the speech had not been one of Peel's best, The Times of 3 July felt moved to praise it as a reminder of his best efforts. The text was published in more than one popular pamphlet version: 'Price One Penny Peel's Last Words.'

Those involved in the international peace movement, which was undergoing an upsurge of activity about 1850, were glad after this speech to claim Peel in death as a friend to their cause – more so than he had actually been in life. An elaborate engraving was published from St John's Wood, London, 'Dedicated to the Friends of Peace, to Endear the Memory of Sir Robert Peel, Bart.' 'Who at freedom's call nobly devoted himself to extend Commerce – to secure the blessings of plenty – and to foster universal brotherhood "to the farthest verge of the green earth".' The engraving included a portrait of Peel, plus his coat of

[17] J. S. M. Anderson, The Dead Yet Speaking, A Sermon Preached at St. George's, Brighton . . . after the Death of Sir Robert Peel (1850); F. W. Robertson, Sermons Preached at Brighton (1886), IV, pp. 61–6.
[18] J. H. Gurney, A Pastor's Warning: Suggested by the Lamented Death of Sir Robert Peel. A Sermon Preached in St. Mary's Church, Marylebone (1850).

arms; and it illustrated nine places linked with his career. These included Constitution Hill, 'where his horse floundered'; and the dining-room at Whitehall Gardens, 'Lo! here the patriot sunk, for ever free'.

A street ballad, 'The Poor Man's Lamentation for the Death of Sir Robert Peel', devoted separate verses to the themes of cheap bread and universal peace:

> Alas, great Robert now is dead
> Who modified our Laws,
> Who took the duty off our Bread,
> And gain'd so much applause.
>
> *   *   *
>
> Let all the warlike nations round
> Lay down their arms of steel,
> And let both truth and grace be found
> In all the acts of Peel.

Eight years later John Bright was still reminding the public of Peel's last speech, and claiming that it lent support to the views of the peace party: 'that last, that beautiful, that most solemn speech, which he delivered with an earnestness and a sense of responsibility as if he had known he was leaving a legacy to his country'.[19]

The Radical *Nonconformist* published on 10 July 1850 one of the fullest of the immediate assessments of Peel's character and career. It admitted that the suddenness of his death had heightened feeling. But other statesmen had died suddenly – Romilly, Castlereagh, Canning, Huskisson – without producing so general a sense of loss. Why was Peel so much missed? Because he 'seemed to be the living representative of this age's political possibilities. Men gauged, not indeed the inherent worth, but the feasibility of future changes, by their suppositions as to what Sir Robert Peel would do.' The aristocracy accepted his estimate of what concessions must be made, and how to make them safely. The people trusted him to make such concessions work in practice. 'The Whigs are like the servant in the parable, who said, "I go, sir," but went not – Peel resembled him who refused, but afterwards repented, *and went*. "And went." This is the secret of Sir Robert's place in the respectful and grateful recollections of Englishmen. His performances outdid his promises.' In the end, remarked the *Nonconformist*, this unusual method had come to be widely appreciated.

Nevertheless, the *Nonconformist* concluded that by the time of Peel's death his work had been done. It did not share the view that he had much more to offer. He had been 'mainly a conservative', who would never have come to advocate those further organic reforms which the *Nonconformist* thought to be necessary. In particular, Peel would have always opposed both

[19] Bright, *Speeches*, p. 467.

disestablishment of the Church of England and further parliamentary reform. 'We did not participate in the common opinion, that he would have become a man of the people.' In this sense of 'a man of the people' the *Nonconformist* was surely right.

7

The Victorians and Peel: *c.*1850–1900

I

How could Peel be best remembered? It quickly became clear that the Victorian public would not be satisfied to remember him just by his works – by his law reforms; by the policemen on the streets; by free trade in general; or even by 'cheap bread' in particular. *Punch* did indeed try to convert this last benefit into a monument in the mind. *Punch*'s 'Monument to Peel' (12 October 1850) showed a pyramid of loaves with the inscription 'Cheap Bread' and with a working-class family happily eating a meal in front of the pyramid. But the Victorians liked to have lasting physical reminders of their heroes, large statues in public and small artefacts at home. Peel was an obvious subject for both. In this instance, however, the most striking of all memorial schemes did not end with a statue. It became known as the Working Men's Memorial of Gratitude to Sir Robert Peel, and it even provided some statistical evidence of the wide extent of working-class mourning for Peel.

An article in the *Spectator* of 20 July 1850 warned of 'The Public Subscription Traders' who had got up collections in the past for such abortive ventures as Queen Caroline's plate; George IV's Irish emerald crown; and a Peel monument in 1846. This last was certainly a subscription which came to nothing. A fund for a Peel statue to be funded by pennies from working men was proposed by 'Alfred', A. S. Kydd, a Chartist barrister, in four letters to the *Morning Advertiser* between 25 June and 9 July 1846. A central organizing committee was apparently formed, chaired by Colonel Perronnett Thompson, the veteran free trader. From July to September 1846 the *Morning Advertiser* printed lists of penny subscriptions, many of them collected in London public houses. The paper reported on 26 September that it had banked 9,000 pence. 'Alfred' had complained, however, that only the *Advertiser* among the London dailies, and *Lloyd's Weekly* among the Sundays, were giving publicity to the venture. He noticed how the Manchester free-trade papers had remained 'ominously silent'. 'Alfred' tried to demonstrate that a Peel fund need not clash with the £75,000 testimonial fund for Richard Cobden. Nevertheless, it does seem that the one collection harmed the other. Cobden needed the money: Peel did not need a statue. It is unclear what happened to the pennies collected.

Four years later the man who took the lead over the Working Men's Memorial was Joseph Hume, the veteran Radical Member of Parliament. He enjoyed a deserved reputation for acuteness and probity in financial matters. Peel and Hume had clashed in the Commons at intervals down the years; and in 1835 Peel, ever sensitive, had written stiffly to Hume about aspersions apparently damaging to his honour. Hume was able to explain his words away, and mutual respect grew steadily thereafter, even though Peel's manner towards Hume was sometimes bantering. Peel recognized the value of Hume's independent criticism of authority, and of his passion for economy in government. Hume, for his part, came to admire Peel's constructive intentions as a Minister. By the end of 1840 Hume was telling Bonham that he was withdrawing his support from the Whigs. And when Peel was forming his administration in the next year, Graham even suggested Hume for the office of Vice-President of the Board of Trade, which went to Gladstone.[1]

By the time of Peel's conversion to the side of Corn Law repeal Hume had become an open admirer. When Peel was briefly out of office in December 1845, Hume wrote to him to express the hope that he would continue his 'powerful support' for free trade. Peel thanked Hume 'for the justice you have frequently done to the motives by which I have been influenced in public life', even though they had 'greatly differed occasionally'. In the debate on the Address in January 1846, Hume emphasized how it was much more honourable for Peel to admit mistake over the Corn Laws than to cling to error. The test of his present views was not their acceptability to his party but their value to the country. Hume told the Commons that nine-tenths of the people wanted repeal. Cobden complained that Villiers was 'badgered . . . even by such men as Jos. Hume, for introducing the annual League motion for total and immediate repeal. 'The Peel fever is upon them, and they seem to have no faith in anyone else.' Hume deeply regretted Peel's determination to resign in June 1846. 'No one ever left power carrying with him so much of the sympathy of the people.' But after hearing Peel's resignation speech two days later, Hume wrote to say that he now understood why Peel could not do otherwise.[2]

The *Manchester Guardian*'s London correspondent (6 July 1850) thought it appropriate that Hume, for whom Peel had shown 'marked regard' of recent years, should have moved the adjournment of the Commons upon Peel's death. But Hume characteristically did not stop at simply making this gesture. On 6

---

[1] Peel to Hume, 20 March 1835; Hume to Peel, 20 March 1835 (Add. MSS 40417, ff. 290, 292); Bonham to Peel, 12 December 1840 (Add. MSS 40428, f. 462); Graham to Peel, 6 August 1841 (Add. MSS 40318, f. 296).

[2] Hume to Peel, 29 June 1846 (Add. MSS 40594, f. 440); McCord, *Anti-Corn Law League*, p. 202.

July a letter from him appeared in *The Times* which drew attention to the formation of a committee of tradesmen with the purpose of collecting penny subscriptions for 'a poor man's monument to the memory of Sir Robert Peel'. The idea seems to have originated among workmen in the Pentonville district of London. Their letter to Hume, asking him to be a trustee, was copied into *The Times*. Hume gladly accepted. He had present as well as past politics in mind, for he was well aware of the revival of protectionist agitation. He wrote privately two days later to George Wilson, former chairman of the Anti-Corn Law League, urging the Manchester repealers actively to support the scheme. 'We want the Millions more than the Money to support the Corn Law repeal.'[3] On 9 July Richard Cobden published in *The Times* a letter which he had sent to the Pentonville committee agreeing to become a patron of the venture. Cobden quoted the famous conclusion to Peel's resignation speech. 'In piling up the pence of the working classes into a pyramid to his memory, let me suggest that the above passage be inscribed upon its base.'

The subsequent history of the scheme was recorded by Hume in letters to *The Times* over the next two years, reprinted in many other papers. By 18 July 1850 a letter from Hume was offering advice about how money should be collected, as he could not reply individually to the 'multitude' of enquiries about this. He advised the formation of local collection committees, which would appoint receivers. A central committee was being formed in London to decide upon the best use of the money. The idea of erecting a 'monument', such as Cobden had assumed, was obviously now in doubt. The word had been replaced in Hume's letter by 'testimonial', so that Hume now wrote of 'The Working Men's Testimonial to the Memory of the late Sir Robert Peel'. Cobden had suggested that, to prevent fraud, the collection of pennies should take place everywhere on the same day. He spoke on 18 July at an organizing meeting in the old League rooms in Manchester. He recommended the formation of committees in every town; the circulation of handbills through every mill; and door-to-door collection of pennies.[4]

The key meeting to complete the central organization of the scheme was held at the Whittington Club, 'late Crown & Anchor Tavern', Strand, London, on 7 August. Hume took the chair, flanked by Cobden, Bright and four other Members of Parliament. *The Times* (8 August) described the occasion as 'numerously attended, but very disorderly'. The great majority of those present were favourably disposed; 'but a considerable number of Chartists, coster-mongers, and others had taken their seats close to the platform.' Bronterre O'Brien, the Chartist leader, spoke, and blamed Peel for creating the 'new police', and for denying the social and political rights of the people. In this same

[3] Hume to Wilson, 8 July 1850 (Wilson Papers, Manchester Reference Library).

[4] Cobden to Wilson, 15, 25 July 1850 (Wilson Papers, Manchester Reference Library); *Manchester Examiner*, 13, 20 July 1850.

spirit the *Red Republican* of 3 August, in an article hostile to the Peel memorial scheme, had offered to sum up his career in a single sentence: '*he first patronized the landlords, then the moneylords, and left the Proletarians to shift for themselves.*' A fortnight later the *Red Republican* was conceding that Peel was 'not a cruel man by nature'; but as a high politician he had kept the people in slavery. 'What need of any other monument, while these perambulating Peelers grace (?) the streets of the metropolis?' Richard Oastler, the ten-hours agitator on the Radical right, joined these critics from the Radical left. He had never trusted Peel. He continued to oppose free trade into the 1850s, because he believed that unrestricted trade required uncontrolled hours of work. An article to this effect, and against a Peel monument, appeared in the *Trades Advocate and Herald of Progress* for 21 September 1850. But Oastler was answered by the editor, who praised cheap bread and urged the working classes to seek help not through protectionist legislation but through trade unions.[5]

Joseph Hume reported to the 7 August London meeting that 167 local collecting committees had been formed. Enough money had been given by noblemen and gentlemen to defray management expenses; so that all subscriptions 'from 1d upwards to 1s' would be devoted entirely towards the memorial. On a motion from Cobden, it was agreed that collection day should be 31 August. Hume was elected chairman of the central committee. A young costermonger urged that the money raised should be employed for educational purposes. Another young man argued likewise. The outcome was that a rider was attached to the original motion, recognizing the propriety of considering use of the fund for educational improvement. This seems to have been the origin of the plan which was eventually adopted.

A letter from Hume appeared in *The Times* of 5 September to announce that the closing date for receipt of money had been extended from 31 August to 17 September. Another letter in *The Times* of 28 January 1851 reported that £1,450 had been subscribed. An enquiry about the progress of the scheme appeared in the paper of 25 November. This produced a reply from Hume, published four days later, which reported that the subscription list was now closed, with about £1,700 in the bank. He promised that early action would follow. But not until *The Times* of 12 April 1852 did Hume report that auditors had now certified the accounts to be in good order. A total of £1,737 0s 6d had been collected, 'chiefly in penny subscriptions' from 3,504 towns and villages, plus about 250,000 individual subscribers. Some four or five thousand circulars had been sent out, at a cost of £295 14s 9d; but the central committee members would meet this cost themselves, so as to keep the fund intact. A further letter from Hume to *The Times* of 24 May 1852 reported that the committee had now decided to spend the money upon the purchase of books

---

[5] *Morning Post*, 1 July 1846; R. L. Hill, *Toryism and the People* (1929), pp. 172–3, 222–3; C. Driver, *Tory Radical, The Life of Richard Oastler* (1970), ch. 39.

'suitable to the working classes'. Each book was to be distinctively bound and stamped in remembrance of Peel's gift of 'untaxed bread'; with copies distributed to public libraries, mechanics' institutes or reading rooms open to the working classes. This became the essence of the scheme as eventually established by deed of indenture dated 10 May 1854. This deed described the penny subscription as having been undertaken throughout the United Kingdom to institute a working men's memorial to Peel 'for his successful legislation in abolishing the Tax on Bread'. Hume, Graham and Russell were appointed trustees of the fund of £1,737 0s 6d 'subscribed by over Four hundred thousand Working Men', which had been invested in consols. The principal was to be kept intact, while the interest was to be expended annually by the Council of University College, London, to promote the mental improvement of the working classes through the distribution of books, maps 'and other aids to knowledge excepting pecuniary aids'.

The memorial indenture survives in the archives of University College, London, as does a manuscript subscription book of fifty-five pages. With its long catalogue of penny subscriptions from humble people, this book casts unique light upon the extent of working-class admiration for Peel. Most, but not quite all, subscribers seem to have given just one penny. Bearing in mind that £1,737 0s 6d is 416,886 pence, the total number of workmen subscribing would therefore seem to have been as claimed. The following were among the entries:

	£	s	d
351 Mutual Imprt. Socy. at Charlton New Mills, Manchester	1	9	3
28 Messengers & others in Her M's Treasury	5	1	0
55 Printers D. News office		5	7
804 Letter carriers, London district, with balance of halfpence collected to cover expenses	3	17	10
14,071 Amount collected by Morning Advertiser	52	12	7
19 Queen's Prison per Capt. Hudson, R. N.	1	4	6
1102 L. & Brighton & S. Coast Ry. per C. Francis	19	1	0
176 Stocking makers, Agrcult. labrs. etc. of Wolvey, North Warwickshire		14	8

Bookplate for Working Men's Memorial of Gratitude

32 Messrs. Debenham & Co. 44					
Wigmore Street				2	8
25 Bank of England Workmen				2	1
29 Houses of Parliament					
Watchmen, Firemen, & doormen				2	5
315 Houses of Parliament					
Carvers empd. there	£1	14	9		
Bricklayers & labourers		6	1		
Masons & labourers	£3	13	6		
Plasterers		2	9	5 17	1
119 Guards & Porters L. & N. W.					
Railway – Euston Station				18 8	0
424 Per Mr. Ed. Green from					
"Working Men of Pontefract"				1 15	4
201 Model Lodging House					
Westminster – per James Archer				16	9
446 Shipwrights, Labourers etc.					
Deptford Dock Yard				3 0	11
752 Sheerness Dockyard					
per Mr. Sidney Smith				5 8	3
72 Nottingham Journal Off.				6	0
30,902 Manchester district per					
Jos. Hicken				128 15	2

Many collections taken in London public houses featured in the list. The final grand total at 17 March 1854 was given in the subscription book as £1,740 10s 11d.

University College, London, which Hume had helped to found, administered the scheme through a committee. This first met on 8 August 1855, and agreed to spend '£130 at the least' on books. The first distribution came in February 1856. Books were given to the Camberwell Institute for the Industrial Classes; the Walworth Literary and Scientific Institution; the Horsleydean Temperance Mutual Instruction Society; and the Bermondsey and Horsleydean Mutual Improvement Association. Certain institutions had been named in the original regulations for priority treatment because they were situated in places which had contributed generously to the scheme. These named institutions included the Manchester Free Library and the Salford Royal Museum and Library. Copies of books supplied to these two bodies have survived, with their special bookplates. The Manchester Free Library received in June 1856 six science publications of the Cavendish Society; plus W. Truran, *The Iron Manufacture of Great Britain theoretically and practically considered*

(1855); *The Engineers' & Machinists' Drawing Book* (1855); M. Alcan, *Essai sur l'industrie des matieres textiles* (1847); Jones Quain, *Elements of Anatomy* (1848); H. Shaw, *The Decorative Arts Ecclesiastical and Civil of the Middle Ages* (1851); an Arabic Grammar; and T. Wright, *Early Christianity in Arabia* (1855).[6]

The annual disbursement seems to have settled down at £45, reduced to £42 in 1891 to allow for clerical overheads. Sidney Webb, the pioneer socialist, was a committee member in the eighteen nineties; and Professors A. E. Housman and A. F. Pollard served in turn as chairmen. The regulations were amended in 1908 to limit distribution of books to institutions not in receipt of state or municipal aid. Applications for books had dried up by 1947; and since 1948 the yearly income from the fund has been given to the adult-class department of the National Central Library.

II

The success of this memorial scheme did not check the demand for statues of Peel. These came to be erected in most of the largest towns (London, Manchester, Birmingham, Liverpool, Leeds, Bradford, Glasgow); as well as in some smaller places (Salford, Tamworth, Montrose, Preston, Bury, Blackburn, Huddersfield). 'We are living,' wrote the *Athenaeum* (10 August 1850) six weeks after Peel's death, 'our readers know, in an age emphatically of statues and testimonials.' Why did the Victorians want statues? More useful visible memorials to the great dead were often recommended as preferable. *The Sunday Times* (21 July 1850) suggested, for example, that Peel's well-known concern for suffering artists and men of letters would make appropriate the foundation of an asylum for such people, with a school for their children. A correspondent to the *Manchester Courier* (13 July 1850) argued that 'pillars and statues, in the course of time, become rather vestiges of historical research'. Gladstone was recorded as saying in 1866 that monuments were little use in commemorating people, 'and that those who were worth remembering were so without monuments'.[7] Yet Victorian promoters of statues refused to be discouraged. Part of their motivation was certainly a wish to ornament the new public places of their rapidly expanding towns. But beyond ornamentation lay moral purpose. A statue was regarded as a reminder of virtue and a source of inspiration, as the *Manchester Guardian* of 11 September 1852 emphasized with regard to the Peel statue at Bury: 'the public recognition of merit in this respect re-acts on the people who render it, and tends to make them that which they admire.' In the same spirit, the *Preston Chronicle* (20 July 1850) had

---

[6] Manchester Free Library, Donations Book 1851–63, ff. 367–8.
[7] B. Russell and Patricia Russell (eds), *The Amberley Papers* (1966) I, p. 512.

recommended the erection of a local statue of Peel to remind those, and 'especially the young', who worked in manufactures and trade 'that the greatest of English statesmen was the son of a cotton spinner'. Lord Houghton remarked at the inauguration of the Huddersfield Peel statue in 1873 how good it was that 'every poor child who comes through this square . . . should ask his mother who that man was who stands there, and that she should tell him, as far as her knowledge goes, how great and how good was that man'.[8]

The eagerness of the Victorians to erect statues did not mean that they were uncritical of the statues which their sculptors provided. Complaints about poor quality were so regular that it was even once suggested in despair that at every great man's death a statue should be pulled down rather than one more put up.[9] Early Victorian sculpture lacked freshness of touch. F. T. Palgrave dismissed most contemporary public statuary as 'feeble, or ugly, or lifeless'. He blamed the system of open competition run by committees, which inhibited creative freedom.[10] The *Builder* (17 April 1852), quoted by *The Times*, even forecast that 'the traditions of the statesman and the requirements of the committees' would render the Peel statues so much alike that a single figure might as well be designed by one first-rate sculptor, and then electrotyped for the different towns. In reality, there was enough interest among sculptors to generate strong competition for commissions. Evidence has survived of how Calder Marshall lobbied for the Manchester work. Such was obviously his custom, for he had written boldly to Peel himself in 1846 after hearing rumours of plans for statues of heroes of the recent Sikh war. Within days of Peel's death he was sending letters to the Mayor of Manchester and other influential figures in the city.[11] *The Times* of 10 October 1850 carried an article on 'The Peel Statues and the Sculptors'. This recorded which sculptors had been given which commissions. Small models had been made by several contestants, and were already on display. Behnes had produced one of Peel in modern dress; Calder Marshall of Peel in a cloak, 'a sort of medium between the ancient classical and the modern nonclassical'. The temptation to dress Victorian gentlemen in Roman togas was strong.

What had Peel himself looked for in public statues? Characteristically, he emphasized the first importance of a good likeness. 'No allegories will be half so interesting to Posterity, nor will the figure of fame or Britannia be regarded with the same satisfaction with which people will look on the most faithful remembrance of the man himself that can be procured.' In this spirit he hoped

---

[8] *Builder*, 15 November, 6 December 1851; *Huddersfield Daily Chronicle*, 4 June 1873.

[9] *Huddersfield Daily Chronicle*, 4 June 1873. See R. Gunnis, *Dictionary of British Sculptors 1660–1851* (new ed., n.d.); and B. Read, *Victorian Sculptors* (1982).

[10] F. T. Palgrave, *Essays on Art* (1866), p. 251.

[11] Calder Marshall to Peel, 4 May 1846 (Add. MSS 40591, f. 129); Calder Marshall to C. Swain, 17 July 1850 (Swain Autograph Letters and Manuscripts, Manchester Reference Library).

that the statue of Sir Sidney Smith, the hero of Acre, would be exactly life-size. Also that the inscription would be in English, 'and in very unexaggerated language'.[12] About 1844 Peel seems to have contemplated the idea of establishing state scholarships to support English students who wished to study sculpture at Rome. He asked the opinion of John Gibson, who resided there, and who was the leading English-born sculptor of the day. Peel had visited his Rome studio, and owned one of his works. But the scholarship idea was not adopted.[13]

It was fortunate that Peel did not live to see some of the statues of himself. One correspondent to the *Preston Chronicle* of 20 July 1850, who signed only as 'An Admirer of All Truly Great Men', warned against the erection of numerous local monuments, done on the cheap. His fear of unsightly Peel memorials in every town and village did not come to pass; but neither did his wish for just three national monuments 'on a grand and noble scale', in London, Manchester and Bury. A proposal to Parliament for a Peel statue at public expense in Westminster Abbey was made by Lord John Russell, the Prime Minister, ten days after Peel's death. This statue was erected in the south transept in September 1853. It was life size, in pure white marble, placed on a pedestal of blue veined marble. *The Times* (10 September) found it a good representation of Peel in the act of addressing the Commons. The *Illustrated London News* (1 October), however, thought that by clothing Peel in a toga Gibson had lost 'the peculiarly simple but manly bearing of our great social reformer'. A granite statue by Behnes in Cheapside, London, was uncovered with little ceremony in July 1855. Peel was portrayed wearing contemporary dress, although with trousers so fashionably tight that one observer likened them to rubber pants. *The Times* (27 July) nevertheless concluded that 'the manner and character of the original are preserved'. The statue in Parliament Square, paid for by Peel's closest friends, was found acceptable only at the third attempt. The first version, by Marochetti, was rejected in 1863 as too large for the original site in New Palace Yard. A second try by the same sculptor, at his own expense, was put in the same place in January 1868; but it was removed by resolution of the House of Commons, and melted down to provide the bronze for a fresh attempt by Matthew Noble. This was his fourth statue of Peel. It was unveiled in December 1876, and removed to Parliament Square in the following year.[14]

What seems to have been the earliest monument to Peel was erected in a cemetery at Forfar in 1851. It was not a statue but an elaborate canopy by

[12] Peel to Goulburn, 11 October 1842 (Add. MSS 40443, f. 280); Peel to Croker, 28 December 1842 (Add. MSS 40521, f. 57).

[13] Mrs Rose Lawrence to Peel, 8 February 1843; Peel to Mrs Lawrence, 9 February 1843 (Add. MSS 40524, ff. 252, 254); T. Matthews, *Biography of John Gibson R.A.* (1911), p. 104.

[14] *The Times*, 18 January 1877; Lord Edward Gleichen, *London's Open-air Statuary* (1928), pp. 34, 127; T. Fontane, *Journeys to England* (1939), p. 112.

James MacLaren in the Greek style, designed to provide cover for a bust of Peel. But this bust, by William Anderson of Perth, was not ready until two years later. An inscription on the front of the monument expressed the gratitude of the town for repeal of the Corn Laws. Forfar had been a strong Chartist centre.[15]

The earliest full-sized statue of Peel to be unveiled was a bronze at Salford on 8 May 1852. This was the first of Noble's four attempts. Nearly thirty years later an article in the *Pendleton Reporter* (16 July 1881) remembered with satisfaction how £1,200 had been raised by local public subscription, one-third of it from working people. The best available site had been chosen, in front of the museum and library and in full view of the main entrance to Peel Park. Peel was shown in the pose he adopted when speaking in the House of Commons. The *Manchester Guardian* (12 May 1852) reported that those who had known him found the likeness to be 'faultless'. Peel's resignation appeal for remembrance was inscribed on the granite pedestal. The words were said to be still read attentively a generation later: 'visitors stay to admire the statue as a work of art and to read the words which touch a sympathetic chord in every breast.'

Preston's statue was inaugurated on the last day of the same month. It was the work of a local self-taught sculptor, Thomas Duckett, and it proved to be both crude in finish and a poor likeness. None the less, the inauguration was celebrated as a local gala day with workplaces closed. A bronze statue by Noble was unveiled in Peel's home town of Tamworth in July 1852. The *Illustrated London News* (31 July) complained about the 'severity of expression', but thought that Peel's attitude as a speaker had been well caught. A total of £1,100 had been raised in subscriptions which ranged from one penny to £50.[16]

The Leeds statue by Behnes was set up in August 1852.[17] It was the first large bronze to be cast in one piece in England. The sum of £1,800 had been collected, and contemporaries were satisfied that the likeness was a good one. The Mayor of Leeds emphasized that it would be valued not principally as a work of art, 'far more as an image of a statesman'. The Leeds branch of Hyam's, the 'national tailor', took the opportunity to issue an advertisement in rhyme in the local press (*Leeds Mercury*, 21 August 1852):

> *Mementoes* rise on every side,
>   Fit tributes of his worth;
> His name's revered – his loss is mourned,

[15] *Builder*, 5 March 1853; C. Rogers, *Monuments and Monumental Inscriptions in Scotland* (1872) II, p. 230.

[16] *The Times*, 27 April 1857.

[17] See Melanie Stafford, 'Peel's statue in Leeds – a first for town and country', *Leeds Art Calendar* (1982).

Throughout the mighty earth!
Whilst *Yorkshire* nobly has awoke
Its feelings to reveal,
And LEEDS devotedly has given
A *Statue unto Peel*!

Peel gained immortal honour by cheapening the price of bread.
HYAM has won his popularity by cheapening the price of clothing.

SAMUEL HYAM.
NATIONAL TAILOR, CLOTHIER, AND OUTFITTER,
42, BRIGGATE, LEEDS.

In the same month a Peel statue by Ritchie was unveiled in Montrose, where
Joseph Hume was the local Member of Parliament.[18]

Bury, which claimed Peel as a native son, erected both a Peel statue and a
Peel column. They were inaugurated in September 1852, with Peel's son,
Frederick, to the fore. He had recently been elected as the local Member of
Parliament. The statue in bronze by Baily was lifelike; but it was destined to
become most noticed for the way Peel's waistcoat fastened the wrong way.
This does not seem to have been noticed on the day. *The Times* (10 September)
reported the 'singular scene', with working people gathering round the statue
for hours after the ceremonies had ended to cheer and shout. The *Illustrated
London News* (18 September) claimed, more indulgently, that the groups
which gathered 'talked affectionately of the man who had brought cheap bread
into their homes'. The column on Holcombe Hill reached 120 feet high, with
the one word 'Peel' inscribed on its base. It was designed, explained the
Manchester Guardian of 12 September, 'to attract attention from a distance,
rather than to afford a specimen of architectural beauty on a near inspection'.

Manchester's statue, inaugurated in October 1853, was the product of much
deliberation. The idea of a Peel statue had first been locally aired at the time of
repeal of the Corn Laws. A letter had appeared in the *Manchester Guardian* of
20 May 1846 urging the erection of a figure in recognition of Peel's services to
free trade, and in the knowledge that Manchester was 'without a public
monument of any description'. A sharp answering letter appeared in the next
issue. This insisted that a statue of Cobden must come first. 'To whom is the
credit of Magna Charta due . . . to King John, perhaps? What next?' No move
was made in 1846. But upon Peel's death four years later the Mayor of
Manchester was immediately asked to call a meeting of leading citizens to
discuss a memorial. They met on 8 July. The same issue of the *Manchester
Guardian* (13 July) which reported Peel's funeral, also reported the widespread
enthusiasm among both the middle and working classes for starting memorial
schemes. The Conservative *Manchester Courier* was as well disposed towards

---

[18] *Illustrated London News*, 28 August 1852.

INAUGURATION OF THE STATUE OF THE LATE SIR ROBERT PEEL, AT BURY.

Unveiling the Peel statue at Bury: *Illustrated London News*, 18 September 1852

the idea of a local statue as its Liberal rivals, although a sarcastic letter did appear in the *Courier* of 3 August which suggested that any Peel monument should be surmounted by a weather-cock.

The history of Manchester's Peel statue from conception to unveiling was summarized in a handwritten account which survives in the Manchester Reference Library. The large sum of £5,143 16s 2d was raised by public subscription. A site for the statue was chosen in August 1850, in front of the infirmary; the figure was to be cast in bronze 'in an erect position, and of colossal size'. Whether or not Peel should be dressed in classical garb aroused discussion; but contemporary dress was finally chosen, 'as far as practicable'. Eleven sculptors were invited to compete. Gibson declined. Calder Marshall was among the chosen number, and was eventually successful. Only the chairman of the selection committee, the Bishop of Manchester, knew which model statuettes had been submitted by which sculptors. So Calder Marshall seems to have won the commission on merit, not because of his speedy lobbying. But the Bishop did argue for Calder Marshall's model in committee, and this was chosen by eleven votes to nine.[19] Tens of thousands visited a public exhibition in Manchester of all the statuettes submitted. Calder Marshall was paid 4,000 guineas in four instalments. The statue was cast in June 1853, and sent by rail from London on 1 October. The grand inauguration took place eleven days later.

All three Manchester newspapers gave elaborate coverage to the event in their numbers for 15 October. The *Illustrated London News* carried a drawing of the statue, as it did of most of the Peel figures. The *Manchester Guardian* described the erection of a local representation of Peel as 'a duty which we owed to public education'. The *Manchester Examiner* remarked that it was Manchester's first public monument; that it was fitting for Peel, with his family links with local industry, to take pride of place; and fitting also that Gladstone, his pupil, should be present as chief speaker at the inauguration. Gladstone himself wrote in his diary of the 'great assemblage – of men almost exclusively, & working men. There I spoke, to the croaking of my voice.' Gladstone's speech praised Peel's industriousness, his 'purity of conscience' and his determination to serve the public good. Gladstone expressed particular satisfaction that the statue was not hidden in 'some gilded hall', but was prominent on a main throughfare. He was probably thinking of the Liverpool statue of Peel, also by Noble, which was to be placed next year in St George's Hall.

The Manchester statue showed Peel in contemporary dress, but with an ample cloak draped loosely over his shoulders. This gave a vaguely classical air to the figure, especially from the rear and side views. The base was adorned with two supporting statues – that on the left representing commerce and manufactures; that on the right representing art and science. The latter was holding a book, which had been cast hollow so as to allow the organizing committee to deposit inside a record of the inauguration. The newspapers agreed that here was a fine statue, lifelike yet dignified.

Birmingham's bronze statue by Hollins was not ready until August 1855. *The Times* (28 August) pointed out how noteworthy it was that a statue had been erected in Birmingham at all. This was the place where fifteen years earlier Peel had been assaulted by the mob, on account especially of his currency views. 'Times and circumstances have, however, since that period wonderfully changed.' The crowd present at the unveiling was said by the *Birmingham Journal* (29 August) to have been as large as that at the famous reform meeting on Newhall Hill in 1832. The Crimean War was being fought, and the chairman of the organizing committee remarked that contemporaries had cried out during the Commons debates on the war, 'Oh for one hour of Peel'. The

---

[19] *Manchester Guardian*, 8 June 1851; Watkin, *Journal*, p. 265.

Journal believed that the sculptor had succeeded 'in conveying the sharp outlines which the wear and tear of official life had begun to carve on the statesman's handsome countenance'. The figure also took account of Peel's awkwardness with his legs, although some present at the inauguration assumed this to be a flaw: 'we saw several endeavouring to get themselves into the pose which such a curve of the limb involved, but both right leg and body had to yield ere they were successful.'

The Bradford statue, the third from Behnes, was inaugurated in November 1855; Glasgow's figure, by Mossman, followed in June 1859. A long-delayed addition was made at Huddersfield in June 1873.[20] Proposals for a statue there had foundered in the 1850s because of differences between 'the Gentlemen's Committee' which wanted a London sculptor, and 'the Working Men's Committee' which wanted a Leeds man. As a result, the two committees between them collected only a small part even of the £300 expected to be sufficient, which was itself a very low target. In 1869 a new beginning was made, with a competition which resulted in the design submitted by William Theed the Younger being successful. The total cost was £1,000. The *Huddersfield Daily Chronicle* of 4 June 1873 described the crowds at the inauguration as larger than any ever before seen at a ceremony in the town. The statue showed Peel enveloped in the robes of Chancellor of the Exchequer. It may have been forgotten that he had held this office only during his brief first Ministry. On the back of the pedestal were inscribed the concluding words from Peel's resignation speech.

The chief speaker at Huddersfield was Lord Houghton, who as Richard Monckton Milnes had voted for repeal in 1846. He expressed satisfaction that such large crowds could be gathered to remember someone who had been dead for twenty-three years. He recited the epitaph raised by Peel's children in Drayton Church, which he described as one of the most afflicting that he had ever read: 'To the Right Honourable Sir Robert Peel, to whom the people have raised many monuments in many places, and his children have raised this where he lies buried.'

Not only large statues, but small busts, engravings, medals and other items for display at home became part of the business of remembering Sir Robert Peel. 'The virtues of the time are giving daily increasing employment to the manufacturers of busts and silver teapots.' So observed the *Athenaeum* of 10 August 1850. The *Manchester Guardian* of 11 September 1852 exclaimed that Lord Derby, the protectionist leader, might achieve a tomb in Westminster Abbey; but 'when will he get a corner in the market place of a dozen English towns, or a niche in the households of the people?'

Within days of Peel's death the newspapers were full of advertisements of mementoes. *The Times* of 4 July announced as 'just published, price 2d', a

---

[20] Huddersfield Cuttings Book 5, f. 24 (Huddersfield Reference Library).

short account of Peel's life and death. 'Be particular to ask for Elliot's authentic edition.' Another short life was advertised to be sent 'free for three postage stamps ... a succinct and well digested account of the domestic and Parliamentary career, up to his last memorable speech on the foreign question, on Friday last.' By 8 July George Routledge was publicising in *The Times* a new one-shilling life, 'Political and Social, as Subject and Citizen, as Legislator and Minister, and as Patron of Learning and the Arts'. Next day *The Times* was advertising cheap engraved portraits. Read & Co. of Fleet Street offered a new likeness 'at the nominal price of 6d ... to place the possession within the means of every admirer of so true a patriot'. A rival advertisement promised 'the only authentic PORTRAIT of this great Statesman as he appeared delivering his brilliant and last speech': prints 2s 6d, proofs 5s. The earliest advertisement for a mourning bust also appeared in *The Times* of 9 July. 'Mr. HOGARTH has the honour to inform the friends of the eminent statesman that he has entrusted to him for publication a BUST, executed from the original marble, for which Sir ROBERT PEEL sat at the instigation of a most intimate friend. Price – small size, in Parian, £1 1s; life size, in composition, £5 5s.' The original bust, 'admirably executed by an Italian artist', was on view in Hogarth's gallery. This may have been the bust of Bienaimé. In *The Times* of 28 August Linnell's portrait of Peel was advertised as on view at White's gallery in Maddox Street. 'His peculiar and characteristic expression is at once recognized.' The *Art Journal* for November 1850 advertised a parian bust copied from an original by George Abbott, done about 1830. It was tactfully described as showing Peel 'during the "better" part of his life; at that period of his age when a likeness is most desirable to be preserved for posterity.' It was of 'convenient size for the mantel-piece or drawing room table'. Large numbers of these busts were made, in parian or bronze. On the last day of 1850 *The Times* announced a new engraving of the best-liked of all portraits of Peel, that by Lawrence, showing him in his prime a quarter of a century earlier.

Staffordshire-ware pieces produced at Peel's death have already been mentioned, notably the model of Peel on horseback which seems to have been inspired by an engraving which had appeared in the *Illustrated London News*. Medals produced to commemorate repeal of the Corn Laws have also been noticed. Others appeared at Peel's death. One of them in the British Museum, a medallet only half an inch across showing Peel on horseback, may have been the likeness distributed free in Nottingham, as advertised in the *Nottingham Journal* of 12 July 1850:

Given Away!!

An Obituary Medal
of the late
Sir Robert Peel Bart.,

Staffordshire-ware figure of Peel on horseback (1850)

To every Purchaser at Skidmore's Cheap Book
and Stationery Shop, Clumber Street, on and
after Friday, July 12th.

The best mourning medal in the British Museum collection shows a handsome head and shoulders of Peel on the obverse, and a broken column plus a weeping Britannia on the reverse. Beneath Britannia appears a good summary of the reasons why Peel was being mourned:

HIS DEATH WAS DEEPLY DEPLORED BY MEN OF ALL SHADES OF POLITICAL OPINION, AS THE LOSS OF A GREAT PRACTICAL STATESMAN, EARNESTLY DEVOTED TO THE WELFARE OF HIS COUNTRY, AND A GENEROUS FRIEND TO LITERATURE, AND ART.

III

The feeling that Peel was the man to handle crises in peace, and Wellington the man to face emergencies in war, had consolidated during the late 1840s. This sense of great men in reserve was suddenly shattered by Peel's unexpected death; although Wellington's death two years later, aged 83, hardly came as a surprise. 'The Duke' had become even more subject than Peel to public adulation. His opposition to the Reform Bill had brought him widespread unpopularity during the 1830s; but by the 1840s, as he slipped into semi-retirement, this began to be forgotten, or least forgiven, while the victory of Waterloo was gratefully remembered. The Wellington monument, with its over-large statue of the Duke on horseback, erected at Hyde Park Corner in September 1846, was an architectural disaster; yet not one for which Wellington himself was responsible. His state funeral, by contrast, on 18 November 1852, was hailed as a triumph of elaborate mourning.[21]

Like Peel, Wellington had ended up above party. But whereas Peel had reached that position by developing and acting upon his own opinions, Wellington reached it by ceasing to do so. This point was made by *The Times* (16 September 1852) in its obituary editorial. 'It was not that the Duke had no opinions, or predilections of his own; he had them as strongly as other men, and they were of a decidedly aristocratic origin; but he freely gave them up for the good of his country.' Greville remembered (18 September) how, for example, although always blaming Peel for breaking up the Conservative party in 1846, Wellington had abandoned his resistance to Corn Law repeal out of respect for Peel's judgement. The two men were now remembered together in

[21] See J. Physick, *The Wellington Monument* (1970); and J. Morley, *Death, Heaven and the Victorians* (1971), ch. 7.

the general estimation as public servants above party. *The Times* (31 December 1859) observed in its retrospect of the 1850s that their deaths had left an unfilled gap. 'No statesman has since taken the place in public estimation which was occupied by Wellington and Peel, in their later years, irrespective of party opinion and feeling.'

Yet, while Wellington's patriotic reputation remained unquestioned through the Victorian years, Peel's career became the subject of recurring discussion by politicians, journalists and historians. The wisdom of free trade was no longer in much dispute by the later 1850s, and did not again become so until the 'great depression' of the 1870s and 1880s. The question could nevertheless still be asked whether Peel should have acted as he did in 1846. Should he, as leader of a political party hitherto committed to maintaining the Corn Laws, not only have abandoned that policy but have himself taken the lead in guiding repeal through Parliament? And should he have been willing to do this even to the extent of readily breaking up the party which he had done much to create? Should he, furthermore, have turned round over the Corn Laws in 1846 when he had already turned round over Catholic Emancipation in 1829? Was not such changeability damaging to all public faith in public men?

These questions, asked in anger in 1846, now featured more calmly but still prominently in Erskine May's *Constitutional History of England* (1861–3). This major work of constitutional scholarship devoted a whole chapter to 'Party', which ended with a review of 'the evils and merits of party'. Was party confrontation a desirable basis for the conduct of political business in Parliament or in the constituencies? Only after careful consideration did Erskine May come down in favour of such confrontation in politics. He noticed how persistent was the desire among the public for politicians to rise above party; how at public meetings calls to act without reference to party always met with applause. He concluded, however, that although there was much to condemn in the history of parties, there was more to commend. Government without party soon became absolutism, because rulers without opposition tended to become despots. Party was essential to the working of representative institutions, since through party every major interest could be represented. 'The majority governs: but the minority is never without sympathy, representation, and hope.' Erskine May concluded that Peel was entitled to the gratitude of his country for promoting necessary measures; but that because he had twice betrayed his party, he was disqualified from governing again. 'Every one was sensible that so long as party ties and obligations should continue to form an essential part of parliamentary government, the first statesman of his age had forfeited all future claim to govern.'

Only if party connections were regarded as secondary was it possible to imagine that Peel might have returned to office if he had lived. J. A. Roebuck argued that 'the nation looked with eager expectation to his future career' because people cared little for party. 'He rose in their affections in proportion as he lost the favour of his party.' Jellinger Symons agreed. He forecast in *Sir Robert Peel As a Type of Statesmanship* (1856) that Peel would have returned to promote 'sweeping reforms', before handing over the Premiership to 'the Right Honourable Richard Cobden, then and long previously a member of his Cabinet'.[22]

The Times, which still pursued its own line of independence towards all parties, long doubted the usefulness of the party contest. At the end of 1853 it praised Lord Aberdeen's coalition Government because it constituted a step towards the demise of party, with national affairs 'in the hands of those best able to administer them'. Future historians, suggested *The Times*, might regard 1853 as the year when the parliamentary system 'had reached its highest perfection'. Aberdeen's Ministry was Peelite-dominated, and opposed by the Derby–Disraeli Conservatives. Disraeli remained convinced that Peel's 'betrayal' of his party in 1846 had undermined trust in all politicians. He emphasized this in his biography of Lord George Bentinck, published in 1852. Consistency was essential to the smooth running of the political system. Otherwise, argued Conservatives, the way was open for sudden shifts of policy at the whim of temporary majorities in Parliament. Disraeli contended that this was how Peel had won his way from 1841: 'the whole tendency of his policy was to render our institutions mere forms . . . no one with all his conservative language more advanced revolution.'[23]

Radicals, Liberals and Peelites, by contrast, looked back to repeal of the Corn Laws as a triumph of reason over party prejudice; not a dangerous precedent, but evidence that the system could respond in emergency. G. H. Francis's 'critical biography', published in 1852, contrasted 'ultra-Tory' and 'Liberal' views about Peel. The former believed that Peel's treachery towards the landed interest had been 'long-planned'. 'The manufacturer's son was now to raise up his order by destroying the aristocracy.' The 'Liberal' view, on the other hand, was that Peel had achieved 'a moral elevation' by the way he shook off party once in office. 'The public, the nation, were, from that hour, his party. He became a demagogue, speaking by acts of parliament.'[24]

At the time of the unveiling of the Birmingham statue, *The Times* of 30 August 1855 suggested that most contemporaries praised Peel in a spirit of tunnel vision. They remembered him as the man who had delivered 'cheap bread'. They chose to forget his previous commitments as a party leader:

> Peel's symbolical is quite separate from his personal character. While the latter is liable to infinite controversy and misconception, the former is clear from all doubt and difficulty. The last action of his political life has

[22] Symons, *Peel*, p. 189.

[23] Disraeli, *Bentinck*, p. 309. See R. E. McGowen and W. L. Arnstein, 'The mid-Victorians and the two-party system', *Albion*, 11 (1979), pp. 242–58.

[24] Francis, *Peel*, pp. 11–19.

completely eclipsed all the others, and the statues that rise to his memory stand simply and solely as the effigy of the man who broke the fetters of Protection.

This narrow materialist explanation seemed to overlook a higher dimension in the character of Peel's popularity. It forgot the sense of admiration for Peel's self-sacrifice in 1846, sacrifice which had involved not merely loss of the prestigious leadership of a great party but also courageous self-exposure to hurtful charges of treachery. In 1846 *The Times* of 6 July had itself emphasized how anticipation of future material benefits was elevated by gratitude for Peel's present courage: 'the singular merit of the statesman in the popular eyes is his unprecedented sacrifice to attain a good for his country.'

Walter Bagehot linked his assessment of Peel the politician to an unflattering personal assessment. 'Was there ever such a dull man?,' asked Bagehot in 1852. 'Can any one, without horror, foresee the reading of his memoirs?'[25] These were being edited by Peel's executors, Lord Mahon and Edward Cardwell. The first part, dealing with Catholic Emancipation, appeared in 1856; a second part, covering 1834–5 and repeal of the Corn Laws, came out in 1857. These volumes contained much correspondence to and from Peel, with a linking commentary mainly written during his retirement in the late 1840s. The care taken to present his case showed how much it mattered to Peel to be understood both by contemporaries and by posterity – how much he had felt hurt by the charges of false motives. The *Memoirs* certainly presented Peel's case well; and they served to reinforce the sympathy of those already inclined to be favourable. *Punch* (17 May 1856), for example, noticed how £100 from royalties on the first volume had been donated to the Literary Fund. 'From the tomb of Sir Robert speaks the spirit that, when in the flesh and bated by the dogs of party, still beneficently thought of the wants of spasmodic Haydon; still, by sympathy in words and act, smoothed the dying pillow of poor Tom Hood.'

Walter Bagehot's notice of this first volume in the *National Review* for July 1856 was to be often reprinted and to be long remembered for its succession of seductive aphorisms:

Public opinion, as it is said, rules; and public opinion is the opinion of the average man.

A constitutional statesman is in general a man of common opinions and uncommon abilities.

No man has come so near our definition of a constitutional statesman – the powers of a first-rate man and the creed of a second-rate man.

He was converted at the conversion of the average man.

[25] St John Stevas (ed.), *Collected Works of Walter Bagehot*, IV (1962), p. 51.

> You scarcely think of such a mind as acting; it seems always acted upon.

> He scarcely ever said anything which struck you in a moment to be true; he never uttered a sentence which for a moment any body could deny to be plausible.

This view of Peel as able in response but weak in origination failed to consider his policy after 1832 as a whole, or to take account of the evidence hidden away in then still unpublished papers and letters of how Peel could indeed look ahead. Maybe Bagehot would have written differently a year later, after reading the second volume of *Memoirs*. But even this volume, by concentrating upon 1834–5 and 1845–6, perhaps encouraged the impression that Peel was capable of decisive response to sudden challenges but did not take longer or wider views.

Peel's House of Commons speeches had been collected in book form three years before publication of his *Memoirs*. These speeches appeared, however, in four badly printed and unedited volumes. Not surprisingly, such an unattractive collection, which contrived both to omit all Peel's important extra-parliamentary addresses and to be not quite complete even with regard to his Commons speeches, was said to have sold poorly. Regret was expressed at intervals over the lack of a good select edition of Peel's speeches. But Peel himself, without giving reasons, had refused permission in 1846 for publication of such a selection.[26]

Anthony Trollope, in his novel *The Three Clerks* (1858), inclined to praise Peel with faint damns.

> He has taught us a great lesson, that a man who has before him a mighty object may dispense with those old-fashioned rules of truth to his neighbours and honesty to his own principles, which should guide us in ordinary life. At what point ordinary life ends, at what crisis objects may be considered great enough to justify the use of a dispensing power, that he has not taught us.

Trollope thought it at least 'suspicious' that each time Peel chose to promote the views of his political opponents, this meant that he retained office. Trollope accepted that the Corn Laws needed to be repealed, but it was not necessary that Peel should himself have led the way. Peel would be remembered as a politician without policy, as a statesman without principle, as a worshipper at the altar of expediency. His bad example might be copied, and not only in politics. 'It creeps with gradual, but still with sure and quick motion, into all the doings of our daily life.'

---

[26] Dr John Sheil to Peel, 14 May 1846; Stephenson to Sheil, 16 May 1846 (Add. MSS 40591, ff. 429, 433); H. Jephson, *The Platform* (1892) II, p. 597; Lord Rosebery, 'Sir Robert Peel', *Anglo-Saxon Review*, I (1899), p. 97.

Three later Prime Ministers were to express their dislike of Peel's political example. The future Lord Salisbury, in the *Quarterly Review* for April 1865, quoted a passage from the *Memoirs* in which Peel justified his abandonment of party on grounds of higher national interest. Salisbury accepted that the 'suicidal' nature of Peel's actions confirmed his sincerity. But his errors remained open to blame. He had betrayed his followers, hardly aware that he had obligations towards them as well as they towards him: 'it is no slight calamity that he should himself have devised and have handed down for the misguidance of others, a perverted conception of duty.' He should have insisted upon remaining out of office in December 1845, letting repeal be passed less hastily, 'under the ordeal of legitimate party conflict'. In this spirit, as Conservative leader in 1886, Salisbury refused to countenance cooperation with Gladstone to impose an above-party solution of the Irish question through the sudden enactment of Home Rule.

Salisbury's nephew and successor as Conservative leader, A. J. Balfour, several times explicitly refused to condone, let alone to follow, the example of Peel. Most notably during the 'peers versus people' crisis of 1909–11, when Lloyd George and others took soundings about the formation of a national government, Balfour gave them no encouragement. 'I cannot become another Robert Peel in my Party.'[27] And yet, although their leaders refused to follow his example, many Conservatives seem to have recalled Peel to the ranks of their heroes within a generation of his death, refusing to be deterred by his insistence upon putting nation before party. This was made very clear in T. E. Kebbel's *History of Toryism* (1886):

His very name seems a synonym for all that is safe, judicious, business-like, sound, and practical. In spite of the great schisms of 1829 and 1846, we cannot help looking back upon him as a man whom any party would have been wise to follow. We cannot help it. Nor can I doubt that if he had been spared, his old followers would again have fallen under the spell, and again have mustered under his banner.

No new interpretations of Peel's career resulted from the publication in 1891 and 1899 of C. S. Parker's *Sir Robert Peel from His Private Papers*. The first volume covered Peel's work to 1827; the two later volumes went to 1850. This was the long-delayed official life. First Goldwin Smith and then Edward Cardwell had agreed to write it, but had given up. Parker had been Cardwell's private secretary, and then a Liberal Member of Parliament. His three volumes were a compilation, not a rounded biography; letters to and from Peel were printed at length, but under much silent editing and conflation. Parker expanded but did not alter the case made by Peel himself in his *Memoirs*. Much of Peel's revealing correspondence with his friend, J. W. Croker, and with the

<hr />

[27] Blanche E. C. Dugdale, *Arthur James Balfour* (1939) I, pp. 25–9; II, pp. 54–5.

Duke of Wellington, had already been published in Wellington's post-war *Despatches* (1867–80) and in *The Croker Papers* (1884).

Lord Rosebery, the recent Liberal Prime Minister, reviewed Parker's two later volumes for the *Anglo-Saxon Review* in June 1899. This brilliant sketch was immediately republished in book form. Rosebery argued that Peel's action in 1846 had encouraged Disraeli's unscrupulous coup over the Second Reform Act in 1867, which had delivered a blow to trust in politicians which was still being felt. Rosebery compared Peel's action over Catholic Emancipation with his action over the Corn Laws. 'Granted that he was right in the first transition, he should not have repeated it: the character of public men cannot stand two such shocks: we incline as it were to the old verdict of, "Not guilty, but don't do it again".' Yet reviewers of Parker's *Peel* in the *Quarterly* and *Edinburgh Reviews* for April 1899 each put the emphasis the other way – that Peel was blameworthy for acting only out of expediency in 1829, whereas in 1846 he had genuinely changed his mind.

J. R. Thursfield's sketch, published in 1891 as one of Macmillan's 'Twelve English Statesmen' series, edited by John Morley, was an able development of the line that Peel 'had insight but not foresight'. Thursfield, however, did not blame Peel for his attitude towards party: 'party is only a great instrument if it is subordinate to patriotism.' C. S. Parker rightly emphasized in the 1899 preface to his second volume how Peel revealed himself in his private papers to have lacked neither foresight nor ideas. Yet a *Times* reviewer (7 February 1899) still insisted upon drawing a distinction between Peel as a legislator and Peel as a statesman. The reviewer accepted that Peel showed skill in diagnosing the disease and in prescribing a cure; if, however, he had possessed the foresight of a statesman, 'the disease would never have become so desperate, nor would the physician have been dismissed'.

So, at the end of the century, *The Times* was as reserved as ever in its appreciation of Peel. But there was much less qualification in the columns of two other publications which shared with *The Times* the status of national institutions in print, the *Encyclopaedia Britannica* and the *Dictionary of National Biography*. The article on Peel in the *Encyclopaedia Britannica* of 1858 was written by Goldwin Smith, and revised by C. S. Parker for the 1885 edition. It was the more persuasive for not claiming too much. Peel, it pointed out, had carried many reforms, even if he had not originated the demand for them: 'of what he did nothing has been undone.' People would reflect 'that as a parliamentary statesman he could not govern without a party, and that it is difficult to govern at once for a party and for the whole people.' Peel may not have been a model statesman, if by model was meant 'a great administrator and party leader, a great political philosopher, and a great independent orator, all in one. But if the question is, whether he was a ruler loved and trusted by the English people, there is no arguing against the tears of a nation.'

The author of the 1895 article in the *Dictionary of National Biography* was

Peel's grandson, George Peel. This article emphasized how Peel had created a party of the right which was not a party of reaction. 'In an age of European revolutions, Peel may alone be said to have had the foresight and the strength to form a conservative party, resting not on force or on corruption, but on administrative capacity, and the more stable portion of the public will.'

In this same spirit, at the time of the one hundred and fiftieth anniversary of the Tamworth Manifesto in 1984, Conservative Ministers were to claim Peel as deserving remembrance for being the founder of modern Conservatism. *The Times* of 22 September 1984, in the tart tradition of its Victorian predecessor, pointed out that if this were true, the brand of Conservatism in question was that of R. A. Butler and Edward Heath rather than that of Margaret Thatcher.

But how much, near the end of the twentieth century, is Peel remembered for anything at all? Augustine Birrell remarked in a review of Parker's *Peel* in the *Contemporary Review* for May 1899 that the British public usually mourned its statesmen briefly, gave each one an epithet, and then forgot them. 'Thus, Pitt is majestic, Fox generous, Canning splendid, Palmerston patriotic, John Russell plucky, Disraeli romantic, Gladstone religious.' Peel had attracted no dismissive epithet, claimed Birrell, because he was still remembered for the range of great reforms which constituted 'his imperishable fame'. Birrell seemed to have overlooked the adjective 'practical', so often used by and about Peel. Moreover, if in 1899 his reforms were still remembered, his work was not destined to stay in the public mind long into the new century. Although Joseph Chamberlain's tariff reform campaign from 1903 reopened discussion about free trade and cheap bread, Chamberlain's free-trade opponents invoked the memory of Cobden much more often than that of Peel. Morley's *Life of Cobden* was reprinted in 1903 in a cheap shilling edition as part of their counter-attack. Morley was much more readable than Parker. The Peel statues were, of course, still standing; and it is interesting to notice how Harold Wilson in his television series, *A Prime Minister on Prime Ministers*, published in book form in 1977, remembered reading as a boy the famous resignation last words inscribed on the Huddersfield statue: 'political leaders of today can recall seeing them – learning them by heart – as boys.' And yet, in the Huddersfield of the 1920s and 1930s, young Wilson may already have been exceptional in his awareness. The town's local newspaper was writing plainly in 1934 that 'to the present generation the name of Sir Robert Peel conveys nothing, and probably few persons have even taken the trouble to read the inscription on the base of the statue.'[28] When the Blackburn statue was taken down from the top of 'Peel Buildings' in the same year, the *Blackburn Times* (11 August 1934) even expressed uncertainty about whether the figure was that of the statesman or of his father. A photograph with the report shows clearly enough that the figure was indeed of the Prime Minister, in a characteristic speaking pose. It was

---

[28] Huddersfield Cuttings Book 5, f. 24.

destroyed soon after the photograph was taken. 'We were informed yesterday by the general foreman of the contractors that he had mentioned the removal of the statue to a number of people, but they did not seem interested in its preservation, so it was broken up.'

Contrastingly, it was during this same period that Peel scholarship was given greater depth by the deposit of the voluminous Peel papers in the British Museum. First, Dr George Kitson Clark, and then Professor Norman Gash, began their long and productive researches into the life and times of Peel. And yet all their endeavours have not brought Peel's name back into informed public awareness. During the past thirty years even the word 'bobby' has fallen out of use, to be replaced by less sympathetic nicknames for policemen. A slip which may be revealing occurred in Martin Pugh's *Making of Modern British Politics* (1982), a book of generally commendable accuracy. References to Peel in the index appear under 'Peel, Sir John'. The same confusion of two Peels led the *Lake District Restaurant Guide* for 1984 to mention the Parkside Restaurant, 'where John Peel was born', with the reassurance that 'anything less like an establishment where our police force was founded would indeed be hard to find'. At least, this confusion of identities was spotted by a reader of *Punch* (18 July 1984). But, thanks to a tuneful song, it does seem that John Peel, the huntsman, is now better remembered than Robert Peel, the statesman.

8

Conclusion

The later career of Sir Robert Peel – from the time of the passing of the first Reform Act in 1832 until his death in 1850 – was a career conducted through difficult years of running crisis. This crisis was two-sided. On the one hand lay problems of adjustment to the great changes in social and economic life brought about by the industrial revolution. On the other hand were problems of adjustment in the conduct of the political life of the nation under the newly reformed system. Peel, more than any other politician of his day, was involved in finding answers to both these sets of problems. In each context he showed himself to be characteristically 'practical'. This was a favourite word of Peel's, much used both by him and by others about him.

Peel's policies – notably his economic measures with a social purpose, centring upon the extension of free trade and culminating in the repeal of the Corn Laws in 1846 – have been much studied by historians. This book has set out to break new ground by looking less at the content of Peel's policies and more at his presentation of them within the new political situation; at the same time it has traced the developing response of the Victorian press and public to that presentation.

The Reform Act had increased the electorate by at least one-half, to some 650,000 (perhaps even 800,000) male voters; and it had also considerably redistributed the constituencies. Although there was to be no further major constitutional change through legislation for a generation after 1832, much innovation in political practice was required to meet the new situation, both at Westminster and in the constituencies. Peel saw this to be inevitable. Although he had strongly opposed the passing of the Reform Act, he now set out to make the reformed system work. He wanted it to work, however, in as traditional a spirit as possible. He knew that the authority of the House of Commons had been much increased over recent years, and that of the Lords and of the Crown proportionately reduced. He did not want this 'popular' tendency to go any further, because he feared that it would mean the end of the balanced constitution which had served the country well since the revolution of 1688. Nor did he want the authority and influence of the Church of England as the established religion in support of that constitution to be lessened. He dismissed all calls for disestablishment, even when made in the name of religious equality. Toleration did not require equality. Further alteration in the machinery of Church or state would, in Peel's view, threaten confidence and stability. 'Property' would feel itself in danger. Peel, indeed, feared that it was already in danger, from the inflammatory influence of Chartist and other demagogues. The example of the French Revolution was continuously in his mind during the 1830s and 1840s. Only at the very end of his life did he begin to feel confident, thanks in large part to the economic and psychological effects of his own measures, that a French Revolution would not be attempted in England.

The House of Commons was the main forum for national political debate, and Peel deliberately chose to spend his whole political life as a Member. His personal standing in the House became unequalled, with his speeches usually heard there with great attention and increasingly reported verbatim in the press. These speeches were intended to give a clear lead both to the Commons and to the country. Peel was determined that the increased standing of the lower House after 1832 should not mean that it took control of Ministers. Certainly, an administration could not survive in office without House of Commons approval; but Peel was sure that only a strong executive Cabinet, in succession to the personal rule of the Sovereign, could provide good government. Radicals wanted Members of Parliament to be mandated on certain issues. Peel always insisted that they should act as representatives, not delegates. This then left them free to respond to proposals – perhaps unexpected proposals such as the 1842 income tax or the 1845 Maynooth scheme – which Ministers had declared to be in the national interest.

Uncertainty about the three-sided relationship between the executive, the legislature, and the electorate left much room for differences about the place of 'party' in politics, and about the role of public opinion. What, indeed, was 'the public'? Did it mean only the electorate, mainly middle class; or did it include, even at elections, any or all of those non-electors who comprised some 80 per cent of the adult male population? Were 'the public' and 'the people' the same? 'The people' were often equated with the middle classes, and Peel seems to have accepted this equation. He remained fearful of 'the masses'. This was a new word of the 1830s, which Richard Cobden used without qualms, but which carried overtones for Peel of 'the mob' and therefore of violence. Yet Peel wanted to serve the interests of all, rich and poor, electors and non-electors alike. But he always found it easier to work *for* the unenfranchised millions that to work *with* them. Hence his embarrassed description of his reception at Blackburn in 1834, 'not from a radical but a conservative assemblage (mob I must not call them)' (p. 82).

In particular, Peel remained hostile to 'pressure from without'. He regarded the working-class and largely extra-parliamentary Chartist movement as a challenge to the parliamentary system, not merely because of its demand for universal suffrage but also because of its methods of 'eternal agitation' (p. 127). He felt much the same even about the middle-class Anti-Corn Law League. He eventually admitted to being influenced by the arguments of its leader, Richard Cobden; but only 'in the House of Commons' (p. 237). He believed that mass meetings were always likely to become platforms for extreme opinions. He recognized the role of meetings called by constituted authorities, and of petitions arising therefrom; but he saw no justification for systematic political campaigning year after year. 'We hate the pressure from without' (p. 73).

The press played a prominent role in extra-parliamentary agitation; but it was also taking an increasing part in the interplay between parliamentary politics at Westminster and opinion in the constituencies. How then did Peel regard the role of the press? His opponents often claimed that he did not read newspapers because he despised them. This was untrue and unfair. Peel accepted that it was his duty, both as Leader of the Opposition and as Prime Minister, to study the foremost London dailies, weeklies and quarterlies; and he was glad when supporters sent him copies of provincial papers which contained significant items. Peel accepted that newspapers must now perform an important service by reporting to the public the speeches of politicians in Parliament, not least his own. He very much wanted outside opinion to understand his policies. 'My speech will, no doubt, be in the possession of everyone tomorrow morning.' So he remarked during his first Corn Law speech in 1846 (p. 36). But just as he was never prepared to vary his policies to humour opinion inside Parliament, so he was not prepared to alter his line or language simply to win approval outside.

While welcoming the reporting role of the press, Peel was uneasy about its pretensions to represent and to influence public opinion. During the Reform Bill crisis, he had complained that the press was trying to make and unmake Ministries. He had perforce to accept, however, that leading articles in major newspapers, plus longer pieces in the weekly, monthly and quarterly journals, contributed towards the creation and articulation of a climate of opinion. As early as 1820 he was noticing what he called 'the tone of England – of that great compound of folly, weakness, prejudice, wrong feeling, right feeling, obstinacy, and newspaper paragraphs, which is called public opinion' (p. 13).

During the 1830s and 1840s the newspaper with much the largest circulation was *The Times*, which was selling 40,000 copies daily by 1850. If Victorian public opinion had one voice, this was it, as Peel himself realized. His feelings towards *The Times* varied from the generally favourable during the mid and late 1830s, when Barnes was editor, to the often exasperated during the next decade, under the editorship of Delane. *The Times* showed its independence by keeping all politicians always on probation. In the end, however – before, during and after the Corn Law crisis of 1846 – Peel's reputation expanded regardless of reservations about his personality which

The Times tried to maintain, even while accepting most of his policies. *The Times* could not restrain the growth of Peel's good name. Here was a rare rebuff for the paper, which has hitherto passed unnoticed.

The primacy of *The Times* as an outlet for publicity was recognized when Peel gave it, along with the avowedly Conservative *Morning Herald* and *Morning Post*, the text of the Tamworth Manifesto for publication on 18 December 1834. This document has always been hailed as a major innovation in constitutional practice. Peel had become Prime Minister because William IV had suddenly dismissed his Whig Ministers. This was the last time that a Sovereign felt free so to exercise the royal prerogative. Conversely, the manifesto showed Peel as a Prime Minister for the first time addressing the national electorate at the time of a general election. Peel's action can, however, be easily misunderstood, if it is taken out of the context of its own time. Ultimately, such election appeals from party leaders were to become part of the democratic process. But in 1834, far from wanting to encourage 'democracy', Peel was seeking to resist its progress. Peel called for support from 'that class which is much less interested in the contentions of party, than in the maintenance of order and the cause of good government'. So 'order' was placed first by Peel; and 'good government' did not mean radical reform. He promised to respect 'the spirit of the Reform Bill', but not by adopting 'every popular impression of the day' (p. 70).

In this progressive but far from democratic spirit, Peel asked for the support of that middle opinion to which he was repeatedly to appeal during the rest of his career – that floating and usually silent majority who, if they had votes, might vote for party candidates at elections but who did not do so as partisans. The *Maidstone Gazette* noticed Peel's successful call to moderate men at the time of the Corn Law Repeal: 'the depositories of that common sense for which our nation is celebrated; who seldom take an active part in politics, but who invariably throw their weight into the scale in opposition to every proved and tangible public grievance' (p. 16).

Peel's reputation for 'manliness' in the eyes of such people was observed to be growing even before his 1834 Tamworth appeal. His restrained handling of the Catholic Emancipation issue in 1829, despite much abuse over his change of side, was said to have won Peel increased respect. So was his steady, but not factious, opposition to the Reform Bills of 1831–2. He asked in the Tamworth Manifesto for a 'fair trial', and he seems genuinely to have expected to be given one as the King's chosen Minister. Significantly, however, the 1835 general election was the first for which the newspapers published lists of candidates with attached party labels. Peel had noticed this, but had not admitted that party loyalties were becoming paramount. 'I am not alarmed at the lists that are published ... I cannot but think that many of those who are classed as Reformers entertain opinions not far different from my own' (p. 75). But the Lichfield House compact between the Whigs and the Irish meant that Peel's hopes of regularly attracting votes from the Opposition side were not to be realized. His proposals were steadily voted down, regardless of their merits. Upon his resignation, after only four months in office, addresses poured in from the country condemning such 'excess of party zeal' (p. 77).

Peel himself was never to be a party zealot; but he now realized that he must build up his party's position in Parliament and in the country, so that he could eventually return to power at the head of a clear majority, visible in advance of taking office. This he achieved at the general election of 1841. For six years from 1835 he had acted as a busy party leader, speaking often at Westminster and at intervals in his Tamworth constituency and elsewhere. On all occasions when he spoke as Conservative party leader during the 1830s he took care not to appear as a *partisan* leader. Then from 1841 to 1845 he went on to become a constructive Prime Minister, who was still the leader of the Conservative party but who was a leader seen to be acting increasingly *apart* from his party. Finally, during and after the Corn Law crisis of 1846, finding himself resisted by about two-thirds of his backbenchers, Peel deliberately placed himself not merely apart from the Conservative party but *above* all parties, in Parliament and outside.

Peel went into the 1841 general election expecting to win. The Conservatives had been gaining ground steadily through the two earlier general elections of 1835 and 1837, and at subsequent by-elections. Given the continuing importance of local issues and local influence, too much must not be claimed for Peel's personal contribution in 1841. On the other hand, Peel's vigorous but not partisan leadership had been noticed in all constituencies. Perhaps it gained him most credit in the larger boroughs, with their concentrated electorates. These returned forty-four Conservatives. This block of seats gave the Conservatives their overall majority of at least seventy-eight. Victory under Peel's leadership was the more noteworthy for being, despite the natural Conservative strength in the rural seats, the only occasion between the First and Second Reform Acts when the party gained a House of Commons majority.

While from 1841 Peel was making his apart-from-party stance increasingly apparent, dissatisfaction was growing among Conservative backbenchers. At the same time, contrasting approval for his measures and his approach to politics was developing outside Parliament, even among newspapers and voters who had not supported him at the general election. Admittedly, one noticeable strand of opinion, although praising many of Peel's measures upon their merits, was still careful not to praise their sponsor. But some organs, such as the *Spectator* and *Fraser's Magazine*, quickly gave Peel full personal credit for his new boldness. 'For the first time in his life Sir Robert Peel has been seen to act from the impulses of his own mind . . . for the first time ought the question of his being "a great man" to be considered' (p. 20).

By the end of 1845 Peel's reputation as a successful Prime Minister, who had promoted great measures regardless of party constraints, was already considerable. He remained, however, leader of the Conservative party, and still apparently an advocate of the Corn Laws. It needed his sacrifice of that party leadership, his abandonment of the Corn Laws and the bearing of much abuse from his own backbenchers before he began to reach a still higher level of popularity. During a few weeks early in 1846 Peel deliberately advanced from acting apart from party to acting above party. He had been surprised by the strength and rancour of the protectionist resistance to repeal; but he did not doubt that he could and should overcome it, even by collecting majorities which contained two Whig votes for every 'Peelite' vote. The maintenance of party unity and superficial policy consistency seemed to him to be a secondary consideration in a time of national crisis. Moreover, he believed that he was really being guided by an underlying consistency to Conservative principles, in that the concession of repeal would demonstrate the responsiveness of the existing system of government and thereby undermine the demand for further constitutional change.

Disraeli, on the other hand, claimed that Peel's repudiation of the Corn Laws, which he had been elected in 1841 to defend, was bound dangerously to weaken public trust in public men. Party commitment was, in Disraeli's view, 'embodied public opinion' (p. 176). Peel's critics also felt that his action was the more deplorable because of his previous volte-face over Catholic Emancipation, which had been forgiven but never quite forgotten. Peel seemed to be making a habit of, and even claiming virtue for, a course of political untrustworthiness. The protectionist *Morning Herald* concluded that he had offended 'not merely against party but *against morals*' (p. 208). Peel answered that a Prime Minister's reading of the present national interest must override all earlier party commitments. And majority opinion in the country, even more than inside Parliament, quickly agreed with him. 'His measure satisfies only moderate men – that is, the many.' So explained the *Liverpool Journal* perceptively (p. 203).

Long-standing charges that Peel had always been motivated by mere expediency, and by desire to retain office, were now widely felt to have been discredited by his willingness to sacrifice himself for the sake of repeal. *Punch*, an increasingly accurate barometer of middle-class opinion, moved right round from still deep distrust of Peel as 'the Knave of Spades' in November 1845 to sympathy at the abuse being heaped upon him and to congratulation for his achievement by the time of his resignation (p. 158). Lower down the social scale, readers of the Chartist *Northern Star* were urged to hail 'the ALL-MIGHTY measures of this mental Hercules' (p. 186).

How provincial public opinion had now become well informed and shrewd, thanks especially to newspaper guidance, was illustrated each week in the *Liverpool Journal*'s 'Talk on Change'. 'The general talk is . . . that there will be no dissolution; that Sir Robert Peel is safe in a majority of 90.' Such was an early and accurate forecast in January 1846 (p. 203). Four years later at Peel's death, the same paper's 'Talk on Change' was recalling his 'moral heroism perfectly unexampled' (p. 279).

The famous peroration to Peel's resignation speech of 29 June 1846 asked for remembrance from 'those whose lot it is to labour' (p. 236). This was the first time that Peel had made such a direct appeal to non-electors, although his speech of 15 May had defined 'the greatest object' of any Minister as the elevation of the social conditions 'of that class of the people with whom we are brought into no direct relationship by the exercise of the elective franchise'. Even now, however, although Peel hoped for gratitude, he was still careful throughout the Corn Law crisis never to call for any outside agitation in his support.

Between 1846 and 1850 Peel's above-party attitude in the Commons made many Peelites increasingly restless; but the Victorian public took this attitude only as pleasing evidence of Peel's continuing statesmanlike purpose. 'His party,' explained the *Weekly Dispatch*, 'was the nation' (p. 276). Peel the man and Peel the statesman were now viewed by many with equal satisfaction. Although Peel was usually shy and aloof in his dealings with individuals, except close friends, his personal image in the public eye had gradually warmed over the years. There was increasing acceptance that he 'had a heart' (p. 109). He was remembered at the last as a good as well as a great man, always guided by Christian conscience, who had died an exemplary death just as he had lived an exemplary life. Public awareness of his happy family circle, and of his active support for the arts and sciences, had both added perceptibly to his reputation. 'Had not Sir Robert Peel been a minister he would have been a Maecenas' (p. 242).

Clearly, Peel had touched what Carlyle called 'the dumb heart of England' (p. 240). He had reached the hearts and minds of millions of the middle classes, who normally went about their business with an uncommitted eye on politics. He had reached even more millions of the working classes, as they struggled for a living, usually with little time to spare for politics. His admirers and mourners were, in the words of the *Northern Star*, 'the great mass of the people, whose political predilections are of a moderate description, and who do not take part in political struggles' (p. 277). This testimony was the more convincing for coming from a newspaper which was itself intensely political. The *Star* subsequently issued Peel's portrait for inclusion among its gallery of popular heroes – a remarkable tribute. Even more remarkable was the huge number of contributors to the Working Men's Memorial of Gratitude, about 400,000 working people. Here was a unique measure of Peel's popularity.

Yet none of Peel's great reforms had been chosen for him either by the middle or by the working classes. He had seemed even to relish his own unresponsiveness. 'We have not acted in deference to popular clamour', he explained about his 1845 budget, 'for we have selected taxes for reduction and abolition against which there has been no agitation' (p. 146). Nevertheless,

Peel's masterfulness in deciding for himself, and in acting in his own way and in his own time, had seemed only to increase popular trust in his judgment. The man who had steadily opposed the passing of the Reform Act, and who to his dying day distrusted 'democracy', died the hero equally of the newly enfranchised, propertied middle classes, and of the unenfranchised, property-less masses. This shared admiration for Peel was no freak of opinion. In troubled and changing times, he had satisfied the majority of the British people of all classes that the reformed political system, under strong leadership, was capable of reacting purposefully to their needs. In this way, even though not in all ways, Peel was the first 'modern' Prime Minister. The point was well expressed by Carlyle (p. 240):

> Let this merit never be forgotten in Sir Rt., that he could do without articulate backing, and depend upon the inarticulate; which indeed argues a strong man.

Index